Jekka's
COMPLETE HERB BOOK

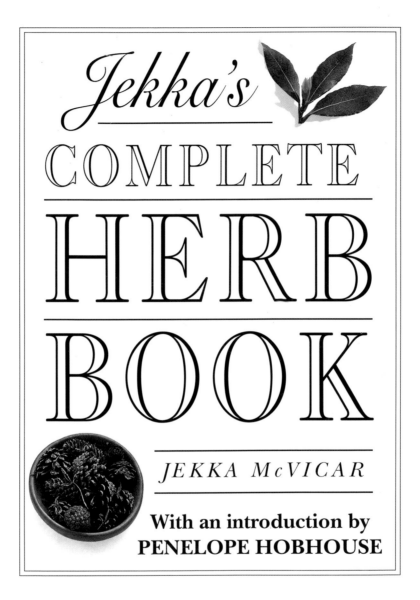

Jekka's COMPLETE HERB BOOK

JEKKA McVICAR

With an introduction by
PENELOPE HOBHOUSE

KYLE CATHIE LIMITED

To Mac, Hannah and Alistair

First published in Great Britain in 1994 by
Kyle Cathie Limited
20 Vauxhall Bridge Road, London SW1V 2SA

This edition published 1994
Reprinted 5 times

ISBN 1 85626 161 1

Book Design by Geoff Hayes

Printed and bound in Hong Kong
South China Printing Co. (1988) Ltd.

Jessica McVicar is hereby identified as the author of this work in
accordance with Section 77 of the Copyright, Designs and Patents
Act, 1988.

A Cataloguing in Publication record for this title is available
from the British Library

Acknowledgements
With many thanks to Mac for all his support, Anthea for turning up
in the nick of time, Kyle for taking the gamble, Piers for all his
reading and Penny for her compliments.

Photographic acknowledgements
Plant photography by Jekka McVicar and Sally Maltby. All other
photography by Michelle Garrett except: Roast Beef and Horseradish pages 38-39 by Roger Phillips; Lily of the Valley page 69
courtesy of Rowden Garden; Elderberry Sorbet page 173 by Sally
Maltby; Turmeric and Green and Black Cardamoms page 215 by
Peter Knab; pages 220 and 235 by Derek St Romaine.

CONTENTS

INTRODUCTION

In Western civilization ancient herbals, dating back to the *De Materia Medica* of Dioscorides written in the first century AD, described plants for their healing virtues. In his great work the Greek physician named and described five hundred plants actually seen by him, as well as how to observe their growth, how to gather and store the 'flowers and sweet scented things' in 'dry boxes of Limewood' and the moister medicines in more suitable containers. The earliest extant copy of his manuscript, written and illustrated in the sixth century and known as the *Codex Vindobonensis*, is in Vienna. His plants came from the Mediterranean basin and scholars over the centuries have worked to find and identify them.

In the next 1500 years herbals came to include and emphasize the culinary as well as the medicinal uses, sometimes a mixture of fanciful myth and magic, at others the down-to-earth practicalities of culture and preparation. The best known in Britain is John Gerard's *Herball* written in 1597, much more a treatise on gardening than just a catalogue of plants considered for their 'vertues' as simples or in cooking. It is treasured because of the practical nature of his descriptions, many based on his own personal knowledge of growing them in his garden at Holborn. By 1596, of course, he was growing plants newly arrived from east of the Mediterranean and from the New World, pushing out the frontiers of plant and herb knowledge.

In 1994 Jekka McVicar grows three hundred varieties of herbs in her nursery. In this very practical book she brilliantly assembles information on species and varieties, their cultivation and garden use, and their medicinal, culinary and cosmetic properties, as well as uses for aromatherapy. For appropriate herbs she provides recipes, her writing evocative of scent and taste.

The old favourites are here but, in addition, for each genus she amplifies the range of species and cultivars to cover those most useful as well as most garden-worthy. For anyone who has seen her stands, set up as decorative herb gardens at Chelsea or Hampton Court, it will be axiomatic that her book is also a guide to growing herbs aesthetically, including plans for herb gardens designed for all occasions. Jekka describes in detail how to sow, propagate from cuttings and how to maintain and grow the herbs – even how to turn them into ornamental topiary subjects. It is a book on herbs which has, without sacrificing plant information, expanded into an encyclopedia on making and enjoying herb gardens, in which their aromatic leaves and scented flowers can be enjoyed by all the senses.

Growing herbs, with their poetic and historical associations, has a connotation of 'usefulness' which serves a moral purpose when ordinary decorative gardening can seem too full of display and artistry. Jekka McVicar strikes a happy balance between industry and pleasure, between history – she looks back to the old herbalists for facts and then amplifies these in the light of contemporary knowledge – and modern use. It is particularly good to be reminded of herbal remedies scientifically approved today. She encourages us to know and grow a great number of herbs which are unfamiliar to many of us, and to experiment with them. She leads us through her growing processes with a clarity not always discovered in 'how-to' books and her recipes sound practical as well as enticing.

Penelope Hobhouse

'Excellent herbs had our fathers of old, Excellent herbs to ease their pain'
'Our Fathers of Old' by Rudyard Kipling

AUTHOR'S NOTE

Herbs have been used since man has been on Earth as a food and a medicine. There are few plants capable of providing the sheer pleasure of herbs; they are the most generous of plants, aromatic and attractive, useful in both the home and the garden, health-giving and healthy.

The increasing interest in herbs is part of a movement towards a healthier lifestyle, symbolizing a more natural approach. Herbs are used in cooking, in domestic products, alternative medicines and cosmetics; and they affect the quality of life in many ways.

The most extraordinary feature of herbs is their incredible versatility. You may think of a particular herb as having mainly culinary or medicinal properties and then discover it has other useful applications. Thyme, for example, provides the raw material for cooking, medicines and aromatherapy.

What is a herb? It can be argued that all useful plants are herbs. *The Oxford English Dictionary* defines them as 'plants of which the leaves, stem or flowers are used for food or medicine, or in some way for their scent or flavour'. To elaborate, a herb can be any plant used as an ingredient in food or drink for flavour or preservative properties, in medicine for health-giving properties, or in perfume, cosmetics or aromatherapy as a fixative, for flavour or aroma or as a cleansing agent. That herbs do you good is in no doubt, improving your health, appearance or sense of well-being.

When I started working on a herb farm eighteen years ago the only people to come and buy herbs were witches, warlocks and vegetarians. Now it is anybody and everybody. The increase in demand over the past decade has been caused by the public's growing awareness of the infinite variety of herbs, and their use in herbalism, cosmetics and cooking all over the world. The need to conserve plants has also increased people's knowledge of herbs. Growing traditional plants, with their vast histories of use, is immensely satisfying.

Jekka's Herb Farm was established as a specialist wholesale nursery in 1985, and I now cultivate over three hundred varieties, using the principles of organic growing. We exhibit at many of the major flower shows throughout the year, including the Chelsea Flower Show, Hampton Court Palace

Flower Show and at the Royal Horticultural Society Halls in Westminster for the autumn shows. There I witness the enthusiasm that herbs create, and the hunger for information on growing techniques and the different uses to which herbs can be put.

This book is to satisfy that hunger and is intended to guide the reader through the fascinating world of herbs, providing not only practical information on the growing and use of each herb but also the mythical, magical and historical context.

Herbs have been my life for almost 2 decades now. In this book I have tried to convey to you just some of the pleasure working with herbs can bring.

HOW TO USE THIS BOOK

This book comprises two main sections:

The A–Z of Herbs details information for each specific herb and is arranged alphabetically by the botanical Latin name. I have included:

The botanical Latin and family names
Other names including folk and country names by which the herb is known
Natural habitat including native country and area of distribution
Species: this identifies some of the other closely related plants of the same species together with any unique properties. For many species there are so many varieties it would be impossible to name them all.
Propagation: detailing helpful tips that will make all the difference between success and failure. Techniques for seed, cuttings and layerings are given.
garden cultivation gives the preferred position and soil type. It details specific tasks for maintaining the plant at its best, its likes and dislikes, watering requirements and winter protection needs.
Container growing: whether indoors or outdoors I give type of compost together with watering and feeding requirements.
Pests and diseases: where a particular herb is susceptible to pests or diseases, treatments and any preventative measures are detailed.
Yearly maintenance provides a quick check on tasks necessary throughout the year.
harvest gives the parts of the plant to harvest, together with the best time for harvesting, depending on the eventual use and method of storing.
Uses: this details known uses for individual herbs and is subdivided into culinary, medicinal and other uses, demonstrating the vast number of ways herbs have been used throughout history.

General details of herb growing
Propagation: what you need to propagate your plant, whether it be by seed cutting or layering, or division. Detailed step-by-step instructions are provided for each method.
planning your herb garden: useful tips when you take the first step in planning a herb garden, together with plans for ten herb gardens.
Container growing: including useful tips for growing herbs successfully in pots, indoor or outdoor.
Harvesting: including instruction on methods of harvesting, drying, storing and freezing.
Herb oils, vinegars and preserves gives methods of making delicious produce from the garden.
Natural dyes provides step-by-step instructions on how to dye your own material to the natural colours which have again become fashionable.
Pests and diseases refers to the major pests and diseases and the strategies best adopted to cure, and prevent reoccurrence of, problems.
Yearly calendar provides a check list of tasks to be performed month by month, and also identifies the herbs available for harvest.
Botanical names explains the relationship between the family, genus and species of plants.

The A-Z of Herbs

Achillea ageratum (decolorans)

ENGLISH MACE

From the family Compositae

Native of Switzerland, now cultivated in northern temperate countries. This culinary herb is little known and under-used.

English mace belongs to the *Achillea* genus, named after Achilles, who is said to have discovered the medicinal properties of the genus. There is no direct historical record of English mace itself apart from the fact it was discovered in Switzerland in 1798.

English Mace in Spring
Achillea ageratum (decolorans)

SPECIES

Achillea ageratum (decolorans)
English Mace
Hardy perennial. Ht 30-45cm (12-18in) when in flower. Spread 30cm (12in). Clusters of small cream flowers that look very Victorian in summer. Leaves brightish green, narrow and very deeply serrated.

CULTIVATION

Propagation
Cuttings
This is the best method for the propagation of a large number of plants. Take softwood cuttings in late summer, protect from wilting as they will be very soft. Use the bark, peat mix of compost. When well-rooted, harden off and plant out in the garden 30cm (12in) apart.

Division
If you require only a few plants it is best to propagate by division. Either divide the plant in early spring – it is one of the first to appear – or in autumn. Replant in the garden in a prepared site. As this is a hardy plant it will not need protection, but if

you leave division until the frosts are imminent, winter the divided plants in a cold frame or cold greenhouse.

Pests and Diseases
Mace, in most cases, is free from pests and disease.

Maintenance
Spring: Divide established plants.
Summer: Cut back flowers. Take softwood cuttings.
Autumn: Divide established plants if needed.
Winter: Does not need protection.

Garden Cultivation
This fully hardy plant, which even flourishes on my heavy soil, prefers a sunny, well-drained site. It starts the season off as a cluster of low-growing, deeply serrated leaves and then develops long flowering stems in summer. Cut back after flowering for a fresh supply of leaves and to encourage a second flowering crop. When in flower this plant may need staking in a windy exposed site.

Harvest
Cut fresh leaves when you wish. For freezing, which is the best method of preserving, cut before flowering and freeze in small containers.

Pick the flowers during the summer. Collect in small bunches and hang upside down to dry.

Both flowers and leaves dry particularly well.

CULINARY

The chopped leaves can be used to stuff chicken, flavour soups, stews, and to sprinkle on potato salads, rice and pasta dishes. The leaf has a mild, warm, aromatic flavour and combines well with other herbs.

Chicken with English Mace in Foil

Serves 4

4 chicken breasts
2 tablespoons yoghurt
2 tablespoons Dijon mustard
Salt and fresh ground black pepper
Bouquet garni herb oil (or olive oil)
6 tablespoons of chopped English mace
Juice of 1 lemon

Pre-heat oven to 190°C 375°F or Gas mark 5. Mix the yoghurt and mustard together and coat the chicken pieces on all sides. Sprinkle with salt and pepper. Cut 4 pieces of foil and brush with herb or olive oil. Lay the chicken breasts in the foil and scatter a thick layer of English mace on each piece. Sprinkle with lemon juice. Wrap in the foil, folding the ends very tightly so no juices can escape. Lay the packets on a rack in the oven, cook for 30 minutes. Serve with rice and a green salad.

OTHER USES

Flowers in dried flower arrangements.

English Mace
Achillea ageratum (decolorans)

CONTAINER GROWING

For a tall flowering plant this looks most attractive in a terracotta pot. Make sure it has a wide base to allow for its height later in the season. Use the bark, peat, grit mix of compost. Water regularly throughout the growing season and give a liquid feed (according to manufacturer's instructions) in the summer months during flowering. Cut back after flowering to stop the plant from toppling over and encourage new growth. As this plant dies back in winter, allow the compost to become nearly dry, and winter the container in a cold greenhouse or cold frame.

Achillea millefolium

YARROW

Also known as Nosebleed, Millefoil, Thousand Leaf, Woundwort, Carpenter's Weed, Devil's Nettle, Mille Foil, Soldier's Woundwort and Noble Yarrow. From the family Compositae.

Yarrow is found all over the world in waste places, fields, pastures and meadows. It is common throughout Europe, Asia and North America.

This is another very ancient herb. It was used by the Greeks to control haemorrhages, for which it is still prescribed in homeopathy and herbal medicine today. The legend of Achilles refers to this property – it was said that during the battle of Troy, Achilles healed many of his warriors with yarrow leaves. Hence the name, 'Achillea'.

It has long been considered a sacred herb. Yarrow stems were used by the Druids to divine seasonal weather. The ancient Chinese text of prophecy, *I Ching*, The Book of Changes, states that 52 straight stalks of dried yarrow, of even length, were spilled to foretell the future instead of the modern way of using 3 coins.

It was also associated with magic. In Anglo-Saxon times it was said to have a potency against evil, and in France and in Ireland it is one of the Herbs of St John. On St John's Eve, the Irish hang it up in their houses to avert illness.

There is an old superstition, which apparently still lingers in remote parts of Britain and the United States, that if a young girl tickles her nostrils with sprays of yarrow and her nose starts to bleed, it proves her lover's fidelity:

'Yarrow away, Yarrow away, bear a white blow?
If my lover loves me, my nose will bleed now.'

Yarrow *Achillea millefolium*

SPECIES

Achillea millefolium
Yarrow
Hardy perennial. Ht 30-90cm (1-3ft), spread 60cm (2ft) and more. Small white flowers with a hint of pink appear in flat clusters from summer to autumn. Its specific name, **millefolium**, means 'a thousand leaf', which is a good way to describe these darkish green, aromatic, feathery leaves.

Achillea millefolium 'Fire King'
Hardy perennial. Ht and spread 60cm (24in). Flat heads of rich, red, small flowers in flat clusters all summer. Masses of feathery dark green leaves. This has an upright habit and is a vigorous grower.

Achillea 'Coronation Gold'
Hardy perennial. Ht 1m (3ft), spread 60cm (2ft). Large flat heads of small golden flowerheads in summer that dry well for winter decoration. Masses of feathery silver leaves.

Achillea Moonshine
Hardy perennial. Ht 60cm (24in), spread 50cm (20in). Flat heads of bright yellow flowers throughout summer. Masses of small feathery grey/green leaves.

CULTIVATION

Propagation
Seed
For reliable results sow the very small seed under cool protection in autumn. Use either a proprietary seeder or the cardboard trick and sow into prepared seed or plug trays. Leave the trays in a cool greenhouse for the winter. Germination is erratic. Harden off and plant out in the garden in spring. Plant 20-30cm (8-12in) apart, remembering that it will spread. As this is an invasive plant, I do not advise sowing direct into the garden.

Division
Yarrow is a prolific grower, producing loads of creeping rootstock in a growing season. To stop the invasion, divide by digging up a clump and replanting where required, in the spring or early autumn.

Pests and Diseases
Yarrow is free from both.

Maintenance
Spring: Divide established clumps.
Summer: Dead-head flowers, and cut back after flowering to prevent self-seeding.
Autumn: Sow seeds. Divide established plants.
Winter: No need for protection, very hardy plant.

Garden Cultivation
Yarrow is one of nature's survivors. Its creeping rootstock and ability to self-seed ensure its survival in most soils.

It does well in seaside gardens, as it is drought-tolerant. Still, owners of manicured lawns will know it as a nightmare weed that resists all attempts to

Salad made with 3 Wild herbs

irradicate it.
Yarrow is the plant doctor of the garden, its roots secretions activating the disease resistance of nearby plants. It also intensifies the medicinal actions of other herbs and deepens their fragrance and flavour.

Harvest
Cut the leaves and flowers for drying as the plant comes into flower.

CONTAINER GROWING

Yarrow itself does not grow well in containers. However, the hybrids, and certainly the shorter varieties, can look stunning. Use the bark, grit, peat mix of compost and feed plants with liquid fertilizer during the flowering season, following the manufacturer's instructions. Cut back after flowering and keep watering to a minimum in winter. No variety is suitable for growing indoors.

CULINARY

The young leaves can be used in salads. Here is an interesting salad recipe:

Salad made with 3 Wild Herbs
Equal parts of yarrow, plantain and water cress
A little garlic
½ cucumber
Freshly chopped or dried chives and parsley
1 medium, boiled cold potato
Salad dressing consisting of lemon and cream, or lemon and oil, or lemon and cream and a little apple juice.

Select and clean herbs. Wash carefully and allow to drain. Cut the yarrow and plantain into fine strips. Cube cucumber and potato into small pieces. Leave watercress whole and arrange in bowl. Add herbs and other vegetables and salad dressing and mix well.

OTHER USES
Flowerheads may be dried for winter decoration.
This unassuming plant harbours great powers. 1 small leaf will speed decomposition of a wheelbarrow full of raw compost.
Infuse to make a copper fertilizer.

WARNING

Yarrow should always be taken in moderation and never for long periods because it may cause skin irritation. It should not be taken by pregnant women. Large doses produce headaches and vertigo.

MEDICINAL

Yarrow is one of the best known herbal remedies for fevers. Used as a hot infusion it will induce sweats that cools fevers and expels toxins. In China, yarrow is used fresh as a poultice for healing wounds. It can also be made into a decoction for wounds, chapped skin and rashes, and as a mouthwash for inflamed gums.

Aconitum napellus

MONKSHOOD

Also known as Friar's Cap, Old Woman's Night-cap, Chariots Drawn by Doves, Blue Rocket, Wolf's Bane and Mazbane. From the family Ranunculaceae.

Various species of monkshood grow in temperate regions. They can be found on shady banks, in deciduous woodlands and in mountainous districts. They are all poisonous plants.

One theory for the generic name, *Aconitum*, is that the name comes from the Greek 'akoniton', meaning dart. This is because the juice of the plant was used to poison arrow tips and was used as such by the Arabs and ancient Chinese. Its specific name *napellus* means 'little turnip', a reference to the shape of the root. It was the name used by Theophrastus, the Greek botanist (370-285BC), for a poisonous plant.

This plant has been known through out history to kill both animals and man. In the 16th century Gerard commented in his Herbal on its 'fair and good bluey flowers in shape like helmet which are so beautiful that man would think they were of some excellent virtue'. Appearances should not be trusted. 150 years later, Miller in his garden dictionary wrote, 'Monks Hood was in almost all old gardens and not to be put in the way of children less they should prejudice themselves therewith.'

As late as 1993 a West Country flower seller had to be hospitalized after handling Monkshood, *Aconitum* ssp, outside pubs in Salisbury and Southampton.

Monkshood *Aconitum napellus*

SPECIES

Aconitum napellus
Monkshood
Hardy perennial. Ht 1.5m (5ft), spread 30cm (1ft). Tall slender spires of hooded, light blue/indigo/blue flowers in late summer. Leaves mid-green, palm shaped and deeply cut. There is a white flowered version, **A. napellus 'Albidum'**, which grows in the same way.

Aconitum napellus ssp. napellus Anglicum Group
Monkshood
Hardy perennial. Ht 1.5m (5ft), spread 30cm (1ft). Tall slender spires of hooded, blue/lilac flowers in early/mid-summer. Leaves mid-green, wedged shaped, and deeply cut. One of a few plants peculiar to the British Isles, liking shade or half-shade along brooks and streams. Grows only in a few areas in south-west Britain. Probably the most dangerous of all British plants.

CULTIVATION

Propagation
Seed
Sow the small seed under protection either in the autumn (which is best) or spring. Use prepared seed or plug trays. Cover with Perlite. Germination can be erratic, an all-or-nothing affair. The seeds do not need heat to germinate. In spring, when the seedlings are large enough to handle, plant out into a prepared, shady site 30cm (12in) apart. Wash your hands after handling the seedlings; even better wear thin gloves. The plant takes 2-3 years to flower.

Division
Divide established plants throughout the autumn, so long as the soil is workable. Replant in a prepared site in the garden – remember the gloves. You will notice when splitting the plant that the tap root puts out tubicals or daughter roots with many rootlets. Remove and store in a warm dry place for planting out later.

Pests and Diseases
For obvious reasons this plant does not suffer from pests, and it is usually disease free.

Maintenance
Spring: Plant out autumn-grown seedlings.
Summer: Cut back after flowering.
Autumn: Sow seeds, divide established plants.
Winter: No need to protect fully hardy.

Garden Cultivation
In spite of the dire warnings this is a most attractive plant, which is hardy and thrives in most good soils.
   Position it so that it is not accessible. Plant at the back of borders, or under trees where no animals can eat it or young fingers fiddle with it. It is useful for planting in the shade of trees as long as they are not too dense.
   It is important always to teach people which plants are harmful, and which plants are edible. If you remove all poisonous plants from the garden, people will not learn which to respect.

Harvest
Unless you are a qualified herbalist I do not recommend harvesting.

CONTAINER GROWING

Because of its poisonous nature, I cannot whole-heartedly recommend that it be grown in containers. But if you know you can control the situation, it does look very attractive in a large container surrounded by heartsease (**Viola tricolour**). Use the bark, peat, grit mix of compost, water regularly throughout the summer months. Liquid feed in summer only.

WARNING

The symptoms of **Aconitum** poisoning are a burning sensation on the tongue, vomiting, abdominal pains and diarrhoea, leading to paralysis and death. Emergency antidotes, which are obtainable from hospitals, are atropine and strophanthin.

Monkshood (Aconite) *Aconitum napellus* **growing with dill**

MEDICINAL

Aconitum is one of the most potent nerve poisons in the plant kingdom and is contained in proprietory analgesic medicines to alleviate pain both internally and externally. These drugs can only be prescribed by qualified medical practitioners. Tinctures of monkshood are frequently used in homeopathy.
   Under no circumstances should monkshood ever be prepared and used for self-medication.

CULINARY

None

Agastache foeniculum

ANISE HYSSOP

**Also known as Giant Hyssop, Anise Hyssop, Blue Giant Hyssop,
Fennel Hyssop, Fragrant Giant Hyssop. From the family Labiatae.**

Anise hyssop is a native of North America, the
Mosquito Plant and *A. mexicana*
'*Brittonastrum mexicana*' are from Mexico,
and *A. rugosa* is from Korea.
   There are few references to the history of this lovely herb.
According to Allen Paterson, Director of the Royal Botanical Garden
in Ontario, it is a close cousin of the Bergamots. It is common in
North American herb gardens and is certainly worth including in any
herb garden for its flowers and scent. The long spikes of purple, blue
and pink flowers are big attractions for bees and butterflies.

SPECIES

Agastache cana
The Mosquito Plant
Half-hardy perennial. Ht
60cm (2ft), spread 30cm
(1ft). Pink tubular flowers in
the summer with aromatic
oval mid-green toothed
leaves.

**Agastache mexicana
'Brittonastrum mexicana'
(or 'Cedronella mexican')**
Half-hardy perennial. Ht 1m
(3ft), spread 30cm (1ft). In
summer whorls of small
tubular flowers in shades
from pink to crimson.
Leaves oval pointed, toothed
and mid-green with an
eucalyptus scent.

Agastache rugosa
Korean Mint
Hardy perennial. Ht 1m
(3ft), spread 30cm (1ft).
Lovely mauve/purple flower
spikes in summer. Distinctly
minty scented mid-green
oval pointed leaves.

Anise Hyssop
Agastache foeniculum

**Agastache
foeniculum**
Anise Hyssop
Hardy perennial.
Ht 60cm (2ft), spread
30cm (1ft). Long purple
flower spikes in summer.
Aniseed scented mid-green
oval leaves.

CONTAINER GROWING

**Not suitable for growing
indoors. However, anise
hyssop and Korean mint
both make good patio
plants provided the
container is at least 25-
30cm (10-12in) diameter.
Use the bark, peat mix of
compost, and a liquid
fertilizer feed only once a
year after flowering. If
you feed the plant
beforehand, the flowers
will be poor. Keep well
watered in summer.**

CULTIVATION

Propagation

Note: *A. mexicana* can only be propagated by cuttings.

Seed

The small fine seeds need warmth to germinate: 17°C (65°F). Use the cardboard method and artificial heating if sowing in early spring.

Use either prepared seed or plug trays or if you have only a few seeds directly into a pot and cover with Perlite. Germination takes 10–20 days.

One can also sow outside in the autumn when the soil is warm, but the young plants will need protection throughout the winter months.

When the seedlings are large enough to handle prick out and pot on using a bark or peat mix of compost. In mid-spring, when air and soil temperature has risen, plant out at a distance of 45cm (18in).

Cuttings

Take cuttings of soft young shoots in spring; when all the species root well. Use 50per cent bark, 50per cent peat mix of compost. After a full period of weaning cuttings should be strong enough to plant out in the early autumn.

Semi-ripe wood cuttings may be taken in late summer, use the same compost mix. After they have rooted, pot up, and winter in a cold frame or cold greenhouse.

Division

This is a good alternative way to maintain a short-lived perennial. In the second or third year divide the creeping roots either by the 'forks back-to-back' method, or by digging up the whole plant and dividing.

Pests and Diseases

Being an aromatic plant, pests keep their distance. Rarely suffers from disease, although seedlings can damp off.

Maintenance

Spring: Sow seeds.
Summer: Take softwood or semi-ripe cuttings late season.
Autumn: Tidy up the plants by cutting back the old flower heads and woody growth. Sow seeds. Protect young plants from frost.
Winter: Protect half-hardy species (and Anise hyssop below –6°C (20°F)) with either agricultural fleece, bark or straw.

Garden Cultivation

All species like a rich, moist soil and full sun, and will adapt very well to most ordinary soils if planted in a sunny situation. All are short lived and should be propagated each year to ensure continuity.

Anise hyssop, although hardier than the other species, still needs protection below –6°C (20°F).

The Mexican half-hardy species need protection below –3°C (26°F).

Harvest

Flowers

Cut for drying just as they begin to open.

Leaves

Cut leaves just before late spring flowering.

Seeds

Heads turn brown as the seed ripens. At the first sign of the seed falling, pick and hang upside down with a paper bag tied over the heads.

OTHER USES

Anise Hyssop, Korean Mint and *Agastache mexicana* all have scented leaves which makes them suitable for potpourris.

Summer fruit cup made with anise hyssop

CULINARY

The two varieties most suitable are –

Anise Hyssop

Leaves can be used in salads and to make refreshing tea. Like borage, they can be added to summer fruit cups. Equally they can be chopped and used as a seasoning in pork dishes or in savoury rice.

Flowers can be added to fruit salads and cups giving a lovely splash of colour.

Korean Mint

Leaves have a strong peppermint flavour and make a very refreshing tea, said to be good first thing in the morning after a night on the town. They are also good chopped up in salads, and the flowers look very attractive scattered over a pasta salad.

Korean mint tea

Alchemilla mollis

LADY'S MANTLE

From the family Rosaceae.

Lady's mantle is a native of the mountains of Europe, Asia and America. It is found not only in damp places but also in dry shady woods.

The Arab 'alkemelych' (alchemy) was thought to be the source of the herb's Latin generic name, *Alchemilla*. The crystal dew lying in perfect pearl drops on the leaves have long inspired poets and alchemists, and was reputed to have healing and magical properties, even to preserve a woman's youth provided she collected the dew in May, alone, in full moonlight, naked, and with bare feet as a sign of purity and to ward off any lurking forces.

In the medieval period it was dedicated to the Virgin Mary, hence Lady's Mantle was considered a woman's protector, and nicknamed 'a woman's best friend', and was used not only to regulate the menstrual cycle and to ease the effects of menopause, but also to reduce inflammation of the female organs. In the 18th century, women applied the leaves to their breasts to make them recover shape after they had been swelled with milk.

It is still prescribed by herbalists today.

Lady's Mantle *Alchemilla mollis*

Alchemilla conjuncta
Lady's Mantle Conjuncta
Hardy perennial. Ht 30cm (12in), spread 30cm (12in) or more. Tiny, greenish-yellow flowers in summer. Leaves star-shaped, bright green on top with lovely silky silver hairs underneath. An attractive plant suitable for ground cover, rockeries and dry banks.

SPECIES

Alchemilla alpina
Alpine Lady's Mantle
Known in America as Silvery Lady's Mantle.
Hardy perennial. Ht 15cm (6in), spread 60cm (24in) or more. Tiny, greenish-yellow flowers in summer. Leaves rounded, lobed, pale green and covered in silky hairs. An attractive plant suitable for ground cover, rockeries and dry banks.

Alchemilla mollis
Lady's Mantle (Garden variety)
Hardy perennial. Ht and spread 50cm (20in). Tiny, greenish-yellow flowers in summer. Large, pale green, rounded leaves with crinkled edges.

Alchemilla xanthochlora (vulgaris)
Lady's Mantle (Wild flower variety)
Also known as Lion's Foot, Bear's Foot and Nine Hooks.
Hardy perennial. Ht 15-45cm (6-18in), spread 50cm (20in). Tiny, bright greenish/yellow flowers in summer. Round, pale green leaves with crinkled edges.

CULTIVATION

Propagation
Seed

Why is it that something that self-seeds readily around the garden can be so difficult to raise from seed? Sow its very fine seed in early spring or autumn into prepared seed or plug trays (use the cardboard method), and cover with Perlite. No bottom heat required. Germination can either be sparse or prolific, taking 2-3 weeks. If germinating in the autumn, winter seedlings in the trays and plant out the following spring when the frosts are over, at a distance of 45cm (18in) apart.

Division

All established plants can be divided in the spring or autumn. Replant in the garden where desired.

Pests and Diseases
This plant rarely suffers from pests or disease.

Maintenance
Spring: Divide established plants. Sow seeds if necessary.
Summer: To prevent self-seeding, cut off flowerheads as they begin to die back.
Autumn: Divide established plants if necessary. Sow seed.
Winter: No need for protection.

Garden Cultivation
This fully hardy plant grows in all but boggy soils, in sun or partial shade. Seed can be sown in spring where you want the plant to flower. Thin the seedlings to 30cm (12in) apart.

 This is a most attractive garden plant in borders or as an edging plant, but it can become a bit of a nuisance, seeding everywhere. To prevent this, cut back after flowering and at the same time cut back old growth.

Early morning dew on
Alchemilla mollis

Harvest
Cut young leaves after the dew has dried for use throughout the summer. Harvest for drying as plant comes into flower.

CONTAINER GROWING

All forms of Lady's Mantle adapt to container growing and look very pretty indeed. Use a soil-based compost, water throughout the summer, but feed with liquid fertilizer (following manufacturer's instructions) only occasionally. In the winter, when the plant dies back, put the container in a cold greenhouse or cold frame, and water only very occasionally. Lady's Mantle can be grown in hanging baskets as a centre piece.

MEDICINAL

Used by herbalists for menstrual disorders. It has been said that if you drink an infusion of green parts of the plant for 10 days each month it will help relieve menopausal discomfort. It can also be used as a mouth rinse after tooth extraction. Traditionally, the alpine species has been considered more effective, although this is not proven.

Leaves laid out for drying

CULINARY

Tear young leaves, with their mild bitter taste, into small pieces and toss into salads. Many years ago Marks & Spencer had a yoghurt made with Lady's Mantle leaves! I wish I had tried it.

OTHER USES
Excellent for flower arranging.
 Leaves can be boiled for green wool dye and are used in veterinary medicine for the treatment of diarrhoea.

Allium

ONIONS

From the family Liliaceae.

T hese plants are widely distributed throughout the world.

The onion goes back to a time before historians, and has been in cultivation so long that its country of origins are now uncertain although most agree that it originated in Central Asia. It was probably introduced to Europe by the Romans. The name seems to have been derived from the Latin word 'unio' meaning a large pearl.

In the Middle Ages it was believed that a bunch of onions hung outside the door would absorb the infection of the plague, saving the inhabitants. From this came the scientific recognition that its sulphur content acts as a strong disinfectant. The juice of the onion was used to heal gunshot wounds and burns caused by gunpowder.

SPECIES

There are many, many varieties of Onion, the following information concerns the two that have herbal qualities.

Allium fistulosum
Welsh Onion
Also known as Japanese Leek.
Evergreen hardy perennial. Ht 60cm-90cm (2-3ft). Flowers of second year's growth greenish yellow in early summer. Leaves, green hollow cylinders. This onion is a native of Siberia and extensively grown in China and Japan. The name Welsh comes from 'walsch' meaning foreign.

Welsh Onion *Allium fistulosum*

Allium cepa Proliferum Group
Tree Onion
Also known as Egyptian Onion, Lazy Man's Onions. Hardy perennial. Ht 90-150cm (3-5ft). Flowers small greenish white appear in early summer in the same place as its bulbs. It grows bulbs underground and then, at the end of flowering, bulbs in the air. Seeing is believing. It originates from Canada. It is very easy to propagate.

Young Tree Onions *Allium cepa* Proliferum Group

CULTIVATION

Propagation
Seed
Welsh onion seed loses its viability within 2 years, so sow fresh in late winter, early spring under protection with a bottom heat of between 15°C (60°F) and 21°C (70°F). Cover with Perlite. When the seedlings are large enough, and after a period of hardening off, plant out into a prepared site in the garden at a distance of 25cm (9in) apart.

The tree onion is not grown from seed.

Division
Each year the Welsh onion will multiply in clumps, so it is a good idea to divide them every 3 years in the spring.

Because the tree onion is such a big grower, it is a good idea to split the underground bulbs every 3 years in spring.

Bulbs
The air growing bulbils of the tree onion have small root systems, each one capable of reproducing another plant. Plant where required in an enriched soil either in the autumn, as the parent plant dies back, or in the spring.

Pests and Diseases
The onion fly is the curse of the onion family especially in late spring, early summer. The way to try and prevent this is to take care not to damage the roots or leaves when thinning the seedlings and also not to leave the thinnings lying around, the scent attracts the fly.

Another problem is downy mildew caused by cool wet autumns; the leaves become velvety and die back. Again, too warm a summer may encourage white rot. Burn the affected plants and do not plant in the same position again.

Other characteristic diseases are neck rot and bulb rot, both caused by a

Botrytis fungus that usually occurs as a result of the bulbs being damaged either by digging or hoeing.

Onions are prone to many more diseases but, if you keep the soil fertile and do not make life easy for the onion fly, you will still have a good crop.

Maintenance

Spring: Sow the seed, divide 3-year-old clumps of Welsh and tree onions.

Plant bulbs of tree onions.
Summer: Stake mature tree onions to stop them falling over and depositing the ripe bulbils on the soil.
Autumn: Mulch around tree onion plants with well-rotted manure. Use a small amount around the Welsh onions.
Winter: Neither variety needs protection.

Garden Cultivation

Welsh Onions
These highly adaptable hardy onions will grow in any well-drained fertile soil. Seeds can be sown in spring after the frosts, direct into the ground. Thin to a distance of 25cm (9in) apart. Keep well watered throughout the growing season. In the autumn give the area a mulch of well-rotted manure.

Tree Onions
Dig in some well-rotted manure before planting. Plant the bulbs in their clusters in a sunny well-drained position at a distance of 30-45cm (12-18in) apart. In the first year nothing much will happen (unless you are one of the lucky ones). If the summer is very dry, water well. In the following year, if you give the plant a good mulch of well-rotted manure in autumn, it grows to 90-150cm (3-5ft) and produce masses of small onions.

Harvest

Welsh onions may be picked at any time from early summer onwards. The leaves do not dry well but can be frozen like those of their cousin, chives. Use scissors and snip them into a plastic bag. They form neat rings; freeze them.

The little tree onions can be picked off the stems and stored; lay them out on a rack in a cool place with good ventilation.

CULINARY

Welsh onions make a great substitute for spring onions, as they are hardier and earlier. Pull and use in salads or stir fry dishes, chop and use instead of chives.

Tree onions provide fresh onion flavour throughout the year. The bulbils can be pickled or chopped raw in salads (fairly strong), or cooked whole in stews and casseroles.

Pissaladière
Serves 4-6

4 tablespoons olive oil (not extra virgin)
20 tree onions, finely chopped
1 clove garlic, crushed
1 dessertspoon fresh thyme, chopped
Salt
Freshly ground black pepper
360g (¾lb) once-risen bread dough
250g (½lb) ripe tomatoes, peeled and sliced
60g (2oz) canned anchovy fillets, drained and halved lengthways
16 large black olives, halved and pitted

Heat the olive oil in a heavy frying pan, add the onions, cover the pan tightly and fry, gently stirring occasionally for 15 minutes. Add the garlic and the thyme and cook uncovered for 15 minutes, or until the onions are reduced to a clear purée. Season to taste and leave to cool. Pre-heat the oven to 200°C (400°F, Gas mark 6).

Pissaladière

Roll the bread dough directly on the baking sheet into a circle 25cm (10in) diameter. Spread the puréed onions evenly over the dough, put the tomato slices on the onions and top with a decorative pattern of anchovy fillets and olives.

Bake for 5 minutes. Reduce the oven temperature to 190°C (375°F, Gas mark 5) and continue to bake for 30 minutes or until the bread base is well risen and lightly browned underneath.

Serve hot with a green herb salad.

OTHER USES

The onion is believed to help ward off colds in winter and also to induce sleep and cure indigestion. The fresh juice is antibiotic, diuretic, expectorant, antispasmodic, so useful in the treatment of coughs, colds, bronchitis, laryngitis and gastroenteritis. It is also said to lower the blood pressure and to help restore sexual potency which has been impaired by illness or mental stress.

CONTAINER GROWING

Welsh onions can be grown in a large pot using a soil-based compost, and make sure it does not dry out. Feed regularly throughout the summer with a liquid fertilizer.

Tree onions grow too tall for containers.

Allium sativum

GARLIC

Also known as Clove Garlic. From the family Liliaceae.

Garlic originates from India or Central Asia and is one of the oldest and most valued of plants. In Greek legend, Odysseus used Moly, a wild garlic, as a charm to keep the sorceress, Circe, from turning him into a pig. The Egyptians used it medicinally. Both the slaves constructing the pyramid of Cheops and the Roman soldiers were given garlic cloves daily to sustain their strength. It was probably the Romans who introduced it into Britain. The common name is said to have been derived from the Anglo-Saxon 'leac', meaning pot herb and 'gar', a lance, after the shape of the stem.

The term for 'leper' in the Middle Ages was 'pilgarlic' because the leper had to peel his own. During the First World War, spaghnum moss was soaked in garlic juice as an antiseptic wound dressing. An old country remedy for whooping cough was to put a clove of garlic in the shoes of the whooper.

A tradition still held in rural New Mexico is that garlic will help a young girl rid herself of an unwanted boyfriend.

Garlic cloves

SPECIES

Allium sativum
Garlic
Hardy perennial grown as an annual. Ht 40-60cm (16-24in). A bulb made up of several cloves (bulblets) enclosed in white papery skin. The cloves vary in colour from white to pink. Green leaves. White or pink round flower head. Only flowers in warm climates.

Allium oleraceum
Field Garlic
Hardy perennial, bulbous plant. Ht up to 84cm (33in). Pink summer flowers.

CULTIVATION

Propagation
Plant the bulbs direct in the ground.

Pests and Diseases
Susceptible to white rot, which causes yellowing of the foliage and white fungal growth on the bulbs. Remove infected plants and avoid using this ground again for garlic.

Maintenance
Spring: Plant the first month into spring. Feed with liquid fertilizer.
Summer: Potash dress garden plants. Dig up bulbs.
Autumn: Plant cloves.
Winter: Protect if the temperature falls below -15°C (5°F).

Garden Cultivation
Plant in full sun, in rich, light and well drained soil from early end-autumn to early spring. Traditionally garlic cloves are planted on the shortest day of the year and harvested on longest. Split the bulb into the cloves and plant individually, pointed end up, into holes 2cm (1in) deep and 15cm (6in) apart. Keep well watered. They will be well matured in summer when the top growth starts to change colour and keel over. Tying the stems in a knot is said to increase the size of the cloves.

Harvest
Ease the bulbs out of the ground when the leaves die down and lose their greenness (mid-late summer). Dry in the sun for a few days if possible, but indoors if there is a danger of rain. Hang them up in a string bag, or plait them into a garlic string. Store somewhere cool and airy.

CONTAINER GROWING

In the spring place a number of individual cloves in a pot (tip up) and position on a sunny windowsill. Feed with liquid fertilizer regularly and harvest the green leaves as one would chives.

COMPANION PLANTING

Garlic, it is said, helps to prevent leaf curl in trees, especially peaches. Also, when planted next to roses it wards off black spot.

OTHER USES

Its juice acts as an insect repellent and neutralizes the poisons of bites and stings.
It is an excellent glue and also enables holes to be made cleanly in glass. Simply crush a clove, rub it onto the glass and let it dry; then cut or drill the hole.

CULINARY

Garlic is a very pungent but indispensible culinary herb. In spring the flavour is lively but from summertime onwards, cloves should be split in half and the green filaments and sheath enclosing them discarded to make the garlic more digestible.

Whole bulbs may be divided into cloves and roasted under a joint of lamb, and slivers of garlic inserted under the surface of meat. The longer garlic is cooked, the milder the flavour.

A peeled clove may be left to stand in a vinaigrette and then discarded before the dressing of the salad. Alternatively, rub a clove around the salad bowl.

Whole cloves flavour bottles of olive oil or wine vinegar.

Garlic butter is a traditional accompaniment to snails.

The Orientals, particularly the Chinese, are great lovers of garlic. Their solution to garlic breath is to offer pods of cardamom seeds to chew at the end of a meal. You may prefer to eat parsley or basil, mint or thyme, all of which reduce the aroma on the breath.

MEDICINAL

It has been shown to reduce blood pressure, evidently it is useful in guarding against strokes. It has also been

Garlic tonic

successful in controlling diarrhoea, dysentery, TB, whooping cough, typhoid and hepatitis. Effective against many fungal infections and it can be used to expel worms. It has even been shown to lower blood sugar levels, suggesting a use in controlling diabetes.

Herbalists consider garlic to be a first-rate digestive tonic and also use it to treat toothache, earache, coughs and colds. A decaying tooth will hurt less if packed with garlic pulp until treatment can be obtained.

Externally, garlic can be applied to insect bites, boils and unbroken chilblains but it may cause an allergic rash if used for too long.

Warning: Can irritate the skin.

Pests and Diseases
Mostly wild garlic is free from pests and diseases.

CULINARY

Pick from end-spring for use in salads, soups or as a vegetable.

OTHER USES
Traditionally, as a liquid household disinfectant.

Alliumursinum

WILD GARLIC

Also known as Wood Garlic, Ransomes, Ramsons, Devil's Posy, Onion Flower, Stinkplant and Bear's Garlic. From the family Liliaceae.

Wild garlic is a native of Europe and Asia, naturalized in many countries in the Northern hemisphere including Britain and North America.

SPECIES

Allium ursinum
Wild Garlic
Hardy perennial. Ht 36-45cm (12-18in).
Clusters of white flowers in spring and summer.

CULTIVATION

Propagation
Seed
It is better to sow straight into the garden.

Division
Divide established plants early autumn, when the flowers have died back.

Maintenance
Spring: If the plant is getting invasive dig up.
Summer: Divide plants in late summer, when the plant has died back.
Autumn: Sow seed.
Winter: No need to protect this herb as it is fully hardy.

Garden Cultivation
Wild garlic likes a moist, fertile soil in a semi-shady to shady spot in the garden. Sow the seed in autumn where the plants are to grow and cover them lightly with soil. Germination will take place in early spring. Wild garlic self-seeds easily; in wet areas it can be invasive.

Wild Garlic *Allium ursinum*

Allium schoenoprasum

CHIVES

From the family Liliaceae

Chives is the only member of the onion group found wild in Europe, Australia and North America, where it thrives in temperate and warm to hot regions. Although one of the most ancient of all herbs, chives were not cultivated in European gardens until the 16th century.

Chives were a favourite in China as long ago as 3,000 BC. They were enjoyed for their delicious mild onion flavour and used as an antidote to poison and to stop bleeding. Their culinary virtues were first reported to the West by the explorer and traveller, Marco Polo. During the Middle Ages they were sometimes known as rush-leeks, from the Greek 'schoinos' meaning rush and 'parson' meaning 'leek'.

Chives *Allium schoenoprasum*

Chives
Allium schoenoprasum

SPECIES

Allium schoenoprasum
Chives
Hardy perennial. Ht 30cm (12in). Purple globular flowers all summer. Leaves green and cylindrical. Apart from being a good culinary herb it makes an excellent edging plant.

Allium schoenoprasum 'fine-leaved'
Extra Fine Leafed Chives
Hardy perennial. Ht 20cm (8in), Purple globular flowers all summer. Very narrow cylindrical leaves, not as coarse as standard chives. Good for culinary usage.

Allium schoenoprasum 'white'
White Chives
Hardy perennial. Ht 20cm (8in). White globular flowers all summer. Cylindrical green leaves. A cultivar of ordinary chives and very effective in a silver garden. Good flavour.

Allium schoenoprasum roseum
Pink Chives
Hardy perennial. Ht 20cm (8in). Pink flowers all summer. Cylindrical green leaves. Also a cultivar of ordinary chives, its pink flowers can look a bit insipid if planted too close to the purple flowered variety. Good in flower arrangements.

Garlic Chive flower
Allium tuberosum

Allium tuberosum
Garlic Chives (Chinese chives)
Hardy perennial. Ht 40cm (16in). White flowers all summer. Leaf mid-green, flat and solid with a sweet garlic flavour when young. As they get older the leaf becomes tougher and the taste coarser.

CULTIVATION

Propagation

Seed

Easy from seed, but they need a temperature of 19°C (65°F) to germinate, so if sowing outside, wait until late spring for the soil to be warm enough. I recommend starting this plant in plug trays with bottom heat in early spring. Sow about 10-15 seeds per 3cm (1in) cell. Transplant either into pots or into the garden when the soil has warmed.

Division

Every few years in the spring lift clumps (made up of small bulbs) and replant in 6-10 bulb-clumps, 15cm (6ins) apart, adding fresh compost or manure.

Pests and Diseases

Greenfly may be a problem on pot-grown herbs. Wash off gently under the tap or use a liquid horticultural soap. Be diligent, for aphids can hide deep down among the bulbs.

Cool wet autumns may produce downy mildew; the leaves will become velvety and die back from the tips. Dig up, split and re-pot affected plants, at the same time cutting back all the growth to prevent the disease spreading.

Chives can also suffer from rust. As this is a virus it is essential to cut back diseased growth immediately and burn it. DO NOT COMPOST. If very bad, remove the plant and burn it all. Do not plant any rust prone plants in that area.

Maintenance

Spring: Clear soil around emerging established plants. Feed with liquid fertilizer. Sow seeds
Summer: Remove the flower stem before flowering to increase leaf production.
Autumn: Prepare soil for next year's crop. Dig up a small clump, pot, bring inside for forcing.
Winter: Cut forced chives and feed regularly.

Garden Cultivation

Chives are fairly tolerant regarding soil and position, but produce the best growth planted 15cm (6in) from other plants in a rich moist soil and in a fairly sunny position. If the soil is poor they will turn yellow and then brown at the tips. For an attractive edging, plant at a distance of 10cm (4in) and allow to flower. Keep newly transplanted plants well watered in the spring, and in the summer make sure that they do not dry out, otherwise the leaves will quickly shrivel. Chives die right back into the ground in winter, but a winter cutting can be forced by digging up a clump in autumn, potting it into a rich mix of compost (bark, peat mix), and placing it somewhere warm with good light.

Harvest

Chives may be cut to within 3cm (1in) of the ground 4 times a year to maintain a supply of succulent fresh leaves. Chives do not dry well. Refrigerated leaves in a sealed plastic bag will retain crispness for seven days. Freeze chopped leaves in ice cubes for convenience.
    Cut flowers when they are fully open before the colour fades for use in salads and sauces.

MEDICINAL

The leaves are mildly antiseptic and when sprinkled onto food they stimulate the appetite and promote digestion.

CONTAINER GROWING

Chives grow well in pots or on a window sill and flourish in a window box if partially shaded. They need an enormous quantity of water and occasional liquid feed to stay green and succulent. Remember too that, being bulbs, chives need some top growth for strengthening and regeneration, so do not cut away all the leaves if you wish to use them next season. Allow to die back in winter if you want to use it the following spring. A good patio plant, easy to grow, but not particularly fragrant.

CULINARY

Add chives at the end of cooking or the flavour will disappear. They are delicious freshly picked and snipped as a garnish or flavour in omelettes or scrambled eggs, salads and soups. They can be mashed into soft cheeses or sprinkled onto grilled meats. Add to sour cream as a filling for jacket potatoes.

COMPANION PLANTING

Chives planted next to apple trees prevent scab, and when planted next to roses can prevent black spot. Hence the saying, 'Chives next to roses creates poses'.

OTHER USES

Chives are said to prevent scab infection on animals.

Chive Butter

Use in scrambled eggs, omelettes and cooked vegetables and with grilled lamb or fish or on jacket potatoes.

100g/4oz/½cup butter
4 tablespoons chopped chives
1 tablespoon lemon juice
Salt and pepper

Cream the chives and softened butter together until well mixed. Beat in the lemon juice and season to taste. Cover and cool the butter in the refrigerator until ready to use; it will keep for several days.

Ajuga reptans

BUGLE

Also known as Common or Creeping Bugle, Bugle Weed, Babies Shoes, Baby's Rattle, Blind Mans Hand, Carpenters Herb, Dead Men's Bellows, Horse and Hounds, Nelson's Bugle, Thunder and Lightening and Middle Comfrey. From the family Labiatae.

The bugle found in Britain is a native of Europe. It is frequently found in mountainous areas and often grows in damp fields, mixed woodland and meadows. The Bugle of North America is a species of Lycopus (Gypsy Weed).

Among the many folk tales associated with bugle is one that its flowers can cause a fire if brought into the house, a belief that has survived in at least one district of Germany.

SPECIES

Ajuga reptans
Bugle
Hardy evergreen perennial. Ht 30cm (1ft), spread up to 1m (3ft). Very good spreading plant. Blue flowers from spring to summer. Oval leaves are dark green with purplish tinge. It is this plant that has medicinal properties.

Ajuga reptans 'Atropurpurea'
Bronze Bugle
As Ajuga reptans but Ht 15cm (6in), spread 1m (3ft). Blue flowers. Deep bronze/purple leaves.

Ajuga reptans 'Multicolor'
Multicoloured Bugle
As Ajuga reptans but Ht 12cm (5in), spread 45cm (18in). Small spikes of blue flowers. Dark green leaves marked with cream and pink.

CULTIVATION

Propagation
Seeds
Sow the small seed in autumn, or spring as a second choice. Cover only lightly with soil. Germination can be slow and erratic.

Division
This method is easy and the only one suitable for cultivars as Bugle produces runners, each having its own root system. Plant out in autumn or spring. Space 60cm (2ft) apart, as a single plant spreads rapidly.

Pests and Diseases
Nothing much disturbs this plant!

Maintenance
Spring: Clear winter debris around established plants. Dig up runners and replant in other areas. Sow seeds. *Summer*: Control established plants by digging up runners.

Autumn: Sow seed, dig up runners of established plants, pot on, using the bark, peat compost, and winter in cold frame, or replant in garden. *Winter*: No protection needed unless very cold -20°C (-6°F).

Garden Cultivation
At close quarters bugle is very appealing and can be used as a decorative ground cover.It will grow vigorously on any soil that retains moisture, in full sun, and it also tolerates quite dense shade. It will even thrive in a damp boggy area near the pond or in a hedgerow or shady woodland area. Guard against leaf scorch on the variegated variety.

Harvest
For medicinal usage the leaves and flowers are gathered in early summer.

CONTAINER GROWING

Bugle makes a good outside container plant especially the variegated and purple varieties. Use the bark, peat mix of compost. Also very effective in hanging baskets.

CULINARY

The young shoots of *Ajuga reptans* can be mixed in salads to give you a different taste. Not mine.

MEDICINAL

An infusion of dried leaves in boiling water is thought to lower blood pressure and to stop internal bleeding. Nowadays it is widely used in homeopathy in various preparations against throat irritation especially in the case of mouth ulcers.

OTHER USES
In some countries it is gathered as cattle fodder.

SPECIES

Aloe vera (barbadensis)
Aloe vera
Half-hardy perennial. Grown outside: ht 60cm (2ft), spread 60cm (2ft) or more. Grown as a house plant: ht 30cm (12in). Minimum temperature 10°C (50°F). Succulent grey/green pointed foliage, from which eventually grows a flowering stem with bell-shaped yellow or orange flowers.

Aloe arborescens 'Variegata'
Half-hardy perennial. Grown outside: ht, spread 2m (6ft). Minimum temperature 7°C (45°F). Each stem is crowned by rosettes of long, blue green leaves with toothed edges and cream stripes. Produces numerous spikes of red tubular flowers in late winter and spring.

Aloe variegata
Partridge-breasted aloe
Half-hardy perennial. A house plant only in temperate climates. Ht 30cm (12in), spread 10cm (4in). Minimum temperature 7°C (45°F). Triangular, white marked, dark green leaves. Spike of pinkish-red flowers in spring.

CULTIVATION

Propagation
Seed
A temperature of 21°C (70°F) must be maintained during germination. Sow onto the surface of a pot or tray and cover with Perlite. Place in a propagator with bottom heat. Germination is erratic – 4 to 24 months.

Division
In summer gently remove offshoots at the base of a mature plant. Leave for a day to dry, then pot into 2 parts compost to 1 part sharp sand mix. Water in and leave in warm place to establish. Give the parent plant a good liquid feed when returning to its pot.

Pest and Disease
Over watering causes it to rot off.

Maintenance
Spring: Give containerized plants a good dust! Spray the leaves with water. Give a good feed of liquid fertilizer.
Summer: Remove the basal offshoots of a mature plant to maintain the parent plant. Re-pot mature plants if necessary.
Autumn: Bring in pots if there is any danger of frost.
Winter: Rest all pot grown plants in a cool room (minimum temp 5°C (40°F); keep watering to the absolute minimum.

ALOE VERA
Aloe vera (barbadensis)
From the family Lilaceae/Aloëaceae

There are between 250 and 350 species of aloe around the world. They are originally native to the arid areas of Southern Africa. In cultivation they need a frost-free environment. Aloe has been valued at least since the 4th century BC when Aristotle requested Alexander the Great to conquer Socotra in the Indian Ocean, where many species grow.

Garden Cultivation
Aloes enjoy a warm, frost-free position – full sun to partial shade – and a free-draining soil. Leave 1m (3ft) minimum between plants.

Harvest
Cut leaves throughout the growing season. A plant of more than 2 years has stronger properties.

CONTAINER GROWING

Compost must be gritty and well drained. Do not over water. Maintain a frost-free, light environment.

Aloe vera *Aloe vera (barbadensis)*

MEDICINAL

The gel obtained by breaking the leaves is a remarkable healer. Applied to wounds it forms a clear protective seal and encourages skin regeneration. It can be applied directly to cuts, burns, and is immediately soothing. Rumour has it that the US Government is building up stocks for use in the event of a nuclear disaster.

COSMETIC

Aloe vera is used in cosmetic preparations, in hand creams, suntan lotions and shampoos.

WARNING

It should be emphasized that, apart from external application, aloes are not for home medication. ALWAYS seek medical attention for serious burns.

Aloysia triphylla (Lippia citriodora)

LEMON VERBENA

From the family Verbenaceae.

Lemon verbena grew originally in Chile. This Rolls Royce of lemon-scented plants was first imported into Europe in the 18th century by the Spanish for its perfume.

MEDICINAL

A tea last thing at night is refreshing and has mild sedative properties; it can also soothe bronchial and nasal congestion and ease indigestion. However, long term use may cause stomach irritation.

SPECIES

Aloysia triphylla (Lippia citriodora)
Lemon Verbena
Half-hardy deciduous perennial. Ht 1-3m (3-10ft), spread up to 2.5m (8ft). Tiny white flowers tinged with lilac in early summer. Leaves pale green, lance shaped and very strongly lemon scented.

CULTIVATION

Propagation
Seeds
The seed only sets in warm climates and should be sown in spring into prepared seed or plug trays and covered with Perlite; a bottom heat of 15°C (60°F) helps. Prick out into 9cm (3½in) pots using the bark, peat, grit mix of compost. Keep in pots for the first 2 years before planting specimens out in the garden 1m (3ft) apart.

Cuttings
Take softwood cuttings from the new growth in late spring. The cutting material will wilt quickly so have

everything prepared. Take semi-hardwood cuttings in late summer or early autumn. Keep in pots for the first 2 years.

Pests and Diseases
If grown under protection you will have to contend with whitefly and red spider mite; spray both with a liquid horticultural soap.

Maintenance
Spring: Trim established plants. Take softwood cuttings. In warm climates sow seed.
Summer: Trim after flowering. Take semi-hardwood cuttings.
Autumn: Cut back, but not hard. Bring in before frosts.
Winter: Protect all winter.

Garden Cultivation
Likes a warm humid climate. The soil should be light, free draining and warm. A sunny wall is ideal. It will need protection against frost and wind, and temperatures below 4°C (40°F). If left in the ground, cover the area around the roots with mulching material.
  In spring give the plant a gentle prune and spray with warm water to help revive it.
  New growth can appear very late so never discard a plant until late summer. Once the plant has started re-shooting, remove the dead tips and prune gently to encourage new growth. At

the end of the growing season, cut the plant back again gently to restore some shape.

Harvest
Pick the leaves any time before they start to wither and darken. Leaves dry very quickly and easily, keeping their colour and scent. Store them in a damp-proof container.

CONTAINER GROWING

Choose a container at least 20cm (8in) wide and use the bark, peat, grit mix of compost. Place the container in a warm, sunny, light and airy spot. Water well throughout the growing season and feed with liquid fertilizer during flowering. Then trim the plant to maintain shape, and trim further during the autumn. In winter move the container into a cold greenhouse, and allow the compost to nearly dry out.

CULINARY

Use fresh leaves to flavour oil and vinegar, drinks, fruit puddings, confectionery, apple jelly, cakes and stuffings. Infuse in finger bowls.
  Add a teaspoon of chopped, fresh leaves to home-made ice cream for a delicious dessert.

OTHER USES

The leaves with their strong lemon scent are lovely in potpourris, linen sachets, herb pillows, sofa sacks. The distilled oil made from the leaves is an essential basic ingredient in many perfumes.

Althaea officinalis

MARSH-MALLOW

Also known as Mortification Root, Sweet Weed, Wymote, Marsh Malice, Mesh-mellice, Wimote, and Althea. From the family Malvaceae.

Marsh-mallow is widely distributed from Western Europe to Siberia, from Australia to North America. It is common to find it in salt marshes and on banks near the sea.

The generic name, *Althaea*, comes from the Latin 'altheo' meaning 'I cure'. It may be the althea that Hippocrates recommended so highly for healing wounds. The Romans considered it a delicious vegetable, used it in barley soup and in stuffing for suckling pigs. In the Renaissance era the herbalists used marsh-mallow to cure sore throats, stomach trouble and toothache.

The soft, sweet marshmallow was originally flavoured with the root of marsh-mallow.

SPECIES

Althaea officinalis
Marsh-Mallow
Hardy perennial. Ht 60-120cm (2-4ft), spread 60cm (2ft). Flowers pink or white in late summer/early autumn. Leaves, grey-green in colour, tear shaped and covered all over with soft hair.

CULTIVATION

Propagation
Seed
Sow in prepared seed or plug trays in the autumn.
Cover lightly with compost and winter outside under glass. Erratic germination takes place in spring. Plant out, 45cm (18in) apart, when large enough to handle.

Division
Divide established plants in the spring or autumn, replanting into a prepared site in the garden.

Pests and Diseases
This plant is usually free from pests and diseases.

Maintenance
Spring: Divide established plants.
Summer: Cut back after flowering for new growth.
Autumn: Sow seeds and winter the trays outside
Winter: No need for protection fully hardy.

Garden Cultivation
Marsh-mallow is highly attractive to butterflies. A good seaside plant, it likes a site in full sun with a moist or wet, moderately fertile soil. Cut back after flowering to encourage new leaves.

Harvest
Pick leaves for fresh use as required; they do not preserve well.
For use either fresh or dried, dig up the roots of 2-year-old plants in autumn, after the flowers and leaves have died back.

MEDICINAL

Due to its high mucilage content (35 percent in the root and 10 percent in the leaf), marsh-mallow soothes or cures inflammation, ulceration of the stomach and small intestine, soreness of throat, and pain from cystitis. An infusion of leaves or flowers serves as a soothing gargle; an infusion of the root can be used for coughs, diarrhoea and insomnia.
The pulverised roots may be used as a healing and drawing poultice, which should be applied warm.

CULINARY

Boil the roots to soften, then peel and quickly fry in butter.
Use the flowers in salads, and leaves, too, which may also be added to oil and vinegar, or steamed and served as a vegetable.

DECOCTION FOR DRY HANDS

Soak 25g (1oz) of scraped and finely chopped root in 150ml (¼pint) of cold water for 24 hours. Strain well. Add 1 tablespoon of the decoction to 2 tablespoons of ground almonds, 1 teaspoon of milk and 1 teaspoon of cider vinegar. Beat it until well blended. Add a few drops of lavender oil. Put into a small screw top pot.

Anethum graveolens

DILL

**Also known as Dillweed and Dillseed.
From the family Umbelliferae.**

A native of southern Europe and western Asia, dill grows wild in the cornfields of Mediterranean countries and also in North and South America. The generic name 'Anethum' derives from the Greek 'Anethon'. 'Dill' is said to come from the Anglo-Saxon 'dylle' or the Norse 'dilla', meaning to soothe or lull. Dill was found amongst the names of herbs used by Egyptian doctors 5,000 years ago and the remains of the plant have been found in the ruins of Roman buildings in Britain.

It is mentioned in the Gospel of St Matthew, where it is suggested that herbs were of sufficient value to be used as a tax payment – oh that that were true today! 'Woe unto you, Scribes and Pharisees, hypocrites! for ye pay tithe of mint and dill and cumin, and have omitted the weightier matters of the law.'

During the Middle Ages dill was prized as protection against witchcraft. While magicians used it in their spells, lesser mortals infused it in wine to enhance passion. It was once an important medicinal herb for treating coughs and headaches, as an ingredient of ointments and for calming infants with whooping cough – dill water or gripe water is still called upon today. Early settlers took dill to North America, where it came to be known as the 'Meeting House Seed', because the children were given it to chew during long sermons to prevent them feeling hungry.

SPECIES

Anethum graveolens
Dill
Annual. Ht 60-150cm (2-5ft), spread 30cm (12in). Tiny yellow/green flowers in flattened umbel clusters in summer. Fine aromatic feathery green leaves.

CULTIVATION

Propagation
Seed
Seed can be started in early spring under cover, using pots or plug trays. Do not use seed trays, as it does not like being transplanted, and if it gets upset it will bolt and miss out the leaf-producing stage.

The seeds are easy to handle, being a good size. Place 4 per plug or evenly spaced on the surface of a pot, and cover with Perlite. Germination takes 2-4 weeks, depending on the warmth of the surrounding area. As soon as the seedlings are large enough to handle, the air and soil temperatures have started to rise and there is no threat of frost, plant out 28cm (9in) apart.

Garden Cultivation
Keep dill plants well away from fennel, otherwise they will cross pollinate and their individual flavours will become muddled. Dill prefers a well-drained, poor soil in full sun. Sow mid-spring into shallow drills on a prepared site, where they will be harvested. Protect from wind. When the plants are

Dill *Anethum graveolens*

large enough to handle, thin out to a distance of 20cm (8in) to give plenty of room for growth. Make several small sowings in succession so that you have a supply of fresh leaves throughout the summer. The seed is viable for 3 years.

The plants are rather fragile and it may be necessary to provide support. Twigs pushed into the ground around the plant and enclosed with string or raffia will give better results than attempting to stake each plant individually.

In very hot summers, make sure that the plants are watered regularly or they will run to seed. There is no need to liquid feed, as this only promotes soft growth and in turn encourages pests and disease.

Pests and Diseases
Watch out for greenfly in crowded conditions. Treat with a liquid horticultural soap if necessary. Be warned, slugs love dill plants.

Maintenance
Spring: Sow the seeds successively for a leaf crop.
Summer: Feed plants with a liquid fertilizer after cutting to promote new growth.
Autumn (early): Harvest seeds.
Winter: Dig up all remaining plants. Make sure all the seed heads have been removed before you compost the stalks, as the seed is viable for 3 years. If you leave the plants to self-seed they certainly will, and they will live up to their other name of Dillweed.

Harvest

Pick leaves fresh for eating at any time after the plant has reached maturity. Since it is quick-growing, this can be within 8 weeks of the first sowing.

Although leaves can be dried, great care is needed and it is better to concentrate on drying the seed for storage.

Cut the stalks off the flower heads when the seed is beginning to ripen. Put the seed heads upside down in a paper bag and tie the top of the bag. Put in a warm place for a week. The seeds should then separate easily from the husk when rubbed in the palm of the hand. Store in an airtight container and the seeds will keep their flavour very well.

CONTAINER GROWING

Dill can be grown in containers, in a sheltered corner with plenty of sun. However, it will need staking. The art of growing it successfully is to keep cutting the plant for use in the kitchen. That way you will promote new growth and keep the plant reasonably compact. The drawback is that it will be fairly short-lived, so you will have to do successive sowings in different pots to maintain a supply. I do not recommend growing dill indoors – it will get leggy, soft and prone to disease.

MEDICINAL

Dill is an antispasmodic and calmative. Dill tea or water is a popular remedy for an upset stomach, hiccups or insomnia, for nursing

Gravlax – the traditional Scandinavian dish of salmon and dill

mothers to promote the flow of milk, and as an appetite stimulant. It is a constituent of gripe water and other children's medicines because of its ability to ease flatulence and colic.

CULINARY

Dill is a culinary herb that improves the appetite and digestion. The difference between dill leaf and dill seed lies in the degree of pungency. There are occasions when the seed is better because of its sharper flavour. It is used as a flavouring for soup, lamb stews and grilled or boiled fish. It can also add spiciness to rice dishes, and be combined with white wine vinegar to make dill vinegar.

Dill leaf can be used generously in many dishes, as it enhances rather than dominates the flavour of food.

Before it sets seed, add one flowering head to a jar of pickled gherkins, cucumbers and cauliflowers for a flavour stronger than dill leaves but fresher than seeds. In America these are known as dill pickles.

Gravlax
Salmon marinaded with dill

This is a traditional Scandinavian dish of great simplicity and great merit. Salmon treated in this way will keep for up to a week in the refrigerator.

420-800g (1½-2lb) salmon, middle cut or tail piece
1 heaped tablespoon sea salt
1 rounded tablespoon caster sugar
1 teaspoon crushed black peppercorns
1 tablespoon brandy (optional)
1 heaped tablespoon fresh dill

Have the salmon cleaned, scaled, bisected lengthways and filleted. Mix remaining ingredients together and put some of the mixture into a flat dish (glass or enamel) large enough to take the salmon. Place one piece of salmon skin side down on the bottom of the dish, spread more of the mixture over the cut side. Add the second piece of salmon, skin up, and pour over the remaining mixture. Cover with foil and place a plate or wooden board larger than the area of the salmon on top. Weigh this down with

weights or heavy cans. Put in the refrigerator for 36-72 hours. Turn the fish completely every 12 hours or so and baste (inside surfaces too) with the juices.

To serve, scrape off all the mixture, pat the fish dry and slice thinly and at an angle. Serve with buttered rye bread and a mustard sauce called Gravlaxsas:

4 tablespoons mild, ready-made Dijon mustard
1 teaspoon mustard powder
1 tablespoon caster sugar
2 tablespoons white wine vinegar

Mix all the above together, then slowly add 6 tablespoons of vegetable oil until you have a sauce the consistency of mayonnaise. Finally stir in 3 to 4 tablespoons of chopped dill.

Alternatively, substitute a mustard and dill mayonnaise.

OTHER USES

Where a salt-free diet must be followed, the seed, whole or ground, is a valuable replacement. Try chewing the seeds to clear up halitosis and sweeten the breath. Crush and infuse seeds to make a nail-strengthening bath.

Dill vinegar

Angelica archangelica

ANGELICA

Also known as European Angelica, Garden Angelica and Root of the Holy Ghost. From the family Umbelliferae.

Angelica in its many forms is a native of Europe, Asia and North America. It is also widely cultivated as a garden plant. Wild angelica is found in moist fields and hedgerows throughout Europe. American angelica is found in similar growing conditions in Canada and north-eastern and northern central states of America.

'Angelica' probably comes from the Greek *angelos*, meaning 'messenger'. There is a legend that an angel revealed to a monk in a dream that the herb was a cure for the plague, and traditionally angelica was considered the most effective safeguard against evil, witchcraft in particular. Certainly it is a plant no self-respecting witch would include in her brew.

Angelica is an important flavouring agent in liqueurs such as Benedictine, although its unique flavour cannot be detected from the others used. It is also cultivated commercially for medicinal and cosmetic purposes.

SPECIES

Angelica archangelica
Angelica
Biennial and short-lived perennial (about 4 years). Ht 1–2.5m (3–8ft), spread 1m (3ft) in second year. Dramatic second-year flowerheads late spring through summer, greenish-white and very sweetly scented. Bright green leaves, the lower ones large and bi- or tri-pinnate; the higher, smaller and pinnate. Rootstock varies in colour from pale yellowish beige to reddish-brown.

Angelica sylvestris
Wild Angelica
Also known as Ground Ash, Jack Jump About, Water Kesh.
Biennial. Ht 1.2–1.5m (4–5ft). White flowers in summer often tinged with pink; smaller than flowers of **A. archangelica**. Lower leaves are large, pinnate and sharply toothed. Stems often have a purple tinge. Rootstock is thick and grey on the outside.

Angelica atropurpurea
American Angelica (left)
Also known as Bellyache Root, High Angelica, Masterwort, Purple Angelica and Wild Angelica.
Biennial. Ht 1.2–1.5m (4–5ft). Flowers resemble those of **A. archangelica** – white to greenish white, late spring through summer. Leaves large and alternately compound. Rootstock purple. The whole plant delivers a powerful odour when fresh.

Angelica sinensis
Chinese Angelica
Also known as Dang Gui, Women's Ginseng.

CULTIVATION

Propagation
Seed
Angelica can only be grown from seed but, as it loses viability after 3 months, sow preferably when fresh, in the autumn. (If for some reason this cannot be done, store in a refrigerator and sow in the spring in tiny pinches.) As seedlings do not transplant well, sow in planting position and thin out all but the best plants once germination has occurred. If transplanting is unavoidable, do it when seedlings are small, before the tap roots are established.

When planting out or thinning seedlings leave 1m (3ft) between plants.

If maintaining for another season mark spot as the plant will die back fully during the winter.

If the plant has flowered and seeded, cut back and dig up roots. If you want thousands more angelicas compost the flower head; if not, bin it.

Pests and diseases
Blackfly can be removed easily with liquid horticultural soap.

Angelica in seed
Angelica archangelica

Maintenance

Spring: Clear ground around existing plants. Plant out autumn seedlings. Sow seed.
Summer: Cut stems of second year growth for crystallizing. Cut young leaves before flowering to use fresh in salads or to dry for medicinal or culinary uses. It cannot be stressed often enough that angelica needs plenty of water and if in summer the leaves turn a yellowish green, it is usually a sign that the plant needs more water.
Autumn: Seed sowing time.
Winter: No need for protection.

Garden Cultivation

Angelica dislikes hot humid climates and appreciates a spot in the garden where it can be in shade for some part of every day. But it can be a difficult plant to accommodate in a small garden, as it needs a lot of space. Site at the back of a border, perhaps near a wall where the plant architecture can be shown off. Make sure that the soil is deep and moist. Add well rotted compost to help retain moisture. Note that angelica dies down completely in winter but green shoots appear quickly in the spring.

Angelica is a biennial plant forming a big clump of foliage in the first summer and dramatic flowers the second, dying after the seed is set. A plant will propagate itself in the same situation if allowed to self-seed. But by cutting back in the autumn, and preventing the flowerhead from seeding, the same plant can be maintained as a short-lived perennial for approximately 4 years.

Harvest

Harvest leaves for use fresh from spring onwards; for drying, from early summer until flowering. Wild angelica is harvested in early autumn.

Pick flowers in early summer for dried flower arrangements.

Collect seeds when they begin to ripen.

Harvest roots for use medicinally in the second autumn immediately after flowering and dry.

CONTAINER GROWING

Angelica is definitely not an indoor plant, though if the container is large enough it can be grown as such. Do not over fertilize and be prepared to stake when in flower. Be wary of the pot toppling over as the plant grows taller.

CULINARY

Young leaves of Wild Angelica can be used as an aromatic in salads and the seeds are used by confectioners in pastry.

Candied Angelica

Angelica is now best known as a decorative confectionery for cakes. There is a bright emerald, apparently plastic, specimen sold commercially as angelica, which cannot compare with home-made, pale green candied angelica; this tastes and smells similar to the freshly bruised stem or crushed leaf of the plant.

Angelica Stems
Granulated sugar
Water
Caster sugar for dusting

Choose young tender springtime shoots. Cut into 8–10cm (3–4in) lengths. Place in a saucepan with just enough water to cover. Simmer until tender, then strain and peel off the outside skin. Put back into the pan with enough water to cover and bring to the boil, strain immediately and allow to cool.

When cool, weigh the angelica stalks and add an equal weight of granulated sugar. Place the sugar and angelica in a covered dish and leave in a cool place for 2 days.

Put the angelica and the syrup which will have formed back into the pan. Bring slowly to the boil and simmer, stirring occasionally, until the angelica becomes clear and has good colour.

Strain again discarding all the liquid, then sprinkle as much caster sugar as will cling to the angelica.

Allow the stems to dry in a cool oven (100°C, 200°F, Gas ¼). If not thoroughly dry they become mouldy later.

Store in an airtight container between grease-proof paper.

Candied Angelica

Stewed rhubarb

If when you cook rhubarb or gooseberries you add young angelica leaves, you will need to add less sugar. It is not that the angelica actually sweetens the fruit but its muscatel flavour cuts through the acidity of the rhubarb.

900g (2lb) rhubarb
225g (8oz) angelica stems
1 orange juice and rind
150ml (5fl oz) water
50g (2oz) sugar

MEDICINAL

Angelica stimulates the circulation. It also has anti-bacterial and anti-fungal properties.

Young leaves can be made into a tea, the flavour resembling China tea. Drink last thing at night for reducing tension, good for nervous headaches, indigestion, anaemia, coughs and colds. The tea made from the root is soothing for colds and other bronchial conditions made worse by damp, cold conditions.

Externally it is used in bath preparations for exhaustion and rheumatic pain. Crushed leaves freshen the air in a car and help prevent travel sickness.

American angelica can be used much as you would its European relatives, but its most common use is medicinal, for heartburn and flatulence.

Chinese angelica is a blood tonic used in Chinese herbal prescriptions.

WARNING

Large doses first stimulate and then paralyse the central nervous system. The tea is not recommended for those suffering from diabetes. Wild angelica can also be used medicinally, though large doses have the effect of depressing the central nervous system.

Wild angelica can be confused with water hemlock, also known as water-dropwort (*Oenanthe crocata*), which is poisonous. Beware.

Anthriscus cerefolium

CHERVIL

From the family Umbelliferae

Chervil *Anthriscus cerefolium*

Native to the Middle East, South Russia and the Caucasus. Cultivated in warm temperate climates where it is now occasionally found growing wild.

Almost certainly brought to Britain by the Romans, it is one of the Lenten herbs thought to have blood-cleansing and restorative properties. It was eaten in quantity in those days, especially on Maundy Thursday.

Gerard, the Elizabethan physician who superintended Lord Burleigh's gardens, wrote in his Herbal of 1636, 'The leaves of sweet chervil are exceeding good, wholesome and pleasant among other salad herbs, giving the taste of Anise seed unto the rest.'

SPECIES

Anthriscus cerefolium
Chervil
Hardy annual (some consider it to be a biennial). Ht 30-60cm (1-2ft), spread 30cm (12in). Flowers, tiny and white, grow in clusters from spring to summer. Leaves, light green and fern-like, in late summer may take on a purple tinge. When young it can easily be confused with cow parsley. However, cow parsley is a perennial and eventually grows much taller and stouter, its large leaves lacking the sweet distinctive aroma of chervil.

Anthriscus cerefolium crispum
Chervil curly leafed
Hardy annual. Grows like the ordinary chervil except that, in my opinion, the leaf has an inferior flavour.

CULTIVATION

Propagation
Seed
The medium-size seed germinates rapidly as the air and soil temperatures rise in the spring provided the seed is fresh (it loses viability after about a year). Young plants are ready for cutting 6-8 weeks after sowing, thereafter continuously providing leaves as long as the flowering stems are removed.

Seed in prepared plug trays if you prefer, and cover with Perlite. Pot on to containers with a minimum 12cm (5in) diameter. But as a typical *Umbelliferae*, with a long tap root, chervil does not like being transplanted, so keep this to a minimum. It can in fact be sown direct into a 12cm (5in) pot, growing it, like mustard and cress, as a cut-and-come-again crop.

Pests and Diseases

Chervil can suffer from greenfly. Wash off gently with a liquid horticultural soap. Do not blast off with a high pressure hose, as this will damage its soft leaves.

Maintenance

Spring: Sow seeds.

Summer: A late sowing in this season will provide leaves through winter, as it is very hardy. Protect from midday sun.

Autumn: Cloche autumn-sown plants for winter use.

Winter: Although chervil is hardy, some cloche protection is needed to ensure leaves in winter.

Garden Cultivation

The soil required is light with a degree of moisture retention. Plant spacing 23-30cm (9-12in). Semi-shade is best, because the problem with chervil is that it will burst into flower too quickly should the weather become sunny and hot and be of no use as a culinary herb. For this reason some gardeners sow between rows of other garden herbs or vegetables or under deciduous plants to ensure some shade during the summer months.

Harvest

Harvest leaves for use fresh when the plant is 6-8 weeks old or when 10cm (4in) tall, and all the year round if you cover with a cloche in winter. Otherwise, freezing is the best method of preservation, as the dried leaves do not retain their flavour.

CONTAINER GROWING

When grown inside in the kitchen chervil loses colour, gets leggy and goes floppy, so unless you are treating it as a cut-and-come-again plant, plant outside in a large container that retains moisture and is positioned in semi-shade.

Chervil looks good in a window box, but be sure that it gets shade at midday.

MEDICINAL

Leaves eaten raw are rich in Vitamin C, carotene, iron and magnesium. They may be infused to make a tea to stimulate digestion and alleviate circulation disorders, liver complaints and chronic catarrh, and fresh leaves may be applied to aching joints in a warm poultice.

CULINARY

It is one of the traditional 'fines herbes', indispensable to French cuisine and a fresh green asset in any meal, but many people in Britain are only now discovering its special delicate parsley-like flavour with a hint of Aniseed. This is a herb especially for winter use because it is easy to obtain fresh leaves and, as every cook knows, French or otherwise, 'Fresh is best'.

Use its leaf generously in salads, soups, sauces, vegetables, chicken, white fish and egg dishes. Add freshly chopped towards the end of cooking to avoid flavour loss.

In small quantities it enhances the flavour of other herbs. Great with vegetables.

OTHER USES

An infusion of the leaf can be used to cleanse skin, maintain suppleness and discourage wrinkles.

Chervil with broad beans

Armoracia rusticana (Cochlearia armoracia)

HORSERADISH

From the family Cruciferae.

Native of Europe, naturalized in Britain and North America. Originally the horseradish was cultivated as a medicinal herb. Now it is considered a flavouring herb. The common name means a coarse or strong radish, the prefix horse often being used in plant to donate a large, strong or coarse plant. In the 16th century it was known in England as Redcol or Recole. In this period the plant appears to have been more popular in Scandinavia and Germany, where they developed its potential as a fish sauce. In Britain horseradish has become strongly associated with roast beef.

SPECIES

Armoracia rusticana (Cochlearia armoracia)
Horseradish
Hardy perennial. Ht 60-90cm (24-35in), spread infinite! Flowers white in spring (very rare). Leaves large green oblongs. The large root, which is up to 60cm (24in) long 5cm (2in) thick and tapering, goes deep into the soil.

Armoracia rusticana 'Variegata'
Hardy perennial. Ht 60-90cm (24-35in), spread also infinite. Flowers white in spring (rare in cool climates). Leaves large with green/cream variegation and oblong shape. Large root which goes deep into the soil. Not as good flavour as **A. rusticana**.

Roast beef is traditionally served with Horseradish

CULTIVATION

Propagation
Root Cuttings
In early spring cut pieces of root 15cm (6in) long. Put them either directly into the ground, at a depth of 5cm (2in), at intervals of 30cm (12in) apart, or start them off in individual pots. These can then be planted out when the soil is manageable.

Division
If you have a perpetual clump it will need dividing; do this in the spring. Remember small pieces of root will always grow, so do it cleanly, making sure that you have collected all the little pieces of root. Replant in a well-prepared site.

Pests and Diseases
Cabbage white caterpillars may feed on the leaves during late summer. The leaves may also be affected by some fungus diseases but this should not be a problem on vigorous plants and should be simply removed and burnt.

Maintenance
Spring: Sow seeds. Plant cuttings in garden.
Summer: Liquid feed with seaweed fertiliser.
Autumn: Dig up roots if required when mature enough.
Winter: No need for protection, fully hardy.

Garden Cultivation
Think seriously if you want this plant in your garden. It is invasive. Once you have it, you have it. It is itself a most tolerant plant, liking all but the driest of soils. But for a good crop it prefers a light, well-dug, rich, moist soil. Prepare it the autumn before with lots of well rotted manure. It likes a sunny site but will tolerate dappled shade.

If large quantities are required, horseradish should be given a patch of its own where the roots can be lifted and the soil replenished after each harvest. To produce strong, straight roots I found this method in an old gardening book. Make holes 42cm (15in) deep with a crow bar, and drop a piece of horseradish 5-8cm (2-3in) long with a crown on the top into the hole. Crown up. Fill the hole up with good rotted manure. This will produce strong straight roots in 2-3 years, some of which may be ready in the first year.

Harvest

Pick leaves young to use fresh, or to dry.

If you have a mature patch of horseradish then the root can be dug up any time for use fresh. Otherwise dig up roots in autumn. Store roots in sand and make sure you leave them in cool dark place for the winter.

Alternatively, wash, grate or slice and dry. Another method is to immerse the whole washed roots in white wine vinegar.

COMPANION PLANTING

Grow near potatoes to improve their disease resistance. Be careful it does not take over.

CULINARY

The reason horseradish is used in sauces, vinegars, and as an accompaniment rather than cooked as a vegetable is that the volatile flavouring oil which is released in grating evaporates rapidly and becomes nothing when cooked. Raw it's a different story. The strongest flavour is from root pulled in the autumn. The spring root is comparatively mild. Fresh root contains calcium, sodium, magnesium and vitamin C, and has antibiotic qualities useful for preserving food.

It can be used grated in coleslaw, dips, pickled beetroot, cream cheese, mayonnaise and avocado fillings.

The young leaves can be added to salads for a bit of zip.

Make horseradish sauce to accompany roast beef, and smoked oily fish.

Avocado Pear with Horseradish Cream

Fresh horseradish root (approx. 15cm (6in) long); preserved horseradish in vinegar can be substituted. If it is, leave out the lemon juice.
1 tablespoon butter
3 tablespoons fresh breadcrumbs
1 apple
1 dessertspoon yoghurt
1 teaspoon lemon juice
Pinch of salt and sugar
1 teaspoon chopped fresh chervil
½ teaspoon each of fresh chopped tarragon and dill
3-4 tablespoons double cream
2 avocado pears (ripe) cut in half with the stones removed

Peel and grate the horseradish, melt the butter and add the breadcrumbs. Fry until brown, and add grated horseradish. Remove from heat and grate the apple into the mixture. Add yoghurt, lemon juice, salt, sugar and herbs. Put aside to cool. Chill in refrigerator.

Just before serving gently fold the cream into the mixture and spoon generously into the avocado pear halves. Serve with green salad and brown toast.

MEDICINAL

Horseradish is a powerful circulatory stimulant with antibiotic properties.

As a diuretic it is effective for lung and urinary infections. It can also be taken internally for gout and rheumatism.

Grate into a poultice and apply externally to chilblains, stiff muscles, sciatica, rheumatic joints, to stimulate blood flow.

Its sharp pungency frequently has a dramatic effect and has been known to clear the sinuses in one breath.

WARNING

Overuse may blister the skin. Do not use it if your thyroid functions is low or if taking thyroxin. Avoid continuous dosage when pregnant or suffering from kidney problems.

OTHER USES

Chop finely into dog food to dispel worms and improve body tone.

Make an infusion 600ml (1 pint) water, 25g (1oz) horseradish roots and dilute 4:1. Spray on apple trees to protect against brown rot.

The roots and the leaves produce a yellow dye for natural dying.

Slice and infuse in milk for a lotion to improve skin clarity.

Horeseradish root

Arnica montana

ARNICA

Also known as Mountain Tobacco, Leopards Bane, Mountain Arnica, Wolfsbane and Mountain Daisy. From the family Compositae.

It is found wild in the mountainous area of Canada, North America, and in Europe, where it is a protected species. Bees love it.

The name 'arnica' is said to be derived from the word 'ptarmikos', Greek for sneezing. One sniff of arnica can make you sneeze.

The herb was known by Methusalus and was widely used in the 16th century in German folk medicine. Largely as a result of exaggerated claims in the 18th century by Venetian physicians, it was, for a short time, a popular medicine.

SPECIES

Arnica montana
Arnica
Hardy perennial. Ht 30–60cm (1–2ft), spread 15cm (6in). Large, single, scented yellow flowers throughout summer. Oval, hairy, light green leaves.

CULTIVATION

Propagation
Seed
Sow the small seed in spring or late summer in either a pot, plug or seed tray, and cover with Perlite. Place trays in a cold frame as heat will inhibit germination. The seed is slow to germinate, even occasionally as long as two years! Once the seedlings are large enough, pot up and harden off in a cold frame.

You can get a more reliable germination if you collect the seed yourself and sow no later than early autumn. After potting up, winter the young plants under protection. They will die back in winter. Plant out in the following spring, when the soil has warmed up, 30cm (1ft) from other plants.

Division
Arnica's root produces creeping rhizomes, which are easy to divide in spring. This is much more reliable than sowing seed.

Pests and Diseases
Caterpillars and slugs sometimes eat the leaves.

Maintenance
Spring: Sow seeds. Divide creeping rhizomes.
Summer: Dead head if necessary. Harvest plant for medicinal use.
Autumn: Collect seeds and either sow immediately or store in an airtight container for sowing in the spring.
Winter: Note the position in the garden because the plants die right back.

Garden Cultivation
Being a mountainous plant it is happiest in a sandy acid soil, rich in humus, and in a sunny position. Arnica is a highly ornamental plant with a long flowering season. It is ideally suited for large rock gardens, or the front of a border bed.

Harvest
Pick flowers for medicinal use in summer, just before they come into full flower. Pick in full flower, with stalks, for drying.

Collect leaves for drying in summer before flowering.

Dig up roots of 2nd/3rd year growth after the plant has fully died back in late autumn/early winter for drying.

MEDICINAL

Arnica is a famous herbal and homeopathic remedy. A tincture of flowers can be used in the treatment of sprains, wounds and bruises, and also to give relief from rheumatic pain and chilblains, if the skin is not broken. Homeopathic doses are effective against epilepsy and sea sickness, and possibly as a hair growth stimulant. It has also been shown to be effective against salmonella.

WARNING

Do not take arnica internally except under supervision of a qualified herbalist or homeopath. External use may cause skin rash or irritation. Never apply to broken skin.

OTHER USES

Leaves and roots smoked as herbal tobacco, hence the name Mountain Tobacco.

Artemisia abrotanum

SOUTHERNWOOD

Also known as Lad's Love and Old Man. From the family Compositae.

This lovely aromatic plant is a native of southern Europe. It has been introduced to many countries and is now naturalized widely in temperate zones.

The derivation of the genus name is unclear. One suggestion is that it honours Artemisia, a famous botanist and medical researcher, sister of King Mausolus (353 BC). Another is that it was named after Artemis or Diana, the Goddess of the Hunt and Moon.

In the 17th century, Culpeper recommended that the ashes of southernwood be mingled with salad oil as a remedy for baldness.

Southernwood *Artemisia abrotanum*

CULTIVATION

SPECIES

Artemisia abrotanum
Southernwood
Deciduous or semi-evergreen hardy perennial. Ht and spread 1m (40in). Tiny insignificant clusters of dull yellow flowers in summer. The abundant olive green feathery leaves are finely divided and carry a unique scent.

Propagation
Seed
It rarely flowers and sets seeds, except in warm climates.
Cuttings
Take softwood cuttings in spring from the lush new growth, or from semi-hardwood cuttings in summer. Use the bark, peat, grit mix of compost. Roots well. It can be wintered as a rooted cutting, when it sheds its leaves and is dormant. Keep the cuttings on the dry side, and in early spring slowly start watering. Plant out 60cm (24in) apart after the frosts have finished.

Pests and Diseases
It is free from the majority of pests and disease.

Maintenance
Spring: Cut back to maintain shape. Take cuttings.
Summer: Take cuttings.
Autumn: Trim any flowers off as they develop.
Winter: Protect the roots in hard winters with mulch.

Garden Cultivation
Southernwood prefers a light soil containing well-rotted organic material in a sunny position. However tempted you are by its bedraggled appearance in winter (hence its name, Old Man) NEVER cut hard back as you will kill it. This growth protects its woody stems from cold winds. Cut the bush hard in spring to keep its shape, but only after the frosts have finished.

Harvest
Pick leaves during the growing season for use fresh. Pick leaves for drying in mid-summer.

CULINARY

The leaves can be used in salads. They have a strong flavour, so use sparingly. It does also make a good aromatic vinegar.

MEDICINAL

It can be used for expelling worms and to treat coughs and bronchial catarrh. A compress helps to treat frost bite, cuts and grazes.

OTHER USES

The French call it Garde Robe, use it as a moth repellent. It is a good fly deterrent, too – hang bunches up in the kitchen, or rub it on the skin to deter mosquitoes.

WARNING

No product containing southernwood should be taken during pregnancy.

Artemisia absinthium

WORMWOOD

Also known as Absinthe and Green Ginger. From the family Compositae.

A native of Asia and Europe, including Britain, it was introduced into America as a cultivated plant and is now naturalized in many places. Found on waste ground, especially near the sea in warmer regions.

Legend has it that as the serpent slithered out of Eden, wormwood first sprang up in the impressions on the ground left by its tail. Another story tells that in the beginning it was called 'Parthenis absinthium', but Artemis, Greek goddess of chastity, benefited so much from it that she named it after herself – 'Artemisia absinthium'. The Latin meaning of 'absinthium' is 'to desist from', which says it all.

Although it is one of the most bitter herbs known, it has for centuries been a major ingredient of aperitifs and herb wines. Both absinthe and vermouth get their names from this plant, the latter being an 18th century French variation of the German 'wermut', itself the origin of the English name Wormwood.

Wormwood was hung by the door where it kept away evil spirits and deterred night-time visitations by goblins. It was also made a constituent of ink to stop mice eating old letters.

It was used as a strewing herb to prevent fleas, hence:

> *'White wormwood hath seed, get a handful or twaine,*
> *to save against March, to make flea to refrain.*
> *Where chamber is sweeped and wormwood is strewn,*
> *no flea for his life, dare abide to be knowne.'*

This extract comes from Thomas Tusser's *Five Hundred Pointes of Good Husbandrie*, written in 1573.

Finally, wormwood is believed to be the herb that Shakespeare had in mind when his Oberon lifted the spell from Titania with 'the juice of Dian's bud', Artemis being known to the Romans as Dian or Diana.

Artemisia absinthium
Wormwood
Partial-evergreen hardy perennial. Ht 1m (40in), spread 1.2m (4ft). Tiny, insignificant, yellow flowerheads are borne in sprays in summer. The abundant leaves are divided, aromatic and grey/green in colour.

Artemisia absinthium 'Lambrook Silver'
Evergreen hardy perennial. Ht 80cm (32in), spread 50cm (20in). Tiny, insignificant, grey flowerheads are borne in long panicles in summer. The abundant leaves are finely divided, aromatic and silver/grey in colour. May need protecting in exposed sites.

Artemisia pontica
Old Warrior
Evergreen hardy perennial. Ht 60cm (24in), spread 30cm (12in). Tiny, insignificant, silver/grey flowerheads are borne on tall spikes in summer. The abundant, feathery, small leaves are finely divided, aromatic and silver/grey in colour. This can, in the right conditions, be a vigorous grower, spreading well in excess of 30cm (12in) .

Artemisia pontica 'Powis Castle'
Evergreen hardy perennial. Ht 90 cm (36in), spread 1.2m (4ft). Tiny, insignificant, greyish-yellow flowerheads are borne in sprays in summer. The abundant leaves are finely divided, aromatic and silver/grey in colour.

Wormwood *Artemisia absinthium*

CULTIVATION

Propagation
Seed

Of the species mentioned above, only wormwood is successfully grown from seed. It is extremely small and best started off under protection. Sow in spring in a prepared seed or plug tray, using the bark, peat, grit mix of compost. Cover with Perlite and propagate with heat, 15-21°C (60-70°F). Plant out when the seedlings are large enough to handle and have had a period of hardening off.

Cuttings

Take softwood cuttings from the lush new growth in early summer; semi-hardwood in late summer. Use the bark, peat, grit mix of compost.

Division

As they are all vigorous growers division is a good idea at least every 3 to 4 years to keep the plant healthy, to stop it becoming woody and to prevent encroaching. Dig up the plant in spring or autumn, divide the roots and replant in a chosen spot.

Pests and Diseases

Wormwood can suffer from a summer attack of blackfly. If it gets too bad, use a liquid horticultural soap, following manufacturer's instructions.

Maintenance

Spring: Sow seeds. Divide established plants. Trim new growth for shape. Take softwood cuttings.
Summer: Take semi-hardwood cuttings.
Autumn: Prune back all the species mentioned to 15cm (6in) of the ground. Divide established plants.
Winter: Protect in temperatures below -5°C (23°F). Cover with agricultural fleece, straw, bark, anything that can be removed in the following spring.

Garden Cultivation

Artemisias like a light well-drained soil and sunshine, but will adapt well to ordinary soils provided some shelter is given. Planting distance depends on spread. Wormwood is an overpoweringly flavoured plant and it does impair the flavour of dill and coriander so do not plant nearby.

Harvest

Pick flowering tops just as they begin to open. Dry. Pick leaves for drying in summer.

CONTAINER GROWING

Artemisia absinthium 'Lambrook Silver' and *Old Warrior* (**Artemisia pontica**) look very good in terracotta containers. Use the bark,

Left: **Artemisia 'Powis Castle'**

peat, grit mix of compost. Only feed in the summer; if you feed too early the leaves will lose their silvery foliage and revert to a more green look. In winter keep watering to the absolute minimum and protect from hard frosts.

OTHER USES

It can produce a yellow dye.

Antiseptic vinegar

This vinegar is known as the 'Four Thieves' because it is said that thieves used to rub their bodies with it before robbing plague victims.

1 tablespoon wormwood
1 tablespoon lavender
1 tablespoon rosemary
1 tablespoon sage
1.1l (1¾) pints vinegar

Put the crushed herbs into an earthenware container. Pour in the vinegar. Cover the container and leave it in a warm sunny place two weeks. Strain into bottles with tight-fitting, non-metal lids. This makes a very refreshing tonic in the bath, or try sprinkling it on work surfaces in the kitchen.

Wormwood Vinegar

Moth-Repellent

Wormwood or southern-wood can be used for keeping moths and other harmful insects away from clothes. The smell is sharp and refreshing and does not cling to your clothes like camphor moth-balls.

Wormwood Moth-Repellant

Bug Ban Recipe

2 tablespoons dried wormwood or southernwood
2 tablespoons dried lavender
2 tablespoons dried mint

Mix the ingredients well and put into small sachets.

MEDICINAL

True to its name, wormwood expels worms especially round- and thread- worms.

WARNING

Not to be taken internally without medical supervision. Habitual use causes convulsions, restlessness and vomiting. Overdose causes vertigo, cramps, intoxication and delirium. Pure wormwood oil is a strong poison, although with a proper dosage there is little danger.

Artemisia dracunculus

TARRAGON

Also known as Estragon. From the family Compositae.

A native of southern Europe, tarragon is now found in dry areas of North America, Southern Asia and Siberia.

'Dracunculus' means little dragon. Its naming could have occurred (via the Doctrine of Signatures) as a result of the shape of its roots, or because of its fiery flavour. Whatever, it was certainly believed to have considerable power to heal bites from snakes, serpents and other venomous creatures.

In ancient times the mixed juices of tarragon and fennel made a favourite drink for the Kings of India.

In the reign of Henry VIII, tarragon made its way into English gardens, and the rhyme, 'There is certain people, and certain herbs, that good digestion disturbs,' could well be associated with tarragon. I love, too, the story that Henry VIII divorced Catherine of Aragon for her reckless use of tarragon.

SPECIES

Artemisia dracunculus
French Tarragon
Half-hardy perennial. Ht 90cm (3ft), spread 45cm (18in). Tiny, insignificant, yellow flowerheads are borne in sprays in summer but rarely produce ripe seed sets except in warm climates. The leaves are smooth dark green, long and narrow, and have a very strong flavour.

Artemisia dracunculus dracunculoides
Russian Tarragon
Hardy perennial. Ht 1.2m (4ft), spread 45cm (18in). Tiny, insignificant, yellow flowerheads in sprays in summer. The leaves are slightly coarser and green in colour, their shape long and narrow. This plant originates from Siberia, so is hardy.

CULTIVATION

Propagation
Seed
Only the Russian variety produces viable seed. A lot of growers are propagating and selling it to the unsuspecting public as French tarragon. If you really want Russian tarragon, sow the small seed in spring, into prepared seed or plug trays, using the bark, peat, grit compost. No extra heat required. When the young plants are large enough to handle, transfer to the garden, 60cm (24in) apart.

Cuttings
Both French and Russian tarragon can be propagated by cuttings.
Roots: Dig up the underground runners in spring when the frosts are finished, pull them apart; do

not cut. You will notice growing nodules, these will reproduce in the coming season. Place a small amount of root – 8-10cm (3-4in) – each with a growing nodule, in a 8cm (3in) pot, and cover with compost. Use the bark, grit, peat mix and place in a warm, well ventilated place. Keep watering to a minimum. When well rooted, plant out in the garden after hardening off, 60cm (24in) apart.

It is possible to take softwood cuttings of the growing tips in summer. You will need to keep the leaves moist, but the compost on the dry side. It works best under a misting unit with a little bottom heat 15°C (60°F).

Division
Divide established plants of either variety in the spring.

Pests and Diseases
Recently there has been a spate of rust developing on French tarragon. When buying a plant, look for tell tale signs – small rust spots on the underneath of a leaf. If you have a plant with rust, dig it up, cut off all foliage carefully, and bin the leaves. Wash the roots free from soil, and pot up into fresh sterile soil. If this fails, place the dormant roots in hot water after washing off all the compost. The temperature of the water should be 40-46°C (105-115°F); over 46°C will damage the root. Leave the roots in the hot water for 5 minutes then replant in a new place in the garden.

Maintenance
Spring: Sow Russian tarragon seeds if you must. Divide established plants. Take root cuttings.
Summer: Remove flowers.
Autumn: Pot up pieces of French tarragon root as insurance.
Winter: Protect French tarragon. As the plant dies back into the ground in winter it is an ideal candidate for either agricultural fleece, straw or a deep mulch.

Garden Cultivation
French Tarragon has the superior flavour of the two and is the most tender. It grows best in a warm dry position, and will need protection in winter. It also dislikes humid conditions. The plant should be renewed every 3 years because the flavour deteriorates as the plant matures.

Russian tarragon is fully hardy and will grow in any conditions. There is a myth going around that it improves the longer it is grown in 1 place. This is untrue, it gets coarse. It is extremely tolerant of most soil types, but prefers a sunny position, 60cm (2ft) away from other plants.

Harvest
Pick sprigs of French tarragon early in the season to make vinegar.

Pick leaves for fresh use throughout the growing season. For freezing it is best to pick the leaves in the mid-summer months.

CONTAINER GROWING

French tarragon grows well in containers. Use the bark, grit mix of compost. As it produces root runners, choose a container to give it room to grow so that it will not become pot bound. At all times make sure the plant is watered, and in the daytime, not at night. It hates having wet roots. Keep feeding to a minimum; overfeeding produces fleshy leaves with a poor flavour; be mean. In winter, when the plant is dormant, do not water, keep the compost dry and the container in a cool, frost-free environment.

CULINARY

Without doubt this is among the Rolls Royces of the culinary herb collection. Its flavour promotes appetite and complements so many dishes – chicken, veal, fish, stuffed tomatoes, rice dishes, and salad dressings, and of course is the main ingredient of Sauce Bernaise.

Chicken Salad with tarragon and grapes
Serves 4-6

1 1.3 kg (3lb) cooked chicken
150ml (5fl oz) mayonnaise
75ml (3fl oz) double cream
1 heaped teaspoon fresh chopped tarragon (½teaspoon dried)
3 spring onions, finely chopped
100g (4oz) green grapes (seedless if not de-piped)
1 small lettuce
A few sprigs water cress
Salt and pepper

Remove the skin from the chicken and all the chicken from the bones. Slice the meat into longish pieces and place in a bowl.

In another bowl mix the mayonnaise with the cream, the chopped tarragon, and the finely chopped spring onions. Pour this mixture over the chicken and mix carefully together. Arrange the lettuce on a dish and spoon on the chicken mixture. Arrange the grapes and the water cress around it.

Serve with jacket potatoes or rice salad.

MEDICINAL

No modern medicinal use. Formerly used for toothache. If nothing else is available, a tea made from the leaves is said to overcome insomnia.

Red Orach
Atriplex hortensis 'Rubra'

T he garden species of orach, *Atriplex hortensis,* originated in Eastern Europe and is now widely distributed in countries with temperate climates. In the past it was called mountain spinach and grown as a vegetable in its own right.

The red form, *Atriplex hortensis* 'Rubra', is still eaten frequently in Continental Europe, particularly with game, and was used as a flavouring for breads.

The common orach, *Atriplex patula,* was considered a poor man's pot herb, which is a fact worth remembering when you are pulling out this invasive annual weed.

SPECIES

Atriplex hortensis
Orach
Hardy annual. Ht 1.5m (5ft), spread 30cm (12in). Tiny greenish (boring) flowers in summer. Green triangular leaves.

Atriplex hortensis 'Rubra'
Red Orach
Hardy annual. Ht 1.2m (4tf), spread 30cm (1ft). Tiny reddish (boring) flowers in summer. Red triangular leaves.

Atriplex patula
Common Orach
Hardy annual. Ht 90cm (3ft) spread 30cm (12in). Flowers similar to orach, the leaves more spear shaped and smaller.

Atriplex hortensis

ORACH

From the family Chenopodiaceae

CULTIVATION

Propagation
Seed
If you wish to have a continuous supply of leaves, start off under protection in early spring, sowing the flat seeds directly into prepared plug trays. Cover with Perlite. When the seedlings are large enough, and after hardening off, plant out in a prepared site in the garden 25cm (10in) apart.

Pests and Diseases
In the majority of cases this herb is pest and disease free.

Maintenance
Spring: Sow seeds.
Summer: Cut flowers before they form.

Autumn: Cut seeds off before they are fully ripe to prevent too much self-seeding.
Winter: Dig up old plants.

Garden Cultivation
This annual herb produces the largest and most succulent leaves when the soil is rich. So prepare the site well with well rotted manure. For Red Orach choose a site with partial shade as the leaves can scorch in very hot summers. The seeds can be sown in rows 60cm (2ft) apart in spring when the soil has warmed. Thin out to 25cm (10in) as soon as the seedlings are large enough, and replant. Water well throughout the growing season.

As this plant is a very rapid grower, it is as well to do 2 sowings to ensure a good supply of young leaves. The

Orach *Atriplex hortensis*

Orach makes an excellent container plant

Red Orach Soup

450g (1lb) potatoes
225g (8oz) young red orach
  leaves
50g (2oz) butter
900ml (1½pt/3¾ cups)
  chicken stock
1 clove garlic, crushed
Salt and black pepper
4 tablespoons sour cream

Peel the potatoes and cut
them into thick slices. Wash
the orach and cut up
coarsely. Cook the potatoes
for 10 minutes in salted
water, drain. Melt the butter
in a saucepan with the
crushed garlic and slowly
sweeten; add the red orach
leaves and gently simmer for
5-10 minutes until soft (if
the leaves are truly young
then 5 minutes will be
sufficient). Pour in the
stock, add the parboiled
potatoes, and bring to the
boil; simmer for a further 10
minutes. When all is soft,
cool slightly then purée in a
blender or liquidize. After
blending, return the soup to
a clean pan, add salt and
pepper to taste, and heat
slowly (not to boiling). Stir
in the sour cream, and serve.

CONTAINER GROWING

The red-leafed orach looks
very attractive in containers,
provided you don't let it get
too tall. Nip out the growing
tip and the plant will bush
out, and do not let it flower.
Use the peat, bark mix of
potting soil. Keep the plant
in semi-shade in high
summer and water well at all
times. If watering in high sun,
be careful not to splash the
leaves, as they can scorch,
especially the red variety.

MEDICINAL

*This herb is no longer used
medicinally. In the past it
was a home remedy for sore
throats, gout, and jaundice.*

Red Orach Soup

red varieties look very
attractive grown as a hedge.
Remove flowering tips as
soon as they appear. This
will help maintain the shape
of the plant.
  If seed is not required, pick
the flowers off as soon as
they appear. To save the
seed, collect before it is fully
ripe, otherwise you will have
hundreds of orach babies all
over your garden and next
door.

Harvest
Pick young leaves to use
fresh as required. The herb
does not dry or freeze
particularly well.

CULINARY

The young leaves can be
eaten raw in salads, and the
red variety looks most
attractive. The old leaves of
both species ought to be
cooked as they become
slightly tough and bitter. It
can be used as a substitute
for spinach or as a vegetable,
served in a white sauce. It is
becoming more popular in
Europe, where it is used in
soups.

Ballota nigra

BLACK HOREHOUND

**Also known as Stinking Horehound, Dunny Nettle, Stinking Roger and Hairy Hound.
From the family Labiatae.**

Black horehound comes from a genus of about 25 species mostly native to the Mediterranean region. Some species have a disagreeable smell and only a few are worth growing in the garden. Black horehound is found on roadsides, hedge banks and in waste places throughout most of Europe, Australia and America.

Ballota nigra, the black horehound, was originally called 'ballote' by the ancient Greeks. It has been suggested that this comes from the Greek word 'ballo' which means 'to reject', 'cast', or 'throw', because cows and other farm animals with their natural instincts reject it. The origin of the common name is more obscure, it could come from the Anglo-Saxon word 'har' which means 'hoar' or 'hairy'.

SPECIES

Ballota nigra
Black Horehound
Hardy perennial. Ht 40-100cm (16-40in), spread 30cm (12in). Purple-pink attractive flowers in summer. The leaves are green and medium sized, rather like the stinging nettle. All parts of the plant are hairy and have a strong, disagreeable smell and taste.

Ballota pseudodictamnus
Half-hardy perennial. Ht 60cm (24in), spread 30cm (12in). White flowers with numerous purple spots in summer. Leaves white and woolly. This plant originated from Crete. The dried calyces look like tiny furry spinning tops; they were used as floating wicks in primitive oil lamps.

Black Horehound *Ballota nigra*

CULTIVATION

Propagation
Seed
Sow the seeds direct into the prepared garden in late summer, thinning to 40cm (16in) apart.

Division
Divide roots in mid-spring.

Pests and Diseases
Rarely suffers from any pests or diseases.

Maintenance

Spring: Dig up established plants and divide; replant where required.

Summer: When the plant has finished flowering, cut off the dead heads before the seeds ripen, so preventing it seeding itself in the garden.

Autumn: Sow seed.

Garden Cultivation

Black horehound will grow in any soil conditions, though it prefers water retentive soil –in fact I have seen it growing in hedgerows throughout England. In the garden, place it in a border The bees love it and the flowers are attractive. Make sure it is far enough back so that you do not brush it by mistake because it does stink.

Harvest

As this is a herbalist's herb, the leaves should be collected before flowering and dried with care.

CONTAINER GROWING

Not recommended, as it is such an unpleasantly smelling plant.

MEDICINAL

Black horehound was used apparently in the treatment of bites from mad dogs. A dressing was prepared from the leaves and laid on the infected part. This was said to have an anti-spasmodic effect.

This is not a herb to be self administered. Professionals use it as a sedative, anti-emetic and to counteract vomiting during pregnancy.

Black Horehound *Ballota nigra*

Borago officinalis

BORAGE

Also known as Bugloss, Burrage, and Common Bugloss. From the family Boraginaceae.

Borage is indigenous to Mediterranean countries, but has now been naturalised in Northern Europe and North America. In fact one can find escapees growing happily on wasteland.

The origin of the name is obscure. The French 'bourrache', is said to derive from an old word meaning 'rough' or 'hairy', which may describe the leaf but the herb's beautiful, pure blue flowers are its feature and are supposed to have inspired the painting of the robes of the Madonna, and charmed Louis XIV into ordering the herb to be planted at Versailles.

The herb's Welsh name translates as 'herb of gladness'; and in Arabic it is 'the father of sweat', which we can accept as borage is a diaphoretic. The Celtic word 'borrach' means 'courage', however, and in this we have an association more credible by far. The Greeks and Romans regarded borage as both comforting and imparting courage, and this belief so persisted that Gerard was able to quote the tag, *Ego borage gaudia semper ago* in his Herbal. It was for courage, too, that borage flowers were floated in stirrup cups given to the Crusaders. Clearly, too, the American Settlers thought sufficiently highly of borage to take the seed with them on their long adventure. Records of it were found in a seed order of an American in 1631, where it was called burradge.

Borage *Borago officinalis*

SPECIES

Borago officinalis
Borage
Hardy annual (very occasionally biennial). Ht 60cm (24in) with hollow, bristly branches and spreading stems. The blue or purplish star-shaped flowers grow in loose racemes from early summer to mid-autumn. The leaves are bristly, oval or oblong. At the base they form a rosette; others grow alternately on either side of the stem.

Borago officinalis 'Alba'
White Borage
Hardy annual. Ht 60cm (2ft). White star-shaped flowers end-spring through summer. Bristly, oval, oblong leaves. Can be used as **B. officinalis**.

CULTIVATION

Propagation
Borage is best grown directly from seed in its final position, as it does not like having its long tap root disturbed. But for an early crop it is as well to start the

seeds under protection. In early spring sow singly in small pots. Transplant to final position as soon as possible after hardening off, when the seedling is large enough and all threat of frosts is over.

Pests and Diseases
Black fly. If you are growing borage as a companion plant this will not worry you, but if it is becoming a nuisance then spray with liquid horticultural soap.
A disease, which can be unsightly at the end of the season, is a form of mildew, but it is not worth using chemicals so late in the year. Dig the plant up and burn.

Maintenance
Spring: Sow seeds. They germinate quickly and plants are full grown in 5-6 weeks.
Summer: Sow seeds. Look out for flower heads turning into seeds – collect or destroy if you do not want borage plants all over the garden. Dead head flowers to prolong flowering season.
Autumn: As the plants begin to die back collect up the old plants. Do not compost the flower heads or next year you will have a garden full of unwanted borage.
Winter: Borage lasts until the first major frost, and some years it is the last flowering herb in the garden.

Garden Cultivation
Borage prefers a well-drained, light, rather poor soil of chalk or sand, and a sunny position. Sow borage seeds 5cm (2in) deep in mid-spring and again in late spring for continuous supply of young leaves and flowers. Thin seedlings to 60cm (24in) apart and from other herbs, as they produce lots of floppy growth.
I have used borage as an exhibit plant at flower shows, and have found that by continuously dead heading the flowers you can maintain a good supply of flowers for longer.

Harvest

Pick flowers fresh or for freezing or drying when they are just fully opened.

Cut the young leaves fresh throughout summer. They do not dry or freeze very successfully.

Collect seed before the plant dies back fully. Store in a light-proof container in a cool place.

COMPANION GROWING

Borage is a good companion plant as the flower is very attractive to bees helping with pollination, especially runner beans and strawberries. Also borage attracts black fly to itself so leaving the other plants alone. Equally if planted near tomatoes it can control tomato worm.

CONTAINER GROWING

It is not suitable for container growing indoors. However, when planted outside in large containers (like a half barrel), borage can be very effective combined with other tall plants like oxeye daisies, poppies and cornflowers.

WARNING

Prolonged use of borage is not advisable. Fresh leaves may cause contact dermatititis.

CULINARY

Be brave, try a young leaf. It may be hairy, some would say prickly, but once in the mouth the hairs dissolve and the flavour is of cool cucumber. Great cut up in salads, or with cream cheese, or added to yoghurt, or even in an egg mayonnaise sandwich. And they give a refreshing flavour to summer cold drinks. Finally fresh leaves are particularly good to use in a salt-free diet as they are rich in mineral salts. Try them combined with spinach or or added to ravioli stuffing.

The flowers are exciting tossed in a salad, floated on top of a glass of Pimms No 1, or crystallized for cake decoration. Also excellent as garnish for savoury or sweet dishes, and on iced soups.

FACIAL STEAM FOR DRY, SENSITIVE SKIN

Place 2 large handfuls of borage leaves in a bowl. Pour over 1.5 litres (3 pints) of boiling water. Stir quickly with a wooden spoon. Using a towel as a tent, place your face about 30cm (12in) over the water. Cover your head with towel. Keep your eyes closed and maintain for about 10-15 minutes. Afterwards rinse your face with tepid cool water. Use a yarrow infusion dabbed on with cotton wool to close pores.

OTHER USES

Dried flowers to add colour to potpourris. Children enjoy stringing them together as a necklace. Add to summer flower arrangements.

As a novelty burn the whole plant – the nitrate of potash will emit sparks and little explosive sounds like fireworks.

Borage and cream cheese

MEDICINAL

In the 1980s borage was found to contain GLA, gamma linoleic acid, an even more valuable medicinal substance than Evening Primrose Oil. But cultivation problems coincided with a dramatic slump in prices because a waste, black currant pulp, provided a cheaper and richer source of GLA. So hopes for the future of borage as a commercial crop have diminished recently, but it deserves more medicinal research.

Borage tea is said to be good for reducing high temperatures when taken hot. This is because in inducing sweat – it is a diaphoretic – it lowers the fever. This makes it a good remedy for colds and flu especially when these infect the lungs as it is also good for coughs. Both leaves and flowers are rich in potassium and calcium and are therefore good blood purifiers and a tonic.

Borage Tea

*Small handful of fresh leaves
600ml/1 pint/2½ cups of
boiling water*

Simmer for 5 minutes.

Natural Night-cap

*3 teaspoons fresh borage leaves
1 cup (250ml) boiling water
1 teaspoon honey
1 slice lemon*

Put the roughly chopped borage leaves into a warmed cup and pour over the boiling water. Cover with a saucer and leave the leaves to infuse for at least five minutes. Strain and add the lemon slice and honey. Drink hot just before retiring to bed.

Variegated box *Buxus sempervirens* 'Elegantissima'

Buxus sempervirens

BOX

Also known as Boxwood and Bushtree. From the family Buxaceae.

Box is a native plant of Europe, Western Asia and North Africa. It has been cultivated widely through out the world and is found in America along the Atlantic coast especially as an ornamental and hedging plant.

The common name, box, comes from the Latin 'buxus' which is in turn derived from the Greek 'puxus' meaning a small box. At one time, box woods were widespread in Europe but the demand for the wood, which is twice as hard as oak, led to extensive felling. Its timber is close-grained and heavy, so heavy in fact that it is unable to float on water. The wood does not warp and is therefore ideal for boxes, engraving plates, carvings, and musical and navigational instruments.

It is not used medicinally now but the essential oil from box was used for the treatment of epilepsy, syphilis and piles, and also as an alternative to quinine in the treatment of malaria. A perfume was once made from its bark and a mixture of the leaves with sawdust has been used as an auburn hair dye.

When it rains, box gives off a musky smell evocative of old gardens, delicious to most people, but not Queen Anne who so hated the smell that she had the box parterres in St James Park (planted for her predecessors, William and Mary, in the last years of the 17th century) torn out.

SPECIES

Buxus balearica
Balearic Box
Half-hardy evergreen. Ht 2m (6ft), spread 1.5m (5ft). Suitable for hedging in mild areas. Has broadly oval, bright green leaves. Planting distance for a hedge 30-40cm (12-15in).

Buxus microphylla
Small Leaved Box
Hardy evergreen. Ht 1m (3ft), spread 1.5m (5ft). Forms a dense mass of round/oblong, dark green, glossy leaves. Attractive cultivar 'Green Pillow', which is good for formal shaping. Planting distance for a hedge 15-23cm (6-9in).

Buxus sempervirens
Common Box
Hardy evergreen. Ht and spread 5m (15ft). Leaves glossy green and oblong. Good for hedges, screening, and topiary. Planting distance for a hedge 37-45cm (15-18in).

Buxus sempervirens 'Elegantissima'
Variegated Box
Hardy evergreen. Ht and spread 1m (3ft). Good variegated gold/green leaves. Susceptible to scorch in hard winter. Trim regularly to maintain variegation. Very attractive as a centre hedging in a formal garden or as specimen plants in their own right. Planting distance for a hedge 30-40cm (12-15in).

Buxus sempervirens 'Handsworthiensis'
Handsworthiensis Box
Hardy evergreen. Ht and spread 3m (10ft). Broad, very dark green leaves. One of the fast growing boxes with a dense habit, ideal for hedging or screening. Planting distance for a hedge 37-45cm (15-18in).

Buxus sempervirens 'Suffruticosa'
Dwarf Box
Hardy evergreen. Ht and spread 45cm (18in). Evergreen dark shrub that forms tight dense mass. Slow grower. This is the architectypal edging in a formal herb garden for patterns and parterres of the knots. It is trimmed to about 15cm (6in) in height when used for hedging. Planting distance for hedge 15-23cm (6-9in).

Buxus wallichiana
Himalayan Box
Hardy evergreen. Ht and spread 2m (6ft). Slow growing. Produces long narrow, glossy, bright green leaves. Planting distance for a hedge 30-40cm (12-15in).

Box *Buxus sempervirens*

BOX 53

CULTIVATION

Propagation

Cuttings: Box is cultivated from cuttings taken in spring from the new growth (see Propagation). Use a bark, grit, peat mix of compost. Keep the cuttings moist but NOT wet, and in a cool place, ideally in shade. They will take 3-4 months to root. If you have a propagator then they will take 6-8 weeks at 21°C (70°F). Use a spray to mist the plant regularly. When rooted, pot up the young plants using a soil based compost or plant out, as per the distances mentioned under species.

Alternatively, take semi-ripe cuttings in summer, using the same compost mix as above. Rooting time approximately 2 months longer than the softwood cuttings, but only 3-4 weeks longer with heat.

Pests and Diseases

If you notice a white deposit on the leaves, look more closely and you will see that some of the leaves have curled up. Inside, you will find a very small caterpillar. These are very difficult to get rid of. The best way is to give the plant a trim (sweep up the cuttings and bin), then spray with derris or a liquid horticultural soap.

Maintenance

Spring: Take stem cuttings. Trim fast growers i.e. **Buxus sempervirens 'Handsworthiensis'**.
Summer: Take semi-ripe cuttings. Trim hedges to promote new growth.
Autumn: Trim if needed but not hard.
Winter: Does not need protection.

Garden Cultivation

The plant is known for its longevity. It is not uncommon for it to live 600 years. Box flourishes on limestone or chalk; it prefers an alkaline soil. But it is very tolerant of any soil provided it is not waterlogged. Box is also fairly tolerant of position, surviving sun or semi-shade.

Hedges are a frame for a garden, outlining, protecting and enhancing what they enclose. The preparation of the planting site for hedges is much the same as for the original herb garden.

Because one will be planting the box plants closer together than when planting individual plants it is important first to feed the soil well by adding plenty of well-rotted manure or garden compost. Width of bed for a boundary hedge should be 60cm (2ft); for small internal hedges 30cm (1ft) wide. Planting distances vary according to species (see above).

If using Common Box or Handsworthiensis Box, the more vigorous growers, trim in spring and prune end summer/early autumn. The slower varieties need a cut only in the summer. In general the right shape for a healthy, dense hedge is broad at the base tapering slightly towards the top, rounded or ridged but not too flat, to prevent damage from heavy snow.

Left: Buxus sempervirens 'Elegantissima'

CONTAINER GROWING

Box, especially the slow growing varities, lend themselves to topiary and look superb in containers. **Buxus sempervirens 'Elegantissima'** looks very attractive in a terracotta pot. They are very easy to maintain. Use a soil based compost. Feed with a liquid fertilizer in spring; water sparingly in winter.

OTHER USES

Boxwood is a favourite timber with cabinet makers, wood engravers and turners because of its non-fibrous structure.

An ornamental mahogany box with boxwood strapping

MEDICINAL

It is advisable not to self-administer this plant; it should be used with caution. Box is used extensively in homoeopathic medicines, a tincture prepared from fresh leaves is prescribed for fever, rheumatism and urinary tract infections.

WARNING

Animals have died from eating the leaves. All parts of the plant, especially the leaves and seeds, are poisonous. It is dangerous to take internally and should never be collected or used for self-medication. Symptoms of poisoning are vomiting, abdominal pain and bloody diarrhoea.

Calamintha

CALAMINT

From the family Labiatae

Calamintha originated in Europe. It is now well established throughout temperate countries, but sadly it is still not a common plant. Calamint has been cultivated since the 17th century. Herbal records show that it used to be prescribed for women.

SPECIES

Calamintha grandiflora
Calamint
Hardy perennial. Ht 37cm (15in), spread 30cm (12in). Square stems arise from creeping rootstock. Dense swirls of lilac pink flowers appear mid-summer to early autumn above mint-scented, toothed, oval leaves.

Calamintha grandiflora 'Variegata'
Hardy perennial. As **C. grandiflora** but with cream variegated leaves.

Calamintha nepeta
Lesser Calamint
Perennial. Ht 30-60cm (12-24in), spread 30cm (12in). Small purple/white flowers from summer to early autumn. Stems and leaves pale grey and covered in fine downy hairs with small greyish leaves. Its wonderful aromatic scent attracts butterflies and bees.

Calamintha sylvatica ssp ascendens
Mountain Balm (Mountain Mint)
Hardy perennial. Ht 30cm (12in), spread 20cm (8in). Pale purple flowers in dense whorls from late summer to early autumn. Leaves mid-

Lesser Calamint
Calamintha nepeta

green, oval, finely toothed and mint scented. A tisane can be made from the leaves.

CULTIVATION

Propagation
Seed
Sow calamint's fine seeds in spring or autumn, either in their eventual flowering position or in trays, covered lightly with Perlite. If autumn sowing in trays leave them outside to over-winter, covered with a sheet of glass. As germination can be tricky, Autumn sowing is sometimes more successful because subjecting the seeds to all weathers – thereby giving the hot and cold treatment – can trigger the

process (see Stratification). When the seedlings are large enough to handle, prick out and plant up into pots, using a bark, grit, peat mix of compost. Alternatively plant them directly into the chosen site in late spring after hardening off.

Cuttings
Take cuttings of young shoots in spring. This is an especially good method for the variegated grandiflora. They take easily, but keep in the shade until fully rooted and do not allow to dry out. Plant out in final position when fully hardened off.

Division
Once the plants are established they can be divided either in the spring or autumn, either by lifting the whole plant or by the double fork method. Replant immediately either into a prepared site or into pots using a bark, peat mix of compost. If this method is chosen in the autumn, keep in a cold frame all winter.

Pests and Diseases
The leaves are aromatic so this plant is left alone by pests.

Maintenance
Spring: Sow seeds. Take cuttings from new growth.
Summer: Cut back after first flowering and keep the plant tidy. Give a feed of liquid fertilizer, this can promote a second flowering.
Autumn: Sow seeds. Cut back new growth after second flowering.
Winter: Protect new growth in frosts below -4°C (25°F). Use either agricultural fleece, bracken, straw, or pine needles.

Garden Cultivation
These plants are indigenous to the limestone uplands and like a sunny position in well-drained soil, low in nutrients. The leaves of **C.g. 'Variegata'** scorch easily and need some shade.

Harvest
Leaves
Pick either side of flowering for use either fresh or dried.

CULINARY

The young minty leaves of the lesser calamint can be added to salads and used to make a refreshing tea.

CONTAINER GROWING

Unsuitable for growing indoors, but can look good growing in containers outside. Use a bark, grit peat mix of compost and a container with a diameter no less than 12cm (5in). **C. g. 'Variegata'** looks particularly striking in a terracotta pot.

MEDICINAL

Infuse dried leaves as a tea for colic, and as an invigorating tonic. Use fresh leaves in a poultice for bruises.

Calomeria amaranthoides (Humea elegans)

INCENSE PLANT

From the family Compositae.

A native of South Australia, Africa and Madagascar.

The Latin, 'Humea', is in honour of Lady Hume of Wormleybury. It was only changed in 1993 to Calomeria.

The incense plant was a favourite of the Victorians, who put it in their front rooms or conservatories.

SPECIES

Calomeria amaranthoides (Humea elegans)
Incense Plant
Tender biennial (sometimes annual). Ht up to 1.8m (6ft), spread 90cm (3ft). Tiny, delicate, coral flower bracts, very numerous on large branches. Large, oblong mid-green leaves.

Warning: Leaves can cause irritation and the same kind of burns as rue. The scent can cause breathing difficulties and when in flower, it has a high pollen count and can trigger asthma attacks.

CULTIVATION

Propagation
Seed
Being a biennial, this is grown from the small seed, which is viable for only a short time. Collect from the plants in the summer, when ripe, and sow immediately into prepared seed or plug trays using the bark, peat compost. Leave the seeds uncovered. Over-winter in a cold frame and cover the seed tray with glass or polythene. Germination is lengthy and very erratic. Pot on seedlings as soon as they appear, taking care not to injure the roots. Grow young plants in a cool, frost-free environment, and keep the roots almost dry through winter. In spring gradually encourage growth by watering and potting on.

Pests and Diseases
As a container-grown plant, it suffers from greenfly and red spider mite. Keep an eye out for these and use a horticultural liquid soap as soon as they appear.

Maintenance
Spring: Prick out first year's plants. Pot up second year's.
Summer: Feed and water regularly. Collect seeds off second year's plant and sow immediately.
Autumn: Protect first year's plants.
Winter: Protect plants from frost. Keep watering to the minimum.

Garden Cultivation
Do not plant outside until the night temperature no longer falls below 4°C (40°F). Plant in an area protected from the wind; even here, a stake is recommended. It prefers a light soil and a sunny position. All in all, it makes a better indoor plant, where the marvellous scent can be enjoyed.

Flowers of the incense plant
Calomeria amaranthoides

Harvest
Collect flowers for drying in summer. Dry for use in potpourris.

CONTAINER GROWING

The incense plant is very ornamental and is the ultimate pot plant, growing to over 1.5m (5ft). It is, however, rarely seen because it needs a good deal of attention and protection.

Use the bark, grit, peat compost, and regularly pot up and liquid feed throughout its short life until a pot size of 30cm (12in) in diameter is reached. Place in full sun and water through the growing season.

OTHER USES

Use in potpourris.

Calendula officinalis

MARIGOLD

Also known as Souci, Marybud, Bulls Eye, Garden Marigold, Holligold, Marybud, Pot Marigold and Common Marigold. From the family Compositae.

Native of Mediterranean and Iran. Distributed throughout the world as a garden plant.

This sunny little flower – the 'merrybuds' of Shakespeare – was first used in Indian and Arabic cultures, before being 'discovered' by the ancient Egyptians and Greeks.

The Egyptians valued the marigold as a rejuvenating herb, and the Greeks garnished and flavoured food with its golden petals. The botanical name comes from the Latin 'calendae', meaning the first day of the month.

In India wreaths of marigold were used to crown the gods and goddesses. In medieval times they were considered an emblem of love and used as chief ingredient in a complicated spell that promised young maidens knowledge of whom they would marry. To dream of them was a sign of all good things; simply to look at them would drive away evil humours.

In the American Civil War, marigold leaves were used by the doctors on the battlefield to treat open wounds.

SPECIES

Calendula officinalis
Marigold
Hardy annual. Ht and spread 60cm (24in). Daisy-like, single or double flowers, yellow or orange: from spring to autumn. Light green, aromatic, lance-shaped leaves.

Marigold
Calendula officinalis

CULTIVATION

Propagation
Seeds
Seeds can be sown in the autumn under protection directly into prepared pots or singly into plug trays, covering lightly with compost. They can be wintered in these containers and planted out in the spring after any frost, 30-45cm (12-18in) apart.

Pests and Diseases
Slugs love the leaves of young marigolds. Keep

night-time vigil with a torch and a bucket, or lay beer traps. In the latter part of the season, plants can become infested with blackfly. Treat this in the early stages by brushing off the fly and cutting away the affected areas, or later on by spraying with a horticultural soap. Very late in the season, the leaves sometimes become covered with a powdery mildew. Cut off those affected and burn them to prevent spreading.

Maintenance

Spring: Sow seeds in garden.
Summer: Dead head flowers to promote more flowering.
Autumn: Sow seeds under protection for early spring flowering.
Winter: Protect young plants.

Garden Cultivation

Marigold is a very tolerant plant, growing in any soil that is not waterlogged, but prefers, and looks best in, a sunny position.

The flowers are sensitive to variations of temperature and dampness. Open flowers forecast a fine day. Encourage continuous flowering by dead heading. It self-seeds abundantly but seems never to become a nuisance.

Marigold seed head

Harvest

Pick flowers just as they open during summer, both for fresh use and for drying. Dry at a low temperature. You can make a colourful oil.

Pick leaves young for fresh use; they are not much good preserved.

CULINARY

Flower petals make a very good culinary dye. They have been used for butter and cheese, and as a poor man's saffron to colour rice. They are also lovely in salads and omelettes, and make an interesting cup of tea.

Young leaves can be added to salads.

Sweet Marigold Buns

Makes 18

100g/4oz softened butter
100g/4oz caster sugar
2 eggs, size 1 or 2
100g/4oz self-raising flour
1 teaspoon baking powder
2 tablespoons fresh marigold petals

Put the butter, sugar, eggs, sifted flour and baking powder into bowl, and mix together until smooth and glossy. Fold in 1½ tablespoons of marigold petals. Turn the mixture into greased bun tins or individual paper cake cases. Sprinkle a few petals onto each bun with a little sugar. Bake in an oven 160°C/325°F/Gas Mark 3 for approximately 25-30 minutes.

CONTAINER GROWING

Marigolds look very cheerful in containers and combine well with other plants. Well suited to window boxes, but not so in hanging baskets, where they will become stretched and leggy.

Use the bark, peat compost. Pinch out the growing tips to stop the plant from becoming too tall and leggy. Dead head flowers to encourage more blooms.

OTHER USES

There are many skin and cosmetic preparations that contain marigold. Infuse the flowers and use as a skin lotion to reduce large pores, nourish and clear the skin, and clear up spots and pimples.

MEDICINAL

Marigold flowers contain antiseptic, anti-fungal and anti-bacterial properties that promote healing. Make a compress or poultice of the flowers for burns, scalds, or stings. Also useful in the treatment of varicose veins, chilblains and impetigo. A cold infusion may be used as an eyewash for conjunctivitis, and can be a help in the treatment of thrush.

The sap from the stem has a reputation for removing warts, corns and calluses.

Marigold skin lotion

Carum carvi

CARAWAY

From the family Umbelliferae

Caraway is a native of Southern Europe, Asia and India and thrives in all but the most humid warm regions of the world. It is commercially and horticulturally cultivated on a wide scale, especially in Germany and Holland.

Both the common and species names stem directly from the ancient Arabic word for the seed, 'karawya', which was used in medicines and as a flavouring by the ancient Egyptians. In fact fossilized caraway seeds have been discovered at Mesolithic sites, so this herb has been used for at least 5,000 years. It has also been found in the remains of Stone Age meals, Egyptian tombs and ancient caravan stops along the Silk Road.

Caraway probably did not come into use in Europe until the 13th century, but it made a lasting impact. In the 16th century when Shakespeare, in *Henry IV*, gave Falstaff a pippin apple and a dish of caraways, his audience could relate to the dish, for caraway had become a traditional finish to an Elizabethan feast. Its popularity was further enhanced 250 or so years later when Queen Victoria married Prince Albert, who made it clear that he shared his countrymen's particular predilection for the seed in an era celebrated in England by the caraway seed cake.

No herb as ancient goes without magical properties of course, and caraway was reputed to ward off witches and also to prevent lovers from straying, a propensity with a wide application – it kept a man's doves, pigeons and poultry steadfast too!

SPECIES

Carum carvi
Caraway
Hardy biennial. Ht in first year 20cm (8in), second year 60cm (24in); spread 30cm (12in). Flower white/pinkish in tiny umbellate clusters in early summer. Leaves feathery, light green, similar to carrot. Pale thick tapering root comparable to parsnip but smaller. This plant is not particularly decorative.

Caraway *Carum Carvi*

CULTIVATION

Propagation
Seed
Easily grown; best sown outdoors in early autumn when the seed is fresh. Preferred situation full sun or a little shade, any reasonable, well-drained soil. For an acceptable flavour it must have full sun.

If growing caraway as a root crop, sow in rows and treat the plants like vegetables. Thin to 20cm (8in) and keep weed free. These plants will be ready for a seed harvest the following summer; the roots will be ready in their second autumn. Caraway perpetuates itself by self-sowing and can, with a little control, maintain the cycle.

If you want to sow in spring, do it either direct in the garden into shallow drills after the soil has warmed, or into prepared plug trays to minimize harmful disturbance to its tap root when potting up. Cover with Perlite. Pot up when seedlings are large enough to handle and transplant in the early autumn.

Pests and Diseases

Caraway occasionally suffers from carrot root fly. The grubs of these pests tunnel into the roots. The only organic way to get rid of them is to pull up the plants and bin them.

Maintenance

Spring: Weed well around autumn sown young plants. Sow seed.
Summer: Pick flowers and leaves.
Autumn: Cut seed heads. Dig up 2nd-year plants. Sow seeds.
Winter: Does not need much protection unless it gets very cold.

Garden Cultivation

Prepare the garden seedbed well. The soil should be fertile, free draining and free of weeds, not least because it is all too easy to mistake a young caraway plant for a weed in its early growing stage. Thin plants when well established to a distance of 20cm (8in).

Harvest

Harvest the seeds in summer by cutting the seed heads just before the first seeds fall. Hang them with a paper bag tied over the seed head or over a tray in an airy place. It was once common practice to scald the freshly collected seed to rid it of insects and then dry it in the sun before storing. This is not necessary. Simply store in an airtight container.

Gather fresh leaves when young for use in salads. They are not really worth drying.

Dig up roots in second autumn as a food crop.

CONTAINER GROWING

Caraway really is not suitable for growing in pots.

Caraway and Cheese Potatoes

CULINARY

When you see caraway mentioned in a recipe it is usually the seed that is required. Caraway seed cake was one of the staples of the Victorian tea table. Nowadays caraway is more widely used in cooking, and in savouries as well as sweet dishes. The strong and distinctive flavour is also considered a spice. It is frequently added to sauerkraut, and the German liqueur, Kummel, contains its oil along with cumin.

Sprinkle over rich meats, goose, Hungarian beef stew – as an aid to digestion. Add to cabbage water to reduce cooking smells. Add to apple pies, biscuits, baked apples and cheese.

Serve in a mixed dish of seeds at the end of an Indian meal both to sweeten the breath and aid digestion.

Caraway root can be cooked as a vegetable, and its young leaves chopped into salads and soups.

Cheese and Caraway Potatoes
Serves 4

4 large potatoes
100gm/4oz/1 cup grated Gruyère cheese
2 teaspoons caraway seeds

Scrub but do not peel the potatoes. Cut them in half length-wise. Wrap in a boat of greaseproof foil and sprinkle each half with some of the grated cheese and a little caraway. Pre-heat the oven to 180°C/350°F/Gas Mark 4 and cook for 35-45 minutes, or until the potatoes are soft.

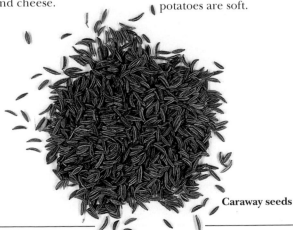

Caraway seeds

MEDICINAL

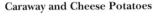

The fresh leaves, roots and seeds have digestive properties.

Chew seeds raw or infuse them to sharpen appetites before a meal, as well as to aid digestion, sweeten the breath, and relieve flatulence after the meal. Safe for children.

An infusion can be made from 3 teaspoons of crushed seeds with ½ cup of water.

OTHER USES

Pigeon fanciers claim that tame pigeons will never stray if there is baked caraway dough in their coot.

Cedronella canariensis (triphylla)

BALM OF GILEAD

Also known as Canary Balm. From the family Labiatae

Although this herb originates from Madeira and the Canary Islands, as indicated by its species name, balm of Gilead is now established in many temperate regions of the world. Many plants have been called balm of Gilead, the common link is that they all have a musky, eucalyptus, camphor-like scent.

The Queen of Sheba gave Solomon a balm of Gilead, which was *Commiphora opobalsamum*, an aromatic desert shrub found in the Holy Land. Today this plant is rare and protected, its export prohibited.

The balm of Gilead mentioned in the Bible ('Is there no balm in Gilead; is there no physician there?') was initially held to be *Commiphora meccanensis* which was an aromatic shrub. However some now say it was oleo-resin obtained from *Balsamodendron opobalsamum*, a plant now thought to be extinct. Whatever is the case, the medicinal balm of Gilead is *Populus balsamifera*. This is balsam poplar, a tree found growing in several temperate countries, which smells heavenly in early summer, while the herb now known as balm of Gilead is *Cedronella canariensis*. This is said to have a similar scent to the Biblical shrubs, perhaps the reason for its popular name.

Balsam poplar *Populus balsamifera*

SPECIES

Cedronella canariensis (triphylla)
Balm of Gilead
Half-hardy perennial, partial evergreen. Ht 1m (3ft), spread 60cm (2ft). Leaves with strong eucalyptus scent, 3 lobes and toothed edges, borne on square stems. Pink or pale mauve, two-lipped flowers throughout summer. Black seed heads.

CULTIVATION

Propagation

Seed

The fairly small seeds should be sown directly on the surface of a prepared pot, plug or seed tray. Cover with a layer of Perlite.

It is a temperamental germinator so bottom heat of 20°C (68°F) can be an asset. If using heat remember not to let the compost dry out, and only water with a fine spray when needed. The seedlings will appear any time between 2–6 weeks. When 2 leaves have formed, prick out and plant in position 1m (3ft) apart.

Cuttings

More reliable than seed. They take readily either in early summer before flowering on new growth or in early autumn on the semi-ripe wood. Use the bark, peat, grit mix of compost .

Pests and Diseases

Being aromatic, aphids and other pests usually leave it alone, but the seedlings are prone to damping off.

Maintenance

Spring: Sow seeds under protection. In a warm garden a mature plant can self-seed; rub the leaves of any self-seedlings to see if it is balm of Gilead or a young nettle (but don't get stung!). At this stage their aroma is the only characteristic which tells them apart.

Plants over-wintered in containers should be repotted if root-bound and given a liquid feed.

Summer: Cut back after flowering to keep it neat and tidy, and also to encourage new growth from which late cuttings can be taken.

Autumn: Take stem cuttings. Collect seed heads.

Winter: Protect from frost.

Balm of Gilead
Cedronella canariensis

Garden Cultivation

Balm of Gilead grows happily outside in sheltered positions. Plant in a well-drained soil in full sun, preferably against a warm, wind-protecting wall. The plant has an upright habit but spreads at the top, so planting distance from other plants should be approximately 1m (3ft).

It is a tender plant which may need protection in cooler climates. If you get frosts lower than –2°C (29°F) protect the plant for the winter, either by bringing it into a cool greenhouse or conservatory or by covering in an agricultural fleece.

Harvest

Pick leaves for drying before the flowers open, when they will be at their most aromatic.

Either pick flowers when just coming into bloom and dry, or wait until flowering is over and collect the black flower heads (good for winter arrangements).

Seeds are ready for extraction when you can hear the flower heads rattle. Store in an airtight container to sow in the spring.

CONTAINER GROWING

Balm of Gilead makes an excellent container plant. A 23–25cm (9–10in) pot will be required for a plant to reach maturity. Use a free-draining compost with bark and grit. Liquid feed a mature plant monthly throughout summer.

When grown in a conservatory, the scent of the leaves perfumes the air especially when the plant is watered or the sun shining on it. Flowers are long lasting and give a good show during the summer. Keep watering to the absolute minimum in the winter months.

MEDICINAL

Crush the leaves in your hand and inhale the aroma to clear your head.

Rub the leaves on skin to stop being bitten by mosquitoes.

Said to be an Aphrodisiac when applied....no comment.

OTHER USES

Dried leaves combine well in a spicy or woody potpourris with cedarwood chippings, rosewood, pineneedles, small fur cones, cypress oil and pine oil.

Add an infusion of the leaves to bath water for an invigorating bath.

'I am sorry to say that Peter was not very well during the evening. His mother put him to bed and made some chamomile tea and she gave a dose of it to Peter, one tablespoon full to be taken at bedtime.'
(*The Tale of Peter Rabbit* by Beatrix Potter)

Chamaemelum nobile

CHAMOMILE

From the family Compositae

Dyers Chamomile
Anthemis tinctoria

Chamomile grows wild in Europe, North America, and many other countries. As a garden escapee, it can be found in pasture and other grassy places on sandy soils.

The generic name, *Chamaemelum,* is derived from the Greek *Khamaimelon,* meaning 'Earth Apple' or 'apple on the ground'.

SPECIES

Chamaemelum nobile
Roman Chamomile
Also known as Garden Chamomile, Ground Apple, Low Chamomile and Whig Plant
Hardy perennial evergreen. Ht 10cm (4in), spread 45cm (18in). White flowers with yellow centres all summer. Sweet smelling, finely divided foliage. Ideal for ground cover. Can be used as a lawn, but because it flowers it will need constant cutting.

Chamaemelum nobile
'Flore Pleno'
Double-flowered Chamomile
Hardy perennial evergreen. Ht 8cm (3in), spread 30cm (12in). Double white flowers all summer. Sweet-smelling, finely divided, thick foliage. Good for ground cover, in between paving stones and lawns. More compact habit than Roman Chamomile, and combines well with Chamomile Treneague.

Chamaemelum nobile
'Treneague' (**Anthemis nobilis** 'Treneague')
Chamomile Treneague
Also known as Lawn Chamomile
Hardy perennial evergreen. Ht 6cm (2.5in), spread 15cm (6in). Non-flowering. Leaves are finely divided and very aromatic. Ideal for ground cover or mow-free lawn. Plant in well-drained soil, free from stones, 10-15cm (4-6in) apart.

Anthemis tinctoria
Dyers Chamomile
Also known as Yellow Chamomile
Hardy perennial evergreen. Ht and spread 1m (3ft). Yellow daisy flowers in the summer. Leaves are mid-green and fern like. Principally a dye plant.

Matricaria recutita
German Chamomile
Also known as Scented Mayweed, Wild Chamomile
Hardy annual. Ht 60cm (24in), spread 10cm (4in). Scented white flowers with conical yellow centres from spring to early summer. Finely serrated aromatic foliage. The main use of this chamomile is medicinal.

CULTIVATION

Propagation
Seed
Dyers, Roman and German chamomiles can be grown from seed. Sow onto the surface of a prepared seed or plug tray. Use a bark, grit, peat compost. Cover with Perlite. Use bottom heat 19°C (65°F). Harden off and plant out or pot on.

Chamomile
Chamaemelum nobile

Cuttings
Double-flowered chamomile and Chamomile Treneague can only be propagated this way.

Take cuttings in the spring and autumn from the offsets or clusters of young shoots. They are easy to grow as they have aerial roots.

Division
All perennial chamomiles planted as specimen plants will benefit from being lifted in the spring of their second or third year and divided.

Pests and Diseases
As all the chamomiles are highly aromatic they are not troubled by pests or disease.

Maintenance
Spring: Collect offshoots, sow seeds. Fill in holes that have appeared in the chamomile lawn. Divide established plants. Give a liquid fertilizer feed to all established plants.
Summer: Water well. Do not allow to dry out. In the first season of a lawn, trim the plants to encourage bushing out and spreading. In late summer collect flowers from the Dyers chamomile and cut the plant back to

Dyers Chamomile
Anthemis tinctoria

6cm (2in) to promote new growth.
Autumn: Take cuttings. Divide if they have become too invasive. Cut back to promote new growth. Give the final feed of the season.
Winter: Only protect in extreme weather.

Garden Cultivation

All the chamomiles prefer a well-drained soil and a sunny situation, although they will adapt to most conditions.

As a lawn plant, chamomile gets more credit than it deserves. Chamomile lawns are infinitely less easy to maintain in good condition than grass lawns. There is no selective herbicide that will preserve chamomile and kill the rest of the weeds. It is a hands-and-knees job.

Prepare the site well, make sure the soil is light, slightly acid, and free from weeds and stones. Plant young plants in plug form. I use a mix of double-flowered and Treneague chamomile at a distance of 10-15cm (4-6in) apart. Keep all traffic off it for at least 12 weeks, and keep it to the minimum during the first year.

If all this seems daunting, compromise and plant a chamomile seat. Prepare the soil in the same way and do not sit on the seat for at least 12 weeks. Then sit down, smell the sweet aroma and sip a cool glass of wine. Summer is on hand . . .

Harvest

Leaves
Gather in spring and early summer for best results. Use fresh or dry.

Flowers
Pick when fully open, around mid-summer. Use fresh or dry. Dyers chamomile flowers should be harvested in summer for their yellow dye.

COMPANION PLANTING

Chamomile has the unique name Physician's Plant because, when planted near ailing plants, it helps to revive them. Roman Chamomile can be planted next to onions to repel flying insects and improve the crop yield.

Chamomile Infusion

Bring 600ml (1 pint) water to the boil. Add a handful of chamomile leaves and flowers. Cover and let it stand for about half a day. Strain.

Spray it onto seedlings to prevent 'damping off'. If there is any liquid left pour it onto your compost heap. This acts like an activator for decomposition.

WARNING

When taken internally, excessive dosage can produce vomiting and vertigo.

CONTAINER GROWING

I would not advise growing chamomiles indoors, as they get very leggy, soft and prone to disease. But the flowers can look very cheerful in a sunny window box. Use Chamomile 'Flore Pleno', which has a lovely double flower head, or the non-flowering *C.* Treneague as an infill between bulbs, with a bark, grit, peat compost.

COSMETIC

Chamomile is used as a final rinse for fair hair to make it brighter. It should be poured over your hair several times. Pour 1 litre (1¾ pints) boiling water over one handful of chamomile flowers and steep for 30 minutes. Strain, cover and allow to cool.

MEDICINAL

German chamomile's highly scented dry flower heads contain up to 1 per cent of an aromatic oil that possesses powerful antiseptic and anti-inflammatory properties. Taken as a tea, it promotes gastric secretions and improves the appetite, while an infusion of the same strength can be used as an internal antiseptic. It may also be used as a douche or gargle for mouth ulcers and as an eye wash.

An oil for skin rashes or allergies can be made by tightly packing flower heads into a preserving jar, covering with olive oil and leaving in the sun for three weeks. If you suffer from overwrought nerves, add five or six drops of chamomile oil to the bath and this will help you relax at night.

Chamomile tea

1 heaped teaspoon chamomile flowers (dried or fresh)
1 teaspoon honey
slice of lemon (optional)

Put the chamomile flowers into a warm cup. Pour on boiling water. Cover and leave to infuse for 3–5 minutes. Strain and add the honey and lemon, if required. Can be drunk either hot or cold.

OTHER USES

Dyers Chamomile can be used as a dye plant. Depending on the mordant, its colour can vary from bright to olive/brown yellow.

German and Double-flowered Chamomile are best for herb pillows and pot pourri.

Chenopodium bonus-henricus

GOOD KING HENRY

Also known as All Good, Good King Harry, Good Neighbour, Wild Spinach, Lincolnshire Asparagus and Mercury. From the family Chenopodiaceae.

Good King Henry comes from a genus (*Chenopodium* spp) that is distributed all over the world and is found growing in all climates. This species (*C. bonus-henricus*) is native to Europe.

Good King Henry was popular from Neolithic times until the last century. Its curious name is taken not from the English king, Henry VIII, as might be expected, but from King Henry IV of Navarre, and to distinguish it from the poisonous Bad Henry (*Mercurialis perennis*).

Gerard in the 17th Century observed that Good King Henry grew in untilled places and among rubbish near common ways, old walls, hedges and fields, and it still does – colonies of the herb can be found on many mediaeval sites.

SPECIES

Chenopodiaceae, the goosefoot family, includes 1,500 rather unattractive plants, some of them important edible plants, for example, spinach and beet.

Chenopodium bonus-henricus
Good King Henry
Perennial. Ht 60cm (24in), spread 45cm (18in). Tiny greenish-yellow flowers in early summer. Leaves green and arrow-shaped (*below right*). Very occasionally a variegated form is found; but the yellow variegation will be difficult to maintain.

Chenopodium album
Fat Hen
Also known as Lambs' Quarters, White Goosefoot, Common Pigweed, All Good and Muckweed
Annual. Ht 60cm-1m (2-3ft). Flowers small, greenish-white, summer to mid-autumn. Green lance-shaped leaves. Its seeds have been identified at Neolithic villages in Switzerland and in the stomach of the Iron Age Tollund Man. Rich in fat and albumen, it appears to have been a food supplement for primitive man.

Good King Henry
Chenopodium bonus-henricus

Chenopodium ambrosioides var. anthelmintium
American Wormseed
Also known as Mexican Tea, and in China as Fragrant Tiger Bones

Annual. Ht 60cm-1.25m (2-4ft). Small greenish flowers from late summer to late autumn. Green lance-shaped leaves. This is native to tropical Central America. Introduced through Mexico, it has become naturalized as far north as New England in the USA. It was introduced into Europe in the 18th century. Mexican Tea was once included in the United States pharmacopoeia but is now restricted to American folk medicine and mainly used for its essential oil, Chenopodium oil, against roundworm and hookworm.

Warning: Poisonous. Use under strict supervision. It causes deafness, vertigo, paralysis, incontinence, sweating, jaundice and

CULTIVATION

Propagation
Seeds
Sow the fairly small seeds early in spring in prepared seed or plug trays for an early crop. Use the bark, grit, peat mix of compost and cover with Perlite. No extra heat required. When the seedlings are large enough to handle and after hardening off, plant out in the garden 25cm (10in) apart. Can be sown direct.

Division
Divide established plants in the spring. You will find even small pieces will grow.

Pests and Diseases
Does not suffer from these.

Maintenance
Spring: Lift and divide established plants. If you wish to grow as an asparagus, blanch the shoots from early spring onwards. As they emerge, earth up with soil.
  Divide and re-pot container-grown plants.
Summer: Give a liquid feed if a second crop of leaves is required.

Good King Henry makes an interesting alternative to asparagus

Autumn: Cut back dying foliage and give the plant a mulch of compost.
Winter: No need for protection.

Garden Cultivation
Good King Henry will tolerate any soil, but if planted in a soil rich in humus, dug deep and well drained in a sunny position, the quality and quantity of the crop will be much improved. Sow directly into prepared soil in the garden in late spring in 1cm (0.5in) drills. Allow 45cm (18in) between rows. Cover the seeds with 6mm (¼in) soil. Germination in warm soil, 10-14 days. When large enough to handle thin to 25cm (10in) apart.
  Keep well watered in dry months. In autumn cover beds with a thin layer of manure. Beds should be renewed every 3 to 4 years.

Harvest
Allow plants 1 year to develop before harvesting. From mid-spring the young shoots can provide an asparagus substitute crop. They should be cut when they are about 15cm (6in) long. Harvest the flowering spikes as they begin to open. Later in the season gather the larger leaves as a spinach substitute as required. Freeze only when used as an ingredient in a cooked dish.

MEDICINAL

The seeds have a gentle laxative effect making them suitable relief for a slightly constipated condition especially in children.
  A poultice (or ointment) cleanses and heals skin sores.

WARNING

Sufferers of kidney complaints or rheumatism should avoid medicinal preparations containing extracts from this plant.

CULINARY

The leaves of Good King Henry and Fat Hen are rich in iron, calcium and Vitamins B_1 and C, and are particularly recommended for anaemic subjects.
  Like all low-growing leaves, Good King Henry must be washed with great care; the slightest suspicion of grit in the finished dish will ruin the meal. Use 2 or 3 changes of water.

OTHER USES
Good King Henry is used as a cough remedy for sheep.
  Whole plant used to fatten poultry.
  Seed is used commercially in the manufacture of shagreen, an artificially granulated untanned leather, often dyed green.
  The whole plant of fat hen can be used as a red or golden dye (*above*).

CONTAINER GROWING

Can be grown outside in a large container, in a rich compost of a bark, peat, grit mix. Needs to be kept well watered throughout the summer and fed once a week to maintain a supply of leaves. Divide each spring and re-pot in fresh compost.

  Steam flower spikes and toss in butter like broccoli.
  Eat young leaves raw in salads. Cook in casseroles, stuffings, soups and purées and savoury pies. They are more nutritious than spinach or cabbage.
  Blanch shoots – dip in hot water, rinse immediately under cold water. Alternatively cut shoots 15cm (6in) long. Steam or boil very quickly. Peel if necessary. Serve hot with melted butter, or cold with a vinaigrette.
  The seed of Fat Hen can be ground into flour and used to make into a gruel.

Cichorium intybus

CHICORY

Also known as Blue Endive, Bunks, Strip for Strip, Blue Sailors, Succory, Wild Chicory and Wild Succory. From the family Compositae.

Chicory
Cichorium intybus

Chicory grows throughout Europe in fields, hedgerows and on the roadside. In Englandand Wales it settles happily on lime rich soils, although it is rarely found in Scotland and Ireland. In Aralia and America it has been naturalized and is found on roadsides and field edges.

Chicory was an important medicinal herb, vegetable and salad plant in ancient Egypt, and in Greek and Roman times. Among the many delightful folk tales about the blue flowers we hear that the flowers are the transformed eyes of a lass weeping for her lover's ship, which never returned. Another from German folklore says that a young girl who could not stop weeping for her dead lover by the side of the road was turned into a flower called wegwort (chicory).

Careful English wives grew chicory among their herbs. It was good for purging and for the bladder. It was a principle of white magic that water distilled from the round blue flowers worked against inflammation and dimness of sight.

Chicory was grown in floral clocks because of the regular opening and closing of its flowers – they open to the sun and close about five hours later – and some gardeners, who have noticed that chicory leaves always align with North, credit the herb with metaphysical significance.

Since the 17th century, dried, roasted and ground roots of chicory have been used to make a drink. Two centuries later, Dickens described in his magazine *Household Words* the extensive cultivation of chicory in England as a coffee substitute.

Chicory leaves *Cichorium intybus*

Among the many varieties of chicory are:

Magdeburg or **Brunswick**
The best for producing roots which can be used as a coffee substitute.

Pain de Sucre (Sugar Loaf)
Looks like lettuce and can be used in the same way. Does not require blanching.

Red Verona
Crimson red foliage, good in salads.

Witloof (Brussels chicory)
This is the one grown for the chicons.

CULTIVATION

Propagation
Seeds
Sow the small seed thinly, either in spring or late summer in prepared pots, plug or seed trays, and cover with Perlite. For rapid germination (7-10 days), sow when freshest, in late summer. Winter the young plants under cover in a cold greenhouse, or on a cold windowsill. Plant these young plants out in the spring, 45cm (18in) apart. The seed can also be sown direct into the garden in spring.

SPECIES

Cichorium intybus
Chicory
Hardy perennial. Ht 1m (3ft), spread 30cm (1ft). Clear blue flowers from mid-summer to mid-autumn. Leaves mid-green, hairy underneath, and coarsely toothed.

Pests and Diseases
Fairly trouble free; keep an eye out for earwigs in the chicons.

Maintenance
Spring: Sow seed under protection for herb garden. Prepare site for outside sowing for chicons.
Summer: Sow seeds in situ for chicons.
Autumn: Dig up roots for forcing, also dig up and dry for coffee. Cut back flowers of plants in herb garden.
Winter: Dig in manure or compost where next year's chicon crop is to be grown.

Garden Cultivation
Seed
Grows easily. Sow in a sunny and open site with a light, preferably alkaline, soil. If you plan to harvest the roots prepare the site well, digging deeply. Thin the seedlings to 15-20cm (6-8in) distance apart in mid- to late summer. Transplant if necessary in the spring remembering that chicory grows fairly tall and looks well at the back of a border or against a fence, and needs to get the early morning sun as its flowers open at sunrise.

Harvest
Roots can be dug up through out the summer, but are usually left until autumn. Lift the root. Shorten to 20cm (8in). Remove all side shoots and leaves, and stack in dry sand in the dark. Dry roots for coffee substitute.
Gather leaves when young for fresh use. Pick before flowering for drying. Collect flowers in early summer either fresh or to dry.

CONTAINER GROWING

As Chicory grows so tall it is not ideally suited to container growing.

CHICONS
These are produced by forcing the roots in warmth and darkness, which blanches the new growth.
Prepare the soil, choosing a part of the garden that is rich in manure and well cultivated. Do not plant in recently manured land because this can cause forking in the roots.
In June sow the seeds. If you sow too early the plants may run to seed in the warm weather. Sow in 1cm (½in) drills, 30cm (12in) apart. Thin the seedlings.
Keep the area well watered in dry weather and weed free.
In late autumn, early winter begin carefully to dig up a few roots for forcing. Cut off the tops just above the crown. Plant the roots close together in a box of loamy soil with the crowns of the roots at soil level. Water and cover with another box. These chicons must remain in total darkness if they are not to become bitter. Put the box where the temperature does not go below 10°C (50°F).
In 4-6 weeks the chicons will be 15-20cm (6-8in) long and ready to harvest. If you break the chicons off carefully, instead of cutting, a second crop will appear. They will be smaller and looser but just as tasty.
The whole process can be repeated. When the remaining plants have died back dig up the roots, trim, and store in sand in a frost proof room, and force as required. One word of warning: do not pick the chicons before you need them because even after an hour in the light they will become limp.

WARNING

Excessive and continued use may impair the function of the retina.

Chicory in salad

MEDICINAL

Chicory, like dandelion, is a gentle but effective, bitter tonic, which increases the flow of bile. It is also a specific remedy for gall stones, and for this reason Galen called it 'friend of the liver'. Like dandelion it has diuretic properties and can be used for treating rheumatism and gout, because it eliminates uric acid from the body.
The roots, in the form of syrup or succory, make an excellent laxative for children.

OTHER USES

Boil the leaves to produce a blue dye.
Grow crop for animal fodder.

CULINARY

Add young leaves and flowers to summer salads, use forced leaves as a winter salad. Toss chicons in salads, or braise in butter as a vegetable dish.
Roasted chicory roots are still widely used as an excellent substitute or adulterant for coffee. Wash, slice and dry in gentle heat (see page000). Roast and grind.
When young the root can be dug up, boiled and served with a sauce.

Convallaria majalis

LILY OF THE VALLEY

Also known as Our Lady's Tears, Fairy's Bells, May Lily, Ladder to Heaven and May Bells. From the family Liliaceae

Lily of the valley is a native of Europe, North America and Canada. Introduced throughout the world in moist cool climates.

According to European folk tales, lily of the valley either originated from the Virgin Mary's tears, shed at the foot of the Cross, or from those shed by Mary Magdalen when she found Christ's tomb.

From the Middle Ages onwards the flowers form the traditional part of a bride's bouquet and are associated with modesty and purity.

In the 16th century they were used medicinally and called Convall Lily. The Elizabethan physician Gerard has this amazing recipe: 'Put the flowers of May lilies into a glass and set it in a hill of ants, firmly closed for 1 month. After which you will find a liquor that when applied appeaseth the paine and grief of gout.'

Lily of the Valley *Convallaria majalis "Vic Pawlowsky's Gold"*

SPECIES

Convallaria majalis
Lily of the Valley
Hardy perennial. Ht 15cm (6in), spread indefinite. White, bell-shaped, scented flowers, late spring to early summer. Leaves mid-green in colour, oval in shape. There are many attractive forms of this plant. The most striking is Vic Pawlowski's Gold which has gold strips running through the leaves. Another is the pink **Convallaria majalis var. rosea** which I think looks insipid next to the white flowering king.

CULTIVATION

Propagation
Seeds
Ripe seeds are seldom formed, and the scarlet berries are highly poisonous, so it is far better to propagate by division.

Division
The plant produces crowns on creeping rhizomes. Divide in the autumn after the plant has finished flowering and the leaves have died back.

Pests and Diseases
Lily of the valley is free from most pests and diseases.

Maintenance
Spring: In very early spring, bring pots into the house for forcing.
Summer: Do nothing!
Autumn: When the plant has died back fully dig up the rhizomes for splitting. Pot up crowns for forcing.
Winter: No need for protection.

Garden Cultivation
Unlike its name, it should be grown not in an open valley but in partial shade. Ideal for growing under trees or in woodlands or in the shade of a fence provided there is not too much competition from other plants.
  To get the best flowers, prepare the site well. The soil should be deeply cultivated with plenty of well-rotted manure, compost or leaf mould. Plant in autumn, 15cm (6in) apart, before the frosts make the soil too hard. Place the crowns upright in the prepared holes with the tips just below the soil.

Harvest
Pick the flowers when in full bloom for drying so that they can be added to potpourri.

CONTAINER GROWING

This plant can be happily grown in pots as long as it is kept in the shade and watered regularly. Use the bark, peat mix of compost. Feed with liquid fertilizer only during flowering. In winter let the plant die down, and keep it in a cool place outside.

MEDICINAL

This plant, like the foxglove, is used in the treatment of heart disease. It contains cardiac glycosides which increase the strength of the heartbeat while slowing and regularising its rate, without putting extra demand on the coronary blood supply.

CULINARY

None – all parts of the plant are poisonous.

WARNING

Lily of the valley should only be used as prescribed by a qualified practitioner and it is restricted. All parts of the plant are poisonous.

Lily of the Valley *Convallaria majalis*

Coriandrum sativum

CORIANDER

Also known as Chinese Parsley, Yuen Sai, Pak Chee, Fragrant Green, Dhania (seed), Dhania Pattar and Dhania Sabz (leaves). From the family Umbelliferae

A native of southern Europe and the Middle East, coriander was a popular herb in England up until Tudor times. Early European settlers in America included seed among the beloved items they took to the New World, as did Spaniards into Mexico.

Coriander has been cultivated for over 3,000 years. Seeds have been found in tombs from the 21st Egyptian Dynasty (1085-945 BC). The herb is mentioned in the Old Testament – 'when the children of Israel were returning to their homeland from slavery in Egypt, they ate manna in the wilderness and the manna was as coriander seeds' – and it is still one of the traditional bitter herbs to be eaten at the Passover when the Jewish people remember that great journey.

Coriander was brought to Northern Europe by the Romans who, combining it with cumin and vinegar, rubbed it into meat as a preservative. The Chinese once believed it bestowed immortality and in the Middle Ages it was put in love potions as an aphrodisiac. Its name is said to be derived from 'koris', Greek for 'bedbug', since the plant smells strongly of the insect.

Coriander *Coriandrum sativum*

Coriander *Coriandrum sativum*

SPECIES

Coriandrum sativum
Coriander
Tender annual. Ht 60cm (24in). White flowers in the summer. The first and lower leaves are broad and scalloped, with a strong, strange scent. The upper leaves are finely cut and have a different and yet more pungent smell. The whole plant is edible. This variety is good for leaf production.

Coriandrum sativum 'Cilantro'
Tender annual. Ht 60cm (24in). Much as **C. sativum**; whitish flowers in summer; also suitable for leaf production.

Coriandrum sativum 'Morocco'
Tender annual. Ht 70cm (28ins). Flowers white with a slight pink tinge in summer. This variety is best for seed production.

CULTIVATION

Propagation
Coriander is grown from seed. Thinly sow its large seed directly into the soil in shallow drills. Lightly cover with fine soil or compost, and water in. Look for results after a period of between 5 and 10 days. Seed sowing may be carried out as often as required between early spring (under glass), and late autumn. When large enough to handle, thin out the seedlings to leave

Coriander seeds

room for growth.

Sowing into seed trays is not recommended because coriander plants do not transplant well once the tap root is established. If they get upset they bolt straight into flower, missing out the leaf production stage.

If a harvest of fresh leaves is required, space the plants 5cm (2in) apart; if of seed, 23cm (9in) apart.

Pests and Diseases

Being a highly aromatic plant coriander is usually free from pests. In exceptional circumstances it is attacked by green fly. If so, do not be tempted to pressure hose the pests off, which will destroy the leaves. Either wash off gently under the tap, and shake the plant gently to remove excess water on the leaves, or use a liquid horticultural soap.

Maintenance

Spring: Sow seeds.
Summer: Sow seeds, cut leaves.
Autumn: Cut seed heads. Sow autumn crop in mild climates. Dig up old plants.
Winter: Once the seed heads have been collected, the plant should be pulled up.

Garden Cultivation

Coriander grows best in a light, well-drained soil, a sunny position and a dry atmosphere. In fact it is difficult to grow in damp or humid areas and needs a good dry summer at the very least if a reasonable crop is to be obtained.

Plant out in cool climates when there is no threat of frost, making sure the final position is nowhere near fennel, which seems to suffer in its presence.

When the plant reaches maturity and the seed set and begin to ripen, the plant tends to loll about on its weak stem and needs staking. On ripening, the seeds develop a delightful orangy scent, and are used widely as a spice and a condiment. For this reason alone, and because the flavour of home-grown seeds is markedly superior to those raised commercially, coriander deserves a place in the garden. If you live in a mild, frost free climate, sow in the autumn for an over-winter crop; but make sure the plants are in full sunlight.

Harvest

Pick young leaves any time. They should be 10cm (4in) in height and bright green.

Watch seed heads carefully, as they ripen suddenly and will fall without warning. Cut the flower stems as the seed smell starts to become pleasant. Cover bunches of about 6 heads together in a paper bag. Tie the top of the bag and hang it upside down in a dry, warm, airy place. Leave for roughly 10 days. The seeds should come away from the husk quite easily and be stored in an airtight container. Coriander seeds keep their flavour well.

CONTAINER GROWING

Coriander can be grown in containers inside with diligence or outside on the windowsill or patio, but for a confined space inside it is not the best choice. Until the seeds ripen the whole plant has an unpleasant smell. Also, being an annual it has a short season. The only successful way to maintain it in a pot is to keep picking the mature leaves. However, if you do decide to grow coriander in a container ensure good drainage with plenty of chippings or broken pot pieces; use a bark, peat compost; and do not over-water in the evening. Like many herbs, coriander does not like wet feet.

MEDICINAL

Coriander is good for the digestive system, reducing flatulence, stimulating the appetite and aiding the secretion of gastric juices.

It is also used to prevent gripe caused by other medication such as senna or rhubarb.

Bruised seed can be applied externally as a poultice to relieve painful joints and rheumatism.

CULINARY

The leaves and ripe seeds have two distinct flavours. The seeds are warmly aromatic, the leaves have an earthy pungency.

Coriander seeds are used regularly in Garam Masala (a mixture of spices) and in curries. Use ground seed in tomato chutney, ratatouille, frankfurters, curries, also in apple pies, cakes, biscuits and marmalade. Add whole seeds to soups, sauces and vegetable dishes.

Add fresh lower leaves to curries, stews, salads, sauces and as a garnish. Delicious in salads, vegetables and poultry dishes. A bunch of coriander leaves with a vinaigrette dressing goes particularly well with hard boiled eggs.

Mushrooms and Coriander
Serves 2

500g (1lb) button mushrooms
2 tablespoons cooking oil
2 teaspoons coriander seeds
1 clove garlic
2 tablespoons tomato purée
300 ml (½pint) dry white wine
salt and pepper
coriander leaf for garnish

Wipe mushrooms and slice in half. Put the oil, wine, coriander seeds and garlic in a large saucepan. Bring to the boil and cover and simmer for 5 minutes. Add the mushrooms and tomato purée. Cook for 5 minutes, by which time the vegetables should be tender. Remove the mushrooms and put in a serving dish. Boil the liquid again for 5 minutes and reduce it by half. Pour over the mushrooms. When cool, sprinkle with some chopped coriander leaf.

Dianthus

PINKS

**Also known as Clove Pink and Gillyflower.
From the family Caryophyllaceae.**

The true pinks are derived from *Dianthus plumarius,* a native of Eastern Europe and introduced to Britain in the 17th century. From then on, numerous varieties have been cultivated. The wild forefather of the carnation, *Dianthus caryophyllus,* is a native of Central and Southern Europe; both species and their varieties are now cultivated throughout the world.

Dianthus comes from the words 'dios', meaning divine, and 'anthos', meaning flower, and was coined by Theophrastus, a Greek botanist who lived in 370-285 BC, alluding to their fragrance and neatness of flower. Both the Romans and Greeks gave pinks a place of honour and made coronets and garlands from the flowers. The strong sweet clove scent has made it popular for both culinary and perfumery purposes for more than 2,000 years. In the 17th century it was recognized that the flowers could be crystallized, and the petals were used in soups, sauces, cordials and wine, and infused in vinegar.

The Cheddar Pink, Cleeve Pink or Cliff Pink, was discovered early in the 18th century by Wiltshire botanist, Samuel Brewer. It became as famous as Cheddar cheese and is mentioned in all the guide books.

SPECIES

Dianthus armeria
Deptford Pink
Evergreen hardy perennial. Ht 30-45cm (12-18in), spread 45cm (18in). Small bunches of little, cerise or pink, unscented flowers in summer. In dull weather the flower closes. Lance-shaped, narrow, dark green leaves. This is a wild plant and is becoming increasingly rare. It looks most attractive growing in a border.

Dianthus caryophyllus
Carnation
Evergreen hardy perennial. Ht 45-60cm (18-24in), spread 45cm (18in). Rose or purply pink flowers, having a spicy sweet scent. Loose mats of narrow, grey/green, lance-shaped leaves.

Dianthus deltoides
Maiden Pink
Evergreen hardy perennial. Ht 15cm (6in), spread 30cm (12in). Small cerise, pink or white flowers are borne singly all summer. Small, narrow, lance-shaped, dark green leaves.
Maiden pinks are a lovely spreading plant for rock gardens or gravely paths.

Dianthus gratianopolitanus syn. Dianthus caesius
Cheddar Pink
Evergreen hardy perennial. Ht 15cm (6in), spread 30cm (12in). Very fragrant, rich pink to magenta, flat flowers are borne singly all summer. Loose mats of narrow, grey/green, lance-shaped leaves.
The Cheddar pink is very rare and a protected species in Britain, but is more common in Europe.

Dianthus plumarius
Pinks
Evergreen hardy perennial. Ht 15cm (6in), spread 30cm (12in). Very fragrant white flowers with dark crimson centres borne singly all summer. Loose mats of narrow, grey/green, lance-shaped leaves.
These are related to the Cheddar pink and are the origin of the Garden pink.

Some old fashioned garden pinks worth looking for:

Dianthus 'Gran's Favourite'
Fragrant semi-double white flowers with deep purple/red centre.

Dianthus 'London Delight'
Fragrant flowers are semi-double and coloured lavender laced with purple.

Dianthus 'Mrs Sinkins'
Heavily scented flower, fringed, fully double, and white.

Dianthus 'Prudence'
Fragrant semi-double flowers, pinkish-white with purple lacing. This variety has a spreading habit.

CULTIVATION

Propagation

Seed

Although pinks can be propagated by seed, they can turn out to be very variable in height, colour and habit. The named forms can only be propagated by cuttings or by layering.

Sow the small seed in the autumn when it is fresh, or in early spring, in prepared seed or plug trays; cover with Perlite. If sown in the autumn the young plants must be wintered under cover. It is critical not to over-water young plants or they will rot off. Allow plenty of air to flow through the greenhouse on warm days – if you open up the cold frame, close it at night. In the spring, when the seedlings are large enough to handle and after a period of hardening off, plant out in the garden about 30cm (1ft) apart.

Cuttings

Stem cuttings can be taken in the spring. Alternatively heel cuttings can be taken in the early autumn (see step 6 of Softwood Cuttings, page 218), using the bark, peat, grit compost. Again, water the compost before taking the cuttings, then keep the compost on the drier side of moist, so helping to prevent disease.

Division

After flowering, the plants can be dug up and divided.

Layering

In late summer plants can be layered.

Pests and Diseases

The main pest is the red spider mite. Use a liquid horticultural soap and spray at first sign of the pest. Alternatively, introduce the natural predator

Phytoseiulus persimilis, following the instructions that will accompany them. Do not use both.

The main disease appears at propagation stage, when the young plants can rot off, usually caused by a fungus attack, triggered off by the compost being too wet. Organically there is nothing one can use to get rid of this; the infected plants must be removed.

Maintenance

Spring: Sow seeds. Take stem cuttings.
Summer: Dead head flowers to prolong flowering. Divide after flowering. Layer plants.
Autumn: Take heal cuttings. Sow seed.
Winter: No need for protection.

Garden Cultivation

Pinks prefer a truly well-drained soil, short of plant nutrient, and a sunny, sheltered site.

They are happy by the sea or growing in a rock garden. With new varieties being developed all the time, many old pinks and carnations have been lost. But you can still find some excellent specialist nurseries that offer a great range.

Harvest

Pick flowers when they are open either to use fresh, or to crystallize the petals or to dry for potpourris or to use for oil or vinegar.

CONTAINER GROWING

Happy in containers, window boxes and tubs as long as their compost is free-draining; so use the bark, peat, grit mix. They combine well with other plants, and look just a bit special on their own. Maiden pinks can look very effective in hanging baskets.

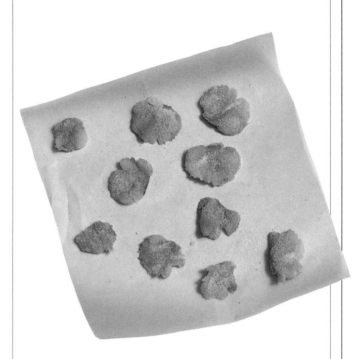

Crystallized dianthus flowers

CULINARY

If you remove a petal from the flower you will notice that it has a white heel. This must be removed before the petals are added to any food as it is very bitter. Add petals to salads, and to fruit pies and sandwiches. Use to flavour sugar and jam, or to make a syrup. Add crystallized flower petals to cakes and decorate puddings.

Infuse the open flowers in almond oil for sweet oil or in wine vinegar for floral vinegar.

Dissected dianthus flowers showing the white heel

MEDICINAL

A tonic cordial can be made from the flower petals and is even better when combined with white wine! Makes an excellent nerve tonic.

OTHER USES

Add dried petals to potpourris, scented sachets, and cosmetic products.

Digitalis purpurea

FOXGLOVE

Also known as Digitalis 'American' Foxglove, Deadmen's Bells, Dogs Fingers, Fairy Fingers, Fairy Gloves, Fringe Flower, Folksglove, Lion Mouths, Ladiesglove, Purple Foxgloves, Witch's Glove, Fairy Glove, Gloves of Our Lady, Bloody Fingers, Fairy Caps and Fairy Thimbles. From the family Scrophulariaceae.

Foxglove grows throughout Europe and North America and is a common wild flower in temperate climates throughout the world, seeding freely in woods and hedgerows.

The principal common name probably derives from the Anglo-Saxon 'foxglue' or 'foxmusic', after the shape of a musical instrument. Judging by its other names it would seem that it was also thought to be a fairy's plant or a goblin's plant, at least in England. Its appearance – its height, the glove shape of the corolla, and the poison of its leaves – seems somehow to beg for its own folklore.

In 1542, Fuchs called it *Digitalis* after the finger-like shape of its flowers but he considered it a violent medicine and it was not until the late 18th century that William Withering used foxglove tea in Shropshire for dropsy that its reputation as a medicinal herb grew. Commercial production of digitalis now takes place mainly in south-east Europe.

SPECIES

There are many extremely attractive species and cultivars. One of the national collections is held by The Botanic Nursery, Atworth, in Wiltshire.

Digitalis grandiflora (Digitalis ambigua)
Yellow Foxglove
Hardy evergreen perennial. Ht 75cm (30in), spread 30cm (12in). Creamy yellow, downward pointing, tubular flowers all summer. Smooth, strongly veined leaves.

Digitalis purpurea
Foxglove (wild, common)
Shortlived perennial, grown as a biennial. Ht 1-1.5m (3-5ft), spread 60cm (2ft). Flowers all shades of pink, purple and red in summer. Rough, mid- to dark green leaves.

Foxglove *Digitalis purpurea*

Digitalis purpurea F. albiflora
White Foxglove
Shortlived perennial, grown as a biennial. Ht 1-1.5m (3-5ft), spread 30-45cm (12-18in). Tubular white flowers all summer. Rough, mid- to dark green leaves.

WARNING

Foxgloves are poisonous and should not be eaten or used domestically. Even touching the plant has been known to cause rashes, headaches and nausea. DO NOT USE without medical direction.

White Foxglove *Digitalis purpurea alba*

If you live in a cold climate -10°C (14°F) protect during the first winter. Use agricultural fleece, straw, bracken or pine needles. In areas where the soil is damp and cold, it is advisable to lift the plants for the first winter and keep them in a cold frame, replanting the following spring.

Harvest
This is not advised unless you are a herbalist or a pharmacist.

MEDICINAL

Foxgloves are grown commercially for the production of a drug the discovery (a major medical breakthrough) of which is a classic example of a productive marriage between folklore and scientific curiosity. Foxgloves contain glycosides which are extracted from second-year leaves to make the heart drug digitalis. For more than 200 years digitalis has provided the main drug for treating heart failure. It is also a powerful diuretic. Although a synthetic form of the drug has been developed, the plant is still grown commercially for the drug industry.

CULTIVATION

Propagation
The seed is very small and fine. Sow in either spring or autumn as carefully as possible, using the cardboard method, either directly onto the prepared ground, or into pots or plug trays. Sow on the surface; do not cover with Perlite, but with a piece of glass, which should be removed as soon as the seedlings appear. No bottom heat required.

Remember, they will not flower the first season.

Pests and Diseases
Foxgloves, on the whole, are pest and disease free.

Maintenance
Spring: Sow seeds. Plant out first-year plants.
Summer: Remove main flowering shoot after flowering.
Autumn: Check round second-year plants for self-sown seedlings, thin out if over-crowded, remove if not required. Pot up a few in case of an exceptionally hard winter.
Winter: In the majority of cases no protection needed.

See Garden Cultivation for the exceptions.

Garden Cultivation
This is one of the most poisonous plants in the flora. Foxgloves will grow in most conditions, even dry exposed sites, but do best in semi-shade and a moist but well-drained acid soil enriched with leaf mould. The rosettes and leaves are formed the first year and the flower spike the second. The plant then dies but usually leaves lots of self-sown babies nearby. Water well in dry weather and remove the centre spike after flowering to increase the size of the flowers on the side shoots.

CONTAINER GROWING

These tall elegant plants do not honestly suit growing in containers. It is possible, but care has to be taken that the plant is not damaged in winds. Use a soil-based compost. Water regularly.

Equisetum arvense

HORSETAIL

Also known as Mare's Tail, Shave Grass, Bottle Brush, Pewter Wort, Snake's Pie, Fairy Spindle, Paddock's Pipes, Cat's Tail and Joint Grass. From the family Equisetaceae.

Horsetail *Equisetum arvense*

This plant is a native of the temperate regions, although some species are found in the tropics where they can grow to a considerable size.

When I first started herb farming I suddenly noticed all these spiky things growing all over the floor of one of my polythene tunnels. Subsequently I discovered it was a very worthy herb, not an invasive weed.

The horsetail is a plant left over from prehistoric times. By the evidence of fossil remains, it has survived almost unchanged since the coal seams were laid. It does not flower but carries spores as do ferns, to which it is related. The fronds have a harsh feel to them, this is because uniquely the plant absorbs large quantities of silica from the soil. The Romans always used horsetail to clean their pots and pans, not just to make them clean but also, thanks to the silica, to make them non-stick. The plant was used in the Middle Ages as an abrasive by cabinet makers and to clean pewter, brass and copper, and for scouring wood containers and milk pans.

No plant, having survived so long, could escape myth and magic. This herb has been associated far and wide with various goblins, toads and snakes, and the Devil.

SPECIES

Equisetum arvense
Horsetail
Hardy perennial. Ht 45cm (18in). The plant does not flower. It grows on a thin creeping rhizome producing 20cm (8in) long grey/brown fertile shoots with 4-6 sheaths in spring. The shoots die off and the spores are spread just like ferns.

CULTIVATION

Propagation
I am not sure that this is necessary, but if you do require a supply of horsetail it may be of merit.

Cuttings
Each piece of horsetail root is capable of reproducing. In summer place small pieces either in a seed or plug tray.

Use the peat, bark mix of compost. Plant out in the following spring when the cuttings are well rooted.

Pests and Diseases
For a plant to have survived so long, it has to be pest- and disease free.

Maintenance
Spring: Make sure the plant is well contained and not wandering off.
Summer: Cut back plants that are beginning to die back to stop the spores spreading.
Autumn: After harvest, cut down to the ground, again to stop the spores spreading.
Winter: No protection necessary; very hardy.

Garden Cultivation
If grown in open ground unconfined, horsetail becomes a permanent inhabitant and is only eradicated with great difficulty. Its root systems have been found to extend down a cliff face 12m (40ft), and breaking the rhizomes stimulates buds on the remainder to sprout and produce more growth.

If horsetail is to be introduced into the garden at all, and to be honest I do not recommend it, it is best confined to a strong container partially sunk into the ground. Leave the rim visible so that the rhizomes cannot penetrate or creep over the top.

Harvest
The green/brown shoots look almost like minute Christmas trees and these are the parts that can be collected during the summer months. Dry them.

CONTAINER GROWING

The only sane way to grow horsetail is in a container using a soil based compost. But be sure to cut it back in the summer to prevent spread by the spores. No need to feed, and it requires little watering. It can look attractive!

CULINARY

It has been eaten as a substitute for asparagus, but I do not recommend it unless you are stuck on a desert island and there is no other food available.

Horsetail nail strengthener

COSMETIC

Horsetail Nail Strengthener
A simple method of improving easily broken nails is to immerse the finger tips in a decoction made by simmering 50g (2oz) of dry or fresh herb in 900ml/1½ pints/3¾cup of water for 20 minutes.

Horsetail Hair Rinse and Tonic
Horsetail provides a good, all-round conditioner and helps the hair to a natural shine.

About 8 horsetail stems 15–20cm (6-8in) long 600ml (1 pint) of boiling water.

Bruise the horsetail stems with a spoon before adding boiling water to make an infusion. Cover and leave until lukewarm then strain off the liquid. After shampooing and rinsing, pour the infusion over the hair and massage into the scalp. Blot up excess moisture with a towel and comb through your hair. Cover your head with a warm towel and wait for 10 minutes before drying hair in the usual way.

Horsetails look like minute Christmas trees

MEDICINAL

This plant is a storehouse of minerals and vitamins, so herbalists recommended it in cases of amnesia and general debility. The tea enriches the blood, hardens fingernails and revitalizes lifeless hair. Its astringent properties help to strengthen the walls of the veins, tightening up varicose veins and help guard against fatty deposits in the arteries. It is also useful when white spots occur on the nails, which indicate a calcium imbalance in the body, as the silica encourages the absorption and use of calcium by the body.

WARNING

It is advised that if you wish to use horsetail that you do it with consultation from a herbalist.

OTHER USES
Stems have a high silica content and can be used after drying to scour metal and polish pewter and fine woodwork.

The whole plant yields a yellow ochre dye.

Echium vulgare

VIPER'S BUGLOSS

Also known as Bugles, Wild Borage, Snake Flower, Blue Devil, Blueweed, Viper's Grass and Snakeflower. From the family Boraginaceae.

This plant originates from the Mediterranean region and is now widespread throughout the northern hemisphere, being found on light porous stones on semi-dry grassland, and waste ground. It is regarded as a weed in some parts of America. To many American farmers this will seem an understatement; they consider it a plague.

The common name, viper's bugloss, developed from the medieval Doctrine of Signatures, which ordained that a plant's use should be inferred from its appearance. It was noticed that the brown stem looked rather like a snake skin and that the seed is shaped like a viper's head. So, in their wisdom, they prescribed it for viper bites, which for once proved right; it did have some success in the treatment of the spotted viper's bite.

SPECIES

Echium vulgare
Viper's Bugloss
Hardy biennial. Ht 2-4ft (60-120cm). Bright blue/pink flowers in the second year. Leaves mid-green and bristly.

CULTIVATION

Propagation
Seed
Viper's bugloss is easily grown from seed. Start it off in a controlled way in spring by sowing the small seed into a prepared seed or plug tray. Cover the seed with Perlite. When the seedlings are large enough to handle, and after a period of hardening off, plant out into a prepared site in the garden, 18in (45cm) apart.

Pests and Diseases
It rarely suffers.

Maintenance
Spring: First year, sow seeds; second year, clear around plants.
Summer: Second year, pick off flowers as they die so that they cannot set seed.
Autumn: First year, leave well alone. Second year, dig up plants and bin. Do not compost unless you want thousands of viper's bugloss plants appearing all over your garden.
Winter: No need to protect first-year plant.

Garden Cultivation
This colorful plant is beautifully marked. Sow the seed in spring directly into the garden. It will grow in any soil and is great for growing on dry soils and sea cliffs. With its long taproot, the plant will survive any drought but cannot easily be transplanted except when very young. The disadvantage is that it self-seeds and is extremely invasive.

Harvest
Gather flowers in summer for fresh use.

CONTAINER GROWING

Because it is a rampant self-seeder, it is quite a good idea to grow it in containers. For the first year it bears only green prickly leaves and is very boring. However, the show put on in the second year is full compensation. Use a soil-based compost; no need to feed. Over-feeding

Viper's Bugloss *Echium vulgare*

will prohibit the flowering. Very tolerant of drought; nevertheless, do water it regularly. Dies back in winter of first year – leave the container somewhere cool and water occasionally.

CULINARY

The young leaves are similar to borage, but they have lots more spikes. It is said you can eat them when young, but I have fought shy of this. The flowers look very attractive in salads. They can also be crystallized.

MEDICINAL

The fresh flowering tips can be chopped up for making poultices for treating boils. Infuse lower leaves to produce a sweating in fevers or to relieve headaches.

OTHER USES

At one time, a red colouring substance for dying fabrics was extracted from the root.

Eruca vesicaria ssp. sativa

SALAD ROCKET

Also known as Rocquette. From the family Cruciferae.

This native of the Mediterranean has only recently found its way back into the British herb garden after an absence of a few hundred years. An annual salad plant with pungent tasting leaves, it is used a great deal in Southern France and Italy. It has been in continuous cultivation since the Romans, who prized the flavour of its leaves and seeds. In England the Elizabethans were extremely partial to it. Some fascinating past uses suggest that it should be taken before a whipping to alleviate the pain, and used as protection against bites of the shrew mouse and other venomous beasts.

SPECIES

Eruca vesicaria ssp. sativa
Salad Rocket
Half-hardy annual. Ht 2-3ft (60-90cm). The flowers are yellowish at first, then in the summer they become whiter with purple veins. The oval lanced-shaped leaves have a nutty flavour.

CULTIVATION

Propagation
This herb is better grown direct in the garden.

Pests and Diseases
This herb rarely suffers from pests and diseases.

Salad Rocket *Eruca vesicaria* ssp. *sativa*

Maintenance
Spring: Sow seeds.
Summer: Pick like mad to prevent flowering.
Autumn: In mild climates sow seeds for winter salads.
Winter: In cooler climates use a cloche for protection.

Garden Cultivation
Sow seed in prepared rows in rich moist soil and a lightly shaded position. In warm countries, sow in autumn to ensure winter leaves. In cooler climates sow in early spring after the last frost, as in severe winters it may not survive. Thin the seedlings to 8in (20cm). It will be ready to pick within 6 to 8 weeks of sowing. It should be gathered before flowering. Be forewarned, late spring sowings are apt to run to seed quickly; if not picked sufficiently, the thin stems of cabbage flowers rise and flavour is lost from the leaves.

Harvest
Harvest leaf within 8 weeks of spring sowing, and keep cutting.

CONTAINER GROWING

Salad rocket is not really suitable for growing in containers, but it is possible. Sow in spring directly into a pot or window box. Use the bark, peat potting soil. Water and pick regularly. Do not use liquid fertilizer, as this makes the leaves too lush and bereft of flavour.

CULINARY

Add the leaves to all forms of salad. The younger leaves have a milder taste than the older ones, which have a definite peppery flavor. Leaves can also be added to sauces and to other vegetable dishes either raw or steamed. This herb is one of many leaves included in the Provençal salad mixture called mesclun.

Right: **Salad rocket in flower**

Salad rocket leaves in salad

MEDICINAL

At one time used medicinally in cough syrup.

Filipendula

MEADOWSWEET

Also known as Bridewort, Meadow Queen, Meadow-Wort, and Queen of the Meadow. From the family Rosaceae.

Meadowsweet can be found growing wild in profusion near streams and rivers, in damp meadows, fens and marshlands, or wet woodlands to 1,000m/3,300ft altitude.

It is a native of Europe and Asia that has been successfully introduced into, and is naturalized in, North America.

The generic name, *Filipendula*, comes from 'filum', meaning thread, 'pendulus', meaning hanging. This is said to describe the root tubers that hang, characteristically of the genus, on fibrous roots.

The common name, meadowsweet, is said to be derived from the Anglo-Saxon word 'medesweete', which itself owes its origin to the fact that the plant was used to flavour mead, a drink made from fermented honey.

It has been known by many other names. In Chaucer's *The Knight's Tale* it is Meadwort and was one of the ingredients in a drink called 'save'. It was also known as Bridewort, because it was strewn in churches for festivals and weddings and made into bridal garlands. In Europe it took its name Queen of the Meadow from the way the herb can dominate a low-lying, damp meadow. In America, it became Gravelroot or Joe Pie Weed (*Eupatorium purpureum*).

In the 16th century, when it was customary to strew floors with rushes and herbs (both to give warmth underfoot and to overcome smells and infections), it was a favourite of Queen Elizabeth I. She desired it above all other herbs in her chambers.

The sap contains a chemical of the same group as salicylic acid, an ingredient of aspirin. It was isolated for the first time in the 19th century by an Italian professor. When the drug company Bayer formulated acetylsalicylic acid, they called it aspirin after the old botanical name for meadowsweet, *Spirea ulmaria*.

SPECIES

Filipendula ulmaria
Meadowsweet
Hardy perennial. Ht 60-120cm (2-4ft), spread 60cm (2ft). Clusters of creamy-white flowers in mid-summer. Green leaf made up of up to 5 pairs of big leaflets separated by pairs of smaller leaflets.

Filipendula ulmaria 'Aurea'
Golden Meadowsweet
Hardy perennial. Ht and spread 30cm (12in). Clusters of creamy-white flowers in mid-summer. Bright golden yellow, divided leaves in spring that turn a lime colour in summer. Susceptible to sun scorch.

Filipendula ulmaria 'Variegata'
Variegated Meadowsweet
Hardy perennial. Ht 45cm (18in) and spread 30cm (12in). Clusters of creamy-white flowers in mid-summer. Divided leaf, dramatically variegated green and yellow in spring. Fades a bit as the season progresses.

Filipendula vulgaris (hexapetala)
Dropwort
Hardy perennial. Ht 60-90cm (2-3ft), spread 45cm (18in). Summertime clusters of white flowers (larger than meadowsweet). Fern-like green leaves.

CULTIVATION

Propagation
Seed

Sow in prepared seed or plug trays in the autumn. Cover lightly with compost (not Perlite) and winter outside under glass. Check from time to time that the compost has not become dry as this will inhibit germination. Stratification is helpful but not essential. Germination should take place in spring. When the seedlings are large enough to handle, plant out, 30cm (12in) apart, into a prepared site.

Division

The golden and variegated forms are best propagated by division. This is easily done in the autumn. Dig up established plant and tease the plantlets apart; they separate easily. Either replant in a prepared site, 30cm (12in) apart, or, if it is one of the decorative varieties, pot up using the bark, peat mix of compost.

Pests and Diseases

Meadowsweet rarely suffers from these.

Maintenance

Spring: Sow seeds if required.
Summer: Cut back after flowering.
Autumn: Divide established plants, sow seed for wintering outside.
Winter: No need for protection.

Garden Cultivation

Meadowsweet adapts well to the garden, but does prefer sun/semi-shade and a moisture retentive soil. If your soil is free-draining, mix in plenty of well-rotted manure and/or leaf mould, and plant in semi-shade.

Harvest

Gather young leaves for fresh or dry use before flowers appear. Pick flowers just as they open and use fresh or dry.

MEDICINAL

The whole plant is a traditional remedy for an acidic stomach.

The fresh root is used in homeopathic preparations and is effective on its own in the treatment of diarrhoea.

The flowers, when made into a tea, are a comfort to flu victims.

Golden Meadowsweet
Filipendula ulmaria 'Aurea'

CULINARY

A charming, local vet who made all kinds of vinegars and pickles gave me to try meadowsweet vinegar. Much to my amazement it was lovely, and combined well with oil to make a different salad dressing, great when used with a flower salad.

I am not a fan of meadowsweet flower fritters so mention them only in passing. The flowers do however make a very good wine, and add flavour to meads and beers. The flowers can also be added to stewed fruit and jams, introducing a subtle almond flavour.

Young leaves can be added to soups, but are not recommended for the faint-hearted!

CONTAINER GROWING

Golden and variegated meadowsweet look very attractive in containers, but use a soil-based compost to make sure moisture is retained. Position in partial shade to inhibit drying out and prevent sun scorch. The plant dies back in winter so leave it outside in a place where the natural weathers can reach it. If you live in an extremely cold area, protect the container from damage by placing in a site protected from continuous frost, but not warm. Liquid feed only twice during flowering.

OTHER USES

A black dye can be obtained from the roots by using a copper mordant.

Use dried leaves and flowers in potpourris.

Meadowsweet *Filipendula ulmaria*

Meadowsweet dye

'So Gladiators fierce and rude,
Mingled it with their daily food,
And he who battled down subdued,
A wreath of Fennel wore.'
Henry Wadsworth Longfellow (1807-82)

Foeniculum vulgare

FENNEL

**Also known as Large Fennel, Sweet Fennel and
Wild Fennel. From the family Umbelliferae.**

It grows wild in Europe and in most temperate countries and is naturalized in the western USA. The generic name, Foeniculum, derives from the Latin 'foenum' which means 'hay', and refers to the foliar structure.

The ancient Greeks thought very highly of fennel and used it as a slimming aid and for treating more than twenty different illnesses. It was also much valued by the Romans in an age of banquets. They ate its leaf, root and seed in salads, and baked it in bread and cakes. Warriors took fennel to keep in good health, while Roman ladies ate it to prevent obesity. In Anglo-Saxon times it was used on fasting days presumably because, as the Greeks had already discovered, it stills pangs of hunger. And more recently, in American Puritan communities, it became known as the Meeting Seeds, because seeds of fennel and dill were taken to church to allay hunger during long services.

In the Middle Ages, fennel was a favourite stewing herb, for not only is it fragrant and flavoursome, it also keeps insects at bay and was used in the kitchen to protect and lend flavour to food which was often far from fresh so making it palatable. In the 16th century Gerard praised it as an aid to eyesight and Culpeper for poison by snakebite or mushrooms.

SPECIES

Foeniculum vulgare
Fennel
Also known as Garden Fennel, Common Fennel, and Green Fennel. Hardy perennial. Ht 1.5m-2.1m (4-7ft), spread 45cm (18in). Lots of small yellow flowers in large umbels in late summer. Soft green feathery foliage.

Foeniculum vulgare 'Purpureum'
Bronze Fennel
As **F. vulgare** Very striking bronze feathery leaves.

Foeniculum vulgare var. dulce
Florence Fennel
Also known as Finocchio Grown as an annual. Ht 75cm-1m (2.5-3ft). Clusters of small yellow flowers in late summer. Leaf feathery and green. The base develops to form a white bulbous sweet vegetable, with a crisp texture and a delicate aniseed flavour.

CULTIVATION

Propagation
Seeds
Sow all varieties early in spring in prepared pots or plug trays, and cover with Perlite.
Bottom heat of 15-21°C (60-70°F) will speed germination. When large enough to handle plant out.

Roots
Division is only really successful if you have a light sandy soil, when roots will divide easily. This should be done in the autumn.

Bronze Fennel *Foeniculum vulgar* *purpureum*

Garden Cultivation

Fennel likes a sunny position in fertile, well-drained, loamy soil. Add an extra layer of sharp sand in the drill on a clay soil. Sow the seed after any frosts, thinning to 50cm (20in) apart. Do not grow fennel near dill or coriander as cross pollination will reduce fennel's seed production.

Fennel grown in a hot dry spot produces a sparse clump, 1.2-1.5m (4-5ft) high, with very thin, highly aromatic leaves. In a decent garden soil, fennel looks more like a dome of green or purple candyfloss.

Even though fennel is perennial, after three years it should be replaced.

Florence Fennel is grown only from seed. Sow in shallow trenches during the early summer in a rich well-composted soil for the bulbous roots to reach maturity by autumn. Thin out to 20cm (9in) apart.

During dry spells water well. When the root swelling is the size of a golf ball, blanch it by drawing some soil around it. After 2-3 weeks, when the size of a tennis ball, harvest.

Pests and Diseases

When the plants are very young root rot may occur if over watered. Green fly may also occasionally infest the plant. This can be treated with horticultural soap.

Maintenance

Spring: Sow seed of all varieties.
Summer: Pick flowering heads to maintain leaf production.
Autumn: Sow seeds in trays and force with heat for use in winter salads.
Winter: Cut back old growth, tidy up round established plants. Fennel will die back into the ground in winter. No need to protect unless temperatures fall below -10°C (14°F).

Harvest

Pick young stems and leaves as required. Freeze leaves or infuse in oil or vinegar.

Collect ripe seeds for sowing or to dry for culinary use. Dig up Florence Fennel bulbs when sufficiently mature and as required

COMPANION PLANTING

Fennel attracts hoverflies so helps keep whitefly at bay.

CONTAINER GROWING

The bronze variety looks especially attractive. Use the bark, grit, peat mix of compost. It may need staking when in flower. In the summer shelter from midday sun, water and feed regularly. Repot each year to maintain health.

OTHER USES

Seed and leaf can be used in facial steams and in baths for deep cleansing. A facial pack made of fennel tea and honey is good for wrinkles.

Finally, a yellow dye substance can be extracted.

MEDICINAL

To make fennel tea put a teaspoon of seeds in a tea cup, add boiling water, cover for 5 minutes, then strain and drink to aid digestion or prevent both heartburn or constipation. A teaspoon of this cooled tea is good for babies with colic. Steep a compress in the tea and place on the eyelid, to ease inflammation or watery eye, or let the solution cool and bathe the naked eye.

Warning: Taken in large doses, the essence can cause convulsions and disturb the nervous system.

Trout with Fennel

CULINARY

Fennel is an additional seasoning for fat meats like pork and stuffings for poultry and lamb. It is as delicious as a salad or vegetable dressing.

Use seeds in sauces, fish dishes and bread; leaves finely chopped over salads and cooked vegetables, and in soups and stuffing for oily fish; and young stems to add an extra crunch to salads.

The bulb of Florence Fennel can be cooked as a root vegetable or sliced or grated raw into sandwiches or salads.

Fish with Fennel
Serves 4

Whole fish – trout, mackerel, mullet (4 fish, 500g/1lb each)
1 cup of fresh sprigs of fennel
1 tablespoon cooking oil
Brandy

Clean the fish and fill with sprigs of chopped green fennel leaves. With a sharp knife score the fish on each side and brush with oil. Season lightly with salt and pepper. Arrange bed of fennel sticks on base of a greased oven-proof dish. Carefully place fish on the sticks and cook in a hot oven

(450°F/230°C/Gas Mark 8) for 15 minutes.

To serve: transfer fennel sticks and fish onto a flat fire proof serving dish. Warm the brandy and pour over the fish and set alight. The fennel will burn and the whole dish becomes deliciously aromatic.

Finocchio Salad (with Florence Fennel)
Serves 2

2 medium-sized fennel bulbs
12 black olives
125g/5oz carton plain yoghurt
1 small lettuce
Juice of 1 lemon,
Chopped parsley

Trim the fennel bulbs and wash carefully. Cut into thin slices. Mix with yoghurt, lemon juice and olives. Arrange the mixture decoratively on a bed of lettuce leaves. Garnish with slices of lemon and chopped parsley.

Fragaria vesca

WILD STRAWBERRY

Also known as Mountain Strawberry, Wood Strawberry and Alpine Strawberry. From the family Rosaceae.

These delightful plants are found mainly in forests, clearings and shady roadsides in the cool temperate climates of Europe, northern Asia and Australia. Other species are found in North America.

Strawberry's name does not in fact originate from a traditional practice of placing straw beneath the berries to keep them clean. Rather, it dates back to the 10th century when the Anglo-Saxon word 'straw' meant small particles of chaff, and which in this case referred to the scattering of pips (achenes) over the surface of the fruit.

Fragaria originates from 'fraga', the old Latin name for 'fragrans' meaning fragrant.

The fruit of this herb is dedicated to Venus and the Virgin Mary.

SPECIES

There are many forms of this small strawberry, some with variegated leaves, some with white fruit; the 2 identified here are the originals.

Fragaria vesca
Wild Strawberry
Hardy perennial. Ht 15-30cm (6-12in), spread 18 cm (7in), more if you include the runners. The flowers have 4 or 5 white petals with a yellow centre in spring to early summer. The leaf is composed of 3 brightish green leaflets with serrated edges.

Fragaria vesca 'semperflorens'
Alpine Strawberry
Hardy perennial. Ht 5-25cm (2-10in), spread 15cm (6in). The flowers have 4 or 5 white petals with a yellow centre from spring to autumn. The leaf is made of 3 brightish green leaflets with serrated edges. True Alpine strawberry does not set down runners, so propagate by seed only.

CULTIVATION

Propagation
Seed
The seed of the strawberry is imbedded all around the surface of the fruit. To collect it, leave the fruit in the summer sun until fully dry and shrivelled; then rub the seed off. Sow in late winter, early spring. Do not cover. A bottom heat of 15°C (60°F) is helpful. Germination will take place in a couple of weeks. Later in spring the seeds can be sown without heat, germination taking the same time. When the seedlings are large enough to handle, transplant to a prepared site in the garden at a distance of 30cm (12in).

Division
The daughter plants are produced on runners and easily propagated by division, each having its own small root system. These can be taken off and replanted where required during the growing season from spring to early autumn.

Pests and Diseases
Obvious pests are slugs and birds, followed closely by children, and at flower shows by members of the public. With all of these there is not a lot one can do, apart from growing enough so that it does not matter. If grown in containers the plants can suffer from mildew. Remove the affected parts and make sure there is plenty of light and air.

Maintenance
Spring: Sow seed. Divide runners.
Summer: Feed with liquid fertilizer.
Autumn: Divide runners if they have become invasive.
Winter: No need for protection.

Wild Strawberry
Fragaria vesca

Strawberries may produce an allergic response.

CULINARY

Eat the fruit fresh in fruit salads or on their own with cream, or use in cakes, pies and syrups and to flavour cordials. If you have enough you can also make jam.

The leaves have a musky flavour and scent. A tea can be made from them, but it is better to combine them with other herbs.

MEDICINAL

The fruit of the wild strawberry (unlike the cultivated varieties) are good for anaemia, bad nerves and stomach disorders. They are also an astringent, diuretic, tonic and laxative.

The leaves can be used to make a gargle and mouthwash for sore gums and mouth ulcers. Strawberry leaf tea is said to be a good tonic for convalescence and is enjoyed by children.

Wild strawberry jam

Garden Cultivation

Wild strawberries prefer a good fertile soil that does not dry out in summer, and either full sun or shade. They grow well in woods and hedgerows and make a marvellous ground cover, the dainty white flowers standing out amongst bright green shiny leaves which, when dry, have a fragrance of musk. The tiny delicious summertime fruits are a terrific bonus and have a good flavour.

Feed regularly with a liquid fertilizer (high in potash) as soon as the fruit begins, following the manufacturer's instructions. Often regarded as a weed by tidy gardeners, if you cannot stand the idea of rampant strawberry plants grow the Alpine variety.

Harvest

Pick leaves as required. If needed for drying, pick before the fruit sets.

Pick fruits as they ripen to eat fresh. They can be frozen.

CONTAINER GROWING

Being small plants they are marvellous in containers, window boxes, even those pots with holes in the side, and also hanging baskets, where the runners look most attractive, trailing over the edge. Use the bark, peat mix of compost. Water and feed with liquid fertilizer regularly, especially when the fruit begins to set.

OTHER USES

The strawberry is used extensively in the cosmetic industry in skin cream manufacture. Mash the fruit and extract juice to add to facepacks to whiten skin and lighten freckles.

Apply cut strawberries to washed face to ease slight sunburn – makes a lovely picture, if you get bored you can always eat them.

Galium odoratum (Asperula odorata)

SWEET WOODRUFF

Also known as New Mowed Hay, Rice Flower, Ladies in the Hay, Kiss Me Quick, Master of the Wood, Woodward and Woodrowell. From the family Rubiaceae.

This is a native of Europe and has been introduced and cultivated in North America and Australia. It grows deep in the woods and in hedgerows.

Records date back to the 14th century, when woodruff was used as a strewing herb, as bed-stuffing and to perfume linen.

On May Day in Germany, it is added to Rhine wine to make a delicious drink called 'Maibowle'.

SPECIES

Galium odoratum (Asperula odorata)
Sweet Woodruff
Hardy perennial. Ht 15cm (6in), spread 30cm (12in) or more. White, star-shaped flowers from spring to early summer. The green leaves are neat and grow in a complete circle around the stem. The whole plant is aromatic.

CULTIVATION

Propagation
Seed
To ensure viability only use fresh seed. Sow in early autumn into prepared seed or plug trays, and cover with compost. Water in well. Seeds require a period of stratification (page 216). Once the seedlings are large enough, either pot or plant out as soon as the young plants have been hardened off. Plant 10cm (4in) apart.

Root Cuttings
The rootstock is very brittle and every little piece will grow. The best time is after flowering in the early summer. Lay small pieces of the root, 2-4cm (1-1.5in) long, evenly spaced, on the compost in a seed tray. Cover with a thin layer of compost, and water. Leave in a warm place, and the woodruff will begin to sprout again. When large enough to handle, split up and plant out.

Pests and Diseases
This plant rarely suffers from pests and diseases.

Maintenance
Spring: Take root cuttings before flowering.
Summer: Dig up before the flowers have set, to check spreading.
Autumn: The plant dies back completely in autumn. Sow seeds.
Winter: Fully hardy plant.

Garden Cultivation
Ideal for difficult places or underplanting in borders, it loves growing in the dry shade of trees right up to the trunk. Its rich green leaves make a dense and very decorative ground cover, its underground runners spreading rapidly in the right situation.

It prefers a rich alkaline soil with some moisture during the spring.

Harvest
The true aroma (which is like new mowed hay) comes to the fore when it is dried. Dry flowers and leaves together in early summer.

CONTAINER GROWING

Make sure the container is large enough, otherwise it will become root-bound very quickly. The compost should be the bark, peat mix. Only feed with liquid fertilizer when the plant is flowering. Position the container in semi-shade and do not over-water.

CULINARY

Add the flowers to salads. Main ingredients for a modern day May Wine would be a bottle of hock, a glass of sherry, sugar, and strawberries, with a few sprigs of woodruff thrown in 1 hour before serving.

MEDICINAL

A tea made from the leaves is said to relieve stomach pain, act as a diuretic, and be beneficial for those prone to gall stones.

Sweet woodruff tea

WARNING

Consumption of large quantities can produce symptoms of poisoning, including dizziness and vomiting.

Glycyrrhiza glabra

LIQUORICE

**Also known as Licorice, Sweet Licorice and Sweetwood.
From the family Leguminosae.**

This plant, which is a native of the Mediterranean region, is commercially grown throughout the temperate zones of the world and extensively cultivated in Russia, Iran, Spain and India. It has been used medicinally for 3,000 years and was recorded on Assyrian tablets and Egyptian papyri. The Latin name *Glycyrrhiza* comes from 'glykys' meaning sweet, and 'rhiza' root.

It was first introduced to England by Dominican friars in the 16th century and became an important crop. The whole of the huge cobbled courtyard of Pontefract Castle was covered by top soil simply to grow liquorice. It is sad that Pontefract cakes are made from imported liquorice today.

Liquorice sticks

SPECIES

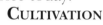

Glycyrrhiza glabra
Liquorice
Hardy perennial. Ht 1.2m (4ft), spread 1m (3ft). Pea-like, purple/blue and white flowers borne in short spikes on erect stems in late summer. Large greenish leaves divided into oval leaflets.

CULTIVATION

Propagation
Seed
The seedlings often damp off. In cooler climates the seed tends not to be viable. Root division is much easier.

Division
Divide when the plant is dormant, making sure the root has 1 or more buds. Place into pots half filled with compost. Cover with compost. Water well and leave in a warm place until shoots appear. Harden off, then plant out in early spring or autumn. If the latter, winter in a cold greenhouse or cold frame.

Pests and Diseases
Largely pest and disease free.

Maintenance
Spring: Divide established plants.
Summer: Do nothing.
Autumn: Divide established plants if necessary.
Winter: In very cold winters protect first year plants.

Garden Cultivation
Liquorice needs a rich, deep, well-cultivated soil.
Plant pieces of the root, each with a bud, directly into a prepared site 15cm (6in) deep and 1m (3ft) apart in early spring or in autumn during the dormant season if the ground is workable and not frosty.
Liquorice does best in long, hot summers, but will need extra watering if your soil is very free draining.

Harvest
Harvest roots for drying in early winter from established 3 or 4 year old plants.

CONTAINER GROWING

Never displays as well as in the garden. Use a soil-based compost. Feed throughout the growing season and water until it dies back.

CULINARY

Liquorice is used as a flavouring in the making of Guinness and other beers.

MEDICINAL

The juice from the roots provides commercial liquorice. It is used either to mask the unpleasant flavour of other medicines or to provide its own soothing action on troublesome coughs. The dried root, stripped of its bitter bark, is recommended as a remedy for colds, sore throats and bronchial catarrh.
Liquorice is a gentle laxative and lowers stomach acid levels, so relieving heartburn. It has a remarkable power to heal stomach ulcers because it spreads a protective gel over the stomach wall and in addition it eases spasms of the large intestine. It also increases the flow of bile and lowers blood cholesterol levels.

WARNING

Large doses of liquorice causes side effects, notably headaches, high blood pressure and water retention.

Helichrysum italicum

CURRY PLANT

From the family Compositae

This plant is from southern Europe and has adapted well to damper, cooler climates. It is the sweet curry scent of its leaves that has caused its recent rise in popularity.

SPECIES

Helichrysum italicum (angustifolium)
Curry Plant
Hardy evergreen perennial. Ht 60cm (24in), spread 1m (3ft). Clusters of tiny mustard yellow flowers in summer. Narrow, aromatic, silver leaves. Highly scented. Planting distance for hedge 60cm (2ft).

Helichrysum italicum 'Dartington'
Curry Plant, Dartington
Hardy evergreen perennial. Ht 45cm (18in), spread 60cm (24in). Compact plant with clusters of small yellow flowers in summer. Grey green, highly scented, narrow leaves (half the size of **H. italicum**). Its compact upright habit makes this a good plant for hedges and edging in the garden. Planting distance for hedge 30cm (1ft).

Curry plant flowers

Helichrysum italicum microphyllum ('Nanum')
Curry Plant Dwarf
Hardy evergreen perennial. Ht 30cm (12in), spread 45cm (18in). Clusters of tiny mustard yellow flowers in summer. Narrow, aromatic, silver leaves. Ideal for formal hedging and knot gardens. Planting distance for hedge 30cm (1ft).

Helichrysum italicum ssp. serotinum
Curry Plant
Hardy evergreen perennial. Ht 60cm (24in), spread 1m (3ft). Broad clusters of small bright yellow flowers, produced on upright white shoots. Narrow, aromatic, silver/grey leaves. Planting distance for hedge 60cm (2ft).

CULTIVATION

Propagation
Seed
I have not known **H. italicum** set good seed. For this reason I advise cuttings.

Cuttings
Take soft cuttings in spring and semi-ripe ones in autumn.

Pests and Diseases
Pests give this highly aromatic plant a wide berth, and it is usually free from disease.

Curry Plant *Helichrysom italicum*

Maintenance
Spring: Trim established plants after frosts to maintain shape and promote new growth. Take soft wood cuttings.
Summer: Trim back after flowering, but not too hard.
Autumn: Take semi-ripe wood cuttings.
Winter: If the temperature falls below -10°C (14°F), protect from frost.

Garden Cultivation
The curry plant makes an attractive addition to the garden and it imparts a strong smell of curry even if untouched. It is one of the most silvery of shrubs and makes a striking visual feature all year round.
  Plant in full sun in a well-drained soil. Do not cut the curry plant as hard back as cotton lavender but it is worth giving a good hair cut after flowering to stop the larger ones flopping and to keep the shape of the smaller ones.
  If it is an exceptionally wet winter, and you do not have a free draining soil, lift some plants, and keep in a cold greenhouse, or cold frame.

Harvest
Pick leaves at any time for fresh use. Pick the flowers when fully open. Dry by hanging in small bunches upside down in an airy place.

CONTAINER GROWING

Dwarf and Dartington curry plants grow happily in large containers (at least 20cm (8in) in diameter). Place in the sun to get the best effect, and do not over water.

CULINARY

There are not many recipes for the curry plant in cooking, and in truth the leaves smell stronger than they taste, but a small sprig stuffed into the cavity of a roasting chicken makes an interesting variation on tarragon.
  Add sprigs to vegetables, rice dishes and pickles for a mild curry flavour. Remove before serving.

OTHER USES

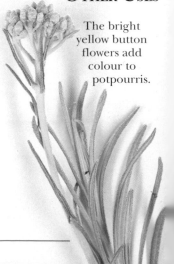

The bright yellow button flowers add colour to potpourris.

Hesperis matronalis
SWEET ROCKET

Also known as Damask Violet and Dame's Violet. From the family Cruciferae.

This sweet-smelling herb is indigenous to Italy. It can now be found growing wild in much of the temperate world as a garden escapee. The old Greek name *Hesperis* was used by Theophrastus, the Greek botantist (370–285 BC). It is derived from 'hesperos', meaning evening, which is when the flowers are at their most fragrant.

SPECIES

Hesperis matronalis
Sweet Rocket
Hardy biennial; very occasionally it will be a perennial, sending out new shoots from the root stock. Ht 60-90cm (2-3ft), spread 25cm (10in). The 4-petalled flowers are all sweetly scented and come in many colours – pink, purple, mauve and white – in the summer of the second year. The leaves are green and lance shaped.
There is a double-flowered form of this plant – *Hesperis matronalis* double form. It can only be propagated by cuttings or division and needs a more sandy loam soil than sweet rocket.

CULTIVATION

Propagation
Seed
Sow the seed in the autumn in prepared seed or plug trays, covering the seeds with Perlite. Winter the young plants in a cold greenhouse for planting out in the spring at a distance of 45cm (18in) apart. Propagated this way it may flower the first season as well as the second.

Pests and Diseases
This herb is largely free from pests and diseases.

White Rocket
Hesperis matronalis var. albiflora

Maintenance
Spring: Sow seed outdoors.
Summer: In the second year dead head flowers to prolong flowering.
Autumn: Sow seed under protection.
Winter: No need to protect.

Garden Cultivation
It likes full sun or light shade and prefers a well-drained fertile soil. The seed can be sown direct into a prepared site in the garden in late spring thinning to 30cm (12in) apart, with a further thinning to 45cm (18in) later on if need be.

Harvest
Pick leaves when young for eating. Pick flowers as they open for using fresh or for drying.

CONTAINER GROWING

Sweet rocket is a tall plant. It looks attractive if 3 or 4 1-year-old plants are potted together, positioned to make the most of the scent on a summer evening. Use the bark, peat, grit mix of compost and water well in summer months. No need to feed.

Purple Rocket
Hesperis matronalis

CULINARY

Young leaves are eaten occasionally in salads. Use sparingly because they are very bitter. The flowers look attractive tossed in salads. They can also be used to decorate desserts.

OTHER USES

Add dried flowers to potpourris for pastel colours and sweet scent.

Humulus lupulus

HOPS

Also known as Hopbind and Hop vine. From the family Cannabaceae.

Native of the Northern temperate zones, cultivated commercially, especially in Northern Europe, North America and Chile.

Roman records from the 1st century AD describe hops as a popular garden plant and vegetable, the young shoots being sold in markets to be eaten rather like asparagus. Hop gardens did not become widespread in Europe until the 9th century. In Britain the hop was a wild plant and used as a vegetable before it became one of the ingredients of beer. It was not until the 16th century that the word hop and the practice of flavouring and preserving beer with the strobiles or female flowers of the *Humulus lupulus* were introduced into Britain by Flemish immigrants, and replaced traditional bitter herbs such as alehoof and alecost.

During the reign of Henry VIII, Parliament was petitioned against the use of the hop, as it was said that it was a wicked weed that would spoil the taste of the drink, ale, and endanger the people. Needless to say the petition was thrown out. The use of hops revolutionized brewing since it enabled beer to be kept for longer.

Hops have also been used as medicine for at least as long as for brewing. The flowers are famous for their sedative effect and were either drunk as a tea or stuffed in a hop pillow to sleep on.

Common Hop
Humulus lupulus

Golden Hop
*Humulus lupulus
'Aureus'*

SPECIES

Humulus lupulus
Common Hop
Hardy perennial, a herbaceous climber. Ht up to 6m (20ft). There are separate female and male plants. The male plant has yellowish flowers growing in branched clusters. They are without sepals and have 5 tepals and 5 stamen. The female plant has tiny greenish yellow, scented flowers, hidden by big scales. The scales become papery when the fruiting heads are ripe. These are the flowers that are harvested for beer. The mid-green leaves have 3 to 5 lobes with sharply toothed edges. The stems are hollow, and are covered with tiny hooked prickles. These enable the plant to cling to shrubs, trees, or anything else. It always entwines clockwise.

Humulus lupulus 'Aureus'
Golden Hop
Hardy perennial, a herbaceous climber. Ht up to 6m (20ft), The main difference between this plant and the common hop is that the leaves and flowers are much more golden, which makes it very attractive in the garden and in dried flower arrangements. It has the same properties as the common hop.

Common Hop *Humulus lupulus*

CULTIVATION

Propagation
Seed
Beer is made from the un-pollinated female flowers. If you grow from seed you will not know the gender for 2 to 3 years, which is the time it takes before good flowers are produced. Obtain seed from specialist seedsmen.

Sow in summer or autumn. The seed is on the medium to large size so sow sparingly; if using plug trays, 1 per cell. Push the seed into and cover it with the compost. Then cover the tray with a sheet of glass or polythene, and leave somewhere cool to germinate – a cold frame, a cold glasshouse, or a garage. Germination can be very erratic. If the seed is not fresh you may need to give the hot/cold treatment.

Warning: As the seed will be from wild hops these should not be grown in areas of commercial hop growing, because they might contaminate the crop.

Cuttings
Softwood cuttings should be taken in spring or early summer from the female plant. Choose young shoots and take the cuttings in the morning as they will loose water very fast and wilt.

Division
In the spring dig up and divide the root stems and suckers of established plants. Replant 1m (3ft) apart against support.

Pests and Diseases
The most common disease is hop wilt. If this occurs, dig up and burn. Do not plant hops in that area again.

Leaf miner can sometimes be a problem. Remove infected leaves immediately.

The golden variety sometimes suffers from sun scorch. If this occurs prune to new growth, and change its position if possible the following season.

Maintenance
Spring: Divide roots and separate rooted stems and suckers. Re-pot container grown plants. Check trellising.
Summer: Sow seed late in the season.
Autumn: Cut back remaining growth into the ground. Give the plants a good feed of manure or compost. Bring containers into a cool place.
Winter: No need for protection.

Garden Cultivation
For successful plants the site should be sunny and open, the soil needs to be rich in humus and dug deeply. It is not generally necessary to tie the plants if good support is at hand. A word of warning, you must dominate the plant. Certainly it will need thinning and encouraging to entwine where you want it to go rather than where it chooses. But remember that it dies back completely in winter. Cut the plant into the ground each autumn and then give it a good feed of manure or compost.

Harvest
Pick young fresh sideshoots in spring. Gather young fresh leaves as required.

Pick male flowers as required. Pick ripe female flowers in early autumn. Dry and use within a few months, otherwise the flavour becomes unpleasant.

CONTAINER GROWING

Hops, especially the golden variety, can look very attractive in a large container with something to grow up. Use a compost made up of the bark, peat mix, and feed regularly with a liquid fertilizer from late spring to mid-summer. Keep well watered in the summer months and fairly dry in winter. It can be grown indoors in a position with good light such as a conservatory, but it seldom flowers. Provide some form of shade during sunny periods. During the winter months, make sure it has a rest by putting the pot in a cool place, keeping the compost on the dry side. Re-pot each year.

OTHER USES

The leaf can be used to make a brown dye. If you live close to a brewery it is worth chatting them up each autumn for the spent hops, which makes either a great mulch or a layer in a compost heap.

WARNING

Contact dermatitis can be caused by the pollen of the female flower. Also, hops are not recommended in the treatment of depressive illnesses because of their sedative effect.

MEDICINAL

Hop tea made from the female flower only is recommended for nervous diarrhoea, insomnia and restlessness. It also helps to stimulate appetite, dispel flatulence and relieve intestinal cramps. A cold tea taken an hour before meals

Hop pillow

is particularly good for digestion.

It can be useful combined with fragrant valerian for coughs and nervous spasmodic conditions. Recent research into hops has shown that it contains a certain hormone, which accounts for the beneficial effect of helping mothers improve their milk flow.

To make a hop pillow, sprinkle hops with alcohol and fill a small bag or pillowcase with them (which all in all is bound to knock you out).

CULINARY

In early spring pick the young side shoots, steam them (or lightly boil), and eat like asparagus. The male flowers can be parboiled, cooled and tossed into salads. The young leaves can be quickly blanched to remove any bitterness and added to soups or salads.

Hyoscyamus niger

HENBANE

Also known as Devil's Eye, Hen Pen, Hen Penny, Hog Bean, Stinking Roger, Symphoniaca, Jusquiamus, Henbell, Belene, Hennyibone Hennebane, Poisoned Tobacco and Stinking Nightshade. From the family Solanaceae.

This native of Europe has become widely distributed worldwide and is found growing on waste ground or roadsides on well-drained sandy or chalk soils.

Two famous deaths are attributed to henbane. Hamlet's father was murdered by a distillation of henbane being poured in his ear, and in 1910 Dr Crippen used hyoscine, which is extracted from the plant, to murder his wife. Every part of the plant is toxic.

Henbane has been considered to have aphrodisiac properties and is the main ingredient in some love potions and witches' brews. It was also placed by the hinges of outer doors to protect against sorcery.

SPECIES

Hyoscyamus niger
Henbane
Annual/biennial. Ht up to 80cm (32in), spread 30cm (12in). Flowers bloom in summer, are yellow/brown or cream, funnel-shaped, and usually marked with purple veins. Leaves are hairy with large teeth, and the upper leaves have no stalks. The whole plant smells foul.

Hyoscyamus albus
White Henbane
Annual. Ht 30cm (12in), spread 30cm (12in). Its summer flowers are pale yellow marked with violet veins, funnel-shaped. Leaves are identical to **H. niger**.

CULTIVATION

Propagation
Seed
Sow the fairly small seeds on the surface of pots or trays in spring, and cover with Perlite. Germination 10-15 days. If you want henbane to behave like a biennial, sow in early autumn, keeping the soil moist until germination (which can be erratic, but on average takes about 14-21 days). Winter the young plants in a cold frame or cold glasshouse. Plant out the following spring at a distance of 30cm (12in).

Pests and Diseases
This plant in the main is free from pests and diseases.

Maintenance
Spring: Sow seed.
Summer: Dead-head flowers to maintain plant (wear gloves).
Autumn: Sow seed for second-year flowers.
Winter: Protect young plants.

Garden Cultivation
Choose the site for planting henbane with care, because it is poisonous. It will tolerate any growing situation but shows a preference for a well-drained sunny site. Sow seeds in late spring. When the seedlings are large enough to handle, thin to 30cm (12in) apart. It can look striking in a mixed border.

Harvest
Collect seed when the head turns brown and begins to open at the end.

CONTAINER GROWING

Inadvisable to grow such a poisonous plant this way.

MEDICINAL

This plant was used for a wide range of conditions which required sedation. The alkaloid hyoscine, which is derived from the green tops and leaves, is used as a hypnotic and brain sedative for the seasick, excitable and insane. It is also used externally in analgesic preparations to relieve rheumatism and arthritis. The syrup has a sedative effect in cases of Parkinson's Disease.

WARNING

The whole plant is poisonous. Children have been poisoned by eating the seeds or seed pods. Use preparation and dosage strictly only under medical direction.

Hypericum perforatum

ST. JOHN'S WORT

Also known as Warriors Wound, Amber, Touch and Heal, Grace of God and Herb of St John. From the family Guttiferae.

This magical herb is found in temperate zones of the world in open situations on semi-dry soils.

Whoever treads on St John's Wort after sunset will be swept up on the back of a magic horse that will charge round the heavens until sunrise before depositing its exhausted rider on the ground.

Besides its magical attributes, *Hypericum* has medicinal properties and was universally known as the 'Grace of God'. In England it cured mania, in Russia it gave protection against hydrophobia and the Brazilians knew it as an antidote to snake bite. St John's Wort ('wort', incidentally, is Anglo-Saxon for 'medicinal herb') has been used to raise ghosts and exorcise spirits. When crushed, the leaves release a balsamic odour similar to incense, which was said to be strong enough to drive away evil sprits. The red pigment from the crushed flowers was taken to signify the blood of St John at his beheading, for the herb is in full flower on 24th June, St John's Day.

Division
Divide established plants in the autumn.

Pests and Diseases
Largely free from pests and diseases.

Maintenance
Spring: Sow seeds.
Summer: Cut back after flowering to stop self-seeding.
Autumn: Divide established clumps.
Winter: No need for protection, fully hardy.

Garden Cultivation
Tolerates most soils, in sun or light shade, but it can be invasive in light soils.

Harvest
Harvest leaves and flowers as required.

OTHER USES

The flowers release a yellow dye with alum, and a red dye with alcohol.

WARNING

St John's Wort has sometimes poisoned livestock. Its use also makes the skin sensitive to light.

MEDICINAL

Oil extracted by macerating the flowers in vegetable oil and applied externally eases neuralgia and the pain of sciatica wounds, varicose veins, ulcers and sunburn. Only take internally under supervision.

SPECIES

Hypericum perforatum
St John's Wort
Hardy perennial. Ht 30-90cm (12-36in), spread 30cm (12in). Scented yellow flowers with black dots in summer. The small leaves are stalkless; covered with tiny perforations (hence **perforatum**), which are in fact translucent glands. This is the magical species.

CULTIVATION

Propagation
Seed
Sow very small seed in spring into prepared seed or plug trays, and cover with Perlite. Germination is usually in 10-20 days depending on the weather. When the seedlings are large enough to handle and after a period of hardening off, plant out 30cm (12in) apart.

CONTAINER GROWING

Can be grown in containers, but it is a bit tall so you do need a large clump for it to look effective. Use a soil based compost. Water in the summer months; only feed with liquid fertilizer twice during the growing season, otherwise it produces more leaf than flower.

'Purge me with Hyssop and I shall be clean'
(Psalm 51, verse 7).

Hyssopus officinalis

HYSSOP

From the family Labiatae.

Hyssop is a native of the Mediterranean region, where it grows wild on old walls and dry banks. It is found as a garden escapee elsewhere in Europe and has been cultivated in gardens for about the last 600 years. It was one of the herbs taken to the New World by the colonists to use in tea, in herbal tobacco and as an antiseptic.

There has been much to-ing and fro-ing about whether common hyssop is the one mentioned in the Bible. Some say it was oregano or savory. However, present thinking is that hyssop is flavour of the month especially since it has been discovered that the mould that produces penicillin grows on its leaf. This may have acted as an antibiotic protection when lepers were bathed in hyssop.

The Persians used distilled hyssop water as a body lotion to give a fine colour to their skin.

Hippocrates recommended hyssop for chest complaints, and today herbalists still prescribe it.

Hyssop *Hyssopus officinalis*

SPECIES

These are the common hyssops, readily available from nurseries and garden centres.

Hyssopus officinalis
Hyssop
Also known as Blue Hyssop Hardy semi-evergreen perennial. Ht 80cm (32in), spread 90cm (36in). Blue flowers from summer to early autumn. Small, narrow, lance-shaped leaves, aromatic and darkish green.

Hyssop *Hyssopus officinalis*

Hyssopus officinalis F. albus
White Hyssop
Semi-evergreen hardy perennial. Ht 80cm (32in), spread 90cm (36in). White flowers from summer to early autumn. Small, narrow, lance-shaped leaves, aromatic, and darkish green in colour.

Hyssopus officinalis ssp. aristatus
Rock Hyssop
Hardy, semi-evergreen, perennial. Ht 30cm (12in), spread 60cm (24in). Dark blue flowers from summer to early autumn. Small, narrow, lance-shaped leaves, aromatic and darkish green.

Hyssopus officinalis roseus
Pink Hyssop
Hardy, semi-evergreen, perennial. Ht 80cm (32in), spread 90cm (36in). Pink flowers from summer to early autumn. Small, narrow, lance-shaped leaves, aromatic and darkish green.

Pink Hyssop
Hyssopus officinalis roseus

CULTIVATION

Propagation
Seeds
In early spring sow the small seeds in plug or seed trays under protection, using the bark and peat mix of compost. Cover with Perlite. If very early in spring, a bottom heat of 15-21°C (60-70°F) would be beneficial. When the seedlings are large enough, either pot up or transplant into the garden after a period of hardening off. Plant at a distance of 30cm (12in) apart. All varieties can be grown from seed with the exception of rock hyssop, which can only be grown from cuttings. However, if you want a guaranteed pink or white hyssop, cuttings are a more reliable method.

Cuttings
In late spring, early summer, take softwood cuttings from the new lush growth and non-flowering stems.

Pests and Diseases

This genial plant rarely suffers from pests or diseases.

Maintenance

Spring: Sow seeds. Trim mature plants. Trim hedges.
Summer: Dead-head flowers to maintain supply, trim after flowering to maintain shape. Trim hedges.
Autumn: Cut back only in mild areas.
Winter: Protect in cold, wet winters and temperatures that fall below -5°C (23°F). Use agricultural fleece, straw, bracken, etc.

Garden Cultivation

This attractive plant, which has only recently become popular again, likes to be planted in conditions similar to rosemary and thyme, a well-drained soil in a sunny position. The seeds can be sown directly into the ground in very late spring or early summer, when the soil is warm. Thin to 30cm (12in) apart if being grown as specimen plants. If for hedging, 18cm (7in).

As all parts of the plant are pleasantly aromatic and the flowers very attractive, plant it where it can be seen and brushed against. The flowers are also attractive to bees and butterflies. For these reasons hyssop makes a very good hedge or edging plant. Trim the top shoots to encourage bushy growth. In early spring, trim the plant into a tidy shape with scissors. To keep the plant flowering in summer, remove the dead heads. Cut back to 20cm (8in) in autumn in mild areas, or trim back after flowering in cold areas. Keep formal hedges well clipped during the growing season.

Harvest

Cut young leaves for drying in summer. The flowers should be picked during the summer too, when they are fully opened. The scent is generally improved with drying.

MEDICINAL

An infusion is used mainly for coughs, whooping cough, asthma and bronchitis, and upper respiratory catarrh. It is also used for inflammation of the urinary tract. Externally it can be used for bruises and burns. It was once a country remedy for rheumatism.

COMPANION PLANTING

Grow near cabbages to lure away cabbage whiteflies. Plant near vines to increase yield.

WARNING

Hyssop should not be used in cases of nervous irritability. Strong doses, particularly those of distilled essential oil, can cause muscular spasms. This oil should not be used in aromatherapy for highly-strung patients, as it can cause epileptic symptoms. Do not use continuously for extended periods. No form of hyssop should be taken during pregnancy.

Hyssop sugar syrup

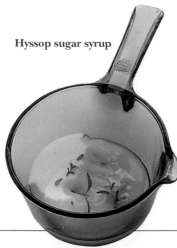

CONTAINER GROWING

Hyssop is a lovely plant in containers. It is happy in plenty of sunshine and prefers a south-facing wall. It also likes dry conditions and its tough leaves are not affected by the fumes of city centres, making it ideal for window-boxes. Equally, it is good on a patio as the scent is lovely on a hot summer's evening. Give it a liquid feed only during the flowering period. Cut back after flowering to maintain shape.

CULINARY

The flowers are delicious tossed in a green salad. In small amounts, leaves aid digestion of fatty foods but as they are somewhat pungent use them sparingly. The herb has a slightly bitter, minty taste and is therefore good flavouring in salads or as an addition to game, meats and soups, stews and stuffings. A good idea is to add a teaspoon of chopped leaf to a Yorkshire pudding batter. Hyssop is still used in Gascony as one of the herbs in bouquet garni and for flavouring a concentrated purée of tomatoes preserved for the winter. It is used in continental sausages and also added to American fruit pies, ¼teaspoon hyssop being sprinkled over the fruit before the top crust goes on.

When making a sugar syrup for fruit, add a sprig of hyssop as you boil the sugar and water; it adds a pleasant flavour, and the sprig can be removed before adding the fruit. When making cranberry pie, use the leaves as a lining for the dish.

Basque-Style Chicken

Serves 6

1.5 kg (3½lb) chicken
4 sweet peppers (2 red, 2 green)
Hyssop olive oil
5 tablespoons dry white wine
4 medium tomatoes, peeled and roughly chopped
6 onions
4 cloves of garlic
1 bouquet garni with a sprig of hyssop
salt and pepper

De-seed and slice the peppers into thin strips. Gently fry them in a small amount of oil until soft. Remove from pan and put to one side. Joint the chicken and gently fry in the oil, turning all the time. Transfer to a casserole, and season with salt and pepper, moisten with the wine, and leave over a gentle heat to finish cooking. Slice the onions and peel the garlic cloves, and soften without colouring in the olive oil in the frying pan. Then add the tomatoes, peppers and bouquet garni, and season. When reduced almost to a cream, turn into the casserole over the chicken and keep on a low heat until ready to serve, about a further 20-30 minutes.

Inula helenium

ELECAMPANE

Also known as Allecampane, July Campane, Elicompane, Dock, Sunflower, Wild Sunflower, Yellow Starwort, Elfdock, Elfwort, Horse Elder, Horse Heal and Scabwort. From the family Compositae.

Inula helenium seed heads

Elecampane originates from Asia whence, through cultivation, it spread across Western Europe to North America and now grows wild from Nova Scotia to Ontario, North Carolina, and Missouri.

Sources for the derivation of the principal common name, Elecampane, and the generic/species name, *Inula helenium*, are not altogether satisfactory, but I have found three possible explanations.

Helen of Troy was believed to be gathering the herb when she was abducted by Paris, hence 'helenium'.

Down through the ages the herb was considered as good medicinally for horse or mule as for man; it was even sometimes called horselene. 'Inula' could come from 'hinnulus' meaning 'a young mule'.

Finally, the Romans called the herb *Enula Campana* (Inula of the fields) from which Elecampane is a corruption.

According to the Roman writer Pliny, the Emperor Julius Augustus enjoyed elecampane so much he proclaimed, 'Let no day past without eating some of the roots candied to help the digestion and cause mirth'. The Romans also used it as a candied sweetmeat, coloured with cochineal. This idea persisted for centuries, and in the Middle Ages, apothecaries sold the candied root in flat pink sugary cakes, which were sucked to alleviate asthma and indigestion and to sweeten the breath. Tudor herbalists also candied them for the treatment of coughs, catarrhs, bronchitis and chest ailments. Their use continued until the 1920s as a flavouring in sweets.

I have discovered an Anglo-Saxon ritual using elecampane – part medicinal, part magical. Prayers were sung of the Helenium and its roots dug up by the medicinal man, who had been careful not to speak to any disreputable creature – man, elf, goblin or fairy – he chanced to meet on the way to the ceremony. Afterwards the elecampane root was laid under the altar for the night and eventually mixed with betony and lichen from a crucifix. The medicine was taken against elf sickness or elf disease.

There is an ancient custom in Scandinavia of putting a bunch of elecampane in the centre of a nosegay of herbs to symbolize the sun and the head of Odin, the greatest of Norse gods.

SPECIES

Inula helenium
Elecampane
Hardy perennial. Ht 1.5-2.4m (5-8ft) spread 1m (3ft) Bright yellow, ragged, daisy-like flowers in summer. The leaves are large, oval-toothed, slightly downy underneath, and of a mid-green colour. Dies back fully in winter.

Inula hookeri
Hardy perennial. Ht. 75cm (30in) spread 45cm (18in). Yellowish green, ragged, daisy-like flowers slightly scented in summer. Lance-shaped hairy leaves, smaller than **I. magnifica**, and mid-green in colour. Dies back fully in winter.

Inula magnifica
Hardy perennial. Ht 1.8m (6ft), spread 1m (3ft). Large, ragged, daisy-like flowers. Lots of large, dark green lance-shaped rough leaves. May need staking in an exposed garden. This is often mistaken for **I. helenium**, the leaf colour is the biggest difference, and on average **I. maginifica** grows much larger. Dies back fully in winter.

chose the point of division carefully. Alternatively remove the offshoots that grow around the parent plant; each has its own root system, so they can be planted immediately in a prepared site elsewhere in the garden. This can be done in autumn or spring.

Pests and Diseases

It rarely suffers from disease, although if the autumn is excessively wet, as the leaves die back, they may suffer from a form of mildew. Simply cut back and destroy the leaves.

Maintenance

Spring: Sow seed. Divide established plants.
Summer: Remove flowerheads as soon as flowering finishes.
Autumn: Cut back growth to stop self-seeding and to prevent the plant from becoming untidy. Remove offshoots for replanting.
Winter: The plant dies back so needs no protection.

Garden Cultivation

Plant in a moist, fertile soil, in full sun, sheltered from the wind (elecampane grows tall and would otherwise need staking). It can look very striking at the back of a border against a stone wall, or in front of a screen of deciduous trees. In a very dry summer it may need watering.

Elecampane *Inula helenium*

Harvest

Dig up second- or third-year roots in the autumn, they can be used as a vegetable, or dried for use in medicine. The flowers are good in autumn flower arrangements and dry well upside down if you cut them just before the seeds turn brown.

CONTAINER GROWING

Elecampane grows too big for most containers and is easily blown over. So it is not advisable

CULINARY

Elecampane has a sharp, bitter flavour. Use dried pieces or cook as a root vegetable.

OTHER USES

Your cat may be interested to know that scientific research indicates that elecampane has a sedative effect on mice.

CULTIVATION

Propagation
Seed
The seed is similar to dandelion; when the plant has germinated you can see the seeds flying all over the garden, which should be all the warning you need... Sow on the surface of a pot or plug tray. Cover with Perlite. Germination is 2-4 weeks, depending on sowing season and seed viability. Prick out and plant 1-1.5m (3-5ft) apart when the seedlings are large enough to handle.

Root Division
If the plant grows too big for its position in the garden, divide in the autumn when the plant has died back. As the roots are very strong

Seeds on a leaf in autumn

MEDICINAL

The main use is for respiratory complaints, at one time specifically for TB. It is still employed in folk medicine as a favourite constituent of cough remedies, and has always been popular both as a medicine and as a condiment.

In America, elecampane oil is used for respiratory, intestinal catarrh, chronic diarrhoea, chronic bronchitis and whooping cough.

A decoction of the root has long been used externally for scabies, herpes, acne and other skin diseases, hence its country name Scabwort.

Recent research shows that the lactines found in the roots are powerful agents against bacteria and fungi.

Elecampane oil

Iris

IRIS

From the family Iridaceae.

Al those mentioned are native of the northern hemisphere and are cultivated in varying conditions, from dry light soil (Orris – Iris 'Florentina') to damp boggy soils (Blue Flag Iris – Iris Versicolor).

The Greek word 'iris', meaning 'rainbow' and the name of the Greek goddess of the rainbow, was appended to describe the plant's variable colours. The iris is one of the oldest cultivated plants – it is depicted on the wall of an Egyptian temple dating from 1500 BC.

In this very large family, 3 stand out for their beneficial herbal qualities. Orris has a violet-scented root which has been powdered and used in perfumes since the ancient Egyptians and Greeks. The Latin Iris 'Florentina' depicts its association with Florence in the early Middle Ages. It is said to be the fleur de lys of French heraldry.

The blue flag iris is the common wetlands plant, native to eastern North America and exported from there to Europe. Employed by the Indians and early settlers as a remedy for gastric complaints, it was included in the United States Pharmacopeia and is still believed in folk medicine to be a blood purifier of use in eruptive skin conditions. Sometimes the plant is known as liver lily because of its purifying effect.

The root of the yellow flag iris, a native of the British Isles, was powdered and used as an ingredient in Elizabethan snuff. It was taken to America and Australia by the earliest settlers.

SPECIES

Iris 'Florentina'
Orris
Also known as Florentine Iris and Oris root.
Hardy perennial. Ht 60cm-1m (2-3 ft). Spread indefinite. Large white flowers tinged with pale lavender and with a yellow beard appear early to mid-summer. Green, sword-shaped leaves. The root stock is stout and rhizomatous with a violet scent. Grows well throughout Europe and North America, except in the warm moist climate of Florida and the Gulf Coast.

Iris germanica
Purple Iris
Also known as Garden Iris, and Flag Iris.
Hardy perennial. Ht 60-90cm (2-3ft), spread indefinite. The fragrant flowers are blue/violet, occasionally white, and form early to mid-summer. Leaves are greyish-green and sword-shaped. The root is thickish rhizome. There are many cultivated varieties. It is grown commercially for the rhizomes and, like **Iris 'Florentina'**, is used in perfumery and pharmaceutical preparations.

Iris pseudacorus
Yellow Iris (Yellow Flag)
Perennial. Ht 40cm-150cm (16in-5ft), spread indefinite. Flowers are bright yellow with radiating brown veins and very slightly scented. They appear early to mid-summer. The root is a thick rhizome from which many rootlets descend.

Yellow Iris *Iris pseudacorus*

Iris versicolor
Blue Flag Iris
Also known as Flag Lily, Fleur de Lys, Flower du Luce, Iris, Liver Lily, Poison Flags, Snake Lily, Water Flag and Wild Iris. Hardy perennial. Ht 30-100cm (12-39in), spread indefinite. Flowers claret-purple-blue in summer. Large, sword-shaped, green leaves. Root large and rhizomatous.

Purple Iris *Iris germanica*

CULTIVATION

Propagation
Seed
All the irises produce large seeds, which take some time to germinate and often benefit from a period of stratification. As the seeds are of a good size, sow directly into an 8cm (3in) pot in autumn, using a peat, grit, bark mix of compost. Water in well, and cover the pots with cling film (to stop the mice eating the seed). Put outside to get the weathers. Check that the compost remains damp. If there is any danger of it drying out, stand the container in water. This is especially important for blue and yellow flag irises.

Division
Divide the rhizome roots in late spring or early autumn. This suits all the varieties. Replant immediately in a prepared site. Leave a decent distance between plants; spread is indefinite.

Pests and Diseases
The only major pest is the iris sawfly. The darkish grey larvae feed along the leaf-margins, removing large chunks. Pupation takes place in the soil beneath or near the host plants, and the adult sawflies are on the wing during early to mid-summer. Cut off infected leaves only if you find them unsightly – the plant will not be weakened. This is an annual pest and there is not much one can do to prevent it.

Maintenance
Spring: Divide roots of mature plants.
Summer: Collect the seeds as soon as ripe.
Autumn: Sow seeds and leave outside.
Winter: Fully hardy; no need for protection.

Garden Cultivation
Orris and common iris prefer a well-drained, rich soil and a sunny situation. When planting, make sure that part of the rhizomes are exposed.
Yellow and blue flag irises are marsh-loving plants, ideal for those with a pond or ditch or piece of boggy ground. They grow happily in semi-shade but need full sun in order to produce the maximum bloom. In deep shade it will not flower at all but will spread quickly by stout underground rhizomes. A measure of control will be necessary.

Harvest
The full violet fragrance of orris will not be apparent until the roots are 2 years old. Dig up these rhizomes in autumn and dry immediately.
Gather yellow flag flowers and roots for use as a dye, in early summer and autumn respectively.
Dig up blue flag roots in autumn and dry.

CONTAINER GROWING

These irises grow on strong rhizomes, so make sure that the container is strong enough, large enough, and so shaped that it will accommodate the plant happily and not blow over.
For the bog lovers use more peat than usual in the compost mix – up the ratio to 75%, but put lots of gravel and broken crocks in the bottom of the container to make up for loss of weight. For the dry gang, use a soil-based compost. Do not let either compost dry out. They become pot-bound very quickly, so split and re-pot every year.

WARNING

Always wash your hands well after handling this plant as it can cause uncontrollable vomiting and violent diarrhoea. Large doses of the fresh root can cause nausea, vomiting and facial neuralgias.

Iris used as a fixative in a potpourri

OTHER USES
The violet-scented, powdered root of orris is used as a fresh scent to linen, a base for dry shampoos, a base for tooth powders, in face-packs, as a fixative in potpourris and as a dry shampoo.
Flowers of yellow flag make a good yellow dye, while the rhizomes yields a grey or black dye when used with an iron mordant.

MEDICINAL

Orris and yellow flag are rarely used medicinally nowadays. However, herbalists still use the blue flag as a blood purifyer acting on the liver and gall bladder to increase the flow of bile, and as an effective cleanser of toxins. It is also said to relieve flatulence and heartburn, belching and nausea, and headaches associated with digestive problems.

CULINARY

Apparently, if you roast the seeds of the yellow flag iris, they make an excellent coffee substitute. Apart from this little gem, I cannot find any culinary uses for irises.

Juniperus communis

JUNIPER

From the family Cupressaceae.

Juniper is widely distributed throughout the world and grows either as a shrub or a small tree. It is a native of the Mediterranean region, but also grows in the Arctic, from Norway to the Soviet Union, in the North and West Himalayas and in North America. It is found on heaths, moorlands, open coniferous forests and mountain slopes.

This widely distributed plant was first used by the ancient Greek physicians and its use has continued right up to modern days. It was believed to cure snake bites and protect against infectious diseases like the plague.

The English word 'gin' is derived from an abbreviation of Holland's 'geneva' as the spirit was first called. This in turn stems from the Dutch 'jenever' meaning juniper.

SPECIES

Juniper is a conifer, a group of trees and shrubs distinguished botanically from others by its production of seeds exposed or uncovered on the scales of the fruit. True to form, it is evergreen and has needle-like leaves.

There are many species and varieties available, **Juniperus communis**, being the main herbal variety. On the varieties detailed below, the flowers are all very similar: male flowers are very small catkins; female flowers are small, globose and berry-like, with usually 3-8 fleshy scales. Over a period of 3 years, these turn blue and then finally black as they ripen.

Irish Juniper
Juniperis communis 'Hibernica'

Juniperus communis 'Compressa'
Juniper Compressa
Hardy evergreen perennial tree. Ht 75cm (30in), spread 15cm (6in). The leaves are small and bluish green, sharply pointed and aromatic. Very slow growing with an erect habit, ideal for rock gardens or containers.

Juniperus communis 'Hibernica'
Irish Juniper
Hardy evergreen perennial tree. Ht 3-5m (10-15ft), spread 30cm (12in). Leaves small and bluish/silvery green, sharply pointed and aromatic. Columnar in shape and with a hint of silver in certain lights. Very slow growing.

Juniperus communis 'Hornibrookii'
Juniper Hornibrookii
Hardy evergreen perennial tree. Ht 50cm (20in), spread 2m (6ft). Leaves small and darkish green, sharply pointed and aromatic. A big carpeting plant.

Juniperus communis 'Rependa'
Prostrate Juniper
Hardy evergreen perennial tree. Ht 20-30cm (8-12in), spread 1-2m (3-6ft). Leaves small and bluish green, sharply pointed and aromatic. A smaller carpeting plant.

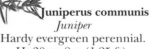

Juniperus communis
Juniper
Hardy evergreen perennial. Ht 30cm-8m (1-25 ft), spread 1-4m (3-12ft) – size of the plant very dependent on where it is growing. Leaves small and bright green, sharply pointed and aromatic.

CULTIVATION

Propagation
Seed
All the species can be propagated by seed. Sow seeds taken from ripe berries in a cold greenhouse, cold frame or cold conservatory in early autumn. As junipers on the whole are extremely slow growing, it is best to grow the seedlings in a controlled environment for 1 or 2 years, before planting out in a permanent position in the garden. Start in seed or plug trays; then, when the seedlings are large enough, pot up into small pots using a soil based compost. This method is the easiest but to be sure of the plant's gender and leaf colour, taking cuttings is more reliable.

Cuttings
It is quite easy to raise juniper from semi-hardwood cuttings taken from fresh current growth in spring or autumn.

Pests and Diseases
Various rusts attack juniper. If you see small rusty spores on the underside of the leaves, cut the branches out and burn them.
Honey fungus attacks many conifers, especially young plants. If this occurs, dig up the plant, making sure you have all the roots, burn it, and plant no further trees in that space.

Maintenance
Spring: Plant out 2-year-old plants. Remove any leaders growing incorrectly in late spring/early summer.
Summer: Take semi-hardwood cuttings.
Autumn: Sow seeds.
Winter: Winter young plants in cold frames, or provide added protection.

Garden Cultivation
Juniper likes an exposed sunny site. It will tolerate an alkaline or neutral soil. Both male and female plants are necessary for berry production. The berries, which only grow on the female bush, can be found in various stages of ripeness on the same plant. Their flavour is stronger when grown in warm climates.
To maintain the shape of the juniper, trim with secateurs to ensure that there is no more than one leader, the strongest and straightest. Remember, when trimming, that most conifers will not make new growth when cut back into old wood, or into branches that have turned brown.

Harvest
Harvest the berries when ripe in late summer. Dry them spread out on a tray, as you would leaves.

CULINARY

Crushed berries are an excellent addition to marinades, sauerkraut and stuffing for guinea fowl and other game birds. Although no longer generally considered as a spice, it is still an important flavouring for certain meats, liqueurs, and especially gin.

Pork chops with juniper

Pork Chops Marinated with Juniper
(serves 4)

Marinade
2 tablespoons olive oil
6 juniper berries, crushed
2 cloves of garlic, crushed
Salt and pepper

Mix the oil, juniper berries, garlic and seasoning together in a bowl.

4 pork chops
25g (1oz) plain flour
275ml (½ pint) dry cider

Lay the pork chops in the base of a shallow dish and cover them with the marinade, turning the chops over once to make sure they are covered. Leave for a minimum of 3 hours, if possible overnight. Remove the chops from the marinade, and reserve it. Heat a large frying pan and add the reserved marinade. When hot, add the pork chops and cook over a moderate heat for about 20 minutes turning the chops regularly. When all traces of pink have gone from the meat, remove from heat, and put the chops on a plate. Return the pan to the heat and stir the flour into the remaining juices. Add the cider and bring to the boil. Return the chops to the sauce in the pan. Heat through slowly, and serve with mashed potato and broccoli.

WARNING

Juniper berries should not be taken during pregnancy or by people with kidney problems. Internal use of the volatile oil must only ever be prescribed by professionals.

MEDICINAL

Juniper is used in the treatment of cystitis, rheumatism and gout. Steamed inhalations of the berries are an excellent treatment for coughs, colds and catarrh.

CONTAINER GROWING

Juniper is slow growing and can look most attractive in pots. Use a soil based compost, starting off with a suitable-sized pot, only potting up once a year if necessary. If the root ball looks happy, do not disturb it. Do not over-water. As the plant is hardy and evergreen, the container will need more protection than the plant during the winter months. Feed during the summer months only with a liquid fertilizer as per manufacturer's guidelines.

Laurus nobilis

BAY

from the family Lauraceae

Bay is an ever-green tree native to southern Europe, and now found throughout the world.

That this ancient plant was much respected in Roman times is reflected in the root of its family name, Lauraceae, the Latin 'laurus' meaning 'praise', and in its main species name, *Laurus nobilis*, the latin 'nobilis' meaning 'famous', 'renowned'. A bay wreath became a mark of excellence for poets and athletes, a symbol of wisdom and glory. The latin 'laureate' means crowned with laurels (synonym for bay), hence Poet Laureate, of course, and the French *baccalaureate*.

The bay tree was sacred even earlier – to Apollo, Greek god of prophecy, poetry and healing. His priestesses ate bay leaves before expounding his oracles at Delphi. As large doses of bay induce the effect of a narcotic, this may explain their trances. His temple had its roof made entirely of bay leaves, ostensibly to protect against disease, witchcraft and lightning. Apollo's son Aesculapius, the Greek god of Medicine, also had bay dedicated to him as it was considered a powerful antiseptic and guard against disease, in particular the plague.

In the 17th-century, Culpeper wrote that 'neither witch nor devil, thunder nor lightening, will hurt a man in the place where a bay-tree is.' He also wrote that 'the berries are very effectual against the poison of venomous creatures, and the stings of wasps and bees.'

SPECIES

Laurus azorica (canariensis)
Canary Island Bay
Perennial evergreen tree. Ht to 6m (20ft). Reddish–brown branches, a colour which sometimes extends to the leaves.

Laurus nobilis
Bay
Also known as Sweet Bay, Sweet Laurel, Laurel, Indian Bay, Grecian Laurel. Perennial evergreen tree. Ht up to 8m (26ft), spread 3m (12ft). Small pale yellow waxy flowers in spring. Green oval berries turning black in autumn. The leaves may be added to stock, soups and stews and are among the main ingredients of bouquet garni. *L. nobilis* is the only bay used for culinary purposes.

Standard Bay tree

Laurus nobilis 'Aurea'
Golden Bay
Perennial evergreen tree. Ht up to 5m (18ft). Small pale yellow waxy flowers in spring. Green berries turning black in autumn. Golden leaves can look sickly in damp, cooler countries. Needs good protection in winter especially from wind scorch and frosts. Trim in the autumn/spring to maintain the golden leaves.

Laurus nobilis F. angustifolia
Willow Leaf Bay
Perennial evergreen tree. Ht up to 7m (23ft). Narrow leafed variety, said to be hardier than *L. nobilis* against wind scorch. This is not strictly true.

Umbellularia californica
Californian Laurel
Perenial evergreen tree. Ht up to 18m (60ft). Pale yellow flowers in late spring. Very pungent/aromatic leaves. Can cause headaches and nausea when the leaves are crushed. NOT culinary.

CULTIVATION

Propagation
Seed
Bay sets seed in its black berries, but rarely in cooler climates. Sow fresh seed on the surface of either a seed or plug tray or directly into pots. Keep warm: 21°C (65°F). Germination is erratic, may take place within 10–20 days, in 6 months, or sometimes even longer. Make sure the compost is not too wet or it will rot the seeds.

Cuttings
Not a plant for the faint hearted. When I started propagating over 20 years ago I thought my bay cuttings were doing really well, but a year later not 1 had properly struck, and three-quarters of them had turned black and died. Out of 100 cuttings only 1 eventually turned into a tree!

A heated propagator is a great help and high humidity is essential. Use either a misting unit or cover the cutting in plastic and maintain the compost or Perlite at a steady moisture. It may be an art but worth the try. Cuttings are taken in late summer 10cm (4in) in length.

Bay *Laurus nobilis* in flower

Division
If offshoots are sent out by the parent plant, dig them up or they will destroy the shape of the tree. Occasionally roots come with them and these then can be potted up, using the bark, peat, grit mix of compost. Place a plastic bag over the pot to maintain humidity. Leave somewhere warm and check from time to time to see if new shoots are starting. When they do, remove the plastic bag. Do not plant out for at least a year.

Layering
Do it in spring. A good method of propagating a difficult plant.

Pests and Diseases
Bay is susceptible to sooty black spots, caused by the scale insect which sticks both to the undersides of leaves and to the stems, sucking the sap. Get rid of them by hand or use a liquid horticultural soap.

Maintenance
Spring: Sow Seeds. Cut back standard and garden bay trees to maintain shape and to promote new growth. Cut back golden bay trees to maintain colour. Check for scale insect and eradicate at first signs. Give container grown plants a good liquid feed.
Summer: Check that young plants are not drying out too much. In very hot weather, and especially if you live in a city, spray-clean container

grown plants with water. Propagate by taking stem cuttings or layering in late summer.
Autumn: Take cuttings of mature plants. Protect container grown plants and young garden plants. Garden plants can be protected either by covering in straw or bracken, if in a sufficiently sheltered position, or by agricultural fleece.
Winter: In severe winters the leaves will turn brown but don't despair. come the spring, it may shoot new growth from the base. To encourage this, cut the plant nearly down to the base.

Garden Cultivation
Bay is shallow rooted and therefore more prone to frost damage. Also, leaves are easily scorched in extremely cold weather or in strong cold winds. Protection is thus essential, especially for bay trees under 2 years old. When planting out, position the plant in full sun, protected from the wind, and in a rich well-drained soil at least 1m (3ft) away from other plants to start with, allowing more space as the tree matures. Mulch in the spring to retain moisture throughout the summer months.

Harvest
Being evergreen leaves can be taken all year round. It is fashionable now to preserve bay leaves in vinegars.
Berries are cultivated for use in laurel oil and laurel butter. The latter is a vital ingredient of laurin ointment, which is used in veterinary medicine.

MEDICINAL

Infuse the leaves to aid digestion and stimulate the appetite.

CONTAINER GROWING

Bay makes a good container plant. Young plants benefit from being kept in a container and indoors for the winter in cooler climates. The kitchen windowsill is ideal. Do not water too much, and let the compost dry out in the winter months.
Large standard bays or pyramids look very effective in half barrels or containers of an equal size. Anything in a container will need extra protection in winter from frosts and wind, so if the temperature drops below –5°C (25°F) bring the plants in.
To produce a standard bay tree, start with a young containerized plant with a straight growing stem. As it begins to grow remove the lower side shoots, below where you want the ball to begin. Allow the tree to grow to 20cm (8in) higher than desired, then clip back the growing tip. Cut the remaining side shoots down to about 3 leaves. When the side shoots have grown a further 4/5 leaves, trim again to 2/3 leaves. Keep

Bay bouquet garni

repeating this until you have a leafy ball shape. Once the shape is established prune with secateurs in late spring and again in late summer to maintain it.

OTHER USES
Place in flour to deter weevil. Add an infusion to a bath to relieve aching limbs.

CULINARY

Fresh leaves are stronger in flavour than dried ones. Use in soups, stews and stocks.

Add leaves to poached fish, like salmon.
Put on the coals of a barbecue.
Put fresh leaves in jars of rice to flavour the rice.
Boil in milk to flavour custards and rice pudding.

Bouquet Garni
I quote from my grandmother's cookbook, *Food for Pleasure*, published in 1950: 'A bouquet garni is a bunch of herbs constantly required in cooking.' The essential herbs in a bouquet garni are bay leaf, parsley and thyme.

Lavandula

LAVENDER

From the family Labiatae.

Native of the Mediterranean region, Canary Isles and India. Now cultivated in different regions of the world, growing in well-draining soil and warm, sunny climates.

Long before the world manufactured deodorants and bath salts, the Romans used lavender in their bath water; the word is derived from the Latin 'lava', to wash. It was the Romans who first introduced this plant to Britain and from then on monks cultivated it in their monastic gardens. Little more was recorded until Tudor times when people noted its fragrance and a peculiar power to ease stiff joints and relieve tiredness. It was brought in quantities from herb farms to the London Herb Market at Bucklesbury. 'Who will buy my lavender?' became perhaps the most famous of all London street cries.

It was used as a strewing herb for its insect-repellent properties and for masking household and street smells. It was also carried in nosegays to ward off the plague and pestilence. In France in the 17th century, huge fields of lavender were grown for the perfume trade. This has continued to the present day.

SPECIES

This is another big family of plants that are eminently worth collecting. I include here a few of my favourites, a few common, a few rare.

Lavandula 'Nana Alba'
Dwarf White Lavender
Hardy evergreen perennial. Ht and spread 30cm (12in). White flowers in summer. Green-grey narrow short leaves. This is the shortest growing lavender and is ideal for hedges.

Old English Lavender
Lavandula x intermedia
Old English Group

Lavandula angustifolia (spica, officinalis)
Common Lavender (English Lavender)
Hardy evergreen perennial. Ht 80 cm (32in), spread 1m (3ft). Mauve/purple flowers on a long spike in summer. Long, narrow, pale greenish-grey, aromatic leaves. One of the most popular and well known of the lavender family.

Lavandula angustifolia 'Alba'
White Lavender
Hardy evergreen perennial. Ht 70cm (28in), spread 80cm (32in). White flowers on a long spike in summer. Long, narrow, pale greenish-grey, aromatic leaves.

Lavandula angustifolia 'Bowles' Variety'
Lavender Bowles
Hardy evergreen perennial. Ht and spread 60cm (24in). Light blue flowers on a medium size spike in summer. Medium-length, narrow grey-greenish, aromatic leaves.

Lavandula angustifolia 'Folgate'
Lavender Folgate
Hardy evergreen perennial. Ht and spread 45cm (18in). Purple flowers on a medium spike in summer. Leaves as above.

Lavandula angustifolia 'Hidcote'
Lavender Hidcote
Hardy evergreen perennial. Ht and spread 45cm (18in). Dark blue flowers on a medium spike in summer. Fairly short, narrow, aromatic, grey-greenish leaves. One of the most popular lavenders. Often used in hedging, planted at a distance of 30-40 cm (12-16 in).

Lavandula angustifolia 'Loddon Blue'
Lavender Loddon Blue
Hardy evergreen perennial. Ht and spread 45cm (18in). Pale blue flowers on a medium-length spike in summer. Fairly short, narrow, grey-greenish, aromatic leaves. Good compact habit. There is another variety called 'Loddon Pink' – same size, same height, with pale pink flowers.

Lavender Hidcote *Lavandula angustifolia 'Hidcote'*

Lavandula angustifolia 'Munstead'
Lavender Dwarf Munstead
Hardy evergreen perennial. Ht and spread 45cm (18in). Purple/blue flowers on a fairly short spike in summer. Medium length, greenish-grey, narrow, aromatic leaves. This is now a common lavender and used often in hedging, planted at a distance of 30-40cm (12-16in).

Lavandula angustifolia 'Rosea'
Lavender Pink/Rosea
Hardy evergreen perennial. Ht and spread 45cm (18in). Pink flowers in summer. Medium length greenish-grey, narrow, aromatic leaves.

Lavandula dentata
Fringe Lavender
(sometimes called French Lavender)
Half-hardy evergreen perennial. Ht and spread 60cm (24in). Pale blue/mauve flowers from summer to early autumn. Highly aromatic, serrated, pale green, narrow leaves. This plant is a native of southern Spain and the Mediterranean region and needs protecting in cold damp winters. It is ideal to bring inside into a cool room in early autumn as a flowering pot plant.

Lavandula x intermedia Dutch group
Lavender Vera
Hardy evergreen perennial. Ht and spread 45cm (18in). Purple flowers in summer on fairly long spikes. Long greenish-grey, narrow, aromatic leaves.

Lavandula x intermedia 'Grappenhall'
Lavender Grappenhall
Hardy evergreen perennial. Ht and spread 1m (3ft). Large pale mauve flowers on long spikes in summer. The flowers are much more open than other species. Long greenish-grey, narrow, aromatic leaves.

Lavandula x intermedia Old English Group
Old English Lavender
Hardy evergreen perennial. Ht and spread 60cm (24in). Light lavender blue flowers on long spikes. Long, narrow, silver/grey/green, aromatic leaves.

French Lavender
Lavandula Stoechas

Lavandula x intermedia 'Seal'
Lavender Seal
Hardy evergreen perennial. Ht 90cm (3ft), spread 60cm (24in). Long flower stems, mid-purple. Long, narrow, silver/grey/green aromatic leaves.

Lavandula x intermedia 'Twickel Purple'
Lavender Twickel Purple
Hardy evergreen perennial. Ht and spread 50cm (20in). Pale purple flowers on fairly short spike. Medium length, greenish-grey, narrow, aromatic leaves. Compact grower.

Lavender Pedunculata
Lavandula stoechas spp pedunculata

Lavandula lanata
Woolly Lavender
Hardy evergreen perennial. Ht 50 cm (20in), spread 45cm (18in). Deep purple flowers on short spikes. Short, soft, narrow, silver-grey aromatic foliage.

Lavandula pinnata
Lavender Pinnata
Half-hardy evergreen perennial. Ht and spread 50cm (20in). The flower spikes are a mixture of **L. angustifolia** and **L. stoechas**, purple in colour. Leaves are fern-like, grey, and slightly aromatic. Could be easily mistaken for an **artemisia**. Protect in winter.

Lavandula stoechas
French Lavender
(sometimes called Spanish Lavender)
Hardy evergreen perennial. Ht 50cm (20in). Spread 60cm (24in). Attractive purple bracts in summer. Short, narrow, grey/green, aromatic leaves.

Lavandula stoechas F. leucantha
White French Lavender
As **L. Stoechas** except white bracts in summer.

Lavendula stoechas ssp pedunculata
Lavender Pedunculata
(sometimes known as Papillon)
Half-hardy evergreen perennial. Ht and spread 60cm (24in). These attractive purple bracts have an extra centre tuft, which is mauve and looks like two rabbit ears. The aromatic leaves are very narrow, grey and longer than the ordinary **stoechas**. Protect in winter.

Lavandula viridis
Lavender Viridis
Half-hardy evergreen perennial. Ht and spread 60cm (24in). This unusual plant has green bracts with a cream centre tuft. The leaves are green, narrow, and highly aromatic. Protect in winter.

**Lavenders – Small
(grow to 45-50cm/18-20in)**
Lavender Folgate, Lavender Hidcote, Lavender Lodden Pink, Lavender Lodden Blue, Lavender Munstead, Lavender Dwarf White, Lavender Twickle Purple.

**Lavenders – Medium
(grow to 60cm/24in)**
Lavender Bowles, Lavender Old English.

**Lavenders – Big
(70cm/28in and above)**
Lavender Grappenhall, Lavender White, Lavender Seal.

Half-hardy Lavenders
Lavender Dentata (50cm/20in), Lavender Lanata (50cm/20in), Lavender Pinnata (50cm/20in), Lavender Stoechas (50cm/20in), Lavender Stoechas Alba (50cm/20in), Lavender Stoechas Pendunculata (60cm/

Fringe Lavender
Lavandula dentata

CULTIVATION

Propagation
Seed
Lavender can be grown from seed but it tends not to be true to species, with the exception of **Lavender Stoechas**.

Seed should be sown fresh in the autumn on the surface of a seed or plug tray and covered with Perlite. It germinates fairly readily with a bottom heat of 4-10°C (40-50°F). Winter the seedlings in a cold greenhouse or cold conservatory with plenty of ventilation. In the spring, prick out and pot on using the bark, peat, grit mix of compost. Let the young plant establish a good size root ball before planting out in a prepared site in the early summer. For other species you will find cuttings much more reliable.

Cuttings
Take softwood cuttings from non-flowering stems in spring. Root in bark, peat, grit mix of compost. Take semi-hardwood cuttings in summer or early autumn from the strong new growth. Once the cuttings have rooted well, it is better to pot them up and winter the young lavenders in a cold greenhouse or conservatory

Lavender viridis
Lavandula viridis

rather than plant them out in the first winter. In the spring, plant them out in well-drained, fertile soil, at a distance of 45-60cm (18-24in) apart or 30cm (12in) apart for an average hedge.

Layering
This is easily done in the autumn. Most hardy lavenders respond well to this form of propagation.

Pests and Diseases
One of the chief pests of lavenders are the cuckoo spit insects and the caterpillars of several types of moth. Cure cuckoo spit by spraying away the foamy white spit with water. Then use a horticultural liquid soap to remove the bugs and caterpillars (follow manufacturer's instructions).

The flowers in wet seasons may be attacked by grey mould and/or botrytis. This can occur all too readily after a wet winter. Cut back the infected parts as far as possible, again remembering not to cut into the old wood if you want it to shoot again.

There is another fungus (**Phoma lavandulae**) which attacks the stems and branches causing wilting and death of the affected branches. If this occurs dig up the plant immediately and destroy, keeping it well away from any other lavender bushes.

Maintenance
Spring: Give a spring hair cut.
Summer: Trim after flowering. Take cuttings.
Autumn: Sow seed. Cut back in early autumn, never into the old wood. Protect all the half-hardy lavenders. Bring containers inside.
Winter: Check seedlings for disease. Keep watering to a minimum.

Garden Cultivation
Lavender is one of the most popular plants in today's herb garden and is particularly useful in borders, edges, as internal hedges, and on top of dry walls. All the species need an open sunny position and a well-drained, fertile soil. But it will adapt to semi-shade as long as the soil conditions are met, otherwise it will die in winter. If you have very cold winter temperatures, it is worth container growing.

The way to maintain a lavender bush is to trim to shape every year in the spring, remembering not to cut into the old wood as this will not re-shoot. After flowering, trim back to the leaves. In the early autumn trim again, making sure this is well before the first autumn frosts. Otherwise the new growth will be too soft and be damaged. By trimming this way, you will keep the bush neat and encourage it to make new growth, so stopping it becoming woody.

If you have inherited a straggly mature plant then give it a good cut back in autumn, followed by a second cut in the spring and then adopt the above routine. If the plant is aged, I would advise that you propagate some of the autumn cuts, so preserving the plant if all else fails.

Harvest
Gather the flowers just as they open, and dry on open trays or by hanging in small bunches.

Pick the leaves any time for use fresh, or before flowering if drying.

Lavender sachets can be used to make good presents or used as moth repellent

CONTAINER GROWING

If you have low winter temperatures, lavenders cannot be treated as a hardy evergreen. Treated as a container plant, however, it can be protected in winter and enjoyed just as well in the summer. Choose containers to set the lavender off; they all suit terracotta. Use a well-drained compost – the peat, bark, grit mix suits them well. The ideal position is sun, but all lavenders will cope with partial shade, though the aroma can be impaired.

Feed regularly through the flowering season with liquid fertilizer, following the manufacturer's instructions. Allow the compost to dry out in winter (not totally, but nearly), and slowly reintroduce watering in spring.

CULINARY

Lavender has not been used much in cooking, but as there are many more adventurous cooks around, I am sure it will be used increasingly in the future. Use the flowers to flavour a herb jelly, or a vinegar. Equally the flowers can be crystallized.

Lavender Biscuits

100g/4oz butter
50g/2oz caster sugar
175g/6oz self-raising flour
2 tablespoons fresh chopped lavender leaves
1 teaspoon lavender flowers removed from spike

Lavender biscuits

Cream the sugar and butter together until light. Add the flour and lavender leaves to the butter mixture. Knead well until it forms a dough. Gently roll out on a lightly floured board. Scatter the flowers over the rolled dough and lightly press in with the rolling pin. Cut into small rounds with cutter. Place biscuits on a greased baking sheet. Bake in a hot oven 450°F/230°C, Gas mark 7 for 10-12 minutes until golden and firm. Remove at once and cool on a wire tray.

Lavender herb jelly

MEDICINAL

Throughout history, lavender has been used medicinally to soothe, sedate and suppress. Nowadays it is the essential oil that is in great demand.

The oil was traditionally inhaled to prevent vertigo and fainting. It is an excellent remedy for burns and stings, and its strong antibacterial action helps to heal cuts. The oil also kills diphtheria and typhoid bacilli as well as streptococcus and pneumococcus.

Add 6 drops of oil to bath water to calm irritable children and help them sleep. Place 1 drop on the temple for a headache relief. Blend for use as a massage oil in aromatherapy for throat infections, skin sores, inflammation, rheumatic aches, anxiety, insomnia and depression. The best oil is made from distillation, and may be bought from many shops.

OTHER USES

Rub fresh flowers onto skin or pin a sprig on clothes to discourage flies. Use flowers in potpourri, herb pillows, and linen sachets, where it makes a good moth repellent.

Levisticum officinale

LOVAGE

Also known as Love Parsley, Sea Parsley, Lavose, Liveche, Smallage and European Lovage. From the family Umbelliferae.

This native of the Mediterranean can now be found naturalized throughout the temperate regions of the world, including Australia, North America and Scandinavia.

Lovage was used by the ancient Greeks, who chewed the seed to aid digestion and relieve flatulence. Knowledge of it was handed down to Benedictine monks by the Romans, who prescribed the seeds for the same complaints. In Europe a decoction of lovage was reputedly a good aphrodisiac that no witch worthy of the name could be without. The name is likely to have come from the Latin 'ligusticum', after Liguria in Italy, where the herb grew profusely.

Because lovage leaves have a deodorising and antiseptic effect on the skin, they were laid in the shoes of travellers in the Middle Ages to revive their weary feet, like latter-day odour eaters.

Lovage *Levisticum officinale*

SPECIES

Levisticum officinale
Lovage
Hardy perennial. Ht up to 2m (6ft), spread 1m (3ft) or more. Tiny, pale, greenish-yellow flowers in summer clusters. Leaves darkish green, deeply divided, and large toothed.
A close relation, **Ligusticum scoticum**, shorter with white clusters of flowers, is sometimes called lovage. It can be used in the same culinary way, but lacks its strong flavour and the growth.

CULTIVATION

Propagation
Seed
Sow under protection in spring into prepared plug or seed trays and cover with Perlite; a bottom heat of 15°C (60°F) is helpful. When the seedlings are large enough to handle and after a period of hardening off, transplant into a prepared site in the garden 60cm (2ft) apart.

Division
The roots of an established plant can be divided in the spring or autumn. Make sure that each division has some new buds showing.

Pests and Diseases
Leaf miners are sometimes a problem. Watch out for the first tunnels, pick off the affected leaves and destroy them, otherwise broad dry patches will develop and the leaves will start to wither away. To control this, cut the plant right down to the ground, burning the affected shoots. Give the plant a feed and it will shoot with new growth. The young growth is just what one needs for cooking.

Maintenance
Spring: Divide established plants.
Summer: Clip established plants to encourage new shoots.
Autumn: Sow seed in garden.
Winter: No need for protection.

Garden Cultivation
Lovage prefers a rich, moist but well-drained soil. Prior to first planting, dig the ground over deeply and manure well. The site can be either in full sun or partial shade. Seeds are best sown in the garden in the autumn. When the seedlings are large enough, thin to

60cm (2ft) apart. It is important that lovage has a period of dormancy so that it can complete the growth cycle.

Lovage is a tall plant, so position it carefully. It will reach its full size in 3-5 years. To keep the leaves young and producing new shoots, cut around the edges of the clumps.

Harvest

After the plant has flowered the leaves tend to have more of a bitter taste so harvest in early summer. I personally believe that lovage does not dry that well and it is best to freeze it. (See page 237 and use the Parsley technique).

Harvest seed heads when the seeds start to turn brown. Pick them on a dry day, tie a paper bag over their heads, and hang upside down in a dry, airy place. Use, like celery seed, for winter soups.

Dig the root for drying in the autumn of the second or third season.

CONTAINER GROWING

Lovage is fine grown outside in a large container. To keep it looking good, keep it well-clipped. I do not advise letting it run to flower unless you can support it. Remember at flowering stage, even in a pot, it can be in excess of 1.5m (5ft) tall.

WARNING

As lovage is very good at reducing water retention, people who are pregnant or who have kidney problems should not take this herb medicinally.

CULINARY

Lovage is an essential member of any culinary herb collection. The flavour is reminiscent of celery. It adds a meaty flavour to foods and is used in soups, stews and stocks. Also add fresh young leaves to salads, and rub on chicken, and round salad bowls.

Crush seeds in bread and pastries, sprinkle on salads, rice and mashed potato. If using the rootstock as a vegetable in casseroles, remove the bitter tasting skin.

Lovage Soup

Serves 4
25g (1oz) butter
2 medium onions, finely chopped
500g (1lb) potatoes, peeled and diced
4 tablespoons finely chopped lovage leaves
850ml (1¼ pints) chicken or vegetable stock
300ml (½ pint) milk or 1 cup cream
Grated nutmeg
Salt and pepper

Melt the butter in a heavy pan and gently sauté the onions and diced potatoes for 5 minutes until soft. Add the chopped lovage leaves and cook for 1 minute. Pour in the stock, bring to the boil, season with salt and pepper, cover and simmer gently until the potatoes are soft (about 15 minutes). Purée the soup through a sieve or liquidizer and return to a clean pan. Blend in the milk or cream, sprinkle on a pinch of nutmeg and heat through. Do not boil OR IT WILL CURDLE. Adjust seasoning. Delicious hot or cold. Serve garnished with chopped lovage leaves.

Lovage and Carrot
Serves 2

2 teaspoons chopped lovage leaves
3 carrots, grated
1 apple, grated
125g (5oz) plain yoghurt
2 tablespoons mayonnaise
1 teaspoon salt (if needed)
Lettuce leaves
1 onion sliced into rings
Chives

Toss together the grated carrots, apple, lovage, mayonnaise and yoghurt. Arrange the lettuce leaves on a serving dish and fill with the lovage mixture. Decorate with a few raw onions rings, chives and tiny lovage leaves.

Lovage as a Vegetable
Treat lovage as you would spinach. Use the young growth of the plant stalks and leaves. Strip the leaves from the stalks, wash, and cut the stalks up into segments. Bring a pan of water to the boil add the lovage, bring the water back to the boil, cover, and simmer for about 5-7 minutes until tender. Strain the water. Make a white sauce using butter, flour, milk, salt, pepper and grated nutmeg. Add the lovage. Serve and wait for the comments!

Lovage soup

MEDICINAL

Lovage is a remedy for digestive difficulties, gastric catarrh and flatulence. I know of 1 recipe from the West Country – a teaspoon of lovage seed steeped in a glass of brandy, strained and sweetened with sugar. It is taken to settle an upset stomach!

Infuse either seed, leaf or root and take to reduce water retention. Lovage assists in the removal of waste products, acts as a deodorizer, and aids rheumatism.

Its deodorizing and antiseptic properties enable certain skin problems to respond to a decoction added to bath water. This is made with 45-60g (1½-2oz) of root stock in 600ml (1 pint) water. Add to your bath.

Lovage, brandy and sugar settles an upset stomach

Lonicera

HONEYSUCKLE

Also known as Woodbine, Beerbind, Bindweed, Evening Pride, Fairy Trumpets, Honeybind, Irish Vine, Trumpet Flowers, Sweet Suckle, and Woodbind. From the family Caprifoliaceae.

'Come into the garden, Maud,
I am here at the gate alone;
And the woodbine spices are wafted abroad,
And the musk of the rose is blown.'
Lord Alfred Tennyson (1809-1892)

Honeysuckle grows all over northern Europe including Britain and can also be found growing wild in North Africa, Western Asia and North America.

Honeysuckle, *Lonicera ssp*, receives its common name from the old habit of sucking the sweet honey-tasting nectar from the flowers. Generically it is said to have been named after the 16th-century German physician, Lonicer.

Honeysuckle was among the plants that averted the evil powers abroad on May Day and took care of milk, the butter and the cows in the Scottish Highlands and elsewhere. Traditionally it was thought that if honeysuckle was brought into the house, a wedding would follow, and that if the flowers were placed in a girl's bedroom, she would have dreams of love.

Honeysuckle's rich fragrance has inspired many poets, including Shakespeare, who called it woodbind after its notorious habit of climbing up trees and hedges and totally binding them up.

'Where oxlips and the nodding violet grows
quite over-canopied with luscious woodbine . . .'
A Midsummer Night's Dream

The plant appeared in John Gerard's 16th-century herbal; he wrote that 'the flowers steeped in oil and set in the sun are good to anoint the body that is benummed and grown very cold'.

SPECIES

There are many fragrant climbing varieties of this lovely plant. I have only mentioned those with a direct herbal input.

Lonicera x americana
American Honeysuckle
Deciduous perennial. Ht up to 7m (23ft). Strongly fragrant yellow flowers starting in a pink bud turning yellow and finishing with orangish pink throughout the summer. The berries are red, and the leaves are green and oval, the upper ones being united and saucer-like.

Lonicera caprifolium
Deciduous perennial. Ht up to 6m (20ft). The buds of the fragrant flowers are initially pink on opening; they then change to a pale white/pink/yellow as they age and finally turn deeper yellow. Green oval leaves and red berries, which were once fed to chickens. The Latin species name, **caprifolium**, means goats' leaf, reflecting the belief that honeysuckle leaves were a favourite food of goats. This variety and **Lonicera periclymenum** can be found growing wild in hedgerows.

Lonicera periclymenum
Deciduous perennial. This is the taller grower of the two common European honeysuckles, and reaches a height of 7m (23ft). It may live for 50 years. Fragrant yellow flowers appear mid-summer to mid-autumn, followed by red berries. Leaves are oval and dark green with a bluish underside.

Lonicera etrusca
Etruscan Honeysuckle
Semi-evergreen perennial. Ht up to 4m (12ft). Fragrant, pale, creamy yellow flowers which turn deeper yellow to red in autumn and are followed by red berries. Leaves oval, mid-green, with a bluish underside. This is the least hardy of those mentioned here, and should be grown in sun on a south facing wall, and protected in winter where temperatures fall below -3°C (23°F).

Lonicera caprifolium

Lonicera japonica
Japanese Honeysuckle
Semi-evergreen perennial. Ht up to 10m (33ft). Fragrant, pale, creamy white flowers turning yellow as the season progresses, followed by black berries. The leaves are oval and mid-green in colour. In the garden it is apt to build up an enormous tangle of shoots and best allowed to clamber over tree stumps or a low roof or walls. Attempts to train it tidily are a lost cause. Still used in Chinese medicine today.

CULTIVATION

Propagation
Seed
Sow seed in autumn thinly on the surface of a prepared seed or plug tray. Cover with glass and winter outside. Keep an eye on the compost moisture and only water if necessary. Germination may take a long time, it has been known to take 2 seasons, so be patient. A more reliable alternative method is by cuttings.

Cuttings
Take from non-flowering, semi-hardwood shoots in summer and root in a bark, grit, peat mix of compost. Alternatively, take hardwood cuttings in late autumn, leave the cuttings in a cold frame or cold greenhouse for the winter.

Layering
In late spring or autumn honeysuckle is easy to layer. Do not disturb until the following season when it can be severed from its parent.

Pests and Diseases
Grown in too sunny or warm a place, it can become infested with greenfly, blackfly, caterpillars and red spider mites. Use a horticultural soap, and spray the pests according to the manufacturer's instructions.

Maintenance
Spring: Prune established plants.
Summer: Cut back flowering stems after flowering. Take semi-hardwood cuttings.
Autumn: Layer established plants. Lightly prune if necessary.
Winter: Protect certain species in cold winters.

Garden Cultivation
This extremely tolerant, traditional herb garden plant will flourish vigorously in the most unpromising sites. Honeysuckle leaves are among the first to appear, sometimes mid-winter, the flowers appearing in very early summer and deepening in colour after being pollinated by the insects that feed on their nectar. Good as cover for an unsightly wall or to provide a rich summer evening fragrance in an arbour.

Plant in autumn or spring in any fertile, well-drained soil, in sun or semi-shade. The best situation puts its feet in the shade and its head in the sunshine. A position against a north or west wall is ideal or on the shady side of a support such as a tree stump, pole or pergola. Prune in early spring, if need be. Prune out flowering wood or climbers after flowering.

MEDICINAL

An infusion of the heavy perfumed flowers can be taken as a substitute for tea. It is also useful for treating coughs, catarrh and asthma. As a lotion it is good for skin infections.

Recent research has proved that this plant has an outstanding curative action in cases of colitis.

Warning: The berries are poisonous. Large doses cause vomiting.

Harvest
Pick and dry the flowers for potpourris just as they open. This is the best time for scent although they are their palest in colour.

Pick the flowers for use in salads as required. Again the best flavour is before the nectar has been collected, which is when the flower is at its palest.

CULINARY

Add flowers to salads.

CONTAINER GROWING

This is not a plant which springs to mind as a good pot plant, certainly not indoors. But with patience, it makes a lovely mop head standard if carefully staked and trained; use an evergreen variety like **Lonicera japonica**. The compost should be a soil based one. Water and feed regularly throughout the summer and in winter keep in a cold frame or greenhouse and only water occasionally.

OTHER USES
Flowers are strongly scented for potpourris, herb pillows and perfumery. An essential oil was once extracted from the plant to make a very sweet perfume but the yield was extremely low.

Honeysuckle flowers in a fresh summer salad

Malva sylvestris

MALLOW

Also known as Billy Buttons, Pancake Plan, and Cheese Flower. From the family Malvaceae.

Native to Europe, Western Asia and North America, it can be found growing in hedgebanks, field edges, and on road sides and wastelands in sunny situations.

The ancient Latin name given to this herb by Pliny was 'malacho', which was probably derived from 'malachi', the Greek word meaning 'to soften', after the mallow's softening and healing properties. Young mallow shoots were eaten as vegetables, and it was still to be found on vegetable lists in Roman times. Used in the Middle Ages for its calming effect as an antidote to aphrodisiacs and love-potions. The shape of its seed rather than its flowers suggested the folk name.

SPECIES

Malva sylvestris
Common Mallow
Also known as High Mallow, Cheese Flower and Country Mallow. Biennial. Ht 45-90cm (18-36in), spread 60cm (24in). Flower, dark pink or violet form, early summer to autumn. Mid-green leaves, rounded at the base, ivy shaped at stem.

Malva rotundifolia
Dwarf Mallow
Also known as Cheese Plant, Low Mallow and Blue Mallow. Annual. Ht 15-30cm (6-12in), a creeper. Purplish-pink, trumpet-shaped flowers from early summer to mid-autumn. Leaves rounded, slightly lobed and greenish. North American native.

Malva moschata
Musk Mallow
Perennial. Ht 30-80cm (12-32ins), spread 60cm (24in). Rose/pink flowers (sometimes white), late summer to early autumn. Mid-green leaves – kidney-shaped at base, deeply divided at stem – emit musky aroma in warm weather or when pressed.

CULTIVATION

Propagation
Seed
Sow in prepared seed or plug trays in the autumn. Cover lightly with compost (not Perlite). Winter outside, covered with glass. Germination is erratic but should take place in the spring. Plant out seedlings when large enough to handle, 60cm (24in) apart.

Cuttings
Take cuttings from firm basal shoots in late spring or summer. When hardened off the following spring, plant out 60cm (24in) apart into a prepared site.

Pests and Diseases
Mallows can catch the hollyhock rust. There is also a fungus that produces leaf spots and a serious black canker on the stems. If this occurs dig up the plants and destroy them. This is a seed-borne fungus and may be carried into the soil, so change planting site the following season.

Maintenance
Spring: Take softwood cuttings from young shoots.
Summer: Trim after flowering.
Autumn: Sow seed.
Winter: Hardy enough.

Garden Cultivation
Mallows are very tolerant of site, but prefer a well-drained and fertile soil (if too damp they may well need staking in summer), and a sunny position (though semi-shade will do). Sow where it is to flower from late summer to spring. Press gently into the soil, 60cm (24in) apart, and cover with a light compost. Cut back stems after flowering, not only to promote new growth, but also to keep under control and encourage a second flowering. Cut down the stems in autumn.

Harvest
Harvest young leaves for fresh use as required throughout the spring. For use in potpourris, gather for drying in the summer after first flowering.

CONTAINER GROWING

Musk mallow is the best variety to grow in a large container. It can look very dramatic and smells lovely on a warm evening. Water well throughout the growing season, but feed only twice. Maintain as for garden cultivation.

CULINARY

Young tender tips of the common mallow may be used in salads or steamed as a vegetable. Young leaves of the musk mallow can be boiled as a vegetable.

Young leaves of the dwarf mallow can be eaten raw in salads or cooked as a spinach.

Musk Mallow salad

MEDICINAL

Marshmallow (**Althaea officinalis**) is used in preference to the mallows (**Malva ssp**) in herbal medicine. However, a decoction can be used in a compress, or in bath preparations, for skin rashes, boils and ulcers, and in gargles and mouth washes.

Marrubium vulgare

WHITE HOREHOUND

Also known as Horehound and Maribeum. From the family Labiatae.

Common throughout Europe and America, the plant grows wild everywhere from coastal to mountainous areas.

The botanical name comes from the Hebrew 'marrob' which translates as 'bitter juice'. The common name is derived from the old English 'har hune' meaning a downy plant.

SPECIES

Marrubium vulgare
White Horehound
Hardy perennial. Ht 45cm (18in), spread 30cm (12in). Small clusters of white flowers from the second year in midsummer. The leaves are green and wrinkled with an underside of a silver woolly texture. There is also a variegated version.

CULTIVATION

Propagation
Seed
The fairly small seed should be sown in early spring in a seed or plug tray, using the bark, grit, peat mix of compost. Germination takes 2-3 weeks. Prick out into pots or transplant to the garden after a period of hardening off.

Cuttings
Softwood cuttings taken from the new growth in summer usually root within 3-4 weeks. Use the bark, grit, peat mix of compost. Winter under protection in a cold frame or cold greenhouse.

Division
Established clumps benefit from division in the spring.

Pests and Diseases
If it is very wet and cold in winter, the plant can rot off.

Maintenance
Spring: Divide established clumps. Prune new growth to maintain shape. Sow seed.
Summer: Trim after flowering to stop the plant flopping and prevent self-seeding. Take cuttings.
Autumn: Divide only if it has dangerously transgressed its limits.
Winter: Protect only if season excessively wet.

Garden Cultivation
White horehound grows best in well-drained, dryish soil, biased to alkaline, sunny and protected from high winds. Seed can be sown direct into a prepared garden in late spring, once the soil has started to warm up. Thin the seedlings to 30cm (12in) distance apart.

Harvest
The leaves and flowering tops are gathered in the spring, just as the plants come into flower, when the essential oil is at its richest. Use fresh or dried.

CONTAINER GROWING

Horehound can be grown in a large container situated in a sunny position. Use a compost which drains well and do not overwater. Only feed after flowering otherwise it produces lush growth which is too soft.

OTHER USES

Infuse the leaf as a spray for cankerworm in trees.
Mix the infusion with milk and put in a dish as a fly killer. Do not spray!

MEDICINAL

White horehound is still extensively used in cough medicine, and for calming a nervous heart; its property, marrubiin, in small amounts, normalizes an irregular heart beat. The plant has also been used to reduce fevers and treat malaria.

A Cold Cure
Finely chop 9 small horehound leaves. Mix 1 tablespoon of honey and eat slowly to ease sore throat or cough. Repeat several times if necessary.

Cough Sweets

100g/4oz of fresh white horehound leaves
½ teaspoon of crushed aniseed
3 crushed cardamom seeds

Put into 600ml/1pint of water and simmer for 20 minutes. Strain through a filter. Over a low heat, dissolve 350g/12oz of white sugar and 350g/12oz of moist brown sugar in the liquid and boil over a medium heat until the syrup hardens when drops are put into cold water. Pour into an oiled tray. Score when partially cooled. Store in wax paper.

Horehound sweets

Melissa officinalis

LEMON BALM

Also known as Balm, Melissa, Balm Mint, Bee Balm, Blue Balm, Cure All, Dropsy Plant, Garden Balm and Sweet Balm. From the family Labiatae.

This plant is a native of the Mediterranean region and Central Europe. It is now naturalized in North America and as a garden escapee in Britain.

This ancient herb was dedicated to the goddess Diana, and used medicinally by the Greeks some 2,000 years ago. The generic name, *Melissa*, comes from the Greek word for bee and the Greek belief that if you put sprigs of balm in an empty hive it would attract a swarm; equally, if planted nearby bees in residence in a hive they would never go away. This belief was still prevalent in medieval times when sugar was highly priced and honey a luxury.

Melissa officinalis
Lemon Balm
Hardy perennial. Ht 75cm (30in), spread 45cm (18in) or more. Clusters of small, pale yellow/white flowers in summer. The green leaves are oval toothed, slightly wrinkled, and highly aromatic when crushed.

Melissa officinalis 'All Gold'
Golden Lemon Balm
Half-hardy perennial. Ht 60cm (24in), spread 30cm (12in) or more. Clusters of small, pale yellow/white flowers in summer. The leaves are all yellow, oval in shape, toothed, slightly wrinkled and aromatic with a lemon scent when crushed. The leaves are prone to scorching in high summer; also more tender than the other varieties.

left: **Lemon balm** *Melissa officinalis* and **Variegated Lemon Balm** *Melissa officinalis 'Aurea'*

In the Middle Ages lemon balm was used to soothe tension, to dress wounds, as a cure for toothache, mad dog bites, skin eruptions, crooked necks, and sickness during pregnancy. It was even said to prevent baldness, and ladies made linen or silk amulets filled with lemon balm as a lucky love charm.

It has been acclaimed the world over for promoting long life. Prince Llewellyn of Glamorgan drank Melissa tea, so he claimed, every day of the 108 years of his life.

Wild claims apart, as a tonic for melancholy it has been praised by herbal writers for centuries and is still used today in aromatherapy to counter depression.

Melissa officinalis 'Aurea'
Variegated Lemon Balm
Hardy perennial. Ht 60cm (24in), spread 30cm (12in) or more. Clusters of small, pale yellow/white flowers in summer. The green/gold variegated leaves are oval, toothed, slightly wrinkled and aromatic with a lemon scent when crushed. This variety is as hardy as common lemon balm. The one problem is that in high season it reverts to green. To maintain variegation keep cutting back, this in turn will promote new growth which should be variegated.

Lemon balm *Melissa officinalis* **in flower**

left: **Variegated Lemon Balm** *Melissa officinalis 'Aurea'*

CULTIVATION

Propagation

Seed

Common Lemon Balm can be grown from seed. The seed is small but manageable, and it is better to start it off under protection. Sow in prepared seed or plug trays in early spring, using the bark, grit, peat mix of compost and cover with Perlite. Germination takes between 10 and 14 days. The seeds dislike being wet so, after the initial watering, try not to water again until germination starts. When seedlings are large enough to handle, prick out and plant in the garden, 45cm (18in) apart.

Cuttings

The variegated and golden lemon balm can only be propagated by cuttings or division. Take softwood cuttings from the new growth in late spring/early summer. As the cutting material will be very soft take extra care when collecting it.

Division

The root stock is compact but easy to divide (autumn or spring). Replant directly into the garden in a prepared site.

Pests and Diseases

The only problem likely to affect lemon balm is a form of the rust virus; cut the plant back to the ground, dispose of all the infected leaves, including any that may have accidentally fallen on the ground.

Maintenance

Spring: Sow seeds. Divide established plants.
Summer: Keep trimming established plants. Cut back after flowering to help prevent self-seeding.
Autumn: Divide established plants, or any that may have encroached on other plant areas.
Winter: Protect plants if the temperature falls below -5°C (23°F). The plant dies back, leaving but a small presence on the surface of the soil. Protect with a bark or straw mulch or agricultural fleece.

Garden Cultivation

Lemon Balm will grow in almost any soil and in any position. It does prefers a fairly rich, moist soil in sunny position with some midday shade. Keep all plants trimmed around the edges to restrict growth and encourage fresh shoots. In the right soil conditions this can be a very invasive plant. Unlike horseradish, the established roots are not difficult to uproot if things get out of hand.

Harvesting

Pick leaves throughout the summer for fresh use. For drying, pick just before the flowers begin to open when flavour is best; handle gently to avoid bruising. The aroma is rapidly lost, together with much of its therapeutic value, when dried or stored.

CULINARY

Lemon Balm is one of those herbs that smells delicious but tastes like school-boiled cabbage water when cooked.
  Add fresh leaves to vinegar.
  Add leaves to wine cups, teas and beers, or use chopped with fish and mushroom dishes. Mix freshly chopped with soft cheeses.
  It has frequently been incorporated in proprietary cordials for liqueurs and its popularity in France led to its name 'Tea de France'.
  It is used as a flavouring for certain cheeses in parts of Switzerland.

Lemon balm with cream cheese

MEDICINAL

Lemon Balm tea is said to relieve headaches and tension and to restore the memory. It is also good to drink after meals to ease the digestion, flatulence and colic. Use fresh or frozen leaves in infusions because the volatile oil tends to disappear during the drying process.
  The isolated oil used in aromatherapy is recommended for nervousness, depression, insomnia and nervous headaches. It also helps eczma sufferers.

OTHER USES

This is a most useful plant to keep bees happy. The flower may look boring to you but it is sheer heaven to them. So plant lemon balm around beehives or orchards to attract pollinating bees.

CONTAINER GROWING

If you live in an area that suffers from very cold winters, the gold form would benefit from being grown in containers. This method suits those with a small garden who do not want a takeover bid from lemon balm. Use the bark, peat, grit mix of compost. Only feed with liquid fertilizer in the summer, otherwise the growth will become too lush and soft, and aroma and colour diminished. Water normally throughout the growing season. Allow the container to become very dry (but not totally) in winter, and keep the pots in a cool, protected environment.

Mentha

MINT

From the family Labiatae.

The *Mentha* family is a native of Europe that has naturalized in many parts of the world, including North America, Australia and Japan. Mint has been cultivated for its medicinal properties since ancient times and has been found in Egyptian tombs dating back to 1,000 BC. The Japanese have been growing it to obtain menthol for at least 2,000 years. In the Bible the Pharisees collected tithes in mint, dill and cumin. Charlemagne, who was very keen on herbs, ordered people to grow it. The Romans brought it with them as they marched through Europe and into Britain, from where it found its way to America with the settlers.

Its name was first used in Greek mythology. There are two different stories, the first that the nymph Minthe was being chatted up by Hades, god of the Underworld. His queen Sephony became jealous and turned her into the plant, mint. The second that Minthe was a nymph beloved by Pluto, who transformed her into the scented herb after his jealous wife took umbrage.

SPECIES

The mint family is large and well known. I have chosen a few to illustrate the diversity of the species.

Mentha arvensis var. piperascens
Japanese Peppermint
Hardy perennial. Ht 60cm-1m (2-3ft), spread 60cm (24in) and more. Loose purplish whorls of flowers in summer. Leaves, downy, oblong, sharply toothed and green grey; they provides an oil (90 per cent menthol), said to be inferior to the oil produced by **M. piperita**. This species is known as English mint in Japan.

Mentha aquatica
Water Mint
Hardy perennial. Ht 15-60cm (6-24in), spread indefinite. Pretty purple/lilac flowers, all summer. Leaves soft, slightly downy, mid-green in colour. The scent can vary from a musty mint to a strong peppermint. This should be planted in water or very wet marshy soil. It can be found growing wild around pounds and streams.

Mentha x gracilis (Mentha x gentilis)
Ginger Mint
Also known as Scotch Mint. Hardy perennial. Ht 45cm (18in), spread 60cm (24in). The stem has whorls of small, 2-lipped, mauve flowers in summer. The leaf is variegated, gold/green with serrated edges. The flavour is a delicate, warm mint that combines well in salads and tomato dishes.

Mentha longifolia
Buddleia Mint
Hardy perennial. Ht 80cm (32in), spread indefinite. Long purple/mauve flowers that look very like buddleia (hence its name). Long grey-green leaves with a musty minty scent. Very good plant for garden borders.

Mentha x piperita
Peppermint
Also known as Mentha d'Angleterre, Mentha Anglais, Pfefferminze and Englisheminze.
Hardy perennial. Ht 30-60cm (12-24in), spread indefinite. Pale purple flowers in summer. Pointed leaves, darkish green with a reddish tinge, serrated edges. Very peppermint scented. This is the main medicinal herb of the genus. There are 2 species worth looking out for – black peppermint, with leaves much darker, nearly brown, and white peppermint, with leaves green, tinged with reddish brown.

above: **Ginger mint**
Mentha x gracilis

Mentha x piperita citrata
Eau de Cologne Mint
Also known as Orange Mint and Bergamot Mint. Hardy perennial. Ht 60-80cm (24-32in), spread indefinite. Purple/mauve flowers in summer. Purple tinged, roundish, dark green leaves. A delicious scent that has been described as lemon, orange, bergamot, lavender, as well as eau de cologne. This plant is a vigorous grower. Use in fruit dishes with discretion. Best use is in the bath.

Mentha x piperita citrata 'Basil'
Basil Mint
Hardy perennial. Ht 45-60cm (18-24in), spread indefinite. Purple/mauve flowers in summer. Leaves green with a reddish tinge, more pointed than Eau de cologne. The scent is unique, a sweet and spicy mint scent that combines well with tomato dishes, especially pasta.

Mentha x piperita citrata 'Lemon'
Lemon Mint
Hardy perennial. Ht 45-60cm (18-24in), spread indefinite. Purple whorl of flowers in summer. Green serrated leaf, refreshing minty lemon scent. Good as a mint sauce, or with fruit dishes.

Mentha pulegium
Pennyroyal
Hardy semi-evergreen perennial Ht 15cm (6in) creeper, spread indefinite. Mauve flowers in spring. Bright green leaves, very strong peppermint scent. There is so much to write about this plant, it has got its own section, see pages 120-121.

Mentha requienii
Corsican Mint
Also known as Rock mint. Hardy semi-evergreen perennial. Ground cover, spread indefinite. Tiny purple flowers throughout the summer. Tiny bright green leaves, which, when crushed, smell strongly of peppermint. Suits a rock garden or paved path, grows naturally in cracks of rocks. Needs shade and moist soil.

Mentha spicata
Spearmint
Also known as Garden mint and Common mint. Hardy perennial. Ht 45-60cm (18-24in), spread indefinite. Purple/mauve flowers in summer. Green pointed leaves with serrated edges. The most widely grown of all mints. Good for mint sauce, mint jelly, mint julep.

Mentha spicata 'Crispa'
Curly Mint
Hardy perennial. Ht 45-60cm (18-24in), spread indefinite. Light mauve flowers in spring. When I first saw this mint I thought it had a bad attack of aphid, but it has grown on me! The leaf is bright green and crinkled, its serrated edge slightly frilly. Flavour very similar to spearmint, so good in most culinary dishes.

left: **Pineapple mint**
Mentha suaveolens 'Variegata'

Mentha spicata 'Moroccan'
Moroccan Mint
Hardy perennial. Ht 45-60cm (18-24in), spread indefinite. White flowers in summer. Bright green leaves with a texture and excellent mint scent. This is the one I use for all the basic mint uses in the kitchen. A clean mint flavour and scent, lovely with yoghurt and cucumber.

Mentha suaveolens
Apple Mint
Hardy perennial. Ht 60cm-1m (2-3ft), spread indefinite. Mauve flowers in summer. Roundish hairy leaves. Tall vigorous grower. Gets its name from its scent, which is a combination of mint and apples. More subtle than some mints, so good in cooking.

Mentha suaveolens 'Variegata'
Pineapple Mint
Hardy perennial. Ht 45-60cm (18-24in), spread indefinite. Seldom produces flowers, all the energy going into producing very pretty cream and green, slightly hairy leaves that look good in the garden. Not a rampant mint. Grows well in hanging baskets.

Apple mint *Mentha sauveolens*

Buddleia mint
Mentha longifolia

Mentha x villosa alopecuroides Bowles' Mint
Bowles Mint
Hardy perennial. Ht 60cm-1m (2-3ft), spread indefinite. Mauve flowers, round, slightly hairy green leaves, vigorous grower. Sometimes called incorrectly Applemint. Has acquired reputation as 'The Connoisseur's Culinary Mint'. Not sure I agree, but mint tastes do vary.

above: **Corsican mint**
Mentha requienii

Pycnanthemum pilosum
Mountain Mint
Hardy perennial. Ht 90cm (3ft), spread 60cm (2ft). Knot-like white/pink flowers, small and pretty in summer. Leaves long, thin, pointed, and grey-green with a good mint scent and flavour. Not a **Mentha**, and therefore not a true mint, and does not spread. Looks very attractive in a border, and is to butterflies. Any soil will support it provided not too rich.

Ginger mint
Mentha x gracilis

CULTIVATION

Propagation
Seed
The seed on the market is not worthwhile – leaf flavour is inferior and quite often it does not run true to species.

Cuttings
Root cuttings of mint are very easy. Simply dig up a piece of root. Cut it where you can see a little growing node (each piece will produce a plant) and place the cuttings either into a plug or seed tray. Push them into the compost (bark, peat mix). Water in and leave. This can be done any time during the growing season. If taken in spring, in about 2 weeks you should see new shoots emerging through the compost.

Division
Dig up plants every few years and divide, or they will produce root runners all over the place. Each bit of root will grow, so take care.
Corsican mint does not set root runners. Dig up a section in spring and divide by easing the plant apart and replanting.

Pests and Diseases
Mint rust appears as little rusty spots on the leaves. Remove them immediately, otherwise the rust will wash off into the soil and the spores spread to other plants. One sure way to be rid is to burn the affected patch. This effectively sterilizes the ground.
Another method, which I found in an old gardening book, is to dig up the roots in winter when the plants are dormant, and clean off the soil under a tap. Heat some water to a temperature of 40-46°C (105°-115°F) and pour into a bowl. Place the roots in the water for 10 minutes. Remove the runners and wash at once in cold water. Replant in the garden well away from the original site.

Maintenance
Spring: Dig up root if cuttings are required. Split established plants if need be.
Summer: Give plants a hair cut to promote new growth. Control the spread of unruly plants.
Autumn: Dig up roots for forcing. Bring in containers.
Winter: Sterilize roots if rust evident during growing season.

Garden Cultivation
Mint is one of those plants that will walk all over the plot if not severely controlled. Also, mint readily hybridizes itself, varying according to environmental factors.
If choosing a plant in a nursery or garden centre rub the leaf first to check the scent. Select a planting site in sun or shade but away from other mints. Planted side by side they seem to loose their individual scent and flavour.
To inhibit spread, sink a large bottomless container (bucket or bespoke frame) in a well-drained and fairly rich soil to a depth of at least 30cm (12in), leaving a small ridge above soil level. Plant the mint in the centre.

Harvest
Pick the leaves for fresh use throughout the growing season. Pick leaves for drying or freezing before the mint flowers.

COMPANION PLANTING

Spearmint or peppermint planted near roses will deter aphids. Buddleia mint will attract hover flies.

OTHER USES

Pick a bunch of eau de cologne mint, tie it up with string, and hang it under the hot water tap when you are drawing a bath. You will scent not only your bath, but the whole house. It is very uplifting (unless you too have a young son, who for some reason thinks it is 'gross').

Curly mint
Mentha spicata 'Crispa' See p117

Chocolate mint mousse

CULINARY

With due respect to their cuisine, the French are always rude about our 'mint sauce with lamb'; they reckon it is barbaric. On the other side of the Channel they use mint less than other countries in cooking. But slowly, even in France, this herb is gaining favour.

Mint is good in vinegars and jellies. Peppermint makes a great tea. And there are many many uses for mint in cooking with fish, meat, yoghurt, fruit, and so on. Here is a recipe for chocoholics like me:

Chocolate Mint Mousse
Serves 2

*100g (4oz) plain dark chocolate
2 eggs, separated
1 teaspoon instant coffee
1 teaspoon fresh chopped mint,
  either Moroccan, spearmint or
  curly
Whipped cream for decoration
4 whole mint leaves*

Melt the chocolate either in a microwave, or in a double saucepan. When smooth and liquid, remove from heat. Beat egg yolks and add to the chocolate while hot (this will cook the yolks slightly). Add coffee and chopped mint.

Leave the mixture to cool for about 15 minutes. Beat the egg whites (not too stiff) and fold them into the cooling chocolate mixture. Spoon into containers. When you are ready to serve put a blob of whipped cream in the middle and garnish with whole leaves.

CONTAINER GROWING (AND FORCING)

Mint is good in containers. Make sure the container is large enough, use a soil-based compost, and do not let the compost dry out. Feed regularly throughout the growing season with a liquid fertilizer. Place the container in semi-shade.

One good reason for growing mint in containers is to prolong the season. This is called forcing. In early autumn dig up some root. Fill a container, or wooden box lined with plastic, with compost. Lay the root down its length and cover lightly with compost. Water in and place in a light, warm glasshouse or warm conservatory (even the kitchen windowsill will do). Keep an eye on it, and fresh shoots should sprout within a couple of weeks. This is great for fresh mint sauce for Christmas.

MEDICINAL

Peppermint is aromatic, calmative, antiseptic, anti-spasmodic, anti-inflammatory, anti-bacterial, anti-parasitic, and is also a stimulant. It can be used in a number of ways for a variety of complaints including gastro-intestinal disorders where anti-spasmodic, anti-flatulent and appetite- promoting stimulation is required. It is particularly useful for nervous headaches, and as a way to increase concentration. Externally, peppermint oil can be used in a massage to relieve muscular pain.

WARNING

The oil may cause an allergic reaction. Avoid prolonged intake of inhalants from the oil, which must never be used by babies.

Black peppermint tea

Mentha pulegium

PENNYROYAL

Also known as European Pennyroyal and Pudding Grass. From the family Labiatae.

This herb is a native of Europe including North Africa and now widespread in comparable climates.

Pulegium is derived from the latin 'pulex', meaning flea because both the fresh plant and the smoke from the burning leaves were used to exterminate the insect.

Puliol was an old French name for Thyme and this plant was designated Royal Thyme, thence Puliol Royale and the corruption Pennyroyal. Today the French name is La Mentha Pouliot, which reflects this history.

Long ago, the wise women of the village used pennyroyal to induce abortion. It has since been used to facilitate menstruation.

The Elizabethan Herbalist John Gerard called it Pudding Grass. He claimed it would purify corrupt water on sea voyages and that it would cure 'swimming in the head and the pains and giddiness thereof'.

Creeping Pennyroyal *Mentha pulegium*

SPECIES

Mentha pulegium
Pennyroyal
Also known as Creeping Pennyroyal.
Semi-evergreen hardy perennial. Ht 15cm (6in). A creeper, spread indefinite. Mauve flowers in late spring. Bright green leaves, very strong peppermint scent.

Mentha pulegium 'Upright'
Pennyroyal Upright
Semi-evergreen hardy perennial. Ht 30cm (12in). Spread indefinite. Mauve flowers in late spring. Bright green leaves, very strong peppermint scent.
The American pennyroyal is **Hedeoma pulegioides** or Rock Pennyroyal. It has a similar aroma and usages to the European pennyroyal.

CULTIVATION

Propagation
Seed
Pennyroyal upright can be grown from seed and come true to species unlike most mints. The seed is very fine, so sow under protection in prepared seed or plug trays in late spring, then cover with Perlite. Germination is 10-20 days. Leave to become well established before planting out in early summer and leave at least 30cm (12in) between plants.

Cuttings

Both can be propagated by root cuttings. Unlike ordinary mint, which travels underground, the pennyroyals travel on the surface, and where the plant touches the soil there a small root system develops.

Dig up a plant in late spring and divide into small clumps. The miniature root systems are ideal for putting in prepared plug trays with the bark, peat, grit mix of compost. Water in well; they will be fully rooted in 4 weeks.

Division

If the plant becomes invasive in the garden, simply remove a section.

Pests and Diseases

Pennyroyal can suffer from leaf rotting mildew if too wet in winter or spring. Pick off any damaged leaves. If the plant is in a container and the weather is mild enough, put it outside and allow the air to get at it. Also, cut back on watering.

Maintenance

Spring: Sow seed. Divide established plants.
Summer: Cut back after flowering.
Autumn: Divide plants. Dig up some plants to winter in a cold frame or greenhouse.
Winter: Although this mint is hardy it hates wet winters followed by frosts. It will also suffer if the temperature falls consistently below -8°C (18°F). It is difficult to protect because if you lay a mulch over it the leaves will rot off. Therefore as a precaution dig up in the Autumn and winter it in a cold frame or greenhouse.

Garden Cultivation

This mint prefers a rich but free-draining soil in a sunny spot, but – this may seem a contradiction – it does like water in summer, so water freely. The creeping pennyroyal can be grown as aromatic ground cover, but make sure that the ground is very free draining, does not get over wet in winter, and offers protection from hard frosts.

Harvest

Pick leaves as required for use fresh. Pick either side of flowering for freezing purposes. Not worth drying.

CONTAINER GROWING

Both pennyroyals are good in containers. When the upright pennyroyal flowers it sends out long branches covered in little circles of mauve flowers. Use the bark, peat, grit mix of compost. Feed during flowering with a liquid fertilizer.

MEDICINAL

It has long been considered dangerous to use when pregnant because it is abortive. However, it has now been found that only the oil produced from the plant is active in this way. This oil, which is highly toxic, also leads to irreversible kidney damage. Therefore it should only be prescribed by a professional.

In a hot infusion this herb has always been a favourite remedy for colds as it promotes sweating.

American Pennyroyal, Hedeoma pulegioides, has similar properties and uses. It is also an antispasmodic and calmative, and is used in minor gastric disturbances, flatulence, nausea, head-aches and menstrual pain.

An excellent insect repellent, pennyroyal can be used to divert the path of ants, too.

CULINARY

This mint has a very strong peppermint scent and flavour, so use sparingly in dishes.

It makes a strong mint sauce, and is a good substitute for peppermint in water ice.

WARNING

Not to be used in pregnancy or if suffering from kidney disease. May cause contact dermatitis.

OTHER USES

If you rub pennyroyal in the path of an army of ants, it will re-route them.

More practically, if you grow pennyroyal outside the kitchen door, it will prevent ants entering the house.

If you rub leaves onto bare skin it acts as a very good insect repellent. Equally, if you rub a leaf on a mosquito or horsefly bite, the itch will disappear. I have rubbed it on a wasp sting and it has brought relief.

Monarda

BERGAMOT

Also known as Oswego Tea, Bee Balm, Blue Balm, High Balm, Low Balm, Mountain Balm and Mountain Mint. From the family Labiatae.

This beautiful plant with its flamboyant flower is a native of North America and is now grown horticulturally in many countries throughout the world.

The species name Monarda honours the Spanish medicinal botanist Dr Nicholas Monardes of Seville who, in 1569, wrote a herbal on the flora of America. The common name, Bergamot, is said to have come from the scent of the crushed leaf which resembles the small bitter Italian Bergamot orange (*Citrus bergamia*), from which oil is produced that is used in aromatherapy, perfumes and cosmetics.

The wild or purple Bergamot (*Monarda didyma*) grows around the Oswego river district near Lake Ontario in the United States. The Indians in this region used it for colds and bronchial complaints as it contains the powerful antiseptic, Thymol. They also made tea from it, hence Oswego Tea that was drunk in many American households, replacing Indian tea, following the Boston Tea Party of 1773.

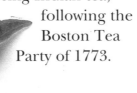

SPECIES

There are many species and cultivars of Bergamot, too many to mention here, so I have included some from each of the species.

Monarda 'Beauty of Cobham'
Bergamot Beauty of Cobham Hardy perennial. Ht 75cm (30in), spread 45cm (18in). Attractive dense 2-lipped pale pink flowers throughout summer. Toothed mid-green aromatic leaves.

Monarda 'Blaustrumpf'
Bergamot Blue Stocking Hardy perennial. Ht 80cm (32in), spread 45cm (18in). Attractive purple flowers throughout summer. Aromatic, green, pointed foliage.

Monarda 'Cambridge Scarlet'
Bergamot Cambridge Scarlet Hardy perennial. Ht 1m (3ft), spread 45cm (18in). Striking rich red flowers throughout summer. Aromatic, slightly hairy leaves of a mid-green colour.

Monarda didyma
Bergamot (Bee Balm Red) Hardy perennial. Ht 80cm (2.5ft), spread 45cm (18in). Fantastic red flowers throughout summer. Aromatic, mid-green foliage.

Monarda 'Schneewittchen'
Bergamot Snow Maiden Hardy perennial. Ht 80cm (2.5ft), spread 45cm (18in). Very attractive white flowers throughout summer. Aromatic, mid-green, pointed leaves.

Monarda 'Croftway Pink'
Bergamot Croftway Pink Hardy perennial. Ht 1m (3 ft), spread 45cm (18in). Soft pink flowers throughout summer. Aromatic green leaves.

Monarda 'Prarienacht'
Bergamot Prarie Night
Hardy perennial. Ht 1m
(3ft), spread 45cm (18in).
Attractive purple flowers
throughout summer.
Aromatic, mid-green,
pointed leaves.

CULTIVATION

Propagation
Seed
Only species will grow true
from seed. Cultivars (i.e.
named varieties) will not.
  Sow the very small seed
indoors in the spring on the
surface of either seed or
plug trays or on individual
pots. Cover with Perlite.
Germination is better with
added warmth 21°C (65°F).
Thin or transplant the
strongest seedlings when
large enough to handle.
Harden off. Plant in the
garden at a distance of 45cm
(18in) apart.

Cuttings
Take first shoots in early
summer, as soon as they are
7.5-10cm (3-4in) long.

Division
Divide in early spring. Either
grow on in pots, or replant
in the garden, making sure
the site is well prepared with
well-rotted compost.
Planting distance from other
plants 45cm (18in).

Pests and Diseases
Bergamot is prone to
powdery grey mildew. At the
first sign remove leaves. If it
gets out of hand cut the
plant back to ground level.
  Young plants are a *bonne
bouche* for slugs!

Maintenance
Spring: Sow seeds of species.
Divide roots. Dig up 3-year-
old plants, divide and
replant.
Summer: Take cuttings of
cultivars and species, if
desired.

Autumn: Cut back to the
ground, and give a good
feed with manure or
compost.
Winter: All perennial
Bergamots die right back in
winter. In hard winters
protect with a mulch.

Garden Cultivation
Bergamot is a highly
decorative plant with long-
lasting, distinctively fragrant
flowers that are very
attractive to bees, hence
the country name Bee Balm.
  All grow well in moist,
nutrient-rich soil, preferably
in a semi-shady spot;
deciduous woodland is ideal.
However, they will tolerate
full sun provided the soil
retains moisture. Like many
other perennials bergamot
should be dug up and
divided every three years,
and the dead centre
discarded.

Harvest
Pick leaves as desired for use
fresh in the kitchen. For
drying, harvest before the
flower opens.
  Cut flowers for drying as
soon as fully opened. They
will dry beautifully and keep
their colour.
  It is only worth collecting
seed if you have species
plants situated well apart in
the garden. If near one
another, cross-pollination
will make the seed variable –
very jolly provided you don't
mind unpredictably mixed
colours. Collect the flower
heads when they turn
brown.

CONTAINER GROWING

Bergamot is too tall for a
window box, but it can look
very attractive growing in a
large pot, say 35-45 cm (14-
18in) across, or tub as long
as the soil can be kept moist
and the plant be given some
afternoon shade.

CULINARY

Pick the small flower petals
separately and scatter over a
green salad at the last
moment. Put fresh leaf in
China tea for an Earl Grey
flavour, and into wine cups
and lemonade. The
chopped leaves can be
added sparingly to salads
and stuffings, and can also
be used in jams and jellies.

Pork Fillets with Bergamot Sauce
Serves 2

2 large pork fillets
75g (3oz/6 tablespoons) butter
2 shallots, very finely chopped
40g (1½oz/2½)tablespoons
  flour
4 tablespoons dry white wine
3½ tablespoons chopped
  bergamot leaves
salt, black pepper
1 tablespoon double cream

Pre-heat the oven to 200°C/
400°F/Gas mark 6.
  Wash the fillets of pork. Pat
dry, season and smear with
half the butter.
  Roast in a shallow greased
tin for 25 minutes. Allow to
rest for 5 minutes before
slicing. Arrange slices in
warmed serving dish.
  Prepare this sauce while
the fillets are in the oven:
Sweat the shallots in half the

butter until soft. Stir in the
flour and cook for about a
minute, stirring all the time.
Whisk in the stock. Simmer
until it thickens, stirring
occasionally. Then slowly
add the wine and 3
tablespoons of the chopped
bergamot. Simmer for
several minutes then season
to taste. Remove from heat,
stir in the cream, pour over
arranged pork slices, garnish
with remaining chopped
bergamot.
  Serve with mashed potato,
and fresh green broccoli.

OTHER USES
Because the dried Bergamot
flowers keep their fragrance
and colour so well, they are
an important ingredient in
potpourris.
  The oil is sometimes used
in perfumes, but should not
be confused with the
similarly smelling bergamot
orange.

MEDICINAL

*Excellent herb tea to relieve
nausea, flatulence, menstrual
pain and vomiting.*
  *Aromatherapists have
found bergamot oil good for
depression, as well as
helping the body to fight
infections.*

Myrrhis odorata

SWEET CICELY

Also known as Anise, Myrrh, Roman Plant, Sweet Bracken, Sweet Fern and Switch.
From the family Umbelliferae.

Sweet Cicely was once cultivated as a pot shrub in Europe and is a native of this region and other temperate countries.

The Greeks called Sweet Cicely 'seselis' or 'seseli'. It is logical to suppose that 'Cicely' was derived from them, 'sweet' coming from its flavour.

In the 16th century John Gerard recommended the boiled roots as a pick-me-up for people who were 'dull'. According to Culpeper, the roots were thought to prevent infection by the plague.

In South Wales, Sweet Cicely is quite often seen growing in graveyards, planted around the head stones to commemorate a loved one.

In the Lake District, Sweet Bracken (Cicely) was not only used in puddings but also for rubbing upon oak panels to make the wood shine and smell good.

CULTIVATION

Propagation
Seed
Sow the seed when ripe in early autumn. Use prepared plug or seed trays and, as the seed is so large, sow only 1 per plug and cover with compost. Then cover the trays with glass and leave outside for the whole winter. The seed requires several months of cold winter temperatures to germinate. Keep a check on the compost, making sure it does not dry out. When germination starts bring the trays into a cold greenhouse. A spring sowing can be

SPECIES

Myrrhis odorata
Sweet Cicely
Hardy perennial. Ht 60-90cm (2-3ft), spread 60cm (2ft) or more. The small white flowers appear in umbels from spring to early summer. The seeds are long, first green, turning black on ripening. The leaves are fern-like, very divided, and smell of aniseed when crushed.

The following plant is called Sweet Cicely in North America. It is unrelated to the European one, but used in a similar way.

Osmorhiza longistylis
Also known as Anise Root, Sweet Anise and Sweet Chervil.
Perennial. Ht 45-90cm (18-36in). Inconspicuous white flowers appear in loose compound umbels in summer. The leaves are oval to oblong and grow in groups of 3. The whole plant has an aniseed odour. Its roots used to be nibbled by children for their anise liquorice flavour.

Sweet Cicely *Myrrhis odorata*

successful provided the seed is first put in a plastic bag mixed with a small amount of damp sharp sand, refrigerated for 4 weeks, and then sown as normal in prepared seed or plug trays. When the seedlings are large enough to handle, which is not long after germination, and after the frosts are over, transplant to a prepared site in the garden, 60cm (2ft) apart.

Root Cuttings

The tap root may be lifted in spring or autumn, cut into sections each with a bud, and replanted either in prepared plug trays or direct into a prepared site in the garden at a depth of 5 cm (2in).

Division

Divide the plant in autumn when the top growth dies down.

Pests and Diseases

Sweet Cicely is, in the majority of cases, free from pests and disease.

Maintenance

Spring: Take root cuttings.
Summer: Cut back after flowering, to produce new leaves and to stop self-seeding.
Autumn: Sow seeds. Divide established plants. Take root cuttings.
Winter: No need for protection.

Garden Cultivation

It is one of the first garden herbs to emerge after winter and is almost the last to die down, and is therefore a most useful plant.

If you have a light well-drained poor soil you may find that Sweet Cicely spreads all round the garden, and when you try to dig out established plants that the tap root is very long; even a tiny bit remaining will produce another plant. On the soil at my farm, which is heavy clay, it is a lovely plant, however, remaining just where it was planted in a

totally controlled fashion.

The situation it likes best is a well-draining soil, rich in humus, and light shade. If the seed is not wanted for propagation or winter flavouring, the whole plant should be cut down immediately after flowering. A new batch of leaves will soon develop.

Sweet Cicely is not suitable for growing in humid areas because it needs a good dormant period before winter to produce its root and lush foliage.

Harvest

Pick young leaves at any time for fresh use.

Collect unripe seeds when green; ripe seeds when dark brown.

The foliage and seed do not dry or freeze, but the ripe seed stores well in a dry container.

Dig up roots for drying in autumn when the plant has died back.

CONTAINER GROWING

As this herb has a very long tap root it does not grow happily in a container. But it can be done. Choose a container that will give the root room to grow, and use the bark, peat mix of compost. Place it in a semi-shady place and keep it well watered throughout the growing season.

MEDICINAL

This herb is now rarely used medicinally. The boiled root is said to be a tonic for the teenager and the elderly.

Sweet Cicely wine

CULINARY

The root can be cooked as a vegetable and served with butter or a white sauce, or allow to cool and chop up for use in salads. Alternatively, it can be eaten raw, or peeled and grated, and served in a French salad dressing. It is difficult to describe the flavour – think of parsnip, add a hint of aniseed. The root makes a very good wine.

Toss unripe seeds, which have a sweet flavour and a nutty texture, into fruit salads. Chop into ice cream. Use ripe seeds whole in cooked dishes such as apple pie, otherwise use crushed.

The leaf flavour is sweet aniseed. Chop finely and stir in salads, dressings and omelettes. Add to soups, stews and to boiling water when cooking cabbage.

Add to cream for a sweeter, less fatty taste. It is a valuable sweetener, especially for diabetics but also for the many people who are trying to reduce their sugar intake.

When cooking tart fruit, such as rhubarb, plums, gooseberries, red or black currants, add 2-4 teaspoons of dried Sweet Cicely. Or, as I do sometimes, mix a handful of large fresh leaves with some lemon balm and add to the boiling water in which the fruit is to be stewed. It gives a delightful flavour and helps to save almost half the sugar needed.

OTHER USES

This is one of the first nectar plants to appear in the spring, so it is valuable to the beekeeper.

Myrtus communis

MYRTLE

From the family Myrtaceae.

Myrtle *Myrtus communis* **in flower**

SPECIES

Myrtus communis
Myrtle
Half-hardy evergreen perennial. Ht and spread 2-3m (6-10ft). Fragrant white flowers from spring to mid-summer, each with a dense cluster of golden stamens; followed by dark, purple-black fruits. The leaves are oval, glossy, dark green and aromatic.

Myrtle communis 'Variegata'
Variegated Myrtle
Half-hardy evergreen perennial. Ht and spread 1-2m (3-6ft). Fragrant white flowers from spring to mid-summer, each with a hint of pink, and a dense cluster of golden stamens; followed by dark, purple-black fruits. Leaves are oval and dark green with silver variegation, and a pink tinge in autumn.

Myrtle communis ssp. tarentina
Tarentina Myrtle
Half-hardy evergreen perennial. Ht and spread 1-2m (3-6ft). Fragrant white flowers from spring to mid-summer, each with a dense cluster of golden stamens; followed by dark, purple-black fruits. Leaves are small and oval, dark green and aromatic. This myrtle is a good hedge in mild areas. Plant 60cm (24in) apart.

Myrtus communis ssp. tarentina 'Microphylla Variegata'
Variegated Tarentina Myrtle
Half-hardy evergreen perennial. Ht 1m (3ft), spread 60cm (2ft). Fragrant white flowers from spring to mid-summer, each with a hint of pink and a dense cluster of golden stamens; followed by dark, purple-black fruits. Leaves are small, oval, and dark green with silver variegation, and a pink tinge in autumn.

I have included the following two because they have only recently been re-classified as **Luma** and are worth looking out for.

Luma chequen (Myrtus chequen)
Half-hardy evergreen perennial. Ht and spread 10m (30ft). Fragrant white flowers from spring to mid-summer, each with a dense cluster of golden stamens; followed by dark purple-black fruits. The leaves are more oblong with a point at the end: glossy dark green and aromatic.

Luma apiculata 'Glanleam Gold' (Myrtus 'Glanleam Gold')
Half-hardy evergreen perennial. Ht and spread 10m (30ft). Fragrant white flowers from mid summer to mid-autumn, each with a hint of pink and a dense cluster of golden stamens; followed by red fruits which darken to deep purple as they ripen. Leaves oval, bright green, edged with creamy yellow.

Myrtle comes from a fragrant genus that is widely distributed in warm temperate and tropical regions of the world.

Myrtle is a direct descendant of the Greek Myrtos, the herb of love. It has been dedicated to Venus and was planted all round her temples. The story goes that Venus transformed one of her priestess called Myrrh into myrtle in order to protect her from an over-eager suitor. Also, Venus herself wore a wreath of myrtle when she was given the Golden Apple by Paris in recognition of her beauty. When she arose out of the sea she was carrying a sprig of myrtle, and to this day it grows very well by the sea, flourishing in the salt air.

Subsequently it was considered an aphrodisiac, and brides carried it in their bouquets or wore wreaths of it at weddings to symbolize love and consistency.

Myrtle *Myrtus communis* **in berry**

Myrtle growing in a hedge

CULTIVATION

Propagation
Cuttings
Take softwood cuttings in spring, semi-hardwood cuttings in summer. As these are tender plants it is as well to grow them on in pots for the first 2 years at least. If you live in an area where the winter temperatures fall continuously below 0°C (32°F) – for variegated varieties 5°C (41°F) – it would be better to leave them in their pots for the winter. Use the bark, peat, grit mix of compost.

Pests and Diseases
In the majority of cases myrtles are free from pests and diseases, but susceptible to root rot from over-watering.

Maintenance
Spring: Trim back growth to regain shape. Take softwood cuttings.

Summer: Take semi-hardwood cuttings.
Autumn: Protect from early frosts.
Winter: Protect in the winter if you live in a frost area.

Garden Cultivation
This lovely, tender, aromatic shrub will grow in fertile well-drained soil in full sun. Where your winters are borderline, plant against a south or west facing wall to restrict the amount of water it receives from rain, and protect it from the winds. If a frost is forecast, cover lightly with an agricultural fleece.
  Trim back growth (where possible) to maintain shape in mid-spring after the frosts have finished.

Harvest
Pick leaves for sweetness and scent when myrtle is in flower; they can be used dried or fresh.
  Preserve the leaves in oil or vinegar for use in cooking.
  Pick flowers for drying just as they open.

CULINARY

Leaves can be added to pork for the final 10 minutes of roasting, or to lamb when barbecuing. They have a spicy flavour.
  After drying, the berries can be ground and used like juniper as a spice for game and venison.

MEDICINAL

The leaves have astringent and antiseptic properties. Rarely used medicinally, but a leaf decoction may be applied externally to bruises and haemorrhoids. Recent research has revealed a substance in myrtle that has an antibiotic action.

CONTAINER GROWING

This plant, when young, is well suited to containers. Use the bark, peat, grit mix of compost. As an evergreen plant, it looks attractive all year round. Place in a cold conservatory away from central heating. Water in the summer months, and allow the compost nearly to dry out in winter. Watch the watering at all times; if ever in doubt give it less rather than more. Feed with a liquid fertilizer during the flowering period.

OTHER USES

Every part of the shrub is highly aromatic and can be used dried in potpourris.

Myrtle potpourri

CATMINT

Nepeta

***Also known as Catnep, Catnip, Catrup, Catswart and Field Balm.
From the family Labiatae.***

Catmint *Nepeta racemosa*

Native to Europe and East and West Asia, but now naturalized in other temperate zones.

The species name may have derived from the Roman town Nepeti, where it was said to grow in profusion.

The Elizabethan herbalist, Gerard, recorded the source of its common name: 'They do call it *herba cataria* and *herba catti* because cats are very much delighted herewith for the smell of it is so pleasant unto them, that they rub themselves upon it and wallow or tumble in it and also feed on the branches and leaves very greedily.'

This herb has long been cultivated both for its medicinal and seasoning properties, and in the hippie era of the late '60s and '70s for its mildly hallucinogenic quality when smoked.

SPECIES

Nepeta cataria, **Nepeta x faassenii** and **Nepeta racemosa** are all called catmint, which can be confusing. However the first is the true herb with the medicinal and culinary properties and, just to be more confusing, is known also as dog mint!

Nepeta racemosa (mussinii)
Hardy perennial. Ht and spread 50cm (20in). Spikes of lavender blue/purple flowers from late spring to autumn. Small, mildly fragrant, greyish leaves. Marvellous edging plant for tumbling out over raised beds or softening hard edges of stone flags. Combines especially well with old-fashioned roses.

Nepeta camphorata
Hardy perennial. Ht and spread 60-75cm (24-30in). Very different from ordinary catmint and very fragrant. Tiny white blooms all summer. Small, silvery grey, aromatic foliage. Prefers a poor, well-drained, dryish soil, not too rich in nutrients, and full sun. However, it will adapt to most soils except wet and heavy.

Nepeta x faassenii
Hardy perennial. Ht and spread 45cm (18in). Loose spikes of lavender blue flowers from early summer to early autumn. Small greyish-green aromatic leaves form a bushy clump.

Nepeta cataria
Dog mint, Nep-in-a-hedge.
Hardy perennial. Ht 1m (3ft), spread 60cm (2ft). White to pale pink flowers from early summer to early autumn. Pungent aromatic leaves. This plant is the true herb. In the 17th century it was used in the treatment of barren women.

CULTIVATION

Propagation
Seed
Sow its small seed in spring or late summer, either where the plant is going to flower or onto the surface of pots, plug or seed trays. Cover with Perlite. Gentle bottom heat can be of assistance. Germination takes from 10-20 days, depending on the time of year (faster in late summer). Seed is viable for 5 years. When large enough to handle, thin the seedlings to 30cm (12in). The seed of **N. camphorata** should be sown in autumn to late winter. This seed will usually flower the following season.

Cuttings
Take softwood cuttings from new growth in late spring through to mid-summer. Do not choose flowering stems.

Catmint 'Six Hills Giant'
Nepeta 'Six Hills Giant'

Catmint *Nepeta cataria*

Division
A good method of propagation particularly if a plant is becoming invasive. But beware of cats! The smell of a bruised root is irresistible. Cats have been known to destroy a specimen replanted after division. If there are cats around, protect the newly divided plant.

Pests and Diseases
These plants are aromatic and not prone to pests. However, in cold wet winters, they tend to rot off.

Maintenance
Spring: Sow seeds.
Summer: Sow seeds until late in the season. Cut back hard after flowering to encourage a second flush.
Autumn: Cut back after flowering to maintain shape and produce new growth. If your winters tend to be wet and cold, pot up and winter this herb in a cold frame.
Winter: Sow seeds of **Nepeta camphorata**.

Garden Cultivation
The main problem with catmint is the love cats have for it. If you have ever seen a cat spaced-out after feeding (hence catnip) and rolling on it, then you will understand why cat lovers love catmint, and why cat haters who grow it get cross with cat neighbours. The reason why cats are enticed is the smell; it reminds them of the hormonal scent of cats of the opposite sex. With all this in mind, choose your planting site carefully.
  Nepeta make very attractive border or edging subjects. They like a well drained soil, sun, or light shade. The one thing they dislike is a wet winter, they may well rot off.
  Planting distance depends on species, but on average plant 50cm (20in) apart. When the main flowering is over, catmint should be cut back hard to encourage a second crop and to keep a neat and compact shape.

Harvest
Whether you pick to use fresh or to dry, gather leaves and flowering tops when young.

CULINARY

Use freshly picked young shoots in salads or rub on meat to release their mintish flavour. Catmint was drunk as a tea before China tea was introduced into the West. It makes an interesting cup!

MEDICINAL

Nepeta cataria is now very rarely used for medicinal purposes. In Europe it is sometimes used in a hot infusion to promote sweating. It is said to be excellent for colds and flu and children's infectious diseases, such as measles. It soothes the nervous system and helps get a restless child off to sleep. It also helps to calm upset stomachs and counters colic, flatulence and diarrhoea.
  In addition, an infusion can be applied externally to soothe scalp irritations, and the leaves and flowering tops can be mashed for a poultice to be applied to external bruises.

COMPANION PLANTING

Planting **Nepeta cataria** near vegetables deters flea beetle.

CONTAINER GROWING

N. x faassenii and **N. racemosa** look stunning in large terracotta pots. The grey green of the leaves and the blue-purple of the flowers complement the terracotta, and their sprawling habit in flower completes the picture. Use a well-draining compost, such as a peat, grit, bark mix. Note: both varieties tend to grow soft and leggy indoors.

OTHER USES

Dried leaves stuffed into toy mice will keep kittens and cats amused for hours.
  The scent of catnip is said to repel rats, so put bunches in hen and duck houses to discourage them.
  The flowers of **Nepeta x faassenii**, and **Nepeta racemosa** are suitable for formal displays.

Ocimum basilicum

BASIL

Also known as Common Basil, St Joseph Wort, and Sweet Basil. From the family Labiatae

Basil is native to India, the Middle East and some Pacific Islands. It has been cultivated in the Mediterranean for thousands of years, but the herb only came to Western Europe in the 16th century with the spice traders and to America and Australia with the early European settlers.

This plant is steeped in history and intriguing lore. Its common name is believed to be an abbreviation of Basilikon phuton, Greek for 'kingly herb', and it was said to have grown around Christ's tomb after the resurrection. Some Greek Orthodox churches use it to prepare their holy water, and put pots of basil below their altars. However, there is some question as to its sanctity – both Greeks and Romans believed that people should curse as they sow basil to ensure germination. There was even some doubt about whether it was poisonous or not, and in Western Europe it has been thought both to belong to the Devil and to be a remedy against witches. In Elizabethan times Sweet Basil was used as a snuff for colds and to clear the brain and deal with headaches, and in the 17th century Culpeper wrote of basil's uncompromising if unpredictable appeal – 'It either makes enemies or gains lovers but there is no in-between.'

SPECIES

Ocimum basilicum
Sweet Basil (Genovese)
Annual. Ht 45cm (18in). A strong scent. Green, medium-sized leaves. White flowers. Without doubt the most popular basil. Sweet basil comes from Genoa in the north of Italy, hence its local name, Genovese. Use sweet basil in pasta sauces and salads, especially with tomato. Combines very well with garlic. Do not let it flower if using for cooking.

Ocimum basilicum 'Cinnamon'
Cinnamon Basil
Annual. Ht 45cm (18in). Leaves olive/brown/green with a hint of purple, highly cinnamon-scented when rubbed. Flowers pale pink. Cinnamon basil comes from Mexico and is used in spicy dishes and salad dressings.

The distinctive leaves of Green Ruffles Basil

Ocimum basilicum var. citriodorum
Lemon Basil (Kemangie)
Annual. Ht 30cm (12in). Light, bright, yellowish green leaves, more pointed than other varieties, with a slight serrated edge. Flowers pale, whitish. Lemon basil comes from Indonesia, is tender in cooler climates, and susceptible to damping off. Difficult to maintain but well worth the effort. Both flowers and leaves have a lemon scent and flavour that enhance many dishes.

Cinnamon basil *Ocimum basilicum 'Cinnamon'*

Ocimum basilicum 'Green Ruffles'
Green Ruffles Basil
Annual. Ht 30cm (12in). Light green leaves, crinkly and larger than sweet basil. Spicy, aniseed flavour, good in salad dishes and combines well with stir-fry vegetables. But it is not, to my mind, an attractive variety. In fact the first time I grew it I thought its crinkly leaves had a bad attack of greenfly. Grow in pots and protect from any frost.

Ocimum basilicum var. minimum
Bush Basil
Annual. Ht 30cm (12in). Small green leaves, roughly half the size of sweet basil. Flowers small, scented and whitish. Spread from Chile throughout South America, where, in some countries, it is believed to belong to the pagan Goddess Erzulie and is carried both as a powerful protector against robbery and by young ladies to keep a lover's eye from roving. Excellent for growing in pots on the windowsill. Delicious added whole to green salads; goes well with ricotta cheese.

Ocimum basilicum var. minimum 'Greek'
Greek Basil (Fine-leaved Miniature)
Annual. Ht 23cm (9in). This basil has the smallest leaves, tiny replicas of the bush basil leaves but, despite their size, they have a good flavour. As its name depicts it originates from Greece. It is one of the easiest basils to look after and is especially good grown in a pot. Use leaves unchopped in all salads and in tomato sauces.

Ocimum basilicum 'Napolitano'
Lettuce-leaved Basil
Annual. Ht 45cm (18in). Leaves very large, crinkled, and with a distinctive flavour, especially good for pasta sauce. Originates in Naples region of Italy and needs a hot summer in cooler countries to be of any merit.

Ocimum basilicum 'Purple Ruffles'
Purple Ruffles Basil
Annual. Ht 30cm (12in). Very similar to straight purple basil (below), though the flavour is not as strong and the leaf is larger with a feathery edge. Flowers are pink. It can be grown in pots in a sunny position outside, but frankly it is a pain to grow because it damps off so easily.

Ocimum basilicum var. purpurascens
Purple Basil
Annual. Ht 30cm (12in) Strongly scented purple leaves. Pink flowers. Very attractive plant with a perfumed scent and flavour that is especially good with rice dishes. The dark purple variety that was developed in 1962 at the University of Connecticut represents something of a breakthrough in herb cultivation not least because, almost exclusively, herbs have escaped the attentions of the hybridizers. The variety was awarded the All American Medal by the seedsmen.

The many diverse shapes and colours of basil

Sacred basil *Ocimum tenuiflorum (sanctum)*

Ocimum basilicum 'Horapha'
Anise Basil (Rau Que)
Annual. Ht 42cm (15in). Leaf olive/purplish. Stems red. Flowers with pink bracts. Aniseed in scent and flavour. A special culinary basil from Thailand. Use the leaves as a vegetable in curries and spicy dishes.

Ocimum tenuiflorum (sanctum)
Sacred Basil (Kha Prao Tulsi)
Annual. Ht 30cm (12in). A small basil with olive/purple leaves with serrated edges. Stems deep purple. Flowers mauve/pink. The whole plant has a marvellously rich scent. Originally from Thailand, where it is grown around Buddhist temples. Can be used in Thai cooking with stir-fry hot peppers, chicken, pork or beef. The Indian-related variety, *sanctum*, is considered kingly or holy by the Hindus, sacred to the Gods Krishna and Vishnu. Being revered it was the chosen herb upon which to swear oaths in courts of Law. It was also used throughout the Indian subcontinent as a disinfectant where malaria was present.

CULTIVATION

Propagation
Seed

All basils can be grown from seed. Sow direct into pots or plug trays in early spring and germinate with warmth. Avoid using seed trays because basil has a long tap root and dislikes being transplanted. Plugs also help minimize damping off, to which all basil plants are prone (see below). Water well at midday in dry weather even when transplanted into pots or containers: basil hates going to bed wet. This minimizes the chances of damping off and will prevent root rot, a hazard when air temperature is still dropping at night.

Plant out seedlings when large enough to handle and the danger of frost has passed. The soil needs to be rich and well drained, and the situation warm and sheltered, preferably with sun at midday. However, prolific growth will only be obtained usually in the greenhouse or in large pots on a sunny patio. I suggest you plant basil in between tomato plants because:

1. being a good companion plant it repels flying insects
2. you will remember to use fresh basil with tomatoes
3. you will remember to water it
4. the situation will be warm and whenever you pick tomatoes you will tend to pick basil, which will encourage bushy growth and prevent it flowering, which in turn will stop the stems becoming woody and the flavour of its leaves bitter.

Pests and Diseases

Greenfly and whitefly may be a problem with pot grown plants. Wash off with liquid horticultural soap.

Seedlings are highly susceptible to damping off, a fungal disease encouraged by overcrowding in overly wet conditions in seed trays or pots. It can be prevented by sowing the seed thinly and widely and guarding against an over-humid atmosphere.

Maintenance

Spring: Sow seeds in early spring with warmth and watch out for damping off; plant out around the end of the season. Alternatively, sow directly into the ground after any frosts.
Summer: Keep pinching out young plants to promote new leaf growth and to prevent flowering. Harvest the leaves.
Autumn: Collect seeds of plants allowed to flower. Before first frosts, bring pots into the house and place on the windowsill. Dig up old plants and dig over the area ready for new plantings.

Garden Cultivation

Garden cultivation is only a problem in areas susceptible to frost and where it is not possible to provide for its great need for warmth and nourishment. In such areas plant out after the frosts have finished; choose a well drained, rich soil in a warm, sunny corner, protected from the wind.

Harvest

Pick leaves when young and always from the top to encourage new growth.

If freezing to store, paint both sides of each leaf with olive oil to stop it sticking to the next and to seal in its flavour.

If drying, do it as fast as you can. Basil leaves are some of the more difficult to dry successfully and I do not recommend it.

The most successful course, post-harvest, is to infuse the leaves in olive oil or vinegar. As well as being useful in your own kitchen, both the oil and the vinegar make great Christmas presents (see Preserving).

Gather flowering tops as they open in the summer and early autumn. Add fresh to salads, dry to potpourris.

CONTAINER GROWING

Basil is happy on a kitchen windowsill and in pots on the patio, and purple basil makes a good centrepiece in a hanging basket. In Europe basil is placed in pots outside houses to repel flies.

Water well at midday but do not over–water. If that is not possible water earlier in the day rather than later and again do not over-water.

OTHER USES

Keep it in a pot in the kitchen to act as a fly repellent, or crush a leaf and rub it on your skin, where the juice repels mosquitoes.

MEDICINAL

Once prescribed as a sedative against gastric spasms and as an expectorant and laxative, basil is rarely used in herbal medicines today. However, leaves added to food are an aid to digestion and if you put a few drops of basil's essential oil on a sleeve and inhale, it can allay mental fatigue. For those that need a zing it can also be used to make a very refreshing bath vinegar, which also acts as an antiseptic.

CULINARY

Basil has a unique flavour, so newcomers should use with discretion otherwise it will dominate other flavours. It is one of the few herbs to increase its flavour when cooked. For best results add at the very end of cooking.

Hints and ideas
1. Tear the leaves, rather than chop. Sprinkle over green salads or sliced tomatoes.
2. Basil combines very well with garlic. Tear into French salad dressing.
3. When cooking pasta or rice, heat some olive oil in a saucepan, remove from heat, add some torn purple basil, toss the pasta or rice in the basil and oil, and serve. Use lemon basil to accompany a fish dish – it has a sharp lemon/spicy flavour when cooked.
4. Add to a cold rice or pasta salad.
5. Mix low fat cream cheese with any of the basils and use in baked potatoes.
6. Basil does not combine well with strong meats such as goat or vension. However, aniseed basil is very good with stir fried pork.
7. Sprinkle on fried or grilled tomatoes while they are still hot as a garnish.
8. Very good with French bread and can be used instead of herb butter in the traditional hot herb loaf. The tiny leaves of Greek basil are best for this because you can keep them whole.
9. Sprinkle on top of pizzas.
10. Basil makes an interesting stuffing for chicken. Use sweet basil combined with crushed garlic, bread crumbs, lemon peel, beaten egg, and chopped nuts.

Pesto Sauce
One of the best known recipes for basil, here is a simple version for 4 people.

1 tablespoon pine nuts
4 tablespoons chopped basil leaves
2 cloves garlic
75g (3oz) Parmesan cheese
6 tablespoons sunflower oil or olive oil (not virgin)

Blend the pine nuts, basil and chopped garlic until smooth. Add the oil slowly and continue to blend the mixture until you have a thick paste. Season with salt to taste. Stir the sauce into the cooked and drained pasta and sprinkle with Parmesan cheese.

Pesto sauce will keep in a sealed container in the fridge for at least a week. It can also be frozen but it is important, as with all herbal mixtures, to wrap the container with at least two thickness of polythene to prevent the aroma escaping.

Pasta with Purple Ruffles Basil

Oenothera

EVENING PRIMROSE

*Also known as Common Evening Primrose, Evening Star, Fever Plant, Field Primrose,
King's Cure-all, Night Willowherb, Scabish, Scurvish, Tree Primrose, Primrose, Moths
Moonflower and Primrose Tree. From the family Onagraceae.*

A native of North America it was introduced to Europe in 1614 when botanists brought the plant from Virginia as a botanical curiosity. In North America it is regarded as a weed, elsewhere as a pretty garden plant.

The generic name, *Oenothera*, comes from the Greek 'oinos' (wine) and 'thera' (hunt). According to ancient herbals the plant was said to dispel the ill effects of wine, but both plant and seed have been used for other reasons – culinary and medicinal – by American Indians for hundreds of years. The Flambeau Ojibwe tribe were the first to realise its medicinal properties. They used to soak the whole plant in warm water to make a poultice to heal bruises and overcome skin problems. Traditionally, too, it was used to treat asthma, and its medicinal potential is still evolving. Oil of Evening Primrose is currently attracting considerable attention worldwide as a treatment for nervous disorders, in particular Multiple Sclerosis. There may well be a time in the very near future when the pharmaceutical industry will require fields of this beautiful plant to be grown on a commercial scale.

The common name comes from the transformation of its bedraggled daytime appearance into a fragrant, phosphorescent, pale yellow beauty with the opening of its flowers in the early evening. All this show is for one night only, however. Towards the end of summer the flowers tend to stay open all day long. (It is called Evening Star because the petals emit phosphorescent light at night.) Many strains of the plant came to Britain as stowaways in soil used as ballast in cargo ships.

Evening Primrose
Oenothera macrocarpa

SPECIES

Oenothera biennis
Evening Primrose
Hardy biennial. Ht 90-120cm (3-4ft), spread 90cm (3ft). Large evening scented yellow flowers for most of the summer. Long green oval or lance-shaped leaves This is the medicinal herb, and the true herb.

Oenothera macrocarpa (missouriensis)
Hardy perennial. Ht 10cm (4in), spread 40cm (16in) or more. Large yellow bell-shaped flowers, sometimes spotted with red, open at sundown throughout the summer. The small to medium green leaves are of a narrow oblong shape.

Oenothera perennis (Pumila)
Hardy perennial. Ht 15-60cm (6-24in), spread 30cm (12in). Fragrant yellow funnel-shaped flowers all summer. The green leaves are narrow and spoon-shaped.

Evening Primrose
Oenothera biennis

CULTIVATION

Propagation
Seeds

Sow in early spring on the surface of pots or plug trays, or direct into a prepared site in the garden. Seed is very fine so be careful not to sow it too thick. Use the cardboard method. When the weather has warmed sufficiently, plant out at a distance of 30cm (12in) apart. Often the act of transplanting will encourage the plant to flower the first year. It is a prolific self-seeder. So once introduced into the garden, it will stay.

Pests and Diseases
This plant rarely suffers from pests or disease.

Maintenance
Spring: Sow seed.
Summer: Dead head plants to cut down on self-seeding.
Autumn: Dig up old roots of second-year growth of the biennials.
Winter: No need to protect.

Garden Cultivation
Choose a well-drained soil in a dry, sunny corner for the best results and sow the seeds in late spring to produce flowers the following year. Thin the seedlings to 30cm (12in) apart, when large enough to handle. After the seed is set, the plant dies. It is an extremely tolerant plant, happy in most situations, and I have known seedlings appear in a stone wall, so be forewarned.

Harvest
Use leaves fresh as required. Best before flowering.
  Pick the flowers when in bud or when just open. Use fresh. Picked flowers will always close and are no good for flower arrangements.

Collect the seeds as the heads begin to open at the end. Store in jar for sowing in the spring.
  Dig up roots and use fresh as a vegetable or to dry.

CONTAINER GROWING

The lower growing varieties are very good in window boxes and tubs. Tall varieties need support from other plants or stakes. None is suitable for growing indoors.

CULINARY

It is a pot herb – roots, stems, leaves, and even flower buds may be eaten. The roots can be boiled – they taste like sweet parsnips, or pickled and tossed in a salad.

MEDICINAL

Soon this plant will take its place in the hall of herbal fame.
  It can have startling effects on the treatment of pre-menstrual tension. In 1981 at St Thomas's Hospital, London, 65 women with PMS were treated. 61 per cent experienced complete relief and 23 per cent partial relief. One symptom, breast engorgement, was especially improved – 72 per cent of women reported feeling better. In November 1982,

Evening Primrose *Oenothera biennis*

an edition of the prestigious medical journal *The Lancet* published the results of a double-blind crossover study on 99 patients with ectopic excema, which showed that when high doses of Evening Primrose Oil were taken, about 43 per cent of the patients experienced improvement of their eczema. Studies of the effect of the oil on hyperactive children also indicate that this form of treatment is beneficial.
  True to the root of its generic name, the oil does appear to be effective in counteracting alcohol poisoning and preventing hangovers. It can help withdrawal from alcohol, easing depression. It helps dry eyes and brittle nails and, when combined with zinc, the oil may be used to treat acne.
  But it is the claim that it benefits sufferers of multiple sclerosis that has brought controversy. It has been recommended for MS sufferers by Professor Field, who directed MS research for the UK Medical Research Council.
  Claims go further – that it is effective in guarding against arterial disease; the effective ingredient, gami-linolelic acid (GLA), is a powerful anti-blood clotter, that it aids weight-loss; a New York hospital discovered that people more

than 10 per cent above their ideal body weight lost weight when taking the oil. It is thought that this occurs because the GLA in Evening Primrose Oil stimulates brown fat tissue... and that in perhaps the most remarkable study of all, completed in Glasgow Royal Infirmary in 1987, it helped 60 per cent of patients suffering from rheumatoid arthritis. Those taking fish oil, in addition to Evening Primrose Oil, fared even better.
  The scientific explanation for these extraordinary results is that GLA is a precursor of a hormone-like substance called PGEI, which has a wide range of beneficial effects on the body. Production of this substance in some people may be blocked. GLA has also been found in oil extracted from blackcurrant seed and borage seed, both of which are now a commercial source of this substance.

OTHER USES

Leaf and stem can be infused to make an astringent facial steam. Add to hand cream as a softening agent.

Origanum

OREGANO & MARJORAM

Also known as Wild Marjoram, Mountain Mint, Winter Marjoram, Winter Sweet, Marjolaine and Origan. From the family Labiatae.

For the most part these are natives of the Mediterranean region. They have adapted to many countries, however, and a native form can now be found in many regions of the world, even if under different common names. For example, *Origanum vulgare* growing wild in Britain is called wild marjoram (the scent of the leaf is aromatic but not strong, the flowers are pale pink); while in Mediterranean countries wild *Origanum vulgare* is known as oregano (the leaf is green, slightly hairy and very aromatic, the flowers are similar to those found growing wild in Britain).

Pot Marjoram *Origanum onites*

Oregano is derived from the Greek 'oros' meaning mountain and 'ganos' meaning joy and beauty. It therefore translates literally as 'joy of the mountain'. In Greece it is woven into the crown worn by bridal couples.

According to Greek mythology, the King of Cyprus had a servant called Amarakos, who dropped a jar of perfume and fainted in terror. As his punishment the gods changed him into oregano, after which, if it was found growing on a burial tomb, all was believed well with the dead. Venus was the first to grow the herb in her garden.

Aristotle reported that tortoises, after swallowing a snake, would immediately eat oregano to prevent death, which gave rise to the belief that it was an antidote to poison.

The Greeks and Romans used it not only as scent after taking a bath and as a massage oil, but also as a disinfectant and preservative. More than likely they were responsible for the spread of this plant across Europe, where it became known as marjoram. The New Englanders took it to North America, where there arose a further confusion of nomenclature. Until the 1940s, common marjoram was called wild marjoram in America, but is now known as oregano. In certain parts of Mexico and the southern states of America, oregano is the colloquial name for a totally unrelated plant with a similar flavour.

Sweet marjoram, which originates from North Africa, was introduced into Europe in the 16th century and was incorporated in nosegays to ward off the plague and other pestilence.

Wild Marjoram
Origanum vulgare

SPECIES

Origanum amanum
Hardy perennial. Ht and spread 15-20cm (6-8in). Open, funnel-shaped, pale pink or white flowers borne above small heart-shaped, aromatic, pale green leaves. Makes a good alpine house plant. Dislikes a damp atmosphere.

Origanum x applei (heraceleoticum)
Winter Marjoram
Half-hardy perennial. Ht 23cm (9in), spread 30cm (12in). Small pink flowers. Very small aromatic leaves which, in the right conditions, are available all year round. Good to grow in a container.

Origanum dictamnus
Ditany of Crete
Hardy perennial. Ht 12-15cm (5-6in), spread 40cm (16in). Prostrate habit, purplish pink flowers that appear in hop-like clusters in summer. The leaves are white and woolly and grow on arching stems. Pretty little plant, quite unlike the other **origanums** in appearance. Tea made from the leaves is considered a panacea in Crete.

Golden Marjoram
Origanum vulgare 'Aureum'

Origanum 'Kent Beauty'
Hardy perennial. Ht 15-20cm (6-8in), spread 30cm (12in). Whorls of tubular pale pink flowers with darker bracts appear in summer on short spikes. Round, oval and aromatic leaves on trailing stems, which give the plant its prostrate habit and make it suitable for a wall or ledge. Decorative more than culinary.

Origanum laevigatum
Hardy perennial. Ht 23-30cm (9-12in), spread 20cm (8in). Summer profusion of tiny, tubular, cerise/pink/ mauve flowers, surrounded by red/purple bracts. Aromatic, dark green leaves, which form a mat in winter. Decorative more than culinary.

Origanum laevigatum 'Herrenhausen'
Hardy perennial. Ht and spread 30cm (12in). Pink/ mauve flowers which develop from deep purple buds in summer. Dark green, aromatic, slightly hairy leaves, with a pink tinge underneath. Decorative, and culinary when no other is available.

Greek Oregano
Origanum vulgare ssp *hirtum.*

Origanum majorana (Origanum hortensis)
Sweet Marjoram
Also known as Knotted Marjoram or Knot Marjoram Half-hardy perennial. Grown as an annual in cool climates. Ht and spread 30cm (12in). Tiny white flowers in a knot. Round pale green leaves, highly aromatic. This is the best variety for flavour. Use in culinary recipes that state marjoram. The leaf is also good for drying, retaining a lot of its scent and flavour.

Origanum onites
Pot Marjoram
Hardy perennial. Ht and spread 45cm (18in). Pink/ purple flowers in summer. Green aromatic leaves that form a mat in winter. Good grower with a nice flavour. Difficult to obtain the true seed; grows easily from cuttings, however.

Origanum rotundifolium
Hardy perennial. Ht 23-30cm (9-12in), spread 30cm (12in). Prostrate habit. The pale pink, pendant, funnel-shaped flowers appear in summer in whorls surrounded by yellow/green bracts. Leaves are small, round, mid-green, and aromatic. Decorative more than culinary.

Origanum vulgare
Oregano
Also known as Wild Marjoram
Hardy perennial. Ht and spread 45cm (18in). Clusters of tiny tubular mauve flowers in summer. Dark green, aromatic, slightly hairy leaves, which form a mat in winter. When grown in its native Mediterranean, it has a very pungent flavour, which bears little resemblance to that obtained in the cooler countries. When cultivated in the garden it becomes similar to pot marjoram.

Origanum vulgare ssp hirtum.
Greek Oregano
Hardy perennial. Ht and spread 45cm (18in). Clusters of tiny tubular white flowers in summer. Grey/green hairy leaves, which are very aromatic and excellent to cook with.

Origanum vulgare 'Aureum'
Golden Marjoram
Hardy perennial. Ht and spread 45cm (18in). Clusters of tiny tubular mauve/pink flowers in summer. Golden, aromatic, slightly hairy leaves, which form a mat in winter. The leaves have a warm aromatic flavour when used in cooking; combines well with vegetables.

Compact Marjoram
Origanum vulgare 'Compactum'

Origanum vulgare 'Aureum Crispum'
Golden Curly Marjoram
Hardy perennial. Ht and spread 45cm (18in). Clusters of tiny tubular mauve/pink/ white flowers in summer. Leaves, small, golden, crinkled, aromatic and slightly hairy, which form a mat in winter. The leaves have a slightly milder savoury flavour (sweeter and spicy) that combines well with vegetable dishes.

Origanum vulgare 'Compactum'
Compact Marjoram
Hardy perennial. Ht 15cm (6in), spread 30cm (12in). Lovely large pink flowers. Smallish green aromatic leaves, which form a mat in winter, have a deliciously warm flavour and combine well with lots of culinary dishes.

Origanum vulgare 'Gold Tip'
Gold Tipped Marjoram
Also known as Gold Splash
Hardy perennial. Ht and spread 30cm (12in). Small pink flowers in summer. The aromatic leaves are green and yellow variegated. Choose the garden site carefully: shade prevents the variegation. The leaves have a mild savoury flavour.

Origanum vulgare 'Nanum'
Dwarf Marjoram
Hardy perennial. Ht 10cm (4in), spread 15cm (6in). White/pink flowers in summer. Tiny green aromatic leaves. It is a lovely, compact, neat little bush, great in containers and at the front of a herb garden. Good in culinary dishes.

CULTIVATION

Propagation
Seed
The following can be grown from seed: **Origanum vulgare**, **Origanum majorana**, **Origanum vulgare ssp hirtum**. The seed is very fine, so sow in spring into prepared seed or plug trays. Use the cardboard trick. Leave uncovered and give a bottom heat of 15°C (60°F). Germination can be erratic or 100 per cent successful. Watering is critical when the seedlings are young; keep the compost on the dry side. As the seed is so fine thin before pricking out to allow the plants to grow. When large enough, either pot on, using the bark, grit, peat mix of compost, or if the soil is warm enough and you have grown them in plugs, plant into the prepared garden.

Cuttings
Apart from the 3 species mentioned above, the remainder can only be propagated successfully by cuttings or division.

Softwood cuttings can be taken from the new growing tips of all the named varieties in spring. Use the bark, grit mix of compost.

Division
A number of varieties form a mat during the winter. These lend themselves to division. In spring, or after flowering, dig up a whole clump and pull sections gently away. Each will come away with its own root system. Replant as wanted.

Pests and Diseases
Apart from occasional frost damage, marjorams and oreganos, being aromatic, are mostly pest free.

Maintenance
Spring: Sow seeds. Divide established plants. Take softwood cuttings.
Summer: Trim after flowering to prevent plants becoming straggly. Divide established plants in late summer.
Autumn: Before they die down for winter, cut back the year's growth to within 6cm (2½in) of the soil.
Winter: Protect pot grown plants and tender varieties.

Garden Cultivation
Sweet marjoram and winter marjoram need a sunny garden site and a well-drained, dry, preferably chalk, soil. Otherwise plant them in containers. All the rest are hardy and adaptable, and will tolerate most soils as long as they are not waterlogged in winter. Plant gold varieties in some shade to prevent the leaves from scorching. For the majority, a good planting distance is 25cm (10in), closer if being used as an edging plant.

Harvest
Leaves
Pick leaves whenever available for use fresh. They can be dried or frozen, or be used to make oil or vinegar.

Flowers
The flowers can be dried just as they open for dried flower arrangements.

CONTAINER GROWING

The **Origanum** species look great in containers. Use the bark, grit, peat mix of compost. Make sure that they are not over-watered and that the gold and variegated forms get some shade at midday. Cut back after flowering and give them a liquid fertilizer feed.

CULINARY

Marjoram and oregano aid the digestion, and act as an antiseptic and as a preservative.

They are among the main ingredients of bouquet garni, and combine well with pizza, meat and tomato dishes, vegetables and milk-based desserts.

Red Mullet with Tomatoes and Oregano
Serves 4-6

4-6 red mullet, cleaned
3 tablespoons olive oil
1 medium onion, sliced
1 clove garlic, chopped
500g (1lb) tomatoes, peeled and chopped
1 green or red pepper, seeded and diced
1 teaspoon sugar
1 teaspoon chopped fresh oregano or ½ teaspoon dried oregano
Freshly milled salt and pepper
Oil for baking or shallow frying

Rinse the fish in cold water and drain on kitchen paper. Heat the olive oil in a pan and cook the onion and garlic slowly until golden brown; add the tomatoes, pepper, sugar and oregano, and a little salt and pepper.

Bring to the boil, then simmer for 20 minutes until thickened.

Bake or fry the fish. Brush them with oil, place in an oiled ovenproof dish and cook at a moderately hot temperature, 190°C (375°F, Gas Mark 5) for 7-8 minutes. Serve with the sauce.

MEDICINAL

This plant is one of the best antiseptics owing to its high Thymol content.

Marjoram tea helps ease bad colds, has a tranquil-lizing effect on nerves, and helps settle upset stomachs. It also helps to prevent sea sickness.

For temporary relief of toothache, chew the leaf or rub a drop of essential oil on the gums. A few drops of essential oil on the pillow will help you sleep.

OTHER USES

Make an infusion and add to the bath water to aid relaxation.

Red mullet with tomatoes and oregano

Papaver

POPPY

From the family Papaveraceae

The poppy is widely spread across the temperate zones of the world. For thousands of years corn and poppy and civilizations have gone together. The Romans looked on poppy as sacred to their corn goddess, Ceres, who taught men to sow and reap.

The ancient Egyptians used poppy seed in their baking for its aromatic flavour.

The field poppy grew on Flanders fields after the battles of World War I and became the symbol of Remembrance Day.

SPECIES

Papaver rhoeas
Field Poppy
Also known as Common Poppy, Corn Poppy, Blind Eyes, Blind Man, Red Dolly, Red Huntsmen, Poppet, Old Woman's Petticoat, Thunderbolt, and Wartflower
Hardy annual. Ht 20-60cm (8-24in), spread 45cm (18in). Brilliant scarlet flower with black basal blotch from summer to early autumn. The mid-green leaf has 3 lobes and is irregularly toothed.

Papaver somniferum
Opium Poppy
Hardy annual. Ht 30-90cm (12-36in), spread 45cm (18in). Large pale lilac, white, purple or variegated flowers in summer. The leaf is long with toothed margins and bluish in colour. There is a double-flowered variety, **P. paeoniaeflorum**.

Papaver commutatum
Ladybird Poppy
Hardy annual. Ht 30-90cm (12-36in), spread 45cm (18in). Red flowers in summer, each with black blotch in centre. Leaf oblong and deeply toothed. Native of Asia Minor.

Meconopsis cambrica
Welsh Poppy
Hardy perennial. Ht 30-60cm (12-24in). Yellow flowers in summer. The green leaves are divided into many leaflets. It differs from **Papaver** in that the seeds are released through slits in the seed heads and not through pepper-pot heads.

WARNING

All parts of the opium poppy, except the ripe seeds, are dangerous and should be used only by trained medical staff.

CULTIVATION

Propagation
Seed
Sow the very fine seed in autumn onto the surface of prepared seed or plug trays, using the bark, peat, grit mix of compost. Cover with glass and leave outside for winter stratification.

In spring, when seedlings are large enough, plant out into the garden in groups.

Pests and Diseases
Largely pest and disease free.

Maintenance
Spring: Plant out in garden.
Summer: Dead head flowers to prolong flowering and prevent self-seeding.
Autumn: Sow seed. Dig up old plants.
Winter: No need to protect.

Garden Cultivation
Poppies all prefer a sunny site and a well-drained fertile soil. Sow in the autumn in a prepared site; press seed into the soil but do not cover.

Thin to 20-30cm (8-12in) apart. Remove the heads after flowering to prevent self-seeding.

Harvest
The ripe seeds can be collected from both field and opium poppies, the seed of which is not narcotic. It must however be ripe, otherwise it will go mouldy in store.

CONTAINER GROWING

Use the bark, peat, grit mix of compost. Place in full sun out of the wind, and water well during the summer. Refrain from feeding as this will produce lots of soft growth and few flowers.

MEDICINAL

The unripe seed capsules of the opium poppy are used for the extraction of morphine and the manufacture of Codeine.

OTHER USES

The oil extracted from the seed of the opium poppy is used not only as a salad oil, and for cooking, but also for burning in lamps, and in the manufacture of varnish, paint and soap.

CULINARY

Sprinkle the ripe seeds on bread, cakes and biscuits for a pleasant nutty flavour. Add to curry powder for texture, flavour, and as a thickener.

Pelargonium

SCENTED GERANIUMS

From the family Geraniaceae.

These form a group of marvellously aromatic herbs which should be used more. Originally native of South Africa, they are now widespread throughout many temperate countries, where they should be grown as tender perennials.

The generic name, *Pelargonium*, is said to be derived from 'pelargos', a stork. With a bit of imagination one can understand how this came about, the seed pods bear resemblance to a stork's bill.

Nearly all the species of scented geranium (the name is a botanical misnomer) came from the Cape of South Africa to England in the mid-17th century. The aromatic foliage found popular assent among Victorians, who used them as houseplants to scent the room. In the early 19th century the French perfumery industry recognized its commercial potential. Oil of Geranium is now not only an ingredient of certain perfumes for men, but also an essential oil in aromatherapy.

SPECIES

There are many different scented geraniums. I am mentioning a few typical of the species that I have a soft spot for. They are a very collectable plant.

Pelargonium 'Attar of Roses'
Half-hardy evergreen perennial. Ht 30-60cm (12-24in), spread 30cm (12in). Small pink flowers in summer. 3-lobed, mid-green leaves that smell of roses.

Pelargonium 'Atomic Snowflake'
Half-hardy evergreen perennial. Ht 30-60cm, (12-24in), spread 30cm (12in). Small pink flowers in summer. Intensely lemon-scented, roundish leaves with silver grey/green variegation.

Pelargonium capitatum
Half-hardy evergreen perennial. Ht 30-60cm (12-24in), spread 30cm (12in). Small mauve flowers in summer, irregular 3-lobed green leaves, rose scented. This is now mainly used to produce geranium oil for the perfume industry.

Pelargonium 'Chocolate Peppermint'
Half-hardy evergreen perennial. Ht 30-60cm (12-24in), spread 1m (3ft). Small white/pink flowers in summer. Large, rounded, shallowly lobed leaves, velvety green with brown marking and a strong scent of chocolate peppermints! This is a fast grower so pinch out growing tips to keep shape.

Pelargonium 'Clorinda'
Half-hardy evergreen perennial. Ht and spread 1m (3ft). Large pink attractive flowers in summer. Large rounded leaves, mid-green and eucalyptus-scented.

Pelargonium crispum
Half-hardy evergreen perennial. Ht and spread 30-60cm (12-24in). Small pink flowers in summer. Small 3-lobed leaves, green, crispy crinkled and lemon scented. Neat habit.

Pelargonium crispum 'Peach Cream'
Half-hardy evergreen perennial. Ht and spread 30-60cm (12-24in). Small pink flowers in summer. Small 3-lobed leaves, green with cream and yellow variegation, crispy crinkled and peach-scented.

A variety of scented geraniums

Pelargonium crispum 'Variegatum'

Half-hardy evergreen perennial. Ht and spread 30-60cm (12-24in). Small pink flowers in summer. Small 3-lobed leaves, green with cream variegation, crispy crinkled, and lemon scented.

Pelargonium Denticulatum Group

Half-hardy evergreen perennial. Ht and spread 1m (3ft). Small pinky-mauve flowers in summer. Deeply cut palmate leaves, green with a lemon scent.

Pelargonium Denticulatum Group 'Filicifolium'

Half-hardy evergreen perennial. Ht and spread 1m (3ft). Small pink flowers in summer. Very finely indented green leaves with a fine brown line running through, slightly sticky and not particularly aromatic, if anything a scent of balsam. Prone to white fly.

Pelargonium Fragrans Group

Half-hardy evergreen perennial. Ht and spread 30cm (12in). Small white flowers in summer. Greyish green leaves, rounded with shallow lobes, and a strong scent of nutmeg/pine.

Pelargonium Fragrans Group 'Fragrans Variegatum'

Half-hardy evergreen perennial. Ht and spread 30cm (12in). Small white flowers in summer. Greyish green leaves with cream variegation, rounded with shallow lobes and a strong scent of nutmeg/pine.

Pelargonium 'Atomic Snowflake'

Pelargonium 'Lemon Fancy' in flower

Pelargonium 'Graveolens'

Rose Geranium

Half-hardy evergreen perennial. Ht 60cm-1m (24-36in). Spread up to 1m (3ft). Small pink flowers in summer. Fairly deeply cut green leaves with a rose/peppermint scent. One of the more hardy of this species, with good growth.

Pelargonium 'Lady Plymouth'

Half-hardy evergreen perennial. Ht and spread 30-60cm (12-24in) Small pink flowers in summer. Fairly deeply cut greyish green leaves with cream variegation and a rose/peppermint scent.

Pelargonium 'Lemon Fancy'

Half-hardy evergreen perennial. Ht 30-60cm (12-24in), spread 30-45cm (12-18in). Smallish pink flowers in summer. Small roundish green leaves with shallow lobes and an intense lemon scent.

Pelargonium 'Lilian Pottinger'

Half-hardy evergreen perennial. Ht 30-60cm (12-24in), spread 1m (3ft). Small whitish flowers in summer. Leaves brightish green, rounded, shallowly lobed with serrated edges. Soft to touch. Mild spicy apple scent.

Pelargonium 'Mabel Grey'

Half-hardy evergreen perennial. Ht 45-60cm (18-24in), spread 30-45cm (12-18in). Mauve flowers with deeper veining in summer. If I have a favourite, this is it: the leaves are diamond shaped, roughly textured, mid-green and oily when rubbed and very strongly lemon-scented.

Pelargonium odoratissimum

Half-hardy evergreen perennial. Ht 30-60cm (12-24in) spread 1m (3ft). Small white flowers in summer. Green, rounded, shallowly lobed leaves, fairly bright green in colour and soft to touch, with an apple scent. Trailing habit, looks good in large containers.

Pelargonium 'Prince of Orange'

Half-hardy evergreen perennial. Ht and spread 30-60cm (12-24in). Pretty pink/white flowers in summer. Green, slightly crinkled, slightly lobed leaves, with a refreshing orange scent. Prone to rust.

Pelargonium quercifolium

Oak-Leafed Pelargonium

Half-hardy evergreen perennial. Ht and spread up to 1m (3ft). Pretty pink/purple flowers in summer. Leaves oak-shaped, dark green with brown variegation, and slightly sticky. A different, spicy scent.

Pelargonium 'Royal Oak'

Half-hardy evergreen perennial. Ht 38cm (15in) spread 30cm (12in). Small pink/purple flowers in summer. Oak-shaped, dark green leaves with brown variegation, slightly sticky with spicy scent. Very similar to **P. quercifolium**, but with a more compact habit.

Pelargonium 'Rober's Lemon Rose'

Half-hardy evergreen perennial. Ht and spread up to 1m (3ft.). Pink flowers in summer. Leaves greyish green – oddly shaped, lobed and cut – with a rose scent. A fast grower, so pinch out the growing tips to maintain shape.

Oak-Leafed Pelargonium
Pelargonium quercifolium

Pelargonium tomentosum

Half-hardy evergreen perennial. Ht 30-60cm (12-24in), spread 1m (3ft). Small white flowers in summer. Large rounded leaves, shallow lobed, velvet grey-green in colour with a strong peppermint scent. Fast grower, so pinch out growing tips to maintain shape. Protect from full sun.

Pelargonium 'Chocolate Peppermint'

Pelargonium 'Attar of Roses'

CULTIVATION

Propagation
Seed
Although I have known scented geraniums to have been grown from seed, I do not recommend this method. Cuttings are much more reliable for the majority. However, if you want to have a go, sow in spring in a peat and grit compost at a temperature no lower than 15°C (59°F).

Cuttings
All scented geraniums can be propagated by softwood cuttings which generally take very easily in the summer. Take cutting about 10-15cm (4-6in) long and strip the leaves from the lower part with a sharp knife. At all costs do not tear the leaves off as this will cause a hole in the stem and the cutting will be susceptible to disease, such as black leg. This is a major caveat for such as **Pelargonium crispum 'Variegatum'**. Use a sharp knife and slice the leaf off, insert the cutting into a tray containing equal parts bark and peat. Water in and put the tray away from direct sunlight. Keep an eye on the compost, making sure it does not thoroughly dry out, but only water if absolutely necessary. The cuttings should root in 2 to 3 weeks. Pot up into separate pots containing the bark, peat, grit mix of compost. Place in a cool greenhouse or cool conservatory for the winter, keeping the compost dry and watering only very occasionally. In the spring re-pot into larger pots and water sparingly. When they start to produce flower buds give them a liquid feed. In early summer pinch out the top growing points to encourage bushy growth.

Pests and Diseases
Unfortunately pelargoniums do suffer from a few diseases.

1 Cuttings can be destroyed by blackleg virus. The cutting turns black and falls over. The main cause of this is too much water. So keep the cuttings as dry as possible after the initial watering.

2 Grey mould (botrytis) is also caused by the plants being too wet and the air too moist. Remove damaged leaves carefully so as not to spread the disease, and burn. Allow the plants to dry out, and increase ventilation and spacing between plants.

3 Leaf gall appears as a mass of small proliferated shoots at the base of a cutting or plant. Destroy the plant, otherwise it could affect other plants.

4 Geraniums, like mint and comfrey, are prone to rust. Destroy the plant or it will spread to others.

5 Whitefly. Be vigilant. If you catch it early enough, you will be able to control it by spraying with a liquid horticultural soap. Follow manufacturer's instructions.

Maintenance
Spring: Trim, slowly introduce watering, and start feeding. Re-pot if necessary. *Summer*: Feed regularly. Trim to maintain shape. *Autumn*: Take cuttings. Trim back plants. Bring in for the winter to protect from frost. *Winter*: Allow the plants to rest. Keep watering to a minimum.

Garden Cultivation
Scented pelargoniums are so varied that they can look very effective grown in groups in the garden. Plant out as soon there is no danger of frost. Choose a warm site with well-drained soil. A good method is to sink the re-potted, over-wintered geraniums into the soil. This makes sure the initial compost is correct, and makes it easier to dig up the pot and bring inside before the first frost.

Harvest
Pick leaves during the growing season, for fresh use or for drying.
    Collect seeds before the seed pod ripens and ripen in paper bags. If allowed to ripen on the plant, the pods will burst, scattering the seeds everywhere.

CONTAINER GROWING

Scented **pelargoniums** make marvellous pot plants. They grow well, look good, and smell lovely. Pot up as described in Propagation. Place the containers so that you can rub the leaves as you walk past.

CULINARY

Before artificial food flavourings were produced the Victorians used scented pelargonium leaves in the bottom of cake tins to flavour their sponges. Why not follow suit? When you grease and line the bottom of a 20cm (8in) sandwich tin, arrange approximately 20 leaves of either **'Lemon Fancy'**, **'Mabel Grey'**, or **'Graveolens'**. Fill the tin with a sponge mix of your choice and cook as normal. Remove the leaves with the lining paper when the cake has cooled. Scented pelargonium leaves add distinctive flavour to many dishes although, like bay leaves, they are hardly ever eaten, being removed after the cooking process. The main varieties used are **'Graveolens'**, **'Odoratissimum'**, **'Lemon Fancy'** and **'Attar of Roses'**.

Geranium Leaf Sorbet

Geranium Leaf Sorbet

12 scented Pelargonium
  graveolens leaves
75g/3oz/6 tablespoons caster
  sugar
300ml/½pint/1¼ cups water
Juice of 1 large lemon
1 egg white
4 leaves for decoration

Wash the leaves and shake them dry. Put the sugar and water in a saucepan and boil until the sugar has dissolved, stirring occasionally. Remove the pan from the heat. Put the 12 leaves in the pan with the sugar and water, cover and leave for 20 minutes. Taste. If you want a stronger flavour bring the liquid to the boil again add some fresh leaves and leave for a further 10 minutes. When you have the right flavour, strain the syrup into a rigid container, add the lemon juice and leave to cool. Place in the freezer until semi-frozen (approximately 45 minutes) – it must be firm, not mushy – and fold in the beaten egg white. Put back into freezer for a further 45 minutes. Scoop into individual glass bowls, and decorate with a geranium leaf.

Rose Geranium Punch

1.2 litre/2pints/5 cups of apple
  juice
4 limes
250g/8oz/1 cup sugar
6 leaves of graveolens
6 drops of green vegetable
  colouring (optional)

Boil the apple juice and sugar and geranium leaves for 5 minutes. Strain the liquid. Cool and add colouring if required. Thinly slice and crush limes, add to the liquid. Pour onto ice in glasses and garnish with geranium leaves.

Graveolens Geranium Butter

Butter pounded with the leaves makes a delicious filling for cakes and sweet biscuits. Spread on bread and top with apple jelly.

WARNING

None of the **crispums** should be used in cooking as it is believed that they can upset the stomach.

Rose Geranium Punch

OTHER USES

In Aromatherapy, Geranium oil is relaxing but use it in small quantities. Dilute 2 drops in 2 teaspoons of soy oil for a good massage, or to relieve pre-menstrual tension, dermatitis, eczema, herpes or dry skin.

Petroselinum

PARSLEY

Also known as Common Parsley, Garden Parsley and Rock Parsley. From the family Umbelliferae.

Parsley in pots

Best known of all garnishing herbs in the West. Native to central and southern Europe, in particular the Mediterranean region, now widely cultivated in several varieties throughout the world.

The Greeks had mixed feelings about this herb. It was associated with Archemorus, the Herald of Death, so they decorated their tombs with it. Hercules was said to have chosen parsley for his garlands, so they would weave it into crowns for victors at the Isthmian Games. But they did not eat it themselves, preferring to feed it to their horses. However, the Romans consumed parsley in quantity and made garlands for banquet guests to discourage intoxication and to counter strong odours.

It was believed that only a witch or a pregnant woman could grow it, and that a fine harvest was only ensured if the seeds were planted on Good Friday. It was also said that if parsley was transplanted, misfortune would descend upon the household.

Parsley *Petroselinum crispum*

SPECIES

Petroselinum crispum
Parsley
Hardy biennial. Ht 30-40cm (12-16in). Small creamy white flowers in flat umbles in summer. The leaf is brightish green and has curly toothed edges and a mild taste. It is mainly used as a garnish.

Petroselinum crispum French (Flat Leafed)
French Parsley
Also known as Broad Leafed Parsley.
Hardy biennial. Ht 45-60cm (18-24in). Small creamy white flowers in flat umbels in summer. Flat dark green leaves with a stronger flavour than **P. crispum**. This is the one I recommend for culinary use.

Petroselinum crispum var. tuberosum
Hamburg Parsley
Also known as Turnip Rooted Parsley.
Perennial, grown as an annual. Root length up to 15cm (6in). Leaf, green and very similar to French parsley.
This variety, probably first developed in Holland, was introduced into England in the early 18th century, but it was only popular for 100 years. The plant is still frequently found in vegetable markets in France and Germany.
Warning: In the wild there is a plant called Fool's Parsley, **Aethusa cynapium**, which looks and smells to the novice like French parsley. Do not be tempted to eat it as it is extremely poisonous.

French Parsley
Petroselinum crispum French

CULTIVATION

Propagation
Seed
In cool climates, to ensure a succession of plants, sow seedlings under cover only in plug trays or pots. Avoid seed trays because, as with all *umbelliferae*, it hates being transferred. Cover with Perlite. If you have a heated propagator, a temperature of 18°C (65°F) will speed up germination. It takes 4-6 weeks without bottom heat and 2-3 weeks with. When the seedlings are large enough and the air and soil temperature have started to rise (about mid-spring), plant out 15cm (6in) apart in a prepared garden bed.

Pests and Diseases
Slugs love young parsley plants. There is a fungus which may attack the leaves. It produces first brown then white spots. Where this occurs the whole stock should be destroyed. Get some fresh seed.

Maintenance
Spring: Sow seed.
Summer: Sow seed. Cut flower heads as they appear on second-year plants.
Autumn: Protect plants for winter crop.
Winter: Protect plants for winter picking.

Garden Cultivation
Parsley is a hungry plant, it likes a good deep soil, not too light and not acid. Always feed the chosen site well in the previous autumn with well-rotted manure.

If you wish to harvest parsley all year round, prepare 2 different sites. For summer supplies, a western or eastern border is ideal because the plant needs moisture and prefers a little shade. For winter supplies, a more sheltered spot will be needed in a sunny position.

The seeds should be sown thinly, in drills 30-45cm (12-18in) apart and about 3cm (1in) deep. Germination is very slow. Keep the soil moist at all times, otherwise the seed will not germinate.

As soon as the seedlings are large enough, thin to 8cm (3in) and then 15cm (6in) apart. If at any time the leaves turn a bit yellow, cut back to encourage new growth and feed with a liquid fertilizer. At the first sign of flower heads appearing remove them if you wish to continue harvesting the leaves. Remember to water well during hot weather. In the second year parsley runs to seed very quickly. Dig it up as soon as the following year's crop is ready for picking, and remove it from the garden.

Hamburg or turnip parsley differs only in the respect that it is a root not a leaf crop. When the seedlings are large enough, thin to 20cm (8in) apart. Water well all summer. The root tends to grow more at this time of year, and unlike a lot of root crops the largest roots taste the best. Lift in late autumn, early winter. They are frost resistant.

Harvest
Pick leaves during first year for fresh use or for freezing (by far the best method of preserving parsley).

Dig up roots of Hamburg parley in the autumn of the first year and store in peat or sand.

CULINARY

Parsley is a widely used culinary herb, valued for its taste as well as its rich nutritional content. Cooking with parsley enhances the flavour of other foods and herbs. In bland food, the best flavour is obtained by adding it just before the end of cooking.

As so many recipes include parsley, here are some basic herb mixtures.

Fines Herbes
You will see this mentioned in a number of recipes and it is a classic for omelettes.

1 sprig parsley, chopped
1 sprig chervil, chopped
Some chives cut with scissors
1-2 leaves French tarragon

Chop up all the herbs finely and add to egg dishes.

Fish Bouquet Garni
2 sprigs parsley
1 spring French tarragon
1 sprig fennel (small)
2 leaves lemon balm

Tie the herbs together in a bundle and add to the cooking liquid.

Boil Hamburg parsley as a root vegetable or grate raw into salads. Use in soup mixes, the flavour resembles both celery and parsley.

CONTAINER GROWING

Parsley is an ideal herb for containers, it even likes living inside on the kitchen windowsill, as long as it is watered, fed, and cut. Use the bark, peat mix of compost. Curly parsley can look very ornamental as an edging to a large pot of nasturtiums. It can also be grown in hanging baskets, (keep well watered), window boxes (give it some shade in high summer), and containers. That brings me to the parsley pot, the one with six holes around the side. Do not use it. As I have already said, parsley likes moisture, and these containers dry out too fast, the holes in the side are small and make it very difficult to water, and the parsley has too big a tap root to be happy.

WARNING

Avoid medicinal use during pregnancy. There is an oil produced from parsley, but it should only be used under medical supervision.

MEDICINAL

All parsleys are a rich source of vitamins including Vitamin C. They are also high in iron and other minerals and contain the antiseptic chlorophyll.

It is a strong diuretic suitable for treating urinary infections as well as fluid retention. It also increases mothers' milk and tones the uterine muscle.

Parsley is a well known breath freshener, being the traditional antidote for the pungent smell of garlic. Chew raw, to promote a healthy skin.

Use in poultices as an antiseptic dressing for sprains, wounds and insect bites.

OTHER USES

A tea made from crushed seeds kills head lice vermin. Pour it over the head after washing and rinsing, wrap your head in a towel for 30 minutes and then allow to dry naturally. Equally, the seeds or leaves steeped in water can be used as a hair rinse.

Parsley tea

Phlomis fruticosa

JERUSALEM SAGE

From the family Labiatae.

Originates from the Mediterranean region but is now cultivated widely as a garden plant.

The generic name, *Phlomis*, was used by Dioscorides, a Greek physician in the first century whose *Materia Medica*, was the standard reference on the medical application of plants for over 1,500 years.

SPECIES

Phlomis fruticosa
Jerusalem Sage
Hardy evergreen perennial. Ht and spread 1.2m (4ft). Whorls of hooded yellow flowers in summer. Grey/green oblongish leaves, slightly wrinkled.

Phlomis italica
Narrow-Leafed Jerusalem Sage
Hardy evergreen perennial. Ht 90cm (36in), spread 75cm (30in). Whorls of lilac pink flowers in mid-summer, borne at the ends of shoots amid narrow, woolly, grey/green leaves.

CULTIVATION

Propagation
Seeds
Sow the medium-size seed in the autumn either into seed or plug trays and cover with a thin layer of compost. Winter in a cold greenhouse or cold frame. Does not need stratification nor heat, just cool temperature. Germination is erratic. When the seedlings are large enough to handle, prick out into pots using the bark, grit, peat mix of compost. Plant the young plants into the garden when there is no threat of frosts.

Cuttings
Take soft wood cuttings in summer from non-flowering shoots; they root easily.

Division
If an established plant has taken over its neighbour's spot, dig up and divide it in the spring; re-plant into a prepared site.

Pests and Diseases
In the majority of cases, this is free from pests and disease.

Maintenance
Spring: Divide established plants if need be.
Summer: Cut back after flowering to maintain shape.
Autumn: Sow seeds.
Winter: Protect outside plants if the winter temperature is persistently below −5°C (23°F).

Garden Cultivation
Jerusalem Sage is an attractive plant, making a fine mound of grey-furred leaves, proof against all but the most severe winter. A prolific summer flowerer, happy in a dry, well-drained, sunny spot. Cut back each year after flowering (late summer) and you will be able to control and maintain its soft grey dome all year round. Do not trim in the autumn as any frost will damage and in some cases kill the plant.

Harvest
Pick leaves for drying before planting flowers.

OTHER USES
The attractive, slightly aromatic leaves are a good addition to a potpourri.

CONTAINER GROWING

Jerusalem Sage is happy if grown in a large container using a soil based compost. Be mean on the feeding and watering as it is a drought-loving plant. Trim back especially after flowering to restrict its rampant growth. Protect during the winter in a cool greenhouse or conservatory. Keep watering to the absolute minimum.

CULINARY

Although not listed amongst culinary herbs, the leaves are pleasantly aromatic. In Greece the leaves are collected from the hillside and, once dried and bundled together with other related species, are hung up for sale. The dried leaves can be used in stews and casseroles.

Jerusalem Sage *Phlomis fruticosa*

Phytolacca americana

POKE ROOT

Also known as Red Ink Plant, Virginia Poke Weed, Pigeon Berry, Coccum, Poke, Indian Poke, American Poke and Cancer Root.
From the family Phytolaccaceae.

This herbaceous plant is a native to the warmer regions of America (especially Florida), Africa and Asia. It has been introduced elsewhere, particularly in the Mediterranean region.

Its generic name is derived from two Greek words: 'phyton' meaning plant and 'lac' meaning lake, referring to the purple/blue dye that flows from some of the *phytolaccas* when crushed.

The herb was introduced to American settlers by the Red Indians, who knew it as Pocan or Coccum, and used it as an emetic for a number of problems. It acquired a reputation as a remedy for internal cancers and was called cancer root.

SPECIES

Phytolacca americana (Phytolacca decandra)
Poke Root
Hardy perennial. Ht and spread 1.2-1.5m (4-5ft). Shallow, cup-shaped flowers, sometimes pink, flushed white and green, borne in terminal racemes in summer. They are followed by round fleshy blackish purple berries with poisonous seeds that hang down when ripe. Oval to lance-shaped mid-green leaves, tinged purple in autumn. There is a variegated form with green and white leaves.

Phytolacca polyandra calvigera
Hardy perennial. Ht and spread 1.2m (4ft). Clusters of shallow, cup-shaped, pink flowers in summer, followed by rounded blackish berries with poisonous seeds. Has brilliant crimson stems, oval to lance-shaped, mid-green leaves that turn yellow in summer through autumn. This plant is a native of China.

CULTIVATION

Propagation
Seed
Sow the seeds fresh in the autumn or spring in prepared seed or plug trays. Cover with Perlite. If sown in the autumn, winter the young plants in a cold greenhouse or cold frame. In the spring, after a period of hardening off, plant them out in a prepared site in the garden, 1m (3ft) apart.

Division
Both species have large root systems that can be divided either in autumn or spring.

Pests and Diseases
Largely free from pests and diseases

Maintenance
Spring: Sow seeds. Divide established plants.
Summer: Cut off the flowers if you do not want berries.
Autumn: Sow seeds. Divide established plants.
Winter: Dies back into the ground; no protection needed.

Garden Cultivation
Plant poke root in sun or shade in a moist, fertile soil, sheltered from the wind. Despite its poisonous seeds, this plant can look marvellous in a garden.

Harvest
It can be used as a pot herb, the young shoots being picked in the spring. But because it is easy to confuse the identity of species, and toxicity varies among them, only do this if you really know what you are doing. So it is better to err on the side of caution and pick some nice fresh sorrel or red orach instead.

Poke Root *Phytolacca americana*

CONTAINER GROWING

It is a tall plant, and when in berry is sufficiently heavy to unbalance even a large pot. Keep the poisonous berries out of reach of children.
If you choose to try it, use the bark, peat, grit compost, water well during the summer months.

MEDICINAL

Herbalists prescribe it for the treatment of chronic rheumatism, arthritis tonsillitis, swollen glands, mumps, and mastitis.
An extract from the roots can destroy snails. This discovery is being explored in Africa as a possible means to control the disease Bilharzia.

WARNING

POISONOUS. When handling either seeds, roots or the mature plant, gloves should be worn. It is toxic and dangerous. It should only be used by professional personnel.

Polygonatum biflorum

SOLOMON'S SEAL

Also known as David's Harp, Jacob's Ladder, Lady's Lockets, Lily of the Mountain, Drop Berry, Seal Root and Sealwort. From the family Lilaceae.

A perennial plant that grows in thick woods and thickets in Europe, Asia and North America.

The plant's generic name, *Polygonatum*, is derived from 'poly', meaning many, and 'gonu', meaning a knee joint, which refers to its many jointed rhizome.

King Solomon, wiser than all men, gave his approval to the use of its roots (said to resemble cut sections of Hebrew characters), as a poultice for wounds, and to help heal broken limbs.

In the 16th century Gerard cited its contribution in the soldering and gluing together broken of bones, when the root might be taken internally (in the form of ale) or applied externally as a poultice.

Solomon's Seal
Polygonatum multiflorum

SPECIES

Polygonatum biflorum
Solomon's Seal
Hardy perennial. Ht 30-80cm (12-32in), spread 30cm (1ft). White waxy flowers tipped with green hang from arching stems in spring to summer. The berries are bluish-black. The leaves are oval to lance shaped and mid-green in colour.

Polygonatum odoratum
Angular Solomon's Seal
Hardy perennial. Ht 60cm (24in), spread 30cm (12in). Produces pairs of fragrant, tubular, bell-shaped, green-tipped, white flowers in spring. The berries and leaves are as **P. biflorum**. A variegated form called **Polygonatum odoratum 'Varigatum'**, which has creamy white striped leaves. Also a double-flowered one **Polygonatum odoratum 'Flore Pleno'**, has scented flowers that look rather like ballet dancers' skirts.

Polygonatum verticillatum
Whorled Solomon's Seal
Hardy perennial. Ht 1.2m (48in) spread 45cm (18in). The flowers are narrow and bell shaped, greenish white in colour, and appear in early summer. Its berries are first red, then dark blue.
The lance-shaped, mid-green leaves grow in whorls.

CULTIVATION

Propagation
Seed
Sow fresh seed in autumn into prepared seed or plug trays, cover with the compost, water in well, then cover with glass, and leave outside for the winter. Remove the glass as soon as germination starts in spring. When the seedlings are large enough plant out in a prepared site. Keep an eye on the watering throughout the first season – before they have developed their creeping rhizomes, young plants dry out quickly.

Division
The plant is best divided just after the stalks die down in autumn, although in dampish weather, division and transplanting can be undertaken any time of year. This method is easier and quicker than seeds.

Pests and Diseases
Sawfly caterpillar is a common pest, you will notice that the leaves have clean cut holes. This will not damage the plant but it can

look unsightly if you have a major attack. Spray with a liquid horticultural soap, at the first sign of attack. Complete eradication is difficult.

Maintenance

Spring: Plant out seedlings.
Summer: Make sure the soil does not dry out.
Autumn: Sow fresh seeds. Divide established plants.

Winter: Protect in the event of a prolonged frost below -10°C (14°F).

Garden Cultivation

This elegant graceful plant is sadly becoming scarce. Plant in groups on their own so that the tall and striking arching stems and waxy green-tipped flowers are shown off to their best. It requires a cool shady situation in fertile well-drained soil. Dig the soil over before planting with some leaf mould, and each winter top dress with extra leaf mould.

Harvest

For medicinal use, dig up and dry the roots of a well-established 3-year-old-plant in the autumn after the foliage has died back.

OTHER USES

The plant has been employed cosmetically to clear freckles and as a skin tonic.

In Turkey the young shoots are harvested and cooked with asparagus.

Solomon's Seal *Polygonatum biflorum* **in flower**

CONTAINER GROWING

Solomon's Seal can be grown in large containers. Use a soil based compost, and top dress in autumn with well-rotted manure or leaf mould. This will also protect it during winter. Position in semi-shade and water well throughout the summer.

WARNING

All parts of the plant are poisonous and should be taken internally only under supervision of a qualified medicinal or herbal practitioner. Large doses can be harmful.

MEDICINAL

The powdered roots and rhizomes make a good poultice for bruises, inflammation and wounds, and a good wash for skin problems and blemishes.

American Indians made a tea of the rootstock to take for women's complaints and general internal pains. They also used it as a wash to counteract the effect of poison ivy.

Polygonatum odoratum contains a substance that lowers the level of blood sugar and has long been used in the Orient for diabetes.

Solomon's seal makes a good skin wash

Polemonium caeruleum

JACOB'S LADDER

***Also known as Blue Jacket, Charity, Jacob's Walking Stick, Ladder to Heaven and Greek Valerian.
From the family Polemoniaceae.***

This European native species grows sparsely over the whole of the temperate regions of the northern hemisphere. It is not as prolific as some of the other closely related species in America.

It was known to the ancient Greeks as 'polemonium', and the root was once administered in wine in cases of dysentery, toothache, and on the bites of poisonous animals.

The leaf, being divided into many segments, has the appearance of a ladder, hence its common name – 'Jacob slept with a stone for a pillow and he dreamed and behold a ladder set upon the earth and the top of it reached to Heaven and behold the Angels of God ascending and descending on it.' (Genesis 28, 12)

As late as the 19th century, it was known as 'Valeranae Graecae' or 'Greek Valerian' and was being used in some European pharmacies. It was predominantly used as an anti-syphilitic agent and in the treatment of rabies. To confuse things, the American Shakers called it 'Abscess' and used it for pleurisy and fevers.

Jacob's Ladder
Polemonium caeruleum

SPECIES

Polemonium caeruleum
Jacob's Ladder
Hardy perennial. Ht and spread 45-60cm (18-24in). Clusters of attractive, cup-shaped, lavender-blue flowers in summer. The mid-green leaves are finely divided into small lance shapes.

Polemonium caeruleum var. lacteum
Jacob's Ladder
Hardy perennial. Ht and spread 45-60cm (18-24in). Cluster of attractive, cup-shaped, lavender-white flowers in summer. Leaves as **P. caeruleum**.

Polemonium reptans
Also known as False Jacob's Ladder or American Greek Valerian.
Hardy perennial. Ht 20-45cm (8-18in), spread 30cm (12in). Cluster of attractive, cup-shaped, blue flowers in summer. The silver/green leaves are finely divided into small lance shapes. The root of this species is bitter in flavour and is employed as an astringent and as an antidote to snake bites.

Other species worth looking out for (both native of western North America) –

Polemonium carneum
Hardy perennial. Ht and spread 45cm (18in). Cluster of attractive, cup-shaped, pink or purple/pink flowers from early summer. Mid-green leaves are finely divided into small lance shapes.

Polemonium pulcherrimum
Hardy perennial. Ht 50cm (20in), spread 30cm (12in). Cluster of attractive, tubular, blue/purple flowers in summer. The mid-green leaves are finely divided into small lance shapes.

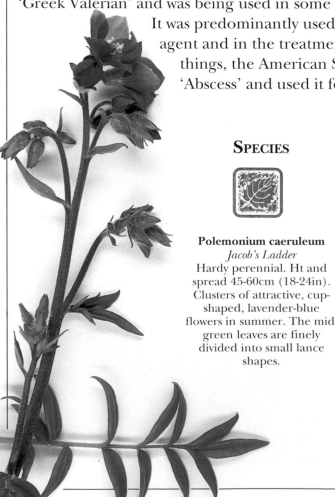

CULTIVATION

Propagation
Seed
For flowering early the following spring, sow the fairly small seeds fresh in autumn into a prepared seed or plug tray. Cover with a thin layer of compost. Leave in a cool/cold greenhouse over winter. They will stay in their trays quite happily through the winter, as long as they are kept frost free. Prick out in spring when the threat of frosts is over and plant directly into the garden, after hardening off, at a distance of 30cm (12in) apart.

For flowering the following season, sow under protection in early spring, or direct in the garden in late spring.

Division
Named varieties must be propagated by division. Divide established plants in the spring. Dig the whole plant up and ease it in half. Replant in a prepared site in the garden.

Pests and Diseases
These plants rarely suffer from pests or disease.

Maintenance
Spring: Sow seeds if not sown the previous autumn. Divide established plants if need be. *Summer*: Dead-head flowers. After flowering, cut back to prevent self-seeding. *Autumn*: Sow seeds under protection. *Winter*: Established plants are hardy and should not need protection.

Garden Cultivation
This lovely shortlived perennial is not particular to site or soil, although it prefers a rich moisture-retaining soil with an addition of lime. It is not fussy about sun or shade, but looks prettier in the sun. In a long, hot summer, make sure the plant gets plenty of extra water. In an average summer it should not need extra watering.

The fairly short flowering season can be prolonged by dead-heading. This is another plant beloved of cats, who seem to take a fancy to the young plants in particular. So, if you live in a catty area, give the young plants some protection.

Harvest
Cut the flowers just as they open for drying. Dry either in small bunches or individual sprays.

CONTAINER GROWING

Jacob's Ladder looks lovely in a container. Use a soil-based compost and do not allow to dry out. Place the container in a semi-shady place to protect if from over-heating in the midday sun. Feed with liquid fertilizer, following manufacturer's instructions, during the flowering period only.

CULINARY

I can find no record of this being used as a culinary herb, and the flowers do not add much flavour when added to salads.

OTHER USES
The dried flowers may not smell, but do look attractive in potpourris.

No longer used for medicinal purposes.

Jacob's Ladder growing in a field

Primula veris

COWSLIP

Also known as Our Lady's Bunch of Keys, St Peter's Keys, Palsywort, Bunch of Keys, Covekeys, Cowflop, Cowstripling, Freckled Face, Golden Drops, Herb Peter, Hot Rod, Long Legs, Nook Maidens, Titsy Totsy, St Peters Herb, Paigale, Coweslop, Cowslap, Fair Bells, Fairy Cups and Keys of Heaven. From the family Primulaceae.

This traditional herb is native to Northern and Central Europe. It has naturalized elsewhere on porous, calcareous soils, meadows and pastures, to an altitude of 2,000m (6,500ft).

In America the plant that is called cowslip is in fact the English marsh marigold (*Caltha palustris*) and is not to be confused with the above.

'Cowslip' is a corruption of 'cowsslop' from the Old English 'cu-sloppe', from which cowslips sprang up in the meadow after a cow had lifted its tail.

The generic name *primula* is from the Latin 'primus', meaning first, after its early flowering in spring. A legend of northern Europe is that St Peter let his keys to Heaven drop when he learned that a duplicate set had been made. Where they fell the cowslip grew, hence the English, French and German common names 'Keys of Heaven', 'Cleft de St Pierre' and 'Schlusselblumen'. The mediaeval *Regimen Sanitatis Salernitanum* recommended the cowslip as a cure for palsy or paralysis, a cure suggested perhaps by the trembling of its nodding flowers?

It is sadly no longer possible for country folk to go out and collect bushels of cowslip flowers to make cowslip wine. This once common grassland flower has now become relatively rare, a casualty of improved farming methods, which do not permit long grass and pastures to settle down and develop perennial flora. However, in East Anglia, where it retains the old alternative name 'paigale', it is beginning to re-establish itself on roadside verges and banked motorway edges in chalk and limestone areas, away from damaging pesticide sprays.

SPECIES

Primula veris
Cowslip
Hardy perennial. Ht and spread 15-20cm (6-8in). Tight clusters of fragrant, tubular, yellow flowers produced on stout stems in spring. Leaves, oval-shaped and mid-green, form a neat clump.

Cowslips are often mistaken for Oxlip (**P. elatior**), which is a hybrid of the cowslip and the primrose (**P. vulgaris**). The difference between the 2 is that oxlip have large pale yellow flowers in a one-sided cluster. Cowslip flowers are much deeper yellow, smaller and there are more in a cluster.

Cowslip *Primula veris*

CULTIVATION

Propagation
Seed
Better sown fresh. Collect the seeds heads in early autumn when the seeds are slightly succulent. Sow the fairly small seeds onto the surface of a prepared pot, seed or plug tray. Cover with glass. Put the container somewhere cool, like a cold frame, cold greenhouse or outside windowsill. Keep an eye on germination, which usually takes 4-6 weeks, and remove glass as soon as the seedling emerges. If you sow in springtime, they will need cold then warm temperatures to break their dormancy – the frost treatment.
  Plant into final position in the garden when the young plants are large enough to handle, or pot up for a spring display.

Division
Being a **primula**, cowslips divide easily. The best time for doing this is in the autumn. Dig up a clump and tease the plants apart. Replant in situ 15cm (6in) apart or pot up. Protect from frost until the roots have come down (this takes 4-6 weeks).

Pests and Diseases
The scourge of all **primula** plants is the vine weevil. I have known them decimate a complete stock of cowslips in a very short time.

Maintenance
Spring: Early in year clear all the winter debris from established plants. Stratify seed if necessary and sow.
Summer: Only dead head if you do not want the seed.
Autumn: Collect seed. Divide established plants.
Winter: No need to protect.

Cowslip wine

Garden Cultivation
Plant cowslips in semi-shade or sun, in a moist but well-drained soil. They prefer lime soil, but do adapt well. They look better grown in clumps rather than on their own, and are ideal for front of border in a spring garden, or for growing in the lawn, although you will have to mow round them until the seeds have set.

Harvest
I am sure no reminder is necessary not to pick or dig up cowslips growing in the wild. This is prohibited in many European countries.
  Pick leaves as required to use fresh. Not really worth drying.
  Pick flowers as they open to use fresh.
  Dig up roots in the autumn for drying.

CONTAINER GROWING

Essentially a wild plant, the cowslip does not thrive inside, but is happy in a container on a windowsill or patio. Use the standard bark, peat compost, and do not allow to dry out. I suggest that the container be in a position that gets some shade at midday.

WARNING

Some **primula** species can cause a form of contact dermatitis characterized by a violent vascular eruption in the fingers and forearms. Hyper-sensitive individuals should avoid these plants.

MEDICINAL

A tea from the flowers is a simple remedy for insomnia, nervous tension and headaches. Cowslip syrup was a country remedy for palsy and paralysis, hence its alternative name 'Palsywort'.
  Cowslip roots are attributed with various medicinal propensities. One, owing to their high saponin content, is to treat whooping cough and bronchitis. Another, attributed to the salicylates present in the root, is to alleviate arthritis. For this reason, in many old herbals, cowslip roots are called **radix arthritica**.

CULINARY

Use leaves in salads and for meat stuffing. Use flowers in cowslip wine and salads.

Cowslip in salad

Primula vulgaris

PRIMROSE

**Also known as Early Rose, Easter Rose, First Rose and May-Flooer.
From the family Primulaceae.**

This herald of spring is a native of Europe.
    The name Primrose originates from the old Latin 'prima', meaning first, and 'rosa', meaning rose.

The polyanthus, which has been known in gardens since the 17th century, probably originates from crosses between coloured forms of the Primrose and the Cowslip.

In the Middle Ages concoctions were made from primroses which were used as a remedy for gout and rheumatism. The flowers were used in the preparation of love potions. An infusion of the roots was taken for nervous headaches.

The plant has become increasingly rare, in part due to the changing countryside. Legislation makes it illegal now to pick or dig up any wild plant and, with more sympathetic farming practices, one can see these plants beginning to re-establish in the hedgerows.

SPECIES

Primula vulgaris
Primrose
Hardy perennial. Ht and spread 15cm (6in). The fresh yellow, sweetly scented flowers with darker yellow centres are borne singly on hairy stems in early spring. Leaves are mid-green and wrinkled.

Primrose *Primula vulgaris*

CULTIVATION

Propagation
Seed
In summer sow the fresh seed when it is still slightly green and before it turns darkish brown and becomes dry. Sow in a prepared seed or plug tray and cover with Perlite. These fresh seeds usually germinate in a few weeks. Either winter in the plug trays, or prick out from seed trays when the seedlings are large enough and winter in pots for planting out into a prepared site the following spring.

The seed that one gets in seed packets should be sown in the autumn or early winter. Do not sow it directly into the ground where it can easily be lost. Water the seeds in; do not cover with compost, but cover with glass or polythene. To help the seeds germinate, leave the trays outside for the winter so that the seeds get the frost (stratification). Sometimes they take 2 years to germinate from the dry state, so leave the seed trays until the following year if nothing appears in the spring, checking the compost occasionally to make sure it does not dry out. When the seedlings are large enough, plant out in a prepared site in the garden 15cm (6in) apart.

Division
Established clumps (from your own or friends' gardens, not from the wild) can be divided very easily in the autumn.

Pests and Diseases
The only major pest to attack the primrose is the

Primrose *Primula vulgaris*

Some **Primula** species can cause a form of contact dermatitis, characterized by a violent vascular eruption in the fingers and forearms. Hyper-sensitive individuals should avoid these plants.

MEDICINAL

Its medicinal use is really in the past, though it is still used occasionally as an expectorant for the treatment of bronchitis. A tisane, which is a mild sedative and good for anxiety and insomnia, can be made from the leaves and flowers.

Primrose salad

Primrose tisane

CULINARY

The flowers are lovely in green salads, and they can be crystallized to decorate puddings and cakes.
  The young leaves make an interesting vegetable if steamed and tossed in butter.

vine weevil. Pollinated primrose flowers produce sticky seeds that attract ants; they then disperse them around the garden, which is why you sometimes see plants where you least expect them.

Maintenance
Spring: Plant out young plants.
Summer: Sow fresh seed.
Autumn: Divide established plants.
Winter: Sow dry seed that needs stratification. No need to protect plants, fully hardy.

Garden Cultivation
When planting primroses bear in mind that their natural habitat is in hedgerows and under deciduous trees and that therefore they prefer a moist soil, and will tolerate heavy soils, in semi-shade. Planted in a very well-sheltered site, they often open early in spring.
  If you are growing primroses in a wild garden make sure you do not cut the grass until mid-summer when the plants will have seeded themselves.

Harvest
Pick flowers for fresh use any time. Pick young leaves to use fresh. In summer collect seed for immediate sowing.

CONTAINER GROWING

Primroses can be grown in containers and look very attractive and heartening especially if spring is damp and miserable. Use a soil-based compost. Keep the plant well watered and feed only occasionally with liquid fertilizer, once in the spring after flowering is sufficient. This is primarily a wild plant and does not benefit from over feeding.

Prostanthera

PROSTANTHERA

Also known as Mint Bush. From the family Labiatae.

These highly attractive aromatic shrubs are natives of Australia.

I have fallen in love with these most generous of flowerers. When exhibiting one in flower at the Chelsea Flower Show some member of the public fell in love with it in equal measure and tried to liberate it from my display!

I can find no historical references other than in the RHS *Dictionary of Gardening*, which states that the generic name, *Prostanthera*, comes from 'prostithemi' to append, and anthera, meaning 'anther', the pollen bearing part of the stamen. This therefore alludes to the appendages usually borne by the anthers.

Prostanthera cuneata

SPECIES

Prostanthera cuneata
Evergreen half-hardy perennial. Ht and spread 60-90cm (2-3ft). Very attractive white flowers with purple spots that look rather like little orchids; late spring, early summer. Round, dark green, slightly leathery and shiny, mint-scented leaves. Can withstand a minimum temperature of -2°C (28°F).

Prostanthera ovalifolia
Evergreen tender perennial. Reaches a height and spread of 1.2m (4ft) in its native country. Attractive purple flowers appear on short leafy racemes throughout the spring and summer. Dark green aromatic leaves. Can only withstand a minimum temperature of 5°C (41°F).

Prostanthera rotundifolia rosea
Evergreen half-hardy perennial. A small tree that reaches a height of 3m (10ft) in it's native country; in cooler climates its a lot smaller. Pretty mauve/purple flowers in spring that last a long time. The dark green leaves (not as dark as **P. cuneata**) are round and mint scented. Can only withstand a minimum temperature of 0°C (32°F).

Prostanthera rotundifolia rosea

Prostanthera sieberi
Evergreen tender perennial. Reaches a height of 2m (6ft), spread 1.5m (5ft) in its native country; in cooler climates it is a lot smaller. The green leaves are small (but larger than the other species mentioned), oval, and coarsely toothed, with a strong mint scent when crushed. Can only withstand a minimum temperature 5°C (41°F).

CULTIVATION

Propagation
Cuttings
Take cuttings either in spring or late summer. Use the bark, peat, grit mix of compost. When the cuttings are well rooted, 8-12 weeks, pot up again using the bark, peat, grit mix and keep in containers for the first year.

Pests and Diseases
Over watering young plants is a killer.

Maintenance
Spring: Take cuttings.
Summer: Cut back after flowering only if necessary.
Autumn: Protect from frosts.
Winter: Protect from hard frosts and excessive water.

Garden Cultivation
In cool climates with persistent frosts they are better grown in a container. However if your climate is mild, plant out in the spring in a warm corner, in a lime-free, well-draining soil at a distance of 60-90cm (24-35in) apart. Rain combined with frost is the killer in winter.

If you want to make a low hedge out of **Prostanthera cuneata** then plant specimens 45cm (18in) apart.

Harvest
Pick leaves in the summer after flowering for drying and inclusion in potpourris.

CONTAINER GROWING

This is a real crowd puller when in flower, and even when not, makes a most attractive aromatic plant. Use the bark, peat, grit mix of compost. Keep young plants on the dry side, but water freely in the growing season.

MEDICINAL

I am sure that a plant that gives off as much scent, and has obviously so much oil in the leaf (**P. cuneata**), will one day have some use.

Prunella vulgaris

SELF HEAL

Also known as Carpenter's Herb, Sticklewort, Touch and Heal, All Heal, Woundwort, Hercules' Woundwort, Blue Curl's, Brownwort and Hock Heal. From the family Labiatae.

This herb is found growing wild throughout all the temperate regions of the Northern Hemisphere, including Europe, Asia and North America. It is found on moist, loamy, well-drained soils, in grass-land, pastures and open woodland, especially in sunny situations.Now introduced into China and Australia.

In strict 16th-century adherence to the Doctrine of Signatures, whereby it was believed that every plant bore an outward sign of its value to mankind, people noted that the upper lip of the flower was shaped like a hook, and as billhooks and sickles were a main cause of wounds in their agrarian society, they decided that the purpose of the herb was to heal wounds (hence Self Heal). They also saw the shape of the throat in the flower, which was why it was introduced to treat diseases of the throat such as quinsy and diphtheria, a propensity with a precedent in Ancient Greece, where physicians used it to cure sore throats and tonsillitis.

SPECIES

Prunella vulgaris
Self Heal
Hardy perennial. Ht 5-30cm (2-12in), spread 15-30cm (6-12in). Clusters of blue/purple flowers all summer. Oval leaves of a bright green.
There is a much rarer white-flowered species, **Prunella laciniata**, which has very deeply cut leaves.

CULTIVATION

Propagation
Seed
Sow the small seeds into prepared seed or plug trays in either spring or autumn and cover with Perlite; no extra heat is required. If an autumn sowing, winter the young plants in a cold frame. In spring, when the plants are large enough, plant out 15-20cm (6-8in) apart.

Division
This plant grows runners that have their own small root systems and is, there-fore, easy to divide. Dig up in the spring or autumn, and split and replant either in the garden or amongst grass.

Garden Cultivation
This plant, which is easy to establish, makes a colourful ground cover with attractive flowers. It is happy in full sun to semi-shade and will

Self Heal *Prunella vulgaris*

grow in most soils, including those that are rather acid, though it does best if the soil is fertile. It can be grown in a lawn, and while the mower keeps its spread and height in check, it will still flower and be much visited by bees and butterflies.

Pests and Diseases
In most cases it is free from pests and disease.

Maintenance
Spring: Sow seed. Divide established plants.
Summer: Cut back after flowering to curtail self-seeding.
Autumn: Divide established plants. Sow seeds.
Winter: No need for protection, fully hardy.

Harvest
Harvest for medicinal use only. Dry the leaves and flowers.

CONTAINER GROWING

Self heal can be grown in containers using a soil based compost. However as it looks a bit insipid on its own it is better combined with plants like heartsease, poppies and cowslips.
Water well during the growing season, but only feed liquid fertilizer twice otherwise it will produce too lush a growth.

MEDICINAL

Used in herbal medicines as a gargle for sore throats and inflammation of the mouth. A decoction is used to wash cuts and to soothe burns and bruises.

Pulmonaria officinalis

LUNGWORT

Also known as Jerusalem Cowslip, Abraham, Isaac and Jacob, Adam and Eve, Bedlam, Cowslip, Beggar's Basket, Bottle of Allsorts, Children of Israel, Good Friday Plant, Lady's Milk, Lady Mary's Tears, Spotted Mary, Thunder and Lightening, Virgin Mary, Virgin Mary's Milkdrops and Virgin Mary's Tears, Spotted Bugloss, Jerusalem Sage, Maple Lungwort, Spotted Comfrey and Spotted Lungwort. From the family Boraginaceae.

L ungwort is a native plant of Europe and northern parts of the USA. It has naturalized in many countries in cool climates, where it grows in shady, moist areas and in woodlands. The markings on the leaves were attributed to the Virgin Mary's milk or her tears; however, the generic name, *Pulmonaria*, comes from 'pulmo' meaning lung, and the common name, Lungwort, conjurs up a rather different image – of diseased lungs – to those blotched markings on the leaves. The Doctrine of Signatures, which held that all plants must be associated either by appearance, smell or habit with the disease which it was said to heal, used it for various lung disorders.

SPECIES

Pulmonaria angustifolia
Hardy perennial. Ht 23cm (9in), spread 20-30cm (8-12in). Flowers pink turning to bright blue in spring. Leaves lance shaped and mid-green with no markings.

Pulmonaria longifolia
Hardy perennial. Ht 30cm (12in), spread 45cm (18in). The flowers start pinkish turning purplish-blue in spring. The leaves are lance shaped, dark green, and slightly hairy with white spots.

Pulmonaria officinalis
Lungwort
Semi-evergreen hardy perennial. Ht 30cm (12in), spread 60cm (24in). Pink flowers turning blue in spring. Leaves oval with blotchy white/cream markings on a mid-green, slightly hairy surface.

Lungwort *Pulmonaria officinalis* **in flower**

Pulmonaria officinalis 'Sissinghurst White'
Semi-evergreen hardy perennial. Ht 30cm (12in), spread 45-60cm (18-24in). White flowers in spring. Leaves white-spotted, mid-green in colour, with a pointed oval shape.

Pulmonaria rubra 'Redstart'
Semi-evergreen hardy perennial. Ht 30cm (12in), spread 60cm (24in). Pink/red flowers in spring. The leaves are long ovals, velvety and mid-green with no markings.

Pulmonaria saccharata 'Mrs Moon'

Semi-evergreen hardy perennial. Ht 30cm (12in), spread 60cm (24in). Flowers start as pink and turn blue in spring. The green leaves are long pointed ovals with clear, creamy white, variable spots.

Note: The American native Virginian cowslip, **Mertensia virginica,** also known as smooth lungwort, belongs to the same Boraginaceae family as Lungwort. The flowers are purple/blue and the leaves lance shaped. It is excellent for shady places. The foliage dies back very early in autumn and leaves a bare patch, so it is not suitable for front of border. Propagate in the same way as the **Pulmonaria spp**.

CONTAINER GROWING

Make sure the container is large enough to give the creeping rhizomes a chance to spread and so prevent the plant from becoming pot bound too quickly. Use a soil-based compost and a frost-hardy container, as these plants do not like coming inside even into a cold greenhouse, where the growth becomes soft and rots off. During the growing season keep the container in a shady spot and water well.

MEDICINAL

Lungwort is a soothing expectorant. The silica it contains restores the elasticity of the lungs. Externally it has been used for healing all kinds of wounds.

Lungwort potpourri

CULTIVATION

Propagation

Seeds
Lungwort seldom produces viable seed; increase your stock by division, but watch out in the garden, where it will self-seed erratically.

Division
Divide established plants either after flowering in late spring or in the autumn.

Pests and Diseases
Lungwort can suffer from powdery mildew when the leaves die back in autumn. Simply remove the damaged leaves and dispose of them.

Maintenance
Spring: Dig up seedlings which mysteriously appear in odd parts of the garden.
Summer: Do nothing.
Autumn: Divide established plants. Cut back growth.
Winter: No need to protect, fully hardy.

Lungwort
Pulmonaria officinalis

Garden Cultivation
This attractive, fully hardy plant prefers a moist but well-drained soil with added leaf mould or well-rotted manure. It is an ideal plant for shady parts of the garden and can not take extreme heat or searing sun. Plant out 30cm (12in) apart in the autumn. Lungwort grows quickly and spreads to provide dense ground cover. Water freely in dry weather.

Harvest
Pick the leaves after flowering in the summer and dry for medicinal use.

Rosmarinus

ROSEMARY

From the family Labiatae.

Rosemary is a shrub that originated in the Mediterranean area and is now widely cultivated throughout the temperate regions. The ancient Latin name means sea-dew. This may come from its habit of growing close to the sea and the dew-like appearance of its blossom at a distance. It is steeped in myth, magic and folk medicinal use. One of my favourite stories about Rosemary comes from Spain. It relates that originally the blue flowers were white. When the Holy family fled into Egypt, the Virgin Mary had to hide from some soldiers, so she spread her cloak over a rosemary bush and knelt behind it. When the soldiers had gone by she stood up and removed her cloak and the blossoms turned blue in her honour. Also connected to the Christian faith is the story that rosemary will grow for 33 years, the length of Christ's life, and then die.

In Elizabethan days, the wedding couple wore or carried a sprig of rosemary as a sign of fidelity. Also bunches of rosemary were tied with coloured ribbon tipped with gold and given to guests at weddings to symbolize love and faithfulness.

Rosemary was burnt in sick chambers to freshen and purify the air. Branches were strewn in courts of law as a protection from gaol fever. During the Plague people used to wear it in neck pouches to sniff as they travelled, and in Victorian times it was carried in the hollow handles of walking sticks for the same reasons.

SPECIES

Rosmarinus officinalis
Rosemary
Evergreen hardy perennial. Ht and spread 1m (3ft). Pale blue flowers in early spring to early summer and then sometimes in early autumn. Needle-shaped dark green leaves are highly aromatic.

Rosmarinus officinalis var. albiflorus
White Rosemary
Evergreen hardy perennial. Ht and spread 80cm (32in). White flowers in early spring to early summer and then sometimes in early autumn. Needle-shaped dark green leaves are highly aromatic.

Rosmarinus officinalis angustissimus 'Corsican Blue'
Corsican Rosemary
Evergreen hardy perennial. Ht and spread 80cm (32in). Blue flowers in early spring to early summer and then sometimes again in early autumn. The needle shaped dark green leaves are highly aromatic. It is much bushier than the standard Rosemary and has a very pungent scent. It is lovely to cook with.

Rosmarinus officinalis 'Aureus'
Golden Rosemary
Evergreen hardy perennial. Ht 80cm (32in), spread 60cm (24in). It hardly ever flowers, but if it does they are pale blue. The thin needle leaves are green splashed with gold. If you did not know better you would think the plant was suffering from a virus. It still looks very attractive.

Rosmarinus officinalis 'Benenden Blue'
Benenden Blue Rosemary
Evergreen hardy perennial. Ht and spread 80cm (32in). Dark blue flowers in early spring to early summer and then sometimes again in early autumn. Leaves are fine needles and fairly dense on the stem, good aroma.

Prostrate Rosemary *Rosmarinus officinalis Prostratus Group*

Miss Jessopp's Upright Rosemary *Rosmarinus officinalis 'Miss Jessopp's Upright'*

Rosmarinus officinalis 'Fota Blue'

Fota Blue Rosemary
Evergreen hardy perennial. Ht and spread 80cm (32in). Very attractive dark blue flowers in early spring to early summer and then sometimes again in early autumn. Very well spaced narrow needle-like dark green leaves, the plant has fairly prostrate habit.

Rosemary officinalis 'Majorca Pink'

Majorcan Pink Rosemary
Evergreen half-hardy perennial. Ht and spread 80cm (32in). Pink flowers in early spring to early summer and then sometimes again in early autumn. The needle-shaped dark green leaves are highly aromatic. This is a slightly prostrate form of Rosemary.

Rosmarinus officinalis 'Miss Jessopp's Upright'

Miss Jessopp's Upright Rosemary
Evergreen hardy perennial. Ht and spread 2m (6ft). Very pale blue flowers in early spring to early summer and then sometimes again in early autumn. This Rosemary has a very upright habit, making it ideal for hedges (see page 162). The leaves are dark green needles spaced closely together, making the plant very bushy.

Rosmarinus officinalis 'Primley Blue'

Primley Blue Rosemary
(Not Frimley which it has been incorrectly called for a few years.)
Evergreen hardy perennial. Ht and spread 80cm (32in). Blue flowers in early spring to early summer and then sometimes again in early autumn. The needle-shaped dark green leaves are highly aromatic. This is a good hardy bushy variety.

Rosmarinus officinalis Prostratus Group (lavandulaceus, repens)

Prostrate Rosemary
Evergreen hardy perennial. Ht 30cm (12in), spread 1m (3ft). Light blue flowers in early spring to early summer and then sometimes again in early autumn. The needle-shaped dark green leaves are highly aromatic. This is a great plant for trailing on a wall or bank.

Rosmarinus officinalis 'Roseus'

Pink Rosemary
Evergreen half-hardy perennial. Ht and spread 80cm (32in). Pink flowers in early spring to early summer and then sometimes again in early autumn. The needle-shaped dark green leaves are highly aromatic.

Rosmarinus officinalis 'Severn Sea'

Severn Seas Rosemary
Evergreen half-hardy perennial. Ht and spread 80cm (32in). Mid-blue flowers in early spring to early summer and then sometimes again in early autumn. The needle-shaped dark green leaves are highly aromatic. The whole plant has a slightly prostrate habit with arching branches.

Rosmarinus officinalis 'Sissinghurst Blue'

Sissinghurst Rosemary
Evergreen hardy perennial. Ht 1.5m (4½ft), spread 1m (3ft). Light blue flowers in early spring to early summer and then sometimes again in early autumn. The plant has an upright habit and grows very bushy. The needle-shaped dark green leaves are highly aromatic.

Rosmarinus officinalis 'Sudbury Blue'

Sudbury Blue Rosemary
Evergreen hardy perennial. Ht and spread 1m (3ft). Mid-blue flowers in early spring to early summer and then sometimes again in early autumn. Good hardy plant. The needle-shaped dark green leaves are highly aromatic.

I have some very old gardening books which make reference to a silver variegated rosemary, as does the RHS *Dictionary of Gardening* (1951) and I have even recently been asked if I grow it. I have yet to find it.

Left to right: **White Rosemary** *Rosmarinus officinalis var. albiflorus*, **Miss Jessopp's Upright Rosemary** *Rosmarinus officinalis 'Miss Jessopp's Upright'*, **Pink Rosemary** *Rosmarinus officinalis 'Roseus'*

CULTIVATION

Propagation
Seed
Rosemary officinalis can, with care, be grown from seed. It needs a bottom heat of 27-32°C (80-90°F) to be successful. Sow in the spring in prepared seed or plug trays, using the bark, peat, grit compost and cover with Perlite. Having got it to germinate be careful not to over-water the seedlings as they are prone to damping off. Harden the young plant off slowly in summer and pot up. Keep it in a pot for the first winter, and plant out the following spring into the required position at a distance of 60-90cm (2-3 ft) apart.

Cuttings
This is a more reliable method of propagation and ensures that you achieve the variety you require.

Softwood: Take these in spring off the new growth. Cut lengths of about 15cm (6in) long. Use the bark, grit, peat mix of compost.

Semi-hardwood: Take these in summer from the non-flowering shoots, using the same compost as for softwood cuttings.

Layering
Rosemary lends itself to layering especially as the branches of several varieties hang down. Layer established branches in summer.

Pests and Diseases
Being an aromatic plant, rosemary really does not suffer too much from pest and disease.

Maintenance
Spring. Trim after flowering. Sow seeds of **Rosemary officinalis**. Take softwood cuttings.
Summer. Feed container plants. Take semi-hardwood cuttings. Layer plants.
Autumn: Protect young tender plants.
Winter. Put a mulch, or straw, or agricultural fleece around all plants.

Garden Cultivation
Rosemary requires a well-drained soil in a sheltered sunny position. It is frost hardy but in cold areas it prefers to grow against a south or south-west facing wall. If the plant is young it is worth giving some added protection in winter. If trimming is necessary cut back only when the frosts are over; if possible leave it until after the spring flowering. Sometimes rosemary looks a bit scorched after frosts, in which case it is worth cutting the damaged plants to healthy wood in spring. Straggly old plants may also be cut back hard at the same time. Never cut back plants in the autumn or if there is any chance of frost, as the plant will be damaged or even killed. On average, despite the story about rosemary growing for 33 years, it is best to replace bushes every 5 to 6 years.

Harvest
As rosemary is evergreen, you can pick fresh leaves all year round as long as you are not greedy. If you need large quantities then harvest in summer and either dry the leaves or make an oil or vinegar.

COMPANION PLANTING

If planted near carrot it repels carrot fly. It is also said to be generally beneficial to sage.

White Rosemary *Rosmarinus officinalis var. albiflorus*

CONTAINER GROWING

Rosemary does well in pots and is the preferred way to grow it in cold districts. The prostrate and less hardy varieties look very attractive and benefit from the extra protection offered by a container. Use the bark, grit, peat mix and make sure the compost is very well drained. Do not over-water, and feed only after flowering.

HEDGES

Rosemary certainly makes an effective hedge; it looks pretty in flower, smells marvellous and is evergreen. In fact it has everything going for it if you have the right soil conditions which, more importantly than ever, must be well drained and carry a bias towards lime. The best varieties for hedges are Primley Blue and Miss Jessopp's. Both are upright, hardy and bushy. Primley Blue has a darker blue flower and I think is slightly prettier. Planting distance 45cm (18in) apart. Again, if you need eventually to trim the hedge, do it after the spring flowering.

CULINARY

This is one of the most useful of culinary herbs, combining with meat, especially lamb, casseroles, tomato sauces, baked fish, rice, salads, egg dishes, apples, summer wine cups, cordials, vinegars and oils.

Vegetarian Goulash
Serves 4

2 tablespoons rosemary olive oil
2 medium onions, sliced
1 dessertspoon wholemeal flour
1 tablespoon paprika
275ml (10fl oz) hot water mixed with 1 teaspoon tomato purée
400gm (14oz) tin Italian tomatoes
2 sprigs 10cm (4in) long Rosemary
225g (8oz) cauliflower sprigs
225g (8oz) new carrots, washed and cut into chunks
250g (8oz) new potatoes, washed and cut into halves
½ green capsium, de-seeded and chopped
150ml (5fl oz) soured cream or Greek yoghurt
Salt and freshly milled black pepper

Vegetarian Goulash

Heat the rosemary oil in a flameproof casserole, fry the onion until soft, then stir in the ¾ of the paprika. Cook for 2 minutes. Stir in the water, tomatoes and sprigs of rosemary. Bring to the boil stirring all the time. Add all the vegetables and the seasonings. Cover and bake in the pre-heated oven (190°C, 375°F, Gas Mark 5) for 30-40 minutes. Remove from oven, carefully take out the rosemary sprigs and stir in the soured cream or yoghurt, plus the remaining paprika. Serve with fresh pasta and/or garlic bread.

OTHER USES

Put rosemary twigs on the barbecue; they give off a delicious aroma. If you have a wood burning stove, a few twigs thrown onto it makes the house smell lovely.

Rosemary is used in many herbal shampoos and the plant has a long reputation as a hair tonic. Use an infusion in the final rinse of a hair wash, especially if you have dark hair, as it will make it shine. (Use chamomile for fair hair.)

Rosemary infusion

MEDICINAL

Like many other essential oils, rosemary oil has anti-bacterial and anti-fungal properties, and it helps poor circulation if rubbed into the effected joints.

The oil may be used externally as an insect repellent. It also makes an excellent remedy for headaches if applied directly to the head.

Rosemary tea makes a good mouthwash for halitosis and is also a good antiseptic gargle. Drunk in small amounts it reduces flatulence and stimulates the smooth muscle of the digestive tract and gall bladder and increases the flow of bile. Put a teaspoon of chopped leaves into a cup and pour on boiling water; cover and leave it to stand for 5 minutes.

An antiseptic solution of rosemary can be added to the bath to promote heathy skin. Boil a handful in 475ml (16fl oz) of water for 10 minutes.

WARNING

The oil should not be used internally. Also, extremely large doses of the leaf are toxic, possibly causing abortion, convulsions and, very rarely, death.

Rumex
SORREL

Also known as Bread and Cheese, Sour Leaves, Tom Thumbs, A Thousand Fingers and Sour Sauce. From the family Polygonaceae.

Buckler Leaf Sorrel
Rumex scutatus

Sorrel is a native plant of Europe, Asia and North America . It has naturalized in many countries throughout the world on rich, damp, loamy, acid soils. The generic name, *Rumex*, comes from the Latin rumo 'I suck'. Apparently, Roman soldiers sucked the leaves to relieve thirst, and their doctors used them as a diuretic.

The name sorrel comes from the old French word 'surelle' meaning 'sour'. The Tudors considered the herb to be one of the best English vegetables; Henry VIII held it in great esteem. In Lapland, sorrel juice has been used instead of rennet to curdle milk.

Sorrel *Rumex acetosa*

SPECIES

Rumex acetosa
Sorrel
Also known as Broad Leafed, Common Sorrel, Garden Sorrel, Meadow Sorrel, and confusingly (see below), French Sorrel.
Hardy perennial. Ht 60-120cm (2-4ft), spread 30cm (1ft). The flowers are small, dull and inconspicuous; colour greenish, turning reddish brown as the fruit ripens. The mid-green leaves are lanced shaped with 2 basal lobes pointing backwards.

Rumex acetosella
Sheep's Sorrel
Hardy perennial. Ht 15-30cm (6-12in), spread indefinite (can be very invasive). The flowers are small, dull and incon-spicuous; colour greenish, turning brown as the fruit ripens. The mid-green leaves are shaped like a barbed spear. It grows wild on heaths and in grassy places, but is rarely found on chalky soil.

Rumex scutatus
Buckler Leaf Sorrel
Also known as French Sorrel.
Hardy perennial. Ht 15-45cm (6-18in), spread 60cm (24in). The flowers are small, dull and inconspicuous; colour greenish, turning brown as the fruit ripens. The mid-green leaves are shaped like squat shields.

CULTIVATION

Propagation
Seed
For an early crop start off under protection in early spring. Sow into prepared seed or plug trays, using the bark, peat compost and covering the seeds with Perlite. Germination is fairly quick, 10-20 days without extra heat. When the seedlings are large enough and the soil has started to warm up, plant out 30cm (12in) apart.

Division
Sorrel is easy to divide and it is a good idea to divide broad leaf sorrel every other year to keep the leaves succulent. Autumn is the best time to do this, replanting in a prepared site.

Pests and Diseases
Wood pigeons, slugs and occasionally leaf miners attack sorrel, but should cause no problems with established plants. Remove the effected leaves, and put out traps for the slugs.

Maintenance
Spring: Sow seed, under protection, in early spring and outdoors from mid-spring.
Summer: Cut off flowers to maintain leaf production and prevent self-seeding. In a hot summer, water regularly to keep the leaves succulent.
Autumn: Divide established plants.
Winter: Fully hardy.

Garden Cultivation

This perennial herb likes a rich acid soil which retains moisture in full sun to partial shade. Sow the seeds in late spring into a prepared site. When germinated, thin seedlings out to a distance of 7.5cm (3in) and finally to a distance of 30cm (12in) apart. Can be grown under cloches to provide leaf throughout the year. The plant tends to run to seed quickly so, to keep the leaves fresh and succulent, remove flowerheads as they appear.

In really warm summers or generally warm climates, sorrel leaves tend to become bitter as the season progresses. A mulch will keep the soil cooler and, once the season cools down, the flavour will improve. Grow buckler leaf sorrel with its smaller leaf, as it is less susceptible.

If sorrel is causing a problem in your garden simply add some lime to eradicate it. It may need a few applications.

Harvest

Pick young leaves throughout the growing season for fresh use and for freezing. Sorrel does not dry well.

CONTAINER GROWING

The buckler variety makes a good low growing pot plant. Use the bark, peat mix of compost, and make sure the container has room for the plant to spread. It is a very useful culinary herb, so for those with a small garden or who live on a chalk soil this makes an ideal container plant. Remember to keep cutting off flowers to keep leaves tender. Water well in the growing season, and feed with liquid fertilizer, especially if you are picking a lot.

Buckler Leaf Sorrel
Rumex scutatus

CULINARY

This is an excellent herb with which to experiment. Use sparingly in soups, omelettes, fish sauces, and with poultry and pork. It is useful for tenderizing meat. Wrap it around steaks or add pounded leaf to a marinade.

Eat leaves raw in salads, especially the buckler leaf sorrel, but reduce the vinegar or lemon in any accompanying dressing to compensate for the increased acidity.

Cook like spinach, changing the cooking water once to reduce acidity.

A Green Sauce

Wash a handful each of sorrel and lettuce leaves and a handful of water cress. Cook in a little water with a whole peeled onion until tender. Remove onion and discard. Allow the (mushy) leaves to cool then add 1 tablespoon (15ml) of olive oil, 1 tablespoon (15ml) of wine vinegar, pepper and salt. Stir until creamy. Serve with fish or cold poultry.

Sorrel and lettuce soup

Serves 4
100g (4oz) sorrel
100g (4oz) lettuce
100g (4oz) potatoes, peeled and
  sliced
50g (2oz) French parsley
50g (2oz) butter
600ml (1 pint) chicken stock
4 tablespoons thin cream.
Wash the sorrel, lettuce and

French parsley, pat dry and roughly chop. Heat the butter in a heavy pan and add the sorrel, lettuce, and parsley. Stew very gently for about 5 minutes, and then add the potato. Mix all together, pour over the heated stock, and simmer covered for 25 minutes. Put in a liquidizer, or, if you are a purist, through a coarse food mill. Return to the pan and heat gently (do not boil). Swirl in some cream just before serving.

OTHER USES

Sorrel is a good dye plant; with an alum mordant it makes a yellow or green dye.

Use juice of the leaf to remove rust, mould and ink stains from linen, wicker and silver.

Sorrel and lettuce soup

MEDICINAL

Sorrel is considered to have blood cleansing and blood improving qualities in a similar way to spinach, which improves the haemoglobin content of the blood. It also contains Vitamin C.

A leaf may be used in a poultice to treat certain skin complaints, including acne.

WARNING

Care has to be taken that sorrel is not used in too great a quantity or too frequently. Its oxalic acid content may damage health if taken in excess. Very large doses are poisonous, causing severe kidney damage.

The herb should not be used medicinally by those predisposed to rheumatism, arthritis, gout, kidney stones or gastric hyperacidity.

The leaf may cause dermatitis.

Ruta graveolens

RUE

Also known as Herb of Grace and Herbygrass. From the family Rutaceae.

Rue is a native of Southern Europe, especially the Mediterranean region, and is found growing in poor free-draining soil. It has established itself in North America and Australia in similar conditions. It has also adapted to the cooler climates and is now naturalized in Northern Europe. Rue was known as Herb of Grace, perhaps because it was regarded as a protector against the Devil, witchcraft and magic.

It was also used as an antidote against every kind of poison from toadstools to snake bites. The Romans brought it across northern Europe to Britain, where it did not gain favour until the Middle Ages, when it was one of the herbs carried in nosegays by the rich as protection from evil and the plague. Also, like rosemary, it was placed near the judge before prisoners were brought out, as protection from the pestilence ridden gaols and goal fever.

It was famous for preserving eyesight and was said to promote second sight, perhaps acting on the third eye. Both Leonardo da Vinci and Michelangelo are supposed to have said that their inner vision had been enhanced by this herb.

SPECIES

Ruta graveolens
Rue
Hardy evergreen perennial. Ht and spread 60cm (24in). Yellow waxy flowers with 4 or 5 petals in summer. Small rounded lobed leaves of a greeny blue colour.

Ruta graveolens 'Jackman's Blue'
Rue Jackman's Blue
Hardy evergreen perennial. Ht and spread 60cm (24in). Yellow waxy flowers with 4 or 5 petals in summer. Small rounded lobed leaves of a distinctive blue colour.

Ruta graveolens 'Variegata'
Variegated Rue
Hardy evergreen perennial. Ht and spread 60cm (24in). Yellow waxy flowers with 4 or 5 petals in summer. Small rounded lobed leaves with a most distinctive cream/white variegation, which is particularly marked in spring, fading in the summer unless the plant is kept well clipped. I have known people mistake the variegation for flowers and try to smell them, which shows how attractive this plant is. Smelling it at close quarters is not, however, a good idea as this plant, like other rues, can cause the skin to blister.

Rue *Ruta graveolens* **is said to have inspired the suit of clubs in playing cards**

CULTIVATION

Propagation
Seed
In spring sow the fine seed using the cardboard technique in prepared plug or seed trays. Use the bark, peat mix of compost and cover with Perlite. You may find that a bottom heat of 20°C (68°F) is helpful. Germination can be an all or nothing affair, it depends on the source of the seed. Young seedlings are prone to damping off, so watch the watering, just keep the compost damp not wet.

Unlike many variegated plants the variegated rue will be variegated from seed. When the seedlings are large enough plant out into a prepared site in the garden at a distance of 45cm (18in).

Cuttings
Take cuttings of new shoots in spring or early summer. Jackman's Blue can only be propagated from cuttings. Use the bark, peat, grit mix of compost for the cuttings; again do not over-water as they can be prone to rot.

Rue Jackman's Blue *Ruta graveolens 'Jackman's Blue'*

Pests and Diseases
Rue is prone to white fly followed by black sooty mould. Treat the white fly with a liquid horticultural soap as soon as the pest appears, following manufacturer's instructions. This should then also control the sooty mould.

Maintenance
Spring: Cut back plants to regain shape. Sow seed. Take softwood cuttings.
Summer: Cut back after flowering to maintain shape.
Autumn: The variegated rue is slightly more tender than the other 2 varieties, so protect when frosts go below -5°C (23°F).
Winter: Rue is hardy and requires protection only in extreme conditions.

Garden Cultivation
All the rues prefer a sunny site with a well-drained poor soil. They are best positioned away from paths or at the back of beds where people won't brush against them accidentally, especially children whose skin is more sensitive than adults. In the spring, and after flowering in the summer (not autumn), cut back all the plants to maintain shape, and the variegated form to maintain variegations.

Harvest
Pick leaves for use fresh when required. No need to preserve.

CONTAINER GROWING

Rue can be grown in containers; use the bark, peat, grit mix of compost. Again position the container carefully so that one does not accidentally brush the leaves. Although it is a drought tolerant plant, in containers it prefers to be watered regularly in summer. Allow to dry in winter, watering only once a month. Feed plants in the spring with liquid fertilizer following the manufacturer's instructions.

MEDICINAL

This ancient medicinal herb is used in the treatment of strained eyes, and headaches caused by eye strain. It is also useful for nervous headaches and heart palpitations, for treating high blood pressure and helping to harden the bones and teeth. The antispasmodic action of its oil and the alkaloids explains its use in the treatment of nervous digestion and colic. The tea also expels worms.

WARNING

Handling the plant can cause allergic reactions or phytol-photodermatitis. If you have ever seen a rue burn, it really is quite serious so do heed this warning.

To minimize this risk do not take cuttings off the plants either when they are wet after rain or when in full sun, as this is when the plant is at its most dangerous. Wait until the plant has dried out or the sun has gone in; alternatively wear gloves.

Must only be used by medical personnel and not at all by pregnant women, as it is abortive. Large doses are toxic, sometimes precipitating mental confusion, and the oil is capable of causing death.

Variegated Rue *Ruta graveolens 'Variegata'*

Rue tea

CULINARY

I seriously cannot believe that people enjoy eating this herb; it is incredibly bitter. It can be added finely chopped with discretion to egg, fish or cheese dishes.

'How can a man grow old who has sage in his garden?'
Ancient Proverb

Salvia

SAGE

From the family Labiatae

This large family of over 750 species is widely distributed throughout the world. It consists of annuals, biennials and perennials, herbs, sub-shrubs and shrubs of various habits. It is an important horticultural group. I have concentrated on the medicinal, culinary and a special aromatic species.

The name Salvia is derived from the Latin 'salveo' meaning I save or heal, because some species have been highly regarded medicinally.

The Greeks used it to heal ulcers, consumption, and snake bites. The Romans considered it a sacred herb to be gathered with ceremony. A special knife was used, not made of iron because sage reacts with iron salts. The sage gatherer had to wear clean clothes, have clean feet and make a sacrifice of food before the ceremony could begin. Sage was held to be good for the brain, the senses and memory. It also made a good gargle and mouthwash and was used as a toothpaste.

There are many stories about why the Chinese valued it so highly, and in the 17th century Dutch merchants found that the Chinese would trade 3 chests of China tea for 1 of sage leaves.

Above: **Sage** *Salvia officinalis*

Right: **Purple Sage** *Salvia officinalis Purpurascens Group*

SPECIES

I have only chosen a very few species to illustrate, they are the main ones used in cooking and medicine – with one exception, with which I begin.

Salvia elegans 'Scarlet Pineapple' (rutilans)
Pineapple Sage
Half-hardy perennial. Ht 90cm (3ft), spread 60cm (2ft). Striking red flowers, mid- to late summer. The leaves are green with a slight red tinge to the edges and have a glorious pineapple scent. This sage is sub-tropical and must be protected from frost during the winter. In temperate climates it is basically a house plant and if kept on a sunny windowsill can be used throughout the year. It can only be grown from cuttings. This is an odd sage to cook with, it does not taste as well as it smells. It is fairly good combined with apricots as a stuffing for pork, otherwise my culinary experiments with it have not met with great success.

Salvia lavandulifolia
Narrowed-Leaved Sage
Also known as Spanish Sage. Hardy evergreen perennial. Ht and spread 45cm (18in). Attractive blue flowers in summer. The leaves are green with a texture, small, thin, and oval in shape and highly aromatic. This is an excellent sage to cook with, very pungent. It also makes a good tea. Can only be grown from cuttings.

Salvia officinalis
Sage
Also known as Common Sage, Garden Sage, Broad Leaved Sage, and Sawge. Hardy evergreen perennial. Ht and spread 60cm (2ft). Mauve/blue flowers in summer. The leaves are green with a texture, thin and oval in shape and highly aromatic. This is the best known sage for culinary use. Can be easily grown from seed. There is also a white flowering sage **Salvia officinalis 'Albiflora'**, which is quite rare.

Salvia officinalis broad-leaved (latifolia)
Broad-Leaved Sage
Hardy evergreen perennial. Ht and spread 60cm (2ft). Very rarely flowers in cool climates, if it does they are blue/mauve in colour. The leaves are green with a texture, larger than the ordinary sage, with an oval shape and highly aromatic. Good for cooking. Can only be grown from cuttings.

Salvia officinalis 'Icterina'
Gold Sage
Hardy evergreen perennial. Ht 45cm (18in), spread 75cm (30in). Very rarely flowers in cool climates, if it does they are blue/mauve in colour. The leaves are green/gold variegated with a texture, small and oval in shape and aromatic. A mild flavour but equally good to cook with. Can only be grown from cuttings.

Clary Sage *Salvia sclarea*

Salvia sclarea
Clary Sage
Also known as Muscatel Sage.
Hardy biennial. Ht 60-90cm (2-3ft), spread 45cm (18in). Colourful flower bracts – blue/purple/lilac with a whitish base in summer. Leaves are often 20-23cm (8-9in) long, soft green in colour and slightly wrinkled. Easily grown from seed. There is another variety, **Salvia sclarea var. turkestanica**, with white flowers tinged with pink.

Salvia officinalis Purpurascens Group
Purple/Red Sage
Hardy evergreen perennial. Ht and spread 70cm (28in). Mauve/blue flowers in summer. The leaves are purple with a texture, a thin oval shape and aromatic. 2 points to think about. If you clip it in the spring, it develops new leaves and looks really good but flowers only a small amount. If you do not clip it and allow it to flower it goes woody. If you then cut it back it does not produce new growth until the spring, so can look a bit bare. So what to do? There is also a variegated form of this purple sage **Salvia officinalis 'Purpurascens Variegata'**. Both of these can only be grown from cuttings.

Salvia officinalis 'Tricolor'
Tricolor Sage
Half-hardy evergreen perennial. Ht and spread 40cm (16in). Attractive blue flowers in summer. The leaves are green with pink, white and purple variegation, with a texture. They are small, thin, and oval in shape and highly aromatic. It has a mild flavour, so can be used in cooking. Can only be grown from cuttings.

CULTIVATION

Propagation
Seed
Common and clary sage grow successfully in the spring from seed sown into prepared seed or plug trays and covered with Perlite. The seeds are a good size. If starting off under protection in early spring, warmth is of benefit – temperatures of 15-21°C (60-70°F). Germination takes 2-3 weeks. Pot up or plant out when the frosts are over at a distance of 45-60cm (18-24in) apart.

Cuttings
This is a good method for all variegated species and the ones that do not set seed in cooler climates. Use the bark, peat mix of compost.
Softwood: Take these cuttings in late spring or early summer from the strong new growth. All forms take easily from cuttings; rooting is about 4 weeks in summer.
Layering: If you have a well-established sage, or if it is becoming a bit woody, layer established branches in spring or autumn.

Pests and Diseases
Sage grown in the garden does not suffer over much from pests and disease. Sage grown in containers, especially pineapple sage, is prone to red spider mite. As soon as you see this pest, treat with a liquid horticultural soap as per the instructions.

Maintenance
Spring: Sow seeds. Trim if needed, and then take softwood cuttings.
Summer: Trim back after flowering.
Autumn: Protect all half-hardy sages, and first-year plants.
Winter: Protect plants if they are needed for fresh leaves.

Purple Sage *Salvia officinalis Purpurascens Group* and **Gold Sage** *Salvia officinalis* 'Icterina'

Garden Cultivation
Sage, although predominately a Mediterranean plant, is sufficiently hardy to withstand any ordinary winter without protection, as long as the soil is well drained and not acid, and the site is as warm and dry as possible. The flavour of the leaf can vary as to how rich, damp, etc, the soil is. If wishing to sow seed outside, wait until there is no threat of frost and sow direct into prepared ground, spacing the seeds 23cm (9in) apart. After germination thin to 45cm (18in) apart. For the first winter cover the young plants with agricultural fleece or a mulch.
To keep the plants bushy prune in the spring to encourage young shoots for strong flavour, and also after flowering in late summer. Mature plants can be pruned hard in the spring after some cuttings have been taken as insurance. Never prune in the autumn as this can kill the plant. As sage is prone to becoming woody, replace the plant every 4-5 years.

Sage Bianco *Salvia blancoana* **has a silvery leaf and prostrate habit**

Broad-Leaved Sage *Salvia officinalis* broad-leaved

Harvest

Since sage is an evergreen plant, the leaves can be used fresh any time of the year. In Mediterranean-type climates, including the southern states of America, the leaves can be harvested during the winter months. In cooler climates this is also possible if you cover a chosen bush with agricultural fleece as this will keep the leaves in better condition. They dry well, but care should be taken to keep their green colour. Because this herb is frequently seen in its dried condition people presume it is easy to dry. But beware, although other herbs may lose some of their aroma or qualities if badly dried or handled, sage seems to pick up a musty scent and a flavour really horrible to taste – better to grow it in your garden to use fresh.

CONTAINER GROWING

All sages grow happily in containers. Pineapple sage is an obvious one as it is tender, but a better reason is that if it is at hand one will rub the leaves and smell that marvellous pineapple scent. Use the bark, grit, peat mix of compost for all varieties, feed the plants after flowering, and do not over-water.

COMPANION PLANTING

Sage planted with cabbages is said to repel cabbage white butterflies. Planted next to vines it is generally beneficial.

OTHER USES

The dried leaves, especially those of pineapple sage, are good added to potpourris.

MEDICINAL

For centuries, sage has been esteemed for its healing powers. It is a first rate remedy as a hot infusion for colds. Sage tea combined with a little cider vinegar makes a gargle which is excellent for sore throats, laryngitis and tonsillitis. *It is also beneficial for infected gums and mouth ulcers.*

The essential oil, known as Sage Clary or Muscatel Oil, is obtained by steamed distillation of the fresh or partially dried flower stems *and leaves. It is used in herbal medicine but more widely in toilet waters, perfumes and soap, and to flavour wine, vermouth and liqueurs.*

Left: **Tricolor Sage** *Salvia officinalis* 'Tricolor'

CULINARY

This powerful healing plant is also a strong culinary herb, although it has been misused and misjudged in the culinary world. Used with discretion it adds a lovely flavour, aids digestion of fatty food, and being an antiseptic it kills off any bugs in the meat as it cooks. It has long been used with sausages because of its preservative qualities. It also makes a delicious herb jelly, or oil or vinegar. But I like using small amounts fresh. The original form of the following recipe comes from a vegetarian friend of mine. I fell in love with it and have subsequently adapted it to include some other herbs.

Hazelnut and Mushroom Roast
Serves 4

A little sage oil (see page 238)
Long grain brown rice (measured to the 150ml (5fl oz) mark on a glass measuring jug)
275ml (10fl oz) boiling water
1 teaspoon salt
1 large onion, peeled and chopped
110g (4oz) mushrooms, wiped and chopped
2 medium carrots, pared and roughly grated
½ teaspoon coriander seed
1 tablespoon soy sauce
110g (4oz) wholemeal breadcrumbs
175g (6oz) ground hazelnuts
1 teaspoon chopped sage leaves
1 teaspoon chopped lovage leaves
Sunflower seeds for decoration
A 900g (2lb) loaf tin, lined with greaseproof paper

Pre-heat the oven (180°C 350°F, Gas Mark 4).

Heat 1 dessertspoon of sage oil in a small saucepan, toss the rice in it to give it a coating of oil, add boiling water straight from the kettle and the teaspoon of salt. Stir, and let the rice cook slowly for roughly 40 minutes or until the liquid has been absorbed.

While the rice is cooking, heat 1 tablespoon of sage oil in a medium sized frying-pan, add the onions, mushrooms, carrots, the ground coriander seed and soy sauce. Mix them together and let them cook for about 10 minutes.

Combine the cooked brown rice, breadcrumbs, hazelnuts, sage and lovage; mix with the vegetables and place the complete mixture in the prepared loaf tin. Scatter the sunflower seeds on top and bake in the oven

Hazelnut and mushroom roast, a delicious dish for vegetarians

for 45 minutes. Leave to cool slightly in the tin. Slice and serve with a home-made tomato sauce and a green salad.

WARNING

Extended or excessive use of sage can cause symptoms of poisoning. Although the herb seems safe and common, it you drink the tea for more than a week or two at a time, its strong antiseptic properties can cause potentially toxic effects.

Sambucus

ELDER

Also known as Boun-tree, Boon-tree, Dogtree, Judas Tree, Scores, Score Tree, God's Stinking Tree, Black Elder, Blackberried, European Elder, Ellhorne and German Elder. From the family Caprifoliaceae.

Elder grows worldwide throughout temperate climates. Its common name is probably derived from the Anglo Saxon 'Ellaern' or 'Aeld', which mean 'fire' or 'kindle', because the hollow stems were once used for getting fires going. The generic name, *Sambucus*, dates from ancient Greek times and may originally have referred to sambuke, a kind of harp made of elderwood. Pipes were made from its branches too, possibly the original Pan pipes. People thought that if you put it on the fire you would see the Devil. They believed it unlucky to make cradle rockers out of it, that the spirit of the tree might harm the child. Again, farmers were unwilling to use an elder switch to drive cattle and one folktale had it that elder would only grow where blood had been shed. Planting it outside the back door was a sure way of protecting against evil, black magic, and keeping witches out of the house, which would never be struck by lightning. It was thought that Christ's cross was made of elderwood.

Common Elder
Sambucus nigra

Red Elder *Sambucus racemosa*

SPECIES

Sambucus canadensis
American Elder
Also known as Black Elder, Common Elder, Rob Elder, Sweet Elder.
Deciduous hardy perennial. Ht 1.5-3.6m (5-12ft). Numerous small white flowers in flat cymes throughout summer. Berries are dark purple in early autumn; its leaves long, sharply toothed and bright green.
Caution: All parts of the fresh plant can poison. Children have even been poisoned by chewing or sucking the bark. Once cooked, however, flowers and berries are safe.
Some Native American tribes use a tea made from the root-bark for headaches, mucous congestion, and to promote labour in childbirth.

Sambucus canadensis 'Aurea'
Deciduous hardy perennial. Ht and spread 4m (12ft). Creamy white flowers in summer, red fruits in early autumn. Large golden yellow leaves.

Sambucus ebulus
Dwarf Elder
Also known as Blood Elder, Danewort, Wild Elder, Walewort.
Deciduous hardy perennial. Ht 60-120cm (2-4ft), spread 1m (3ft). White flowers with pink tips in summer. Black berries in early autumn. Its green leaves are oblong, lance-shaped, and toothed around the edges. Dwarf elder grows in small clusters in Europe and in Eastern and Central States of America.
Warning: All parts of the plant are slightly poisonous and children should be warned not to eat the bitter berries.
It has a much stronger action than its close relative, common elder (**S. nigra**). Large doses cause vertigo, vomiting and diarrhoea, the latter, denoted colloquially as 'the Danes', being the origin of Danewort. Nowadays dwarf elder is rarely used and should be taken internally only under strict medical supervision.

Sambucus nigra
Common Elder
Also known as European Elder, Black Elder, Bore Tree.
Deciduous hardy perennial. Ht 20-23ft (6-7m), spread 4.5m (15ft). Spreading branches bear flat heads of small, star-shaped, creamy-white flowers in late spring and early summer. These are followed in early autumn by drooping branches of purplish-black juicy berries. The flowers and berries are used in industry for cosmetics, jams, jellies and liqueurs.
The leaves are purgative and should not be taken internally; decoctions have an insecticidal effect.
The wood from the adult plant is highly prized by craftsmen.

Sambucus nigra 'Aurea'
Golden Elder
Deciduous shrub. Ht and spread 6m (20ft). Flattened heads of fragrant, star-shaped, creamy-white flowers from early to mid-summer. Black fruits in early autumn. Golden yellow, oval, sharply toothed leaves in groups of usually 5.

Sambucus racemosa
Red Elder
Deciduous hardy perennial. Ht and spread 3-4m (10-13ft). Brown bark and pale brown pith. Flowers arranged in dense terminal panicles of yellowish cream. 'Racemosa' refers to the flower clusters. The fruits are also distinct in being red in drooping clusters. It rarely fruits freely.
Red berried elder is native to central and southern Europe. It has naturalized in Scotland, the northern US and Canada. The fully ripe fruits are used medicinally. Bitter tasting, they may be used fresh or dried, and are high in vitamin C, essential oil, sugar and pectins. Fruits are a laxative and the leaves are a diuretic. This is the most edible and tasty of the elders.
Caution: The seeds inside the berries are poisonous before being cooked.

CULTIVATION

Propagation
Seed
Sow ripe berries 2cm (1in) deep in a pot outdoors. Plant seedlings in semi-shade in the garden when large enough to handle.

Cuttings
Take semi-hardwood cuttings in summer from the new growth. Use the peat, grit mix of compost and winter these cuttings in a cold frame or cold greenhouse. When rooted, either pot on or plant out into a prepared site 30cm (12 in) apart.
Take hardwood cuttings of bare shoots in autumn and replant in the garden 30cm (12in) apart. The following autumn lift and replant.

Pests and Diseases
Rarely suffers from pests or diseases.

Maintenance
Spring: Prune back golden and variegated elders.
Summer: Take semi-ripe cuttings.
Autumn: Take hardwood cuttings. Prune back hard.
Winter: Established plants do not need protection.

Garden Cultivation
Elder tolerates most soils and **S. nigra** is very good for chalky sites. They all prefer a sunny position.
Elder grows very rapidly indeed and self-sows freely to produce new shoots 120cm (4ft) long in one season. It is short-lived.
It is important to dominate elder otherwise it will dominate your garden. Cut back in late autumn, unless it is gold or variegated, when it should be pruned in early spring before growth begins.

Harvest
Handle flower heads carefully to prevent bruising, spread out to dry with heads down on a fine net without touching one another. Pick the fruits in autumn, as they ripen, when they become shiny and violet.

CONTAINER GROWING

Golden varieties of elder can look good in containers, as long as the containers are large enough and positioned to give the plants some shade, to stop the leaves scorching. Use a soil-based compost. Keep well watered, feed with a liquid fertilizer.

CULINARY

WARNING: Berries should not be eaten raw, nor fresh juice used. Be sure to cook very slightly first.

Elderflower Cordial
Pick flowers on a dry sunny day, as the yeast is mainly in the pollen.

4.5 litres/1 gallon of water
700g/1½lb sugar
Juice and thinly peeled rind of 1 lemon
30ml/2 tablespoons of cider or wine vinegar
12 elderflower heads

Bring the water to the boil and pour into a sterilized container. Add the sugar, stirring until dissolved. When cool add the lemon juice and the rind, vinegar and elderflowers. Cover with several layers of muslin and leave for 24 hours. Filter through muslin into strong glass bottles. This drink is ready after 2 weeks. Serve chilled.

OTHER USES

Elderflower water whitens and softens the skin, removes freckles.
The fruits make a lavender or violet dye when combined with alum.

Elderflower sorbet

MEDICINAL

Elderflowers reduce bronchial and upper respiratory catarrh and are used in the treatment of hay fever. Externally a cold infusion of the flowers may be used as an eye wash for conjunctivitis and as a compress for chilblains. A gargle made from elderflower infusion or elderflower vinegar alleviates tonsillitis and sore throats. Elderflowers have a mild laxative action and in Europe have a reputation for treating rheumatism and gout. The berries are a mild laxative and sweat inducing. 'Elderberry Rob' is traditionally made by simmering the berries and thickening with sugar as a winter cordial for coughs and colds.

Elderberry Conserve
(for neuralgia and migraine)

500g/1lb elderberries
500g/1lb sugar

Boil the elderberries with the least quantity of water to produce a pulp. Pass through a sieve and simmer the juice gently to remove most of the water. Add the sugar and stir constantly until the consistancy of a conserve is produced. Pour into a suitable container. Take 2 tablespoons as required.

Sanguisorba minor

SALAD BURNET

Also known as Drumsticks, Old Man's Pepper and Poor Man's Pepper. From the family Rosaceae.

This herb is a native of Europe and Asia. It has been introduced and naturalized in many places elsewhere in the world, especially Britain and the United States. Popular for both its medicinal and culinary properties, it was taken to New England in the Pilgrim Fathers plant collection and called Pimpernel. It is found in dry, free-draining soil in grassland and on the edges of woodland. The name *Sanguisorba* comes from 'sanguis', meaning blood, and 'sorbere', meaning to soak up. It is an ancient herb which has been grown in this country since the 16th century. Traditionally it was used to staunch wounds. In Tudor times Salad Burnet was planted along borders of garden paths so the scent would rise up when trodden on.

SPECIES

Sanguisorba minor
Salad Burnet
Evergreen hardy perennial. Ht 20-60in (8-24in), spread 30cm (12in). Produces small spikes of dark crimson flowers in summer. Its soft mid-green leaves are divided into oval leaflets.

Sanguisorba officinalis
Great Burnet
Also known as Drumsticks, Maidens Hairs, Red Knobs, and Redheads. Perennial. Ht up to 1.2m (4ft), spread 60cm (2ft). Produces small spikes of dark crimson flowers in summer. Its mid-green leaves are divided into oval leaflets. This wild plant is becoming increasingly rare due to modern farming practices.

Salad Burnet
Sanguisorba minor

CULTIVATION

Propagation
Seed
Sow the small flatish seed in spring or autumn into prepared seed or plug trays and cover the seeds with Perlite; no need for extra heat. If sown in the autumn, winter the seedlings under protection and plant out in spring to a prepared site, 30cm (12in) apart. If spring sown allow to harden off and plant out in the same way. As an edging plant it should be planted at a distance of 20cm (8in) apart.

Division
It divides very easily. Dig up an established plant in the early autumn, cut back any excessive leaves, divide the plant and replant in a prepared site in the garden.

Pests and Diseases
This herb is, in the main, free from pests and diseases.

Maintenance
Spring: Sow seeds.
Summer: Keep cutting to stop it flowering, if being used for culinary purposes.

Autumn: Sow seeds if necessary. Divide established plants.
Winter: No protection needed, fully hardy.

Garden Cultivation

This is a most attractive, soft-leaf evergreen and is very useful in both kitchen and garden. That it is evergreen is a particular plus for the herb garden, where it looks most effective as an edging plant. It also looks good in a wild flower garden, where it grows as happily as in its original grassland habitat.

The art with this plant is to keep cutting, which stops it flowering and encourages lots of new growth.

With no special requirements, it prefers chalky soil, but it will tolerate any well-drained soil in sun or light shade. It is deep rooting and very drought resistant.

Harvest

Pick young tender leaves when required. Not necessary to dry leaves (which in any case do not dry well), as fresh leaves can be harvested all year round.

CONTAINER GROWING

Salad Burnet will grow in containers, and will provide an excellent source of soft evergreen leaves throughout winter for those with no garden. Use a soil-based compost. Water regularly, but not too frequently; feed with liquid fertilizer in the spring only. Do not over-feed otherwise the leaf will soften and lose its cool cucumber flavour, becoming more like a spinach. For regular use the plant should not be allowed to flower. Cut back constantly to about 15cm (6in) to ensure a continuing supply of tender new leaves.

CULINARY

Leaves have a nutty flavour and a slight taste of cucumber. The young leaves are refreshing in salads and can be used generously – they certainly enhance winter salads. Tender young leaves can also be added to soups, cold drinks, cream cheeses, or used (like parsley) as a garnish or to flavour casseroles – add at the beginning of cooking. The leaves also make an interesting herbal vinegar.

Salad Burnet combines with other herbs, especially rosemary and tarragon. Serve in a sauce with white fish.

Salad Burnet *Sanguisorba minor*

OTHER USES

Because of its high tannin content, the root of Great Burnet can be used in the tanning of leather.

WARNING

Great Burnet should never be taken in large doses.

This recipe is for a herb butter, which is lovely with grilled fish, either cooked under the grill or on the barbecue, and gives a cucumber flavour to the butter.

75g (3oz) butter
1½ tablespoons chopped Salad Burnet
1 tablespoon chopped garden mint (spearmint)
Salt and black pepper
Lemon juice

Mix the chopped herb leaves together. Melt the butter in a saucepan, add the herbs and simmer on a very low heat for 10 minutes. Season the sauce to taste with salt and pepper, and a squeeze (no more) of lemon. Pour over grilled fish (plaice or sole).

Salad Burnet butter

MEDICINAL

Chewing the leaf assists digestion. An infusion of the whole plant is used for treating haemorrhoids and diarrhoea.

Santolina

COTTON LAVENDER

Also known as Santolina and French Lavender.
From the family Compositae

Cotton lavender is a native of Southern France and the Northern Mediterranean area, where it grows wild on calcareous ground. It is widely cultivated, adapting to the full spectrum of European and Australian climates and to warm-to-hot regions of North America, surviving even an Eastern Canadian winter on well-drained soil.

The Greeks knew cotton lavender as 'abrotonon' and the Romans as 'habrotanum', both names referring to the tree-like shape of the flying branches. It was used medicinally for many centuries by the Arabs. And it was valued in medieval England as an insect and moth repellent and vermifuge.

The plant was probably brought into Britain in the 16th century by French Huguenot gardeners, who were skilled in creating the knot garden so popular among the Elizabethans. Cotton lavender was used largely in low clipped hedges, and as edging for the geometrical beds.

Cotton lavender Rosmarinifolia
Santolina rosmarinifolia ssp. *rosmarinifolia*

SPECIES

Despite its common name, this is not a member of the Lavandula family; rather it is a member of the daisy family.

Santolina chamaecyparissus
Cotton Lavender
Hardy evergreen perennial. Ht 75cm (2.5ft), spread 1m (3ft). Yellow button flowers from mid-summer to early autumn, silver coral like aromatic foliage.

Cotton Lavender
Santolina chamaecyparissus

Santolina chamaecyparissus 'Lemon Queen'
Cotton Lavender 'Lemon Queen'
As 'Edward Bowles', but feathery, deep cut grey foliage.

Santolina pinnata ssp. neapolitana 'Edward Bowles'
Cotton Lavender 'Edward Bowles'
Hardy evergreen perennial. Ht 75cm (2.5ft), spread 1m (3ft). Cream button flowers in summer. Feathery, deep cut, grey/green foliage.

Cotton Lavender 'Lemon Queen'
Santolina chamaecyparissus 'Lemon Queen'

Santolina pinnata ssp. neapolitana
Cotton Lavender 'Neopolitana'
As 'Edward Bowles'.

Santolina rosmarinifolia ssp. rosmarinifolia 'Primrose Gem'
Cotton Lavender Primrose Gem
Hardy evergreen perennial. Ht 60cm (2ft), spread 1m (3ft). Pale yellow button flowers in summer. Finely cut green leaves.

Santolina rosmarinifolia ssp. rosmarinifolia (Virens)
Cotton Lavenda Rosmarinifolia
Also known as *Holy Flax*. As 'Primrose Gem'. Bright yellow button flowers in summer. Finely cut, bright green leaves.

Cotton Lavender Rosmarinifolia
Santolina rosmarinifolia ssp. *rosmarinifolia*

CULTIVATION

Propagation
Seed
Although seed is now available, it is erratic and not worth the effort as germination is poor.

Cuttings
Take 5-8cm (2-3in) soft stem cuttings in spring before flowering, or take semi-ripe stem cuttings from mid-summer to autumn. They root easily without the use of any rooting compound.

Pests and Diseases
Compost or soil that is too rich will attract aphids.

Maintenance
Spring: Cut straggly old plants hard back. Take cuttings from new growth.
Summer: I can not stress enough that after flowering the plants should be cut back or the bushes will open up and lose their attractive shape.
Autumn: Take semi-ripe cuttings, protect them from frost in a cold frame or greenhouse.
Winter: Protect in only the severest of winters.

Garden Cultivation
This elegant aromatic evergreen is ideal for the herb garden as a hedging or specimen plant in its own right. Plant in full sun, preferably in sandy soil. If the soil is too rich the growth will become soft and lose colour. This is particularly noticeable with the silver varieties.
Planting distance for an individual plant 45-60cm (18-24 in), for a hedging 30-38cm (12-15in). Hedges need regular clipping to shape in spring and summer. Do not cut back in the autumn in frosty climates, as this can easily kill the plants. If temperatures drop below -15° C (5°F) protect with agricultural fleece or a layer of straw, spruce or bracken.

Harvest
Pick leaves and dry any time before flowering. Pick small bunches of flower stems for drying, in late summer. They can be dried easily by hanging the bunches upside down in a dry, airy place.

CONTAINER GROWING

Santolina can not be grown indoors, however as a patio plant, a single plant clipped to shape in a large terracotta pot can look very striking. Use a bark, peat compost. Place pot in full sun. Do not over-feed with liquid fertilizer or growth will be too soft.

CULINARY

Cotton lavender (**S. chamaecyparissus**) makes an interesting addition to shortbread biscuits instead of Rosemary. Interesting being the operative word.

MEDICINAL

Although not used much nowadays, it can be applied to surface wounds, hastening the healing process by encouraging scar formation. Finely ground leaves ease the pain of insect stings and bites.

OTHER USES
Lay in drawers, under carpets, and in closets to deter moths and other insects, or make a herbal moth bag.

Herbal Moth Bag

A handful of wormwood
A handful of spearmint
A handful of cotton lavender
A handful of rosemary
1 tablespoon of crushed coriander

Dry and crumble the ingredients, mix together and put in a muslin or cotton bag.

Saponaria officinalis

SOAPWORT

Also known as Bouncing Bet, Bruisewort, Farewell Summer, Fuller's Herb, Joe Run By The Street, Hedge Pink, Dog's Clove, Old Maid's Pink and Soaproot. From the family Caryophyllaceae.

Soapwort, widespread on poor soils in Europe, Asia and Northern America, was used by medieval Arab physicians for various skin complaints. Fullers used soapwort for soaping cloth before it went on the stamps at the mill, and sheep were washed with a mixture of the leaves, roots and water before being shorn.

SPECIES

Saponaria officinalis
Soapwort
Hardy perennial. Ht 30-90cm (1-3ft), spread 60cm (2ft) or more. Compact cluster of small pretty pink or white flowers in summer to early autumn. The leaf is smooth, oval, pointed and mid-green in colour.

Saponaria officinalis 'Rubra Plena'
Double Flowered Soapwort
Hardy perennial. Ht 90cm (3ft), spread 30cm (1ft). Clusters of red, ragged, double flowers in summer. The leaves are mid-green and oval in shape.

Saponaria ocymoïdes
Tumbling Ted
Hardy perennial. Ht 2.5-8cm (1-3in), spread 40cm (16in) or more. Profusion of tiny, flat, pale pink/crimson flowers in summer. Compact or loose sprawling mats of hairy oval leaves.

CULTIVATION

Propagation
Seed
Only Soapwort and Tumbling Ted can be grown from seed. Sow in autumn into prepared seed or plug trays and cover with compost. Place glass over container and leave outside over winter. Germination usually takes place in spring but can be erratic. When large enough, plant 60cm (24in) apart.

Cuttings
Softwood cuttings of the non-flowering shoots can be taken from late spring to early summer.

Division
The creeping root stock is easy to divide in the autumn.

Garden Cultivation
Plant it in a sunny spot, in a well-drained poor soil; rich garden soil makes its already undisciplined habit impossible. Soapwort can become very invasive. Do not plant soapwort around fish ponds because the creeping rhizomes excrete a poison.

Pests and Diseases
Soapwort is largely free from pests and disease.

Maintenance
Spring: Take cuttings.
Summer: Cut back after flowering to encourage a second flowering and to prevent self-seeding.
Autumn: Divide established plants. Sow seed.
Winter: Fully hardy.

Harvest
Pick the leaves when required. Dig up the roots in the autumn and dry for medicinal use.

CONTAINER GROWING

Tumbling Ted is the best species for container growing. Use a soil-based compost. Water well during the growing season, but only feed twice. In winter keep in a cold greenhouse with minimum watering.

MEDICINAL

It has been used not only for treating skin conditions such as eczema, cold sores, boils, and acne but also for gout and rheumatism. It is probably effective because of the anti-inflammatory properties of its saponins.

OTHER USES

The gentle power of the saponins in soapwort makes the following shampoo ideal for upholstery and delicate fibres.

Soapwort Shampoo
15gm (½oz) dried soapwort root or two large handfuls of whole fresh stems
¾ litre (1½pints) water

Crush the root with a rolling pin or roughly chop the fresh stems. If using dried soapwort, prepare by soaking first overnight. Put the soapwort into an enamel pan with water and bring to the boil, cover and simmer for 20 minutes, stirring occasionally. Allow to stand until cool and strain through a fine sieve.

WARNING

This herb should only be prescribed by a qualified herbalist because of the high saponin content which makes it mildly poisonous.

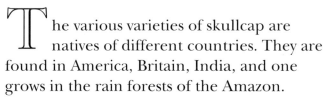

Skullcap
Scutellaria galericulata

Scutellaria
Virginian Skullcap
Scutellaria lateriflora

SKULLCAP

Also known as Helmet Flower, Mad Dog Weed, Blue Skullcap and Blue Pimpernel. From the family Labiatae.

The various varieties of skullcap are natives of different countries. They are found in America, Britain, India, and one grows in the rain forests of the Amazon.

The name *Scutellaria* is derived from 'scutella', meaning a small shield, which is exactly how the seed looks.

The American Indians used *Scutellaria lateriflora* as a treatment for rabies. In Europe it was used for epilepsy.

SPECIES

Scutellaria galericulata
Skullcap
Hardy perennial. Ht 15-50cm (6-20in), spread 30cm (12in) and more. Small purple/blue flowers with a longer spreading lower lip in summer. Leaves bright green and lance shaped with shallow round teeth. This plant is a native of Europe.

Scutellaria minor
Lesser Skullcap
As **S. galericulata** except Ht 20-30cm (8-12in), spread 30cm (12in) and more. Small purple/pink flowers. Leaves lance shaped with 4 rounded teeth. Found on wet land.

Scutellaria lateriflora
Virginian Skullcap
As **S. galericulata** except Ht 30-60cm (12-24in), spread 30cm (12in) and more. Leaves oval and lance shaped with shallow round teeth. Native of America.

CULTIVATION

Propagation
Seed
Sow the small seeds in autumn into prepared seed or plug trays and cover the seeds with compost. Leave the tray outside under glass. If germination is rapid, winter the young seedlings in a cold greenhouse. If there is no germination within 10-20 days leave well alone. The seed may need a period of stratification. In the spring, when the plants are large enough, plant out into a prepared site in the garden 30cm (12in) apart.

Root Cuttings
These produce a rhizomous root from which it is easy to take cuttings. In spring dig up an established clump carefully, for any little bits of root left behind will form another plant. Ensure each cutting has a growing node; place in a seed tray and cover with compost. Put into a cold greenhouse to root.

Division
Established plants can be divided in the spring.

Pests and Diseases
Skullcap is normally free from pests and disease.

Maintenance
Spring: Divide established plants. Take root cuttings.
Summer: Cut back to restrain.
Autumn: Sow seeds.
Winter: No need for protection, fully hardy.

Garden Cultivation
Skullcap tolerates most soils but prefers a well-drained, moisture retentive soil in sun or semi-shade. Make sure this plant gets adequate water.

Harvest
Dry flowers and leaves for medicinal use only.

Virginian Skullcap
Scutellaria lateriflora

CONTAINER GROWING

This herb can be grown in containers but ensure its large root system has room to spread. Use a soil-based compost. Feed only rarely with liquid fertilizer or it will produce too lush a growth and inhibit flowering. Leave outside in winter in a sheltered spot, allowing the plant to die back.

MEDICINAL

The American skullcap is the best medicinal species; the two European species are a little less strong.

It is used in the treatment of anxiety, nervousness, depression, insomnia and headaches. The whole plant is effective as a soothing antispasmodic tonic and a remedy for hysteria and hydrophobia. Its bitter taste also strengthens and stimulates the digestion.

WARNING

Should only be dispensed by a trained herbalist.

Satureja (Satureia)

SAVORY

From the family Labiatae.

Savory is a native of southern Europe and North Africa, especially around the Mediterranean. It grows in well-drained soils and has adapted worldwide to similar climatic conditions. Savory has been employed in food flavouring for over 2,000 year. Romans added it to sauces and vinegars, which they used liberally as flavouring. The Ancient Egyptians on the other hand used it in love potions. The Romans also included it in their wagon train to northern Europe, where it became an invaluable disinfectant strewing herb. It was also used to relieve tired eyes, for ringing in the ears, indigestion, wasp and bee stings, and for other shocks to the system.

Winter Savory *Satureja montana*

SPECIES

Summer Savory
Satureja hortensis

Satureja hortensis
Summer Savory
Also known as Bean Herb. Half-hardy annual. Ht 20-30cm (8-12in), spread 15cm (6in). Small white/mauve flowers in summer. Aromatic leaves, oblong, pointed, and green. A favourite on the Continent and in America, where it is known as the bean herb. It has become widely used in bean dishes as it helps prevent flatulence.

Satureja coerulea
Purple-Flowered Savory
Semi-evergreen hardy perennial. Ht 30cm (12in), spread 20cm (8in). Small purple flowers in summer. The leaves are darkish green, linear and very aromatic.

Satureja montana
Winter Savory
Also known as Mountain Savory. Semi-evergreen hardy perennial. Ht 30cm (12in), spread 20cm (8in). Small white/pink flowers in summer. The leaves are dark green, linear and very aromatic.

Satureja spicigera
Creeping Savory
Perennial. Ht 8cm (3in), spread 30cm (12in). Masses of small white flowers in summer. The leaves are lime greenish and linear. This is a most attractive plant and is often mistaken for thyme or even heather.

CULTIVATION

Propagation
Seed
Only summer and winter savory can be grown from seed, which is tiny, so it is best to sow into prepared seed trays under protection in the early spring, using the cardboard method. The seeds should not be covered as they need light to germinate. Germination takes about 10-15 days – no need to use bottom heat. When the seedlings are large enough, and after a period of hardening off (making quite sure that the frosts have finished), they can be planted out into a prepared site in the garden, 15cm (6in) apart.

Cuttings
Creeping, purple-flowered and winter savory can all be grown from softwood cuttings in spring, using a bark, peat, grit compost. When these have rooted they should be planted out – 30cm (12in) apart for creeping savory, 15cm (6in) apart for the others.

Division
Creeping savory can be divided, as each section has its own root system similar to creeping thymes. Dig up an established plant in the spring after the frosts have finished and divide into as many segments as you require. Minimum size is only dependent on each having a root system and how long you are prepared to wait for new plants to become established. Replant in a prepared site.

Pests and Diseases

Being an aromatic plant savory is, in the main, free from pests and disease.

Maintenance

Spring: Sow seed. Take softwood cuttings. Divide established plants.
Summer: Keep picking and do not allow summer savory to flower, if you want to maintain its flavour.
Autumn: Protect from prolonged frosts.
Winter: Protect.

Garden Cultivation

All the above mentioned savories like full sun and a poor, well-drained soil. Plant summer savory in the garden in a warm sheltered spot and keep picking the leaves to stop it getting leggy. Do not feed with liquid fertilizer, otherwise the plant will keel over.

Winter savory can make a good edging plant and is very pretty in the summer, although it can look a bit sparse in the winter months. Again, trim it from time to time to maintain shape and promote new growth. Creeping savory does not like cold wet winters, or for that matter clay soil, so on this nursery I grow it in a pot (see below). If, however, you wish to grow it in your garden, plant it in a sunny rockery or a well-drained, sheltered corner.

Harvest

For fresh use, pick leaves as required. For drying, pick those of summer savory before it flowers. They dry easily.

CONTAINER GROWING

All savories can be grown in containers, and if your garden suffers from prolonged cold wet winters

Savory is an important constituent of salami

it may be the only way you can grow this delightful plant successfully. Use the bark, peat, grit mix of compost. Pick the plants continuously to maintain shape, especially the summer savory which can get straggly. If you are picking the plants a lot they may benefit from a feed of liquid fertilizer, but keep this to a minimum as they get over eager when fed.

Summer savory, being an annual, dies in winter, creeping savory dies back, the winter savory is a partial evergreen. So, the latter 2 will need protection in winter. Place them in a cool greenhouse or conservatory. If the container cannot be moved, wrap it up in paper or agricultural fleece. Keep watering to the absolute minimum.

MEDICINAL

Summer savory is the plant credited with medicinal virtues and is said to alleviate the pain of bee stings if rubbed on the affected spot. Infuse as a tea to stimulate appetite and to ease indigestion and flatulence. It is also considered a stimulant and was once in demand as an aphrodisiac.

Winter savory is also used medicinally but is inferior.

CULINARY

The two savories used in cooking are winter and summer savory. The other varieties are edible but their flavour is inferior. Summer and winter savory combine well with vegetables, pulses and rich meats. These herbs stimulate the appetite and aid digestion. The flavour is hot and peppery, and so should be added sparingly in salads.

Summer Savory can replace both salt and pepper and is a great help to those on a salt free diet. It is a pungent herb and until one is familiar with its strength it should be used carefully. Summer savory also makes a good vinegar and oil. The oil is used commercially as a flavouring, as is the leaf, which is an important constituent of salami.

The flavour of winter savory is both coarser and stronger, its advantage is that it provides fresh leaves into early winter.

Beans with Garlic and Savory
Serves 3-4

200g (7oz) dried haricot beans
1 Spanish onion
1 carrot, scrubbed and roughly sliced
1 stick celery
1 clove garlic
3 tablespoons olive oil
1 tablespoon white wine vinegar
2 tablespoons chopped summer savory
2 tablespoons chopped French parsley

Soak the beans in cold water overnight or for at least 3-4 hours. Drain them and put them in a saucepan with plenty of water. Bring to the boil slowly. Add half the peeled onion, the carrot and celery, and cook until tender. As soon as the beans are soft, drain and discard the vegetables. Mix the oil, vinegar and crushed garlic. While the beans are still hot, stir in the remaining half onion (thinly sliced), the chopped herbs, and pour over the oil and vinegar dressing. Serve soon after cooling. Do not chill.

Beans with garlic and savory

Sempervivum tectorum

HOUSELEEK

*Also known as Bullocks Eye, Hen and Chickens, Jupiter's Eye, Jupiter's Beard, Live For Ever,
Thunder Plant, Aaron's Rod, Healing Leaf, Mallow Rock and
Welcome-Husband-Though-Never-So-Late. From the family Crassulaceae.*

Originally from the mountainous areas of central and southern Europe, now found growing in many different areas of the world including North America.

The generic name *Sempervivum* comes from the Latin 'semper vivo' meaning 'to live for ever'. The species name, *tectorum*, means 'of the roofs', there being records dating back 2,000 years of houseleeks growing on the tiles of houses. The plant was said to have been given to man by Zeus or Jupiter to protect houses from lightning and fire. Because of this the Romans planted courtyards with urns of houseleek, and Charlemagne ordered a plant to be grown on every roof. This belief continued throughout history and in medieval times the houseleek was thought to protect thatched roofs from fire from the sky and witchcraft. In the Middle Ages the plant was often called Erewort and employed against deafness. When the settlers packed their bags for America they took house-leek with them.

Houseleek *Sempervivum tectorum*

SPECIES

This genus of hardy succulents had 25 species 40 years ago. Now, due to re-classification, it has over 500 different varieties. As far as I am aware only houseleek has medicinal properties.

Sempervivum tectorum
Houseleek
Hardy evergreen perennial. Ht 10-15cm (4-6in) (when in flower) otherwise it is 5cm (2in), spread 20cm (8in). Flowers are star-shaped and pink in summer. The leaves, grey/green in colour, are oval pointed and succulent.

Some other **Sempervivum** worth collecting:

Sempervivum arachnoideum
Cobweb Houseleek
Hardy evergreen perennial. Ht 10-12cm (4-5in), when in flower, otherwise it is 5cm (2in), spread 10cm (4in). Flowers are star-shaped and pink in summer. The leaves, grey/green in colour, are oval pointed and succulent. The tips of the leaves are covered in a web of white hairs.

Sempervivum giuseppii
Hardy evergreen perennial. Ht 8-10cm (3-4in), when in flower, otherwise it is 2cm (1in), spread 10cm (4in). Flowers star-shaped, pink/red in summer. Leaves, grey/green in colour, are oval pointed and succulent and grow into a very compact shape. This **Sempervivum** is a vigorous grower.

Sempervivum montanum
Hardy evergreen perennial. Ht 8-15cm (3-6in), when in flower, otherwise 5cm (2in), spread 10cm (4in). Flowers star-shaped and deep red in summer. Leaves grey/green in colour, oval pointed and succulent.

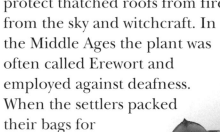

Houseleek *Sempervivum tectorum* **in flower**

Summer: Collect seeds if required from flowering plants.
Autumn: Remove offsets if the plant is becoming too invasive, pot up for following season's display.
Winter: No need for protection.

Garden Cultivation

Basically the soil should be well drained and thin, as they prefer very little to no soil. They will grow anywhere, on weathered rocks and screes and of course rock gardens. Another good place to plant them is between paving stones, or in between other creeping plants like thymes. They can take many years to flower, and when they do they die, but by then there will be many offsets to follow.

Harvest

Pick leaves to use fresh as required. There is no good way of preserving them.

CONTAINER GROWING

If the Romans could do it so can we. Houseleeks do look good in containers and shallow stone troughs. The compost must be poor and very well drained. Use the bark, grit, peat mix but change the ratio to 50 per cent grit, 25 per cent peat, 25 per cent bark. No need to feed, and do not over-water.

CULINARY

The leaves can be added to salad dishes. I think it would be polite to say that it is an acquired taste.

CULTIVATION

Propagation
Seed

Most species hybridize readily, so seed cannot be depended upon to reproduce the species true to type. When you buy seed it often says, 'mixture of several species and varieties' on the packet. It can be good fun to sow these as long as you do not mind what you get; it is even more fun trying to name them as they develop.

The seed is very small, so start off in a seed or plug tray in spring. Sow on the surface. Do not cover except with a sheet of glass. No need for bottom heat. Use the bark, grit, peat compost.

Offsets

All the sempervivum produce offsets that cluster around the base of the parent plant. In spring gently remove them and you will notice each has its own root system. Either put straight into a pot, using the bark, grit, peat mix of compost, or plant where required. Plant 23cm (9in) apart.

Pests and Diseases

Vine Weevil, this scourge of the garden, is very destructive to a number of plants and they like houseleeks. You will know they have been when you see the rosette lying on its side with no roots. See page 242-243 for methods of destroying the pests.

Maintenance

Spring: Sow seeds. Pot up or re-plant offsets.

MEDICINAL

The leaves are an astringent and when broken in half can be applied to burns, insect bites and other skin problems. Press the juice from the leaf onto the infected part. My son, when he goes on hikes or is building dens, always has

some in his pockets – great for clothes washing – for when he gets stung by nettles they are much better than dock when rubbed in.

To soften skin around corns, bind one leaf for a few hours, soak foot in water in attempt to remove corn. Repeat as necessary.

Infuse as a tea for septic throats, bronchitis and mouth ailments. It is also said that chewing a few leaves can ease toothache.

Solidago virgaurea

GOLDENROD

Also known as Woundwort, Aaron's Rod, Cast the Spear and Farewell Summer. From the family Compositae.

This plant is widely distributed throughout Europe including the British Isles, and North America. It is common from the plains to the hills, but especially where the ground is rich in silica.

Its generic name, *Solidago*, is derived from the Latin word 'solido', which means 'to join' or 'make whole', a reference to the healing properties attributed to goldenrod.

The plant, originally called Heathen Wound Herb in Britain, was first imported from the Middle East, where it was used by the Saracens, and it was some time before it was cultivated here. In Tudor times it was available in London but at a price, its expense due to the fact that it was still available only as an import. Gerard wrote, 'For in my remembrance, I have known the dry herb which comes from beyond the sea, sold in Bucklesbury in London for half a crown an ounce,' and went on to say that when it was found growing wild in Hampstead wood, no-one would pay half a crown for 100cwt of it, a fact which the herbalist felt bore out the old English proverb, 'Far fetch and dear, bought is best for ladies.'

From Culpeper, around the same time, we know that goldenrod was used to fasten loose teeth and as a remedy for kidney stones (which it still is).

SPECIES

Solidago odora
Sweet Goldenrod
Also known as Aniseed-Scented Goldenrod, Blue Mountain Tea, Common Goldenrod and Woundweed.
Perennial. Ht 60cm-1.2m (2-4ft), spread 60cm (2ft). Golden-yellow flowers on a single stem from mid-summer to autumn. The green leaf is linear and lance-shaped.

Solidago nemoralis
Grey Goldenrod
Also known as Dyer's Weed, Field Goldenrod and Yellow Goldenrod.
Perennial. Ht 60cm-1m (2-3ft), spread 60cm (2ft). Yellow flowers on large terminals on 1 side of the panicle. Leaves greyish-green or olive-green.

Solidago virgaurea
Goldenrod
Also known as European Goldenrod.
Perennial Ht 30-60cm (12-24in), spread 60cm (2ft). Small yellow flowers from summer to autumn. The green leaves are lance-shaped.

Solidago 'Goldenmosa'
Golden Mimosa
Perennial. Ht 1m (3ft), spread 60cm (2ft). Sprays of mimosa-like yellow flowers from summer to autumn. Lance-shaped green leaves. Attractive border plant. Has no herbal use.

Goldenrod *Solidago virgaurea*

CULTIVATION

Propagation
Seeds
Sow in plug or seed trays in spring. As seed is fine, sow on the surface and cover with Perlite. Germination within 14-21 days without bottom heat. Prick out, harden off, and plant out into prepared site in the garden at a distance of 45cm (18in). Remember, the plant will spread.

Division
Divide established plants in spring or autumn. Dig up the plant, split into required size, half, third, etc., and replant in a prepared site in the garden.

Pests and Diseases
This plant rarely suffers from pests or diseases.

Maintenance
Spring: Sow seeds.
Summer: Enjoy the flowers. If you have rich soil, the plants may become very tall and need support in exposed sites.
Autumn: Divide mature plants.
Winter: No need for protection.

Garden Cultivation
It is an attractive plant and has been taken into cultivation as a useful late-flowering ornamental. It is ideal for the herbaceous border, as it spreads rapidly to form clumps.
In late summer, sprays of bright yellow flowers crowd its branching stems amongst sharply pointed hoary leaves. When planting in the garden, it prefers open conditions and soils that are not too rich and are well drained. It tolerates sun, semi-shade and shade, and being a wild plant it can be naturalized in poor grassland.

Sow seed thinly in spring or autumn in the chosen flowering position, having prepared the site, and cover lightly with soil. When the seedlings are large enough, thin to 30cm (12in) distance apart. (The plant will spread and you may have to do a second thinning.) If sown in the autumn, the young plants may in very cold temperatures need added protection. Use a mulch that they can grow through the following spring, or which can be removed.

Harvest
Collect the flowering tops and leaves in summer. Dry for medicinal use.

Golden Mimosa
Solidago 'Goldenmosa'

CONTAINER GROWING

Golden Rod can be grown in containers, but being a tall plant, it looks much more attractive in a garden border. Use the bark, peat, grit mix of compost and in the summer only give it liquid fertilizer and water regularly. In winter, as the plant dies back, place the container in a cool airy place protected from frost, but not warm. Keep the compost on the dry side.

MEDICINAL

Goldenrod is used in cases of urinary and kidney infections and stones, and catarrh. It also helps to ease backache caused by renal conditions because of its cleansing, eliminative action. It is used to treat arthritis.
A cold compress is helpful on fresh wounds because of its anti-inflammatory properties.
Sweet goldenrod is used as an astringent and as a calmative. The tea made from the dried leaves and flowers is an aromatic beverage and can be used to improve the taste of other medicinal preparations. Native Americans applied lotions made from goldenrod flowers to bee stings.

Stachys officinalis (Betonica officinalis)

BETONY

Also known as Lousewort, Purple Betony, Wood Betony, Bishop's Wort and Devil's Plaything. From the family Labiatae

This attractive plant is native to Europe and still found growing wild in Britain. Betony certainly merits inclusion in the herb garden, but is thought by some to be one of the plant world's frauds. There are so many conflicting stories, all of which are well worth hearing. I leave it to you to decide what is fact or fiction.

The Ancient Egyptians were the first to attribute magical properties to betony. In England, by the 10th century, the Anglo-Saxons had it as their most important magical plant, claiming it as effective against the Elf sickness. In the 11th century it was mentioned in the *Lacnunga* as a beneficial medicinal plant against the Devilish affliction of the body. Later, Gerard wrote in his Herbal, 'Betony is good for them that be subject to the falling sickness,' and went on to describe its many virtues, one of them being 'a remedy against the biting of mad dogs and venomous serpents'.

In the 18th century it was still considered of use in the cure of diverse inflictions, including headaches and drawing out splinters, as well as being used in herbal tobacco and snuff. Today, betony retains an important place in folk medicine even though its true value is seriously questioned.

We owe the name to the Romans, who called the herb first *Bettonica* and then *Betonica*.

Betony *Stachys officinalis*

Betony *Stachys officinalis*

SPECIES

Stachys officinalis
Betony
Hardy perennial. Ht 60cm (24in), spread 25cm (10in). Dense spikes of pink or purple flowers end-spring through summer. Square hairy stems bear aromatic, slightly hairy, round, lobed leaves.

Stachys officinalis 'Alba'
White Betony
Hardy perennial. Ht 60cm (24in), spread 25cm (10in). White flowers end-spring through summer.

CULTIVATION

Propagation
Seed
Grows readily from seed, which it produces in abundance. Sow late summer or spring in planting position and cover very lightly with soil. Alternatively, sow seeds in trays and prick out seedlings into small pots when large enough to handle.

Division
Divide roots of established plants in spring or autumn, replant at a distance of

30cm (12in) from other plants. Alternatively pot up using the bark, peat mix of compost.

Pests and Diseases

Apart from the occasional caterpillar, this plant is pest and disease free.

Maintenance

Spring: Sow seeds. Divide established plants.
Summer: Plant out spring seedlings.
Autumn: Cut back flowering stems, save seeds, divide established plants
Winter: No protection needed.

Garden Cultivation

A very accommodating plant, it will tolerate most soils, but prefers some humus. Flourishes in sun or shade, in fact it will put up with all but the deepest of shade. A wild plant, but it has for centuries been grown in cottage gardens. In the wild flower garden it is a very colourful participant and establishes well either in a mixed bed or in grassland. It is also excellent for the woodland garden.

Harvest

Collect leaves for drying before flowering in late spring/early summer. Use leaves fresh either side of flowering.

Pick flowers for drying and for use in potpourris just as they open. Collect through flowering season to use fresh.

Save seed in early autumn. Store in dry, dark container.

CONTAINER GROWING

Betony grows to great effect in half a beer barrel and combines well with other wild flowers e.g. poppies, oxeye daisy, chamomile. I do not advise it for growing indoors or in small containers.

Betony *Stachys officinalis* **in flower**

OTHER USES

The fresh plant provides a yellow dye. A hair rinse, good for highlighting greying hair, can be made from an infusion of the leaves.

WARNING

Care must be taken if it is taken internally because in any form the root can cause vomiting and violent diarrhoea.

Betony makes a good yellow dye

MEDICINAL

Today opinions differ as to its value. Some authorities consider it is only an astringent while others believe it is a sedative. It is however now chiefly employed in herbal smoking mixtures and herbal snuffs. As an infusional powder, it is used to treat diarrhoea, cystitis, asthma and neuralgia. Betony tea is invigorating, particularly if prepared in a mixture with other herbs. In France it is recommended for liver and gall bladder complaints.

Symphytum officinale
COMFREY

Also known as Knitbone, Boneset, Bruisewort, Knitback, Church Bells, Abraham, Isaac-and-Jacob (from the variation in flower colour) and Saracen's Root. From the family Boraginaceae.

Native to Europe and Asia, it was introduced into America in the 17th century, where it has naturalized.

Traditionally known as Saracen's root, common comfrey is believed to have been brought to England by the Crusaders who had discovered its value as a healing agent – mucilaginous secretions strong enough to act as a bone-setting plaster and which gave it the nickname Knitbone.

The Crusaders passed it to monks for cultivation in their monastic herb gardens, dedicated to the care of the sick.

Elizabethan physicians and herbalists were never without it. A recipe from that time is for an ointment made from comfrey root boiled in sugar and liquorice, and mixed with coltsfoot, mallow and poppy seed. People also made comfrey tea for colds and bronchitis.

But times have changed. Once the panacea for all ills, comfrey is now under suspicion as a carcinogen. In line with its common name 'Bruisewort', research in America has shown that comfrey breaks down the red blood cells. At the same time, the Japanese are investigating how to harness its beneficial qualities: there is a research programme into the high protein and vitamin B content of the herb.

SPECIES

Symphytum 'Bocking 4'
Hardy perennial. Ht 1m (3ft), spread indefinite. Flowers near to violet in colour, in spring and early summer. Thick, solid stems. Large green lance-shaped leaves. Not a particularly attractive plant but it contains almost 35 per cent total protein, the same percentage as in soya beans. Comfrey is an important animal feed in some parts of the world especially Africa.

Symphytum 'Bocking 14'
Hardy perennial. Ht 1m (3ft), spread indefinite. Mauve flowers in spring and early summer. Thin stems. Green oval leaves, tapering to a point. This variety has the highest potash content, which makes it the best for producing liquid manure.

Symphytum 'Hidcote Blue'
Comfrey Hidcote Blue
Hardy perennial. Ht 50cm (20in), spread 60cm (2ft). Pale blue flowers in spring and early summer. Green lance-shaped leaves. Very attractive in a large border.

Symphytum ibericum (grandiflorium)
Dwarf Comfrey
Hardy perennial. Ht 25cm (10in), spread 1m (3ft). Yellow/white flowers in spring. Green lance-shaped leaves. An excellent ground cover plant, having foliage throughout most winters. This comfrey contains little potassium and no allantoin, the crucial medicinal substance.

Dwarf Comfrey
Symphytum ibericum

Symphytum officinale
Comfrey (Wild or Common)
Hardy perennial. Ht and spread 1m (3ft). White/purple/pink flowers in summer. This is the best medicinal comfrey and can also be employed as a liquid feed, although the potassium content is only 3.09 per cent compared to **Bocking 14**'s 7.09 per cent. It makes a first class composting plant, as it helps the rapid breakdown of other compost materials.

Symphytum x uplandicum
Russian Comfrey
Hardy perennial. Ht 1m (3ft), spread indefinite. Pink/purple flowers in

Pink/purple flowers in summer. Green lance-shaped leaves. This is a hybrid which occurred naturally in Upland, Sweden. It is a cross between **S. officinale**, the herbalist's comfrey, and **S. asperum**, the blue-flowered, prickly comfrey from Russia. A very attractive form of this variety is **S. x uplandicum 'Variegatum'**, which has cream and green leaves.

Russian Comfrey
Symphytum x *uplandicum*

CULTIVATION

Propagation
Seed
Not nearly as reliable as root cutting or division. Sow in spring or autumn in either seed or plug trays. Germination slow and erratic.

Root Cuttings
Dig up a piece of root, cut into 2cm (1in) sections, and put these small sections into a prepared plug or seed tray.

Division
Use either the double spade method or simply dig up a chunk in the spring and replant it elsewhere.

Pests and Diseases
Sometimes suffers from rust and powdery mildew in late autumn. In both cases cut the plant down and burn the contaminated leaves.

Maintenance
Spring: Sow seeds. Divide plants. Take root cuttings.
Summer: Cut back leaves for composting, or to use as a mulch around other herbs in the growing season.
Autumn: Sow seeds.
Winter: None needed

Garden Cultivation
Fully hardy in the garden, all the comfreys prefer sun or semi-shade and a moist soil, but will tolerate most conditions. The large tap root can cause problems if you want to move the plant. When doing this make sure you dig up all the root because any left behind will reappear later.

Harvest
Cut leaves with shears from early summer to autumn to provide foliage for making liquid feed. Each plant is able to give four cuts a year if well fed. Cut leaves for drying before flowering.
  Dig up roots in autumn for drying.

CONTAINER GROWING

Comfrey is not suitable for growing indoors, but it can be grown on a patio as long as the container is large enough. Situate in partial shade and give plenty of water in warm weather.

CULINARY

Fresh leaves and shoots were eaten as a vegetable or salad and there is no reason to suppose that it is dangerous to do so now, although it may be best to err on the side of caution until suspicions are resolved.

LIQUID MANURE
A quickly available source of potassium for the organic gardener. One method of extracting it is to put 6kg (14lb) of freshly cut comfrey into a 90 litre (20 gallon) tapped, fibreglass water butt. Do not use metal as rust will add toxic quantities of iron oxide to the liquid manure. Fill up the butt with rain or tap water and cover with a lid to exclude the light. In about 4 weeks a clear liquid can be drawn off from the tap at the bottom. Ideal feed for tomatoes, onions, gooseberries, beans and all potash hungry crops. It can be used as a foliar feed.
  The disadvantage of this method is that the liquid stinks, because comfrey foliage is about 3.4 per cent protein, and when proteins break down they smell.
  An alternative is to bore a hole into the side (just above the bottom) of a plastic dustbin. Stand the container on bricks, so that it is far enough off the ground to allow a dish to be placed under the hole. Pack it solid with cut comfrey, and place something (a heavy lump of concrete) on top to weigh down the leaves. Cover with lid, and in about 3 weeks a black liquid will drip from the hole into dish.
  This concentrate can be stored in a screw top bottle if you do not want to use it immediately. Dilute it 1 part to 40 parts water, and if you plan to use is as a foliar feed, strain it first.

MEDICINAL

Comfrey has received much attention in recent years, both as a valuable healing herb, a source of Vitamin B_{12} and self-proliferate allantoin, and as a potential source of protein.
  Comfrey is also useful as a poultice for varicose ulcers and a compress for varicose veins, and it alleviates and heals minor burns.

WARNING

Comfrey is reported to cause serious liver damage if taken in large amounts over a long period of time.

OTHER USES
Boil fresh leaves for golden fabric dye.
  Comfrey is a good feed for racehorses and helps cure laminitis. For curing septic sores on animals, make a poultice between clean pieces of cotton and tie to the affected places.

Comfrey dye

Tanacetum balsamita

ALECOST

(COSTMARY)

Other names: Bible Leaf, Sweet Mary and Mint Geranium. From the family Compositae

Alecost originated in Western Asia and by the time it reached America in the 17th century, Culpeper wrote of its use in Europe that 'Alecost is so frequently known to be an inhabitant of almost every garden, that it is needless to write a description thereof.'

Since then, in America it has escaped its garden bounds and grows wild in eastern and mid-west States, while in Europe it has become altogether rare. Only recently has interest revived among propagators as well as horticulturalists who, in the space of twenty years, have reclassified alecost twice, from *Chrysanthemum* to *Balsamita* and now to *Tanacetum*.

The first syllable of its common name, alecost, derives from the use to which its scented leaves and flowering tops were put in the Middle Ages, namely to clarify, preserve and impart an astringent, minty flavour to beer. The second syllable, 'cost', comes from *kostos*, Greek for 'spicy'. Literally, 'alecost' means 'a spicy herb for ale'.

The alternative, costmary, by introducing a proper name symbolic of motherhood, conveys another of the plant's traditional uses in the form of a tea.

Religious connotations extend to one other nickname, 'Bible Leaf', which grew out of the Puritan habit of using a leaf of the herb as a fragrant Bible bookmark, its scent dispelling faintness from hunger during long sermons.

SPECIES

**Tanacetum balsamita
(Balsamita major)**
Alecost (costmary)
Hardy perennial. Ht 1m (3ft), spread 45cm (18in). Small white yellow-eyed daisy flowers mid- to late summer. Large rosettes of oval aromatic silvery green leaves.

**Tanacetum balsamita
tomentosum**
Camphor plant
Hardy perennial. Ht 1m (3ft), spread 45cm (18in). Appearance and habit very similar to alecost, but unlike the latter it is not palatable as a culinary herb. Its leaves are an effective moth repellent.

Camphor plant *Tanacetum balsamita tomentosum*

Alecost *Tanacetum Balsamita (Balsamita major)*

CULTIVATION

Propagation
Seed
The seed is fine and thin and cannot be propagated from plants grown in cool climates (the seed not being viable). Obtain seed from a specialist seedsman. Sow in spring onto the surface of a seed or plug tray and cover with Perlite. Use low warmth to encourage germination, and be patient! The seedlings may emerge in 10 days or 2 months, depending on the freshness of the seed. Pot on or plant out into the garden when they are large enough to handle.

Division
The best way to propagate is by division either in spring or autumn. Take a portion of the creeping root from an established plant, and either plant out or pot up using a bark, peat, grit mix of compost. If taking offsets in autumn, it is better to winter the pots in a cold frame.

Garden cultivation
Plant 60cm (2ft) apart and, if possible, in a sunny position. Both alecost and camphor plant will adapt to most conditions but prefer a rich, fairly dry and well-drained soil. Both species will grow in shade but may fail to bloom. But that is no great loss as the flower is not striking. Both die back in winter.

Pests and diseases
Leaves of both are aromatic, so pests are not a problem.

Maintenance
Spring: Divide established plants. Sow seed if available. Feed established plants.
Summer: Plant out seedlings early into permanent positions. Dead head.
Autumn: Trim back flowers. Remove offsets from established plants to prevent them encroaching into others' territory.
Winter: Tidy up dead leaves; they spread disease if left to rot. Bring in potted-up offsets.

Harvest
Pick the leaves for fresh culinary use any time. Both alecost and camphor leaves dry well and retain their sweet aroma. Pick for drying just before flowering for the strongest scent.
The flowers are not worth harvesting for drying.
Only in a warm climate is it worth collecting seeds. Do it when flowers turn brown and centre eye disintegrates on touch. Sow the following year (see Propagation).

CONTAINER GROWING
Neither species lends itself to container growing. They grow soft, prone to disease, are untidy when in flower, tend to be blown over by the wind and make untidy specimens in flower. If there is no other course, dead head to prevent from flowering and do not over-feed with liquid fertilizer.

Alecost *Tanacetum balsamita*
(Balsamita major)

CULINARY

Use only the alecost leaf and very sparingly as it has a sharp tang which can be overpowering. Add finely chopped leaves to carrot soups, salads, game, poultry, stuffing and fruit cakes, or with melted butter to peas and new potatoes. Its traditional value to beer holds good for home brewing.

MEDICINAL

Traditionally in the form of a tea (Costmary or Sweet Mary Tea) to ease the pain of childbirth. It was also used as a tonic for colds, catarrh, stomach upsets and cramps. Rub a fresh leaf of alecost on a bee sting or horse fly bite to relieve pain.

Alecost with new potatoes

OTHER USES

Both alecost and camphor leaves, which are sweet scented like balsam, serve to intensify other herb scents and act as an insect repellent. Add to potpourris or to linen bags or with lavender to make nosegay sachets, or infuse to make a final scented rinse for hair.
Fresh or dried leaves of alecost can be added to baths for a fragrant and refreshing soak.

Alecost potpourri

Tanacetum cinerariifolium (Chrysanthemum cinerariifolium)

PYRETHRUM

From the family Compositae.

This plant is native to Dalmatia but is now cultivated commercially in many parts of the world, including Japan, South Africa and parts of Central Europe.

It has been grown for many years for its insecticidal properties. The derivative was originally known as Dalmatian insect powder but is now better known as Pyrethrum insecticide. I list the two species to contain this natural insecticide.

SPECIES

Tanacetum cinerariifolium (Chrysanthemum cinerariifolium)
Hardy perennial. Ht 30-37cm (12-15in), spread 20cm (8in). Daisy-like flower, white petals with a yellow centre. Leaves green/grey, finely divided, with white down on the underside.

Tanacetum coccineum (Chrysanthemum roseum)
Hardy perennial.Ht 30-60cm (12-24in), spread 30cm (12in). Large flowerhead which can be white or red, and sometimes tipped with yellow. Very variable under cultivation. Vivid green leaves. Native of Iran.

CULTIVATION

Propagation
Seeds
In spring sow into a prepared seed or plug tray and cover with Perlite. Germination is easy and takes 14-21 days. In late spring, when the young plants are large enough and after a period of hardening off, plant out into a prepared site in the garden 15-30cm (6-12in) apart.

Division
Established clumps can be dug up in the spring and divided.

Pests and Diseases
In the majority of cases this plant is free from pests and diseases.

Maintenance
Spring: Sow seed. Divide established plants.
Summer: Dead head flowers to prolong season if not collecting seed.
Autumn: Divide established plants if necessary.
Winter: Fully hardy.

Pyrethrum
Tanacetum cinerariifolium

Garden Cultivation
Pyrethrum likes a well-drained soil in a sunny spot; it is drought tolerant and fully hardy in most winters.

Harvest
The flowerheads are collected just as they open and then dried gently. When they are quite dry, store away from light. The insecticide is made from the powdered dried flower.

CONTAINER GROWING

This herb is very well suited to be grown in containers, especially terracotta. Use the bark, peat, grit compost. Water well during the summer months, but be mean on the liquid fertilizer, otherwise the leaves will become green and it will stop flowering.

MEDICINAL

This herb is rarely used medicinally. Herbalists have found the roots to be a remedy for certain fevers. Recent research has shown that the flowerheads possess a weak antibiotic.

OTHER USES

This is a useful insecticide because it is non-toxic to mammals and does not accumulate in the environment or in the bodies of animals. It acts by paralysing the nervous system of the insects, and can kill pests living on the skin of man and animals. Sprinkle the dry powder from the flowers to deter all common insects, pests, bed bugs, cockroaches, flies, mosquitoes, aphids, spider mites and ants.

To make a spray, steep 28g (1oz) of pyrethrum powder in 28ml (1fl oz) of methylated spirits and then dilute with 14 litres (3 gallons) water. The solution decomposes in bright sunlight. Therefore for maximum effect and to reduce the risk to pollinating insects and bees, spray at dusk.

WARNING

Kills helpful insects and fish.
Wear gloves when processing flowers for insecticide use, as it may cause allergies. When the active ingredient Pyrethrum is extracted it is toxic to humans and animals.

Tanacetum vulgare (Chrysanthemum vulgare)

TANSY

Also known as Bachelor's Buttons, Bitter Buttons, Golden Buttons, Stinking Willy, Hind Heel and Parsley Fern. From the family Compositae.

Tansy is a native to Europe and Asia, and it has managed to become naturalized elsewhere, especially in North America. The name derives from the Greek *athanasia*, meaning immorality. In ancient times it was used in the preparation of the embalming sheets and rubbed on corpses to save them from earthworms or corpse worm.

SPECIES

Tanacetum vulgare
Tansy
Hardy perennial. Ht 90cm (3ft), spread 30-60cm (1-2ft) and more. Yellow button flowers in late summer. The aromatic leaf is deeply indented, toothed and fairly dark green.

Tanacetum vulgare var. crispum
Curled Tansy
As **T. vulgare** except Ht 60cm (24in) and the aromatic leaf is crinkly, curly and dark green.

Tanacetum vulgare 'Isala Gold'
Tansy Isala Gold
As **T. vulgare** except Ht 60cm (24in) and the leaf is golden in colour.

Tansy *Tanacetum vulgare*

Tanacetum vulgare 'Silver Lace'
Tansy 'Silver Lace'
As **T. vulgare** except Ht 60cm (24in) and the leaf starts off white-flecked with green, progressing to full green. If, however, you keep cutting it, some of the variegation can be maintained.

CULTIVATION

Propagation
Seed
Sow the very small seed in spring or autumn in a prepared seed or plug tray and cover with Perlite. Germination takes 10-21 days. Plant out 45cm (18in) apart when the seedlings are large enough to handle. If sown in the autumn, over-winter under protection.

Division
All species produce root runners, so divide in spring or autumn.

Pests and Diseases
Tansy is rarely bothered with pests or disease.

Maintenance
Spring: Sow seed. Divide established clumps.
Summer: Cut back after flowering to maintain shape and colour.
Autumn: Divide established clumps. Sow seeds.
Winter: The plant is fully hardy and dies back into the ground for winter.

Garden Cultivation
Tansy needs to be positioned with care as the roots spread widely. The gold and variegated forms are much less invasive and very attractive in a semi-shaded border. They tolerate most conditions provided the soil is not completely wet.

Harvest
Pick leaves as required. Gather flowers when open.

CONTAINER GROWING

Because of its antisocial habit, container growing is recommended. Use a soil-based compost and a large container, water throughout the growing season, and only feed about twice during flowering. In winter keep on the dry side in a cool place.

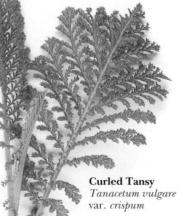

Curled Tansy
Tanacetum vulgare var. *crispum*

OTHER USES

Rub into the coat of your dog or cat to prevent fleas.
Hang leaves indoors to deter flies. Put dried sprigs under carpets. Add to insect repellent sachets. Sprinkle chopped leaves and flowers to deter ants and mice.
It produces a yellow/green woollen dye.

MEDICINAL

Can be used by trained herbalists to expel roundworm and threadworm.
Use tansy tea externally to treat scabies, and as a compress to bring relief to painful rheumatic joints.

WARNING

Use tansy only under medical supervision. It is a strong emmenagogue, provoking the onset of a period, and should not be used during pregnancy. An overdose of tansy oil or tea can be fatal.

Tanacetum parthenium (Chrysanthemum parthenium)

FEVERFEW

Known in America as Featherfew and Febrifuge Plant. From the family Compositae.

Feverfew was probably a native of south-east Europe and spread via the Mediterranean to many parts of the world, including Britain and North America. It is an attractive and robust, vigorous plant, and is found growing in the wild on dry, well-drained soils.

Its common name suggests that the herb was used in the treatment of fevers. It is said to be derived from the Latin 'febrifugia', meaning a substance that drives out fevers. The old herbalists even call it a febrifuge. However, strange as it may seem, the herb was hardly ever employed for the purpose.

Gerard, the Elizabethan herbalist, advised use of the dried plant for 'those that are giddied in the head or have vertigo'. In the 17th century Culpeper advised its use for pains in the head and colds. In the late 18th century it was considered a special remedy for a body racked by too much opium. Nowadays it is used in the treatment of migraines.

Feverfew *Tanacetum parthenium*

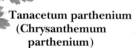

SPECIES

Tanacetum parthenium (Chrysanthemum parthenium)
Feverfew
Hardy perennial. Ht 60cm-1.2m (2-4ft), spread 45cm (18in). White daisy-like flowers from early summer to early autumn. The leaf is mid-green, and a typical chrysanthemum shape.

Tanacetum parthenium 'White Bonnet'
Double-Flowered Feverfew
Hardy perennial. Ht 30cm (12in), spread 45cm (18in). Double white flowers, otherwise as **T. parthenium**.

Tanacetum parthenium 'Aureum'
Golden Feverfew
Hardy perennial. Ht and spread 20-45cm (8-18in). Gold green leaves that remain colourful all year. Otherwise as **T. parthenium**. Growth and colour make Golden Feverfew popular as an edging plant in formal herb gardens and as a partier filling. Particularly conspicuous in winter.

CULTIVATION

Propagation
Seeds
Fine, thin and fairly small, they tend to stick together especially if they get damp. Mix a very small amount of seed with an equally small amount of Perlite or dry sand to make sowing easier. Sow very thinly in spring or early autumn, directly into pots or plug trays. Cover with a final thin layer of Perlite. Germination is usually very rapid, 7-10 days. No need for extra heat. Plant out 30cm (12in) apart, as soon as the seedlings are large enough to handle and hardened off. If sown in autumn, the young plants will need to be wintered under protection.

Division
Dig up established clumps in early autumn. Ease the plants apart, and either replant directly in the positions required or pot up in a standard pot or fancy container for flowers in late spring. Winter in a cold greenhouse or cold frame. Use the bark, peat compost.

Cuttings
Take stem cuttings in the summer, making sure there are no flowers on the cutting material.

Pests and Diseases
Unaffected by the majority of pests and diseases, golden feverfew can suffer from sun scorch; if this occurs cut back and the new growth will be unaffected.

Maintenance
Spring: Sow seeds.
Summer: As flowering finishes cut plant back to restore shape, and remove all flowering heads to

Feverfew in sachets makes a good moth repellant

minimize self-seeding.
Autumn: Divide established clumps. This is the best time for sowing if edging plants are required. Winter young plants in a cold frame.
Winter: No need to protect, fully frost hardy.

Garden Cultivation
Feverfew, while tolerant by nature, is an invasive plant, so choose the site with care. It will grow anywhere, in nooks or crannies, but likes best a loam soil enriched with good manure in a sunny position. Seeds can be sown direct into a prepared site in late spring. When the seedlings are large enough to handle thin to 30cm (12in) apart.

Harvest
Pick leaves before the plant flowers; dry if required for use medicinally. Pick the flowers just as they open; dry hanging upside down.

CONTAINER GROWING

Grown indoors, the plants get stretched and leggy. However, in containers outside all the feverfews flourish. Golden Feverfew, having the most compact

habit, looks very effective in a hanging basket, tub or window-box. Use the bark, peat mix of compost. Keep the plants regularly watered and feed during flowering. Cut back plants after flowering as this will help maintain their shape.

CULINARY

The young leaves of feverfew can be added to salads, but be warned they are very bitter so add sparingly.

MEDICINAL

That feverfew has a propensity to overcome melancholy has been known by herbalists for centuries. However, its ability to soothe headaches was not given much attention until the 1970s when it was thoroughly investigated scientifically, following claims that it reduced migraines. Many clinical trials were held and results, over a six-month period, showed a 70 per cent reduction in migraines, and

43 per cent of the patients felt other beneficial side-effects, including more restful sleep and relief from arthritis. 18 per cent had unpleasant side effects. Golden and double-flowered forms have not been tested, though experience suggests that they will react similarly.
Eat 3 to 5 fresh leaves between a slice of bread every day to reduce migraines. As mentioned before, this is very bitter, so put the leaves in a sandwich (brown bread, of course). To make it more palatable, you could add a sprig of mint, marjoram or parsley. Do NOT eat more.

OTHER USES

A decoction or infusion of the leaves is a mild disinfectant, and the leaves in sachets make a good moth repellent.

WARNING

One side effect associated with taking feverfew is ulceration of the mouth.

Taraxacum officinale

DANDELION

*Also known as Pee in the Bed, Lions Teeth, Fairy Clock, Clock, Clock Flower, Clocks and Watches,
Farmers Clocks, Old Mans Clock, One Clock, Wetweed, Blowball, Cankerwort, Lionstooth,
Priests Crown, Puffball, Swinesnout, White Endive, Wild Endive and Piss-a-beds.
From the family Compositae.*

D andelion is one of nature's great medicines and it really proves that a weed is only a plant out of place! It is in fact one of the most useful of herbs. It has become naturalized throughout the temperate regions of the world and flourishes on nitrogen-rich soils in any situation to a height of 2,000m (6,500ft).

There is no satisfactory explanation why it is called Dandelion, Dents Lioness, Tooth of the Lion in medieval Latin, and Dent de Lion in French. The lion's tooth may be the tap root, the jagged leaf or the parts of the flower.

The Arabs promoted its use in the 11th century. By the 16th it was well established as an official drug. The apothecaries knew it as *Herba taraxacon* or *Herba urinari,* and Culpeper called it Piss-a-beds, all referring to its diuretic qualities.

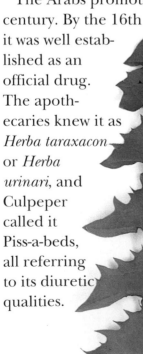

Dandelion
Taraxacum officinale

Dandelion *Taraxacum officinale*

SPECIES

Taraxacum officinale
Dandelion
Perennial. Ht 15-23cm (6-9in). Large, brilliant yellow flowers 5cm (2in) wide, spring to autumn. The flower heads as they turn to seed form a fluffy ball (dandelion clock). Leaves oblong with a jagged edge.

Taraxacum kok-saghyz Rodin
Russian Dandelion
Perennial. Ht 30cm (12in). Similar to the above. Extensively cultivated during the Second World War: latex was extracted from the roots as a source of rubber.

Taraxacum mongolicum
Chinese Dandelion
Perennial. Ht 25-30cm (10-12in). Similar to the above. Used to treat infections, particularly mastitis.

CULTIVATION

Propagation
Seed
Grow as an annual to prevent bitterness developing in the plant. Sow seed in spring on the surface of pots or plug trays. Do not use seed trays as the long tap root makes it difficult to prick out. Cover with a fine layer of Perlite. Germination will be in 3-6 weeks, depending on seed freshness and air temperature. Plant out when large enough to handle.

Root
Sections of the root can be cut and put in either pots, seed or plug trays. Each piece will sprout again, just like comfrey.

Pests and Diseases
Dandelion is rarely attacked by either pest or disease.

Maintenance

Spring: Sow seeds for use as an autumn salad herb.
Summer: Continually pick off the flower buds if you are growing dandelion as a salad crop.
Autumn: Put an up-turned flower pot over some of the plants to blanch them for autumn salads. Sow seed for spring salad crop.
Winter: No protection is needed. For salad crops, if temperatures fall below -10°C (15°F), cover with agricultural fleece or 8cm (3in) of straw or bracken to keep the leaves sweet.

Garden Cultivation

If the dandelion was a rare plant, it would be thought as a highly desirable garden species, for the flowers are most attractive, sweet smelling and a brilliant yellow, and then form the delightful puff balls. Up to that point all is fine. But then the wind disperses the seed all over the garden. And it is very difficult to eradicate when established since every bit of root left behind produces another plant. So, it finds no favour at all with gardeners.

In general, details on how to grow dandelions are superfluous. Most people only want to know how to get rid of them. The easiest time to dig up the plants completely is in the early spring.

Harvest

Pick leaves as required to use fresh, and flowers for wine as soon as they open fully. Dig up roots in autumn for drying.

CONTAINER GROWING

Dandelions do look attractive growing in containers, especially in window boxes, if you can stand neighbours' remarks. But in all seriousness the containers will need to be deep to accommodate the long tap root.

CULINARY

Both the leaves and root have long been eaten as a highly nutritious salad. In the last century, cultivated forms with large leaves were developed as an autumn and spring vegetable. The leaves were usually blanched in the same way as endive. Dandelion salad in spring is also considered a blood cleanser owing to its diuretic and digestive qualities. The leaves are very high in Vitamins A, B, C and D, the A content being higher than that of carrots.

The flowers make an excellent country wine and dandelion roots provide, when dried, chopped and roasted, the best known coffee substitute.

Dandelion wine

Dandelion and Bacon Salad

Serves 4

225g/8oz young dandelion leaves
100g/4oz streaky bacon, diced
1cm/½in slice white bread, cubed
4 tablespoons olive or walnut oil
1 tablespoon white wine vinegar
1 clove garlic, crushed
salt and freshly ground pepper
oil for cooking

Wash and dry the leaves and tear into the salad bowl. Make a vinaigrette using olive oil and vinegar, and season to taste, adding a little sugar if desired. Fry the bacon, crushed garlic and bread in oil until golden brown. Pour the contents of the pan over the leaves and turn the leaves until thoroughly coated. Add the vinaigrette and toss again and serve soon after making.

Dandelion and bacon salad

MEDICINAL

It is one of the most useful medicinal plants, as all parts are effective and safe to use. It is regarded as one of the best herbal remedies for kidney and liver complaints. The root is a mildly laxative, bitter tonic, valuable in treating dyspepsia and constipation. The leaves are a powerful diuretic. However, unlike conventional diuretics, dandelion does not leach potassium from the body as its rich potassium content replaces what the body loses.

The latex contained in the leaves and stalks is very effective in removing corns and in treating warts and verrucas. Apply the juice from the plant daily to the affected part.

The flowers can be boiled with sugar for coughs, but honey has a greater medicinal value.

OTHER USES

As a herbal fertilizer dandelion is a good supply of copper. Pick 3 plants completely: leaves, flowers and all. Place in a bucket, pour over 1 litre (2 pints) boiling water, cover and allow to stand for 30 minutes. Strain through an old pair of tights or something similar. This fertilizer will not store.

A dye, yellow brown in colour, can be obtained from the root and dandelions are excellent food for domestic rabbits, guinea pigs and gerbils. There is one thing for which they are useless, however, flower arrangements . As soon as you pick them and put them in water their flowers close tight.

Teucrium x lucidrys

WALL GERMANDER

***Also known as Ground Oak and Wild Germander.
From the family Labiatae.***

This attractive plant is a native of Europe, and is now naturalized in Britain and other countries in the temperate zone. It is found on dry chalky soils. The Latin *Teucrium* is said to have been named after Teucer, first king of Troy. It is the ancient Greek word for ground oak, its leaves resembling those of the oak tree.

In medieval times, it was a popular strewing herb and a remedy for dropsy, jaundice and gout. It was also used in powder form for treating head colds, and as a snuff.

SPECIES

Teucrium fruticans
Tree Germander
Evergreen hardy perennial. Ht 1-2m (3-6ft), spread 2-4m (6-12ft). Blue flowers in summer. The leaves are aromatic, grey/green with a white underside.

Teucrium chamaedrys 'Variegatum'
Variegated Wall Germander
Evergreen hardy perennial. Ht 45cm (18in), spread 20cm (8in). Pink flowers from mid-summer to early autumn. The leaves are aromatic, dark green with cream/yellow variegation, small, shiny and oval.

Teucrium x lucidrys (chamaedrys)
Wall Germander
Evergreen hardy perennial. Ht 45cm (18in), spread 20cm (8in). Pink flowers from mid-summer to early autumn. The leaves are dark green, small, shiny and oval. When rubbed, they smell pleasantly spicy.

CULTIVATION

Propagation
Seed
Sow the small seeds in spring. Use a prepared seed or plug tray and the bark, peat, grit compost. Cover with Perlite. Germination can be erratic – from 2-4 weeks. When the seedlings are large enough to handle, plant in a prepared site 20cm (8in) apart.

Cuttings
This is a better method of propagating Germander. Take softwood cuttings from the new growth in spring, or semi-hardwood in summer. Ensure compost does not dry fully out and also never gets sodden.

Division
The **teucriums** produce creeping root stock in the spring and are easy to divide. Dig up the plants, split them in half, and replant in a chosen site.

Pests and Diseases
Wall germander hardly ever suffers from pests or disease.

Maintenance
Spring: Sow seeds. Take softwood cuttings. Trim established plants and hedges.
Summer: Trim plants after flowering, take semi-hardwood cuttings.
Autumn: Trim hedges.
Winter: Protect the variegated form when temperatures drop below -5°C (23°F).

Garden Cultivation
Wall germander needs a well-drained soil (slightly alkaline) and a sunny position. It is hardier than lavender and cotton lavender, and makes an ideal hedging or edging plant. To make a good dense hedge, plant at a distance of 15cm (6in). If you clip the hedge in spring and autumn to maintain its shape, you will never need to cut it hard back.

It can also be planted in rockeries, and in stone walls where it looks most attractive. During the growing season it does not need extra water, even in hot summers, nor does it need extra protection in cold winters. The variegated variety is more temperamental, and will require cosseting in the winter in the form of a mulch or agricultural fleece.

Harvest
For drying for medicinal use, pick leaves before the plant flowers, and flowering stems when the flowers are in bud.

CONTAINER GROWING

Both wall germander and the variegated form look good in containers. Use the bark, peat, grit mix of compost. Only feed during the flowering season. Keep on the dry side in winter.

CULINARY

This plant is used extensively in the flavouring of liqueurs.

MEDICINAL

Its herbal use today is minor. However, there is a revival of interest going on, and some use it as a remedy for digestive and liver troubles, anaemia and bronchitis.

Teucrium scorodonia

WOOD SAGE

**Also known as Gypsy Sage, Mountain Sage, Wild Sage and Garlic Sage.
From the family Labiatae.**

This plant is a native of Europe and has become naturalized in Britain and other countries in the temperate zone.

There is not much written about wood sage apart from the fact that, like alecost, it was used in making ale before hops were introduced. However, Gertrude Jekyll recognized its value and with renewed interest in her gardens comes a revival of interest in wood sage.

SPECIES

Teucrium scorodonia
Wood Sage
Hardy perennial. Ht 30-60cm (12-24in), spread 25cm (10in). Pale greenish white flowers in summer. Soft green heart-shaped leaves, which have a mild smell of crushed garlic.

Teucrium scorodonia 'Crispum'
Curly Wood Sage
Hardy perennial. Ht 35cm (14in), spread 30cm (12in). Pale greenish-white flowers in summer. The leaves are soft, oval and olive green with a reddish tinge to their crinkled edges. Whenever it is on show it causes much comment.

CULTIVATION

Propagation
Wood sage can be propagated by seed, cuttings or division. Curly wood sage can only be propagated by cuttings or division.

Seed
Sow the fairly small seed under protection in autumn or spring in a prepared seed or plug tray. Use the bark, peat, grit compost, and cover with Perlite. Germination can be erratic, taking from 2-4 weeks. When the seedlings are large enough to handle, pot up and winter under cover in a cold frame. In the spring, after a period of hardening off, plant out in a prepared site in the garden at a distance of 25cm (10in).

Cuttings
Take softwood cuttings from the new growth in spring, or semi-hardwood cuttings in summer.

Division
Both wood sages produce creeping root stock. In the spring they are easy to divide.

Pests and Diseases
Wood sages are, in the majority of cases, free from pests and disease.

Maintenance
Spring: Sow seeds. Divide established plants. Take softwood cuttings.
Summer: Take semi-hardwood cuttings.
Autumn: Sow seeds.
Winter: No need for protection, the plants die back for the winter.

Garden Cultivation
It grows well in semi-shaded situations, but also thrives in full sun on sandy and gravelly soils. It will adapt quite happily to clay and heavy soils, but not produce such prolific growth.

Harvest
Pick young leaves for fresh use as required.

CONTAINER GROWING

I have grown curly wood sage most successfully in containers. The plain wood sage does not look quite so attractive. Use the bark, grit, peat mix of compost, and plant in a large container – its creeping root stock can too easily become pot-bound. Only feed twice in a growing season, otherwise the leaves become large, soft and floppy. When the plant dies back, put it somewhere cool and keep it bordering on dry.

MEDICINAL

Wood sage has been used to treat blood disorders, colds and fevers, and as a diuretic and wound herb.

CULINARY

The leaves of ordinary wood sage have a mild garlic flavour. When young and tender, the leaves can be added to salads for variety. But go steady, they are slightly bitter.

Wood sage salad

Thymus

THYME

From the family Labiatae.

This is a genus comprising numerous species that are very diverse in appearance and come from many different parts of the world. They are found as far afield as Greenland and Western Asia, although the majority grow in the Mediterranean region. This ancient herb was used by the Egyptians in oil form for embalming. The Greeks used it in their baths and as an incense in their temples. The Romans used it to purify their rooms, and most probably its use spread through Europe as their invasion train swept as far as Britain. In the Middle Ages drinking it was part of a ritual to enable one to see fairies, and it was one of many herbs used in nosegays to purify the odours of disease. Owing to its antiseptic properties, judges also used it along with rosemary to prevent gaol fever.

Common Thyme
Thymus vulgaris

Silver Posie Thyme
Thymus vulgaris 'Silver Posie'

SPECIES

There are so many species of Thyme that I am only going to mention a few of interest. New ones are being discovered each year. They are eminently collectable. Unfortunately their names can be unreliable, a nursery preferring its pet name or one traditional to it, rather than the correct one.

Thymus caespititius (Thymus azoricus)
Caespititius Thyme
Evergreen hardy perennial. Ht 10cm (4in), spread 20cm (8in). Pale pink flowers in summer. The leaves narrow, bright green and close together on the stem. Makes an attractive low growing mound, good between paving stones.

Thymus camphoratus
Camphor Thyme
Evergreen half-hardy perennial. Ht 30cm (12in), spread 20cm (8in). Pink/mauve flowers in summer, large green leaves smelling of camphor. Makes a beautiful compact bush.

Thymus cilicicus
Cilicicus Thyme
Evergreen hardy perennial. Ht 5cm (2in), spread 20cm (8in). Pink flowers in summer. The leaves are bright green, narrow and pointed, growing close together on the stem with an odd celery scent. Makes an attractive low growing mound, good between paving stones.

Thymus x citriodorus
Lemon Thyme
Evergreen hardy perennial. Ht 30 cm (12in), spread 20cm (8in). Pink flowers in summer. Fairly large green leaves with a strong lemon scent. Excellent culinary thyme, combines well with many chicken or fish dishes.

Wild Creeping Thyme
Thymus Praecox spp. arcticus

Thymus x citriodorus 'Archer's Gold'
Archer's Gold Thyme
Evergreen hardy perennial. Ht 10cm (4in), spread 20cm (8in). Pink/mauve flowers in summer. A mound of green/gold leaves. Decorative and culinary, it has a mild thyme flavour.

Thymus x citriodorus 'Bertram Anderson'
Bertram Anderson Thyme
Evergreen hardy perennial. Ht 10cm (4in), spread 20cm (8in). Pink/mauve flowers in summer. More of a round mound than Archers Gold and the leaves are slightly rounder with a more even golden look to the leaves. Decorative and culinary, it has a mild thyme flavour.

Thymus x citriodorus 'Fragrantissimus'
Orange Scented Thyme
Evergreen hardy perennial. Ht 30 cm (12in), spread 20cm (8in). Small pale pink/white flowers in summer. The leaves are small, narrow, greyish green, and smell of spicy orange. Combines well with stir fry dishes, poultry – especially duck, and even treacle pudding.

Thymus x citriodorus 'Golden King'
Golden King Thyme
Evergreen hardy perennial. Ht 30cm (12in) spread 20cm (8in). Pink flowers in the summer. Fairly large green leaves variegated with gold, strongly lemon scented. Excellent culinary thyme, combines well with many dishes, like chicken, fish and salad dressing.

Thymus x citriodorus 'Silver Queen'
Silver Queen Thyme
Evergreen hardy perennial. Ht 30cm (12in) spread 20cm (8in). Pink flowers in the summer. Fairly large leaves, grey with silver variegation, a strong lemon scent. Excellent culinary thyme, combines well with many dishes, like chicken, fish and salad dressing.

Thymus doerfleri
Doerfleri Thyme
Evergreen half-hardy perennial. Ht 2cm (1in), spread 20cm (8in). Mauve/pink flowers in summer, grey, hairy, thin leaves, which are mat forming. Decorative thyme, good for rockeries, hates being wet in winter. Originates from the Balkan Peninsula.

Thymus doerfleri 'Bressingham'
Bressingham Thyme
Evergreen hardy perennial. Ht 2cm (1in), spread 20cm (8in). Mauve/pink flowers in summer. Thin, green, hairy leaves, which are mat forming. Decorative thyme, good for rockeries, hates being wet in winter.

Thymus 'Doone Valley'
Doone Valley Thyme
Evergreen hardy perennial. Ht 8cm (3in), spread 20cm (8in). Purple flowers in summer. Round variegated green and gold leaves with a lemon scent. Very decorative, can be used in cooking if nothing else is available.

Thymus herba-barona
Caraway Thyme
Evergreen hardy perennial. Ht 2cm (1in), spread 20cm (8in). Rose coloured flowers in summer. Dark green small leaves with a unique caraway scent. Good in culinary dishes especially stir fry and meat. It combines well with beef.

Thymus praecox ssp. arcticus
Wild Creeping Thyme
Also known as Mother of Thyme and Creeping Thyme.
Evergreen hardy perennial. Ht 2cm (1in), spread 20cm (8in). Pale mauve flowers in summer. Small dark green leaves which, although mildly scented, can be used in cooking. Wild thyme has been valued by herbalists for many centuries.

Thymus polytrichus 'Porlock'
Porlock Thyme
Evergreen hardy perennial. Ht 30cm (12in), spread 20cm (8in). Pink flowers in summer. Fairly large green leaves with a mild but definite thyme flavour and scent. Excellent culinary thyme. Medicinal properties are anti-bacterial and anti-fungal.

Thymus pseudolanuginosus
Woolly Thyme
Evergreen hardy perennial. Ht 2cm (1in), spread 20cm (8in). Pale pink/mauve flowers for most of the summer. Grey hairy mat-forming leaves. Good for rockeries and in stone paths or walls. Dislikes wet winters.

Thymus pulegioïdes
Broad Leaved Thyme
Evergreen hardy perennial. Ht 8cm (3in), spread 20cm (8in). Pink/mauve flowers in summer. Large round dark green leaves with a strong thyme flavour. Good for culinary uses, excellent for ground cover and good in hanging baskets.

Lemon Thyme
Thymus x *citriodorus*

Thymus richardii ssp. nitidus 'Peter Davis'
Peter Davis Thyme
Evergreen hardy perennial. Ht 8cm (3in), spread 20cm (8in). Attractive pink/mauve flowers in summer. Thin grey/green leaves, mild scent. Very attractive thyme, good in rockeries or formal herb gardens.

Thymus serpyllum var. albus
White Thyme
Evergreen hardy perennial, prostrate form, a creeper. White flowers in summer. Bright green small leaves. Decorative aromatic and good ground cover.

Thymus serpyllum 'Annie Hall'
Annie Hall Thyme
Evergreen hardy perennial, prostrate form, a creeper. Pale pink flowers in summer. Small green leaves. Decorative, aromatic and good ground cover.

Pink Chintz Thyme
Thymus serpyllum 'Pink Chintz'

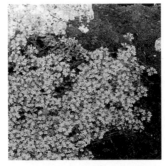

Thymus serpyllum coccineus
Coccineus Thyme
Also known as Creeping Red Thyme.
Evergreen hardy perennial, prostrate form, a creeper. Red flowers in summer. Green small leaves. Decorative, aromatic and good ground cover.

Thymus serpyllum 'Goldstream'
Goldstream Thyme
Evergreen hardy perennial, prostrate form, a creeper. Pink/mauve flowers in summer. Green/gold variegated small leaves. Decorative, aromatic and good ground cover.

Goldstream Thyme
Thymus serpyllum 'Goldstream'

Thymus serpyllum 'Lemon Curd'
Lemon Curd Thyme
Evergreen hardy perennial, prostrate form, a creeper. White/pink flowers in summer. Bright green lemon scented small leaves. Decorative, aromatic and good ground cover. Can be used in cooking if nothing else available.

Thymus serpyllum 'Minimus'
Minimus Thyme
Evergreen hardy perennial, prostrate form, a creeper. Pink flowers in summer. Tiny leaves, very compact. Decorative, aromatic and good ground cover. The leaves grow so close together that it is ideal for growing between pavings and alongside paths.

Thymus serpyllum 'Pink Chintz'
Pink Chintz Thyme
Evergreen hardy perennial, prostrate form, a creeper. Pale pink flowers in summer. Grey green small hairy leaves. Decorative, aromatic and good ground cover. Does not particularly like being wet in winter.

Thymus serpyllum 'Rainbow Falls'
Rainbow Falls Thyme
Evergreen hardy perennial, prostrate form, a creeper. Purple flowers in summer. Variegated green/gold small leaves. Decorative, aromatic and good ground cover.

Thymus serpyllum 'Russetings'
Russetings Thyme
Evergreen hardy perennial, prostrate form, a creeper. Purple/mauve flowers in summer. Small green leaves. Decorative, aromatic and good ground cover.

Thymus serpyllum 'Snowdrift'

Snowdrift Thyme
Evergreen hardy perennial, prostrate form, a creeper. Masses of white flowers in summer. Small green round leaves. Decorative, aromatic and good ground cover.

Thymus vulgaris

Common (Garden) Thyme
Evergreen hardy perennial. Ht 30cm (12in), spread 20cm (8in). Mauve flowers in summer. Thin green aromatic leaves. This is the thyme everyone knows. Use in stews, salads, sauces etc. Medicinal properties are anti-bacterial and anti-fungal.

Thymus vulgaris aureus

Golden Thyme
Evergreen hardy perennial. Ht 30cm (12in), spread 20cm (8in). Pale pink /lilac flowers. Green leaves that turn gold in summer, they have a good flavour and combine well with vegetarian dishes.

Thymus vulgaris 'Lucy'

Lucy Thyme
Evergreen hardy perennial. Ht 30cm (12in), spread 20cm (8in). The thyme sometimes does not flower, and if it does, it is a very pale pink flower and not very prolific. The leaves are very small green. Excellent culinary thyme. Medicinal properties are anti-bacterial and anti-fungal.

Coccineus Thyme

Thymus serpyllum Coccineus **and Snowdrift Thyme**
Thymus serpyllum 'Snowdrift'

Thymus vulgaris 'Silver Posie'

Silver Posie Thyme
Evergreen hardy perennial. Ht 30cm (12in), spread 20cm (8in). Pale pink/lilac flower. The leaves have a very pretty grey/silver variegation with a tinge of pink on the under-side. This is a good culinary thyme and looks very attractive in salads.

Thymus zygis

Zygis Thyme
Evergreen half-hardy perennial. Ht 30cm (12in), spread 20cm (8in). White attractive flowers. Small thin grey/green leaves which are aromatic. This is an attractive thyme which is good for rockeries. Originates from Spain and Portugal, therefore does not like cold wet winters.

Upright Thymes
Up to 30cm (12in):
Caespititius, Archers Gold, Bertram Anderson, Peter Davis.

30cm (12in) and above:
Camphor, Lucy, Lemon, Orange Scented, Golden King, Porlock, Common (Garden), Golden, Silver Posie, Zygis.

Creeping Thymes
Cilicicus, Doerfleri, Bressingham Pink, Doone Valley, Wild Creeping, Woolly, Broad Leaved, White, Annie Hall, Coccineus, Gold Stream, Lemon Curd, Minimus, Pink Chintz, Rainbow Falls, Russetings, Snowdrift.

CULTIVATION

Propagation

To maintain the true plant, it is better to grow the majority of thymes from softwood cuttings. Only a very few, such as common and wild creeping thyme, can be propagated successfully from seed.

Seed
Sow the very fine seed in early spring using the cardboard technique on the surface of prepared trays (seed or plug), using the bark, peat, grit compost and a bottom heat of 15-21°C (60-70°F). Do not cover. Keep watering to the absolute minimum, as these seedlings are prone to damping off disease. When the young plants are large enough and after a period of hardening off, plant out in the garden in late spring/early summer, 23-38cm (9-15in) apart.

Cuttings
Thymes are easily increased by softwood cuttings from new growth in early spring or summer. The length of the cutting should be 5-8cm (2-3in). Use the bark, peat, grit mix of compost. Winter the young plants under protection and plant out the following spring.

Division
Creeping thymes put out aerial roots as they spread, which make them very easy to divide.

Silver Posie Thyme

Thymus vulgaris 'Silver Posie'

Layering
An ideal method for mature thymes that are getting a bit woody. Use either the strong branch method of layering in early autumn or mound layer in early spring.

Pests and Diseases

Being such an aromatic plant it does not normally suffer from pests but, if the soil or compost is too rich, thyme may be attacked by aphids. Treat with a liquid horticultural soap. All varieties will rot off if they become too wet in a cold winter.

Maintenance

Spring: Sow seeds. Trim old plants. Layer old plants.
Summer: Take cuttings of non-flowering shoots. Trim back after flowering.
Autumn: Protect tender thymes.
Winter: Protect containers and only water if absolutely necessary.

Garden Cultivation

Thymes need to be grown in poor soil, in a well-drained bed to give their best flavour. They are drought-loving plants and will need protection from cold winds, hard and wet winters. Sow seed when the soil has warmed and there is no threat of frost. Thin on average to 20cm (8in) apart.
It is essential to trim all thymes after flowering; this not only promotes new growth, but also stops the plant from becoming woody and sprawling in the wrong direction.
In very cold areas grow it in the garden as an annual or in containers and then winter with protection.

Harvest

As thyme is an evergreen it can be picked fresh all year round provided you are not too greedy. For preserving, pick before it is in flower. Either dry the leaves or put them in a vinegar or oil.

chopped thyme leaves over the whole lot. Pour in the wine and enough water just to cover the fish. Bring it to the boil on top of the stove and let it simmer uncovered for 6 minutes for fresh trout, 20 minutes for frozen.

Mix the remaining chopped lemon thyme and garlic chives with the butter. Divide this mixture into 4 equal portions. When the trout are cooked lift them out gently, place on plates with a slice of lemon and the herb butter on the top. Serve with new potatoes.

CONTAINER GROWING

Annie Hall Thyme
Thymus sepyllum 'Annie Hall'

All varieties suit being grown in containers. They like a free-draining poor soil (low in nutrients); if grown in a rich soil they will become soft and the flavour will be impaired. Use the peat, grit, bark mix of compost; water sparingly, keeping the container bordering on dry, and in winter definitely dry – only watering if absolutely necessary, when the leaves begin to lose too much colour. Feed only occasionally in the summer months. Put the container in a sunny spot, which will help the aromatic oils come to the leaf surface and impart a better flavour. Trim back after flowering to maintain shape and promote new growth.

WARNING

Although a medical dose drawn from the whole plant is safe, any amount of the volatile oil is toxic and should not be used internally except by prescription. Avoid altogether if you are pregnant.

CULINARY

Thyme is an aid to digestion and helps break down fatty foods. It is one of the main ingredients of bouquet garni; is good, too, in stocks, marinades, stews; and a sprig or 2 with half an onion makes a great herb stuffing for chicken.

Poached Trout with Lemon Thyme
Serves 4

4 trout, cleaned and gutted
Salt
6 peppercorns (whole)
4 fresh bay leaves
1 small onion cut into rings
1 lemon
1 sprig lemon tyme
1 tablespoon chopped lemon
  thyme leaves
100ml (4fl oz) white wine
2 tablespoons fresh snipped garlic
  chives
75g (3oz) butter

Place the trout in a large frying pan. Sprinkle with salt and add the peppercorns. Place 1 bay leaf by each trout. Put the onion rings on top of the trout, cut half the lemon into slices and arrange this over the trout, add the thyme sprig, and sprinkle some of the

MEDICINAL

Thyme has strong antiseptic properties. The tea makes a gargle or mouthwash, and is an excellent remedy for sore throats and infected gums. It is also good for hangovers.

The essential oil is antibacterial and anti-fungal and used in the manufacture of toothpaste, mouthwash, gargles and other toilet articles. It can also be use to kill mosquito larva. A few drops of the oil added to the bath water helps ease rheumatic pain, and it is often used in liniments and massage oils.

Tropaeolum majus

NASTURTIUM

Also known as Garden Nasturtium, Indian Cress and Large Cress. From the family Tropaeolaceae.

Nasturtiums are native of South America, especially Peru and Bolivia, but are now cultivated worldwide.

The generic name, *Tropaeolum*, is derived from the Latin 'tropaeum' meaning 'trophy' or 'sign of victory'. After a battle was finished, a tree-trunk was set up on the battlefield and hung with the captured helmets and shields. It was thought that the round leaves of the nasturtium looked like shields and the flowers like blood-stained helmets.

It was introduced into Spain from Peru in the 16th century and reached London shortly afterwards. When first introduced it was known as *Nasturcium indicum* or *Nasturcium peruvinum*, which is how it got its common name Indian cress. The custom of eating its petals, and using them for tea and salads, comes from the Orient.

Nasturtium Alaska
Trapaeolum majus 'Alaska'

SPECIES

Tropaeolum majus
Nasturtium
Half-hardy annual. Ht and spread 30cm (12in). Red/orange flowers from summer to early autumn. Round, mid-green leaves.

Tropaeolum majus 'Alaska'
Nasturtium Alaska (Variegated)
Half-hardy annual. Ht and spread 30cm (12in). Red, orange and yellow flowers from summer to early autumn. Round, variegated (cream and green) leaves. Very attractive.

Tropaeolum majus 'Empress of India'
Nasturtium 'Empress of India'
Half-hardy annual. Ht 20cm (8in), spread 30cm (12in). Dark red flowers from summer to early autumn. Round, mid-green leaves.

A few special species of interest:

Tropaeolum peregrinum
Canary Creeper
Tender perennial. Climber: ht 2m (6ft). Small, bright yellow flowers with 2 upper petals that are much larger and fringed from summer until first frost. Grey/green leaves with 5 lobes. In cool areas, best grown as an annual.

Tropaeolum polyphyllum
Hardy perennial. Ht 5-8in (2-3in), spread 30cm (12in) or more. Fairly small yellow flowers from summer to early autumn. Leaves grey green on trailing stems. A fast-spreading plant once established. Looks good on banks or hanging down walls.

Tropaeolum speciosum
Flame Creeper
Hardy perennial. Climber: ht 3m (10ft). Scarlet flowers in summer followed by bright blue fruits surrounded by deep red calyxes in autumn. Leaves green with 6 lobes. This very dramatic plant should be grown like honeysuckle with its roots in the shade and head in the sun.

CULTIVATION

Propagation
Seed

The seeds are large and easy to handle. To have plants flowering early in the summer, sow in early spring under protection directly into prepared pots or cell trays, and cover lightly with compost. Plugs are ideal, especially if you want to introduce the young plants into a hanging basket; otherwise use small pots to allow more flexibility before planting out. When the seedlings are large enough and there is no threat of frosts, plant out into a prepared site in the garden, or into containers.

Cuttings

Take cuttings of the perennial varieties in the spring from the new soft growth.

Pests and Diseases

Aphids and caterpillars of cabbage white butterfly and its relatives may cause a problem. If the infestation is light, the fly may be brushed off or washed away with soapy water.

Maintenance

Spring: Sow seed early under protection, or after frosts in garden.
Summer: Deadhead flowers to enhance flowering season.
Autumn: Dig up dead plants.
Winter: Plan next year.

Garden Cultivation

Nasturtiums prefer a well-drained, poor soil in full sun or partial shade. If the soil is too rich, leaf growth will be made at the expense of the flowers. They are frost-tender and will suffer if the temperature falls below 4°C (40°F).

As soon as the soil has begun to warm and the frosts are over, nasturtiums can be sown directly into the garden. Sow individually 20cm (8in) apart. For a border of these plants sow 15cm (6in) apart. Claude Monet's garden at Giverny in France has a border of nasturtiums sprawling over a path that looks very effective.

Harvest

Pick the flowers for fresh use only; they cannot be dried.
 Pick the seed pods just before they lose their green colour (for pickling in vinegar).
 Pick the leaves for fresh use as required. They can be dried, but personally I don't think it is worth it.

Nasturtium *Tropaeolum majus*

COMPANION PLANTING

This herb attracts blackfly away from vegetables like cabbage and broad beans. It also attracts the hover fly, which attacks aphids. Further, it repels whitefly, woolly aphids and ants. Altogether it is a good tonic to any garden.

CONTAINER GROWING

This herb is excellent for growing in pots, tubs, window boxes, hanging baskets. Use the bark, peat, grit compost. Do not feed, because all you will produce are leaves not flowers, but do keep well watered, especially in hot weather.

MEDICINAL

This herb is rarely used medicinally, although the fresh leaves contain vitamin C and iron as well as an antiseptic substance, which is at its highest before the plant flowers.

WARNING

Use the herb with caution. Do not eat more than 15g (½oz) at a time or 30g (1oz) per day.

CULINARY

I had a group from the local primary school around the farm to talk about herbs. Just as they were leaving I mentioned that these pretty red flowers were now being sold in supermarkets for eating in salads. When a little boy looked at me in amazement, I suggested he try one. He ate the whole flower without saying a word. One of his friends said, 'What does it taste like?' With a huge smile he asked if he could pick another flower for his friend, who ate it and screamed, 'Pepper pepper...' The seeds, flowers and leaves are all now eaten for their spicy taste. They are used in salads also as an attractive garnish. The pickled flower buds provide a good substitute for capers.

Nasturtium Cream Cheese Dip

100g (¼lb) cream cheese
2 teaspoons tender nasturtium
 leaves, chopped
3 nasturtium flowers

Blend the cream cheese with the chopped leaves. Put the mixture into a bowl and decorate with the flowers. Eat this mixture as soon as possible because it can become bitter if left standing.

Urtica

NETTLE

Also known as Common Nettle, Stinging Nettle, Devil's Leaf and Devil's Plaything. From the family Urticaceae.

Common Nettle *Urtica dioica* **in full flower**

This plant is found all over the world. It is widespread on wasteland especially on damp and nutrient-rich soil.

The generic name *Urtica* comes from the Latin 'uro' meaning 'I burn'. The Roman nettle *Urtica pilulifera* originally came to Britain with the invading Roman army. The soldiers used the plants to keep themselves warm. They flogged their legs and arms with nettles to keep their circulation going.

The use of nettles in the making of fabric goes back before history. Nettle cloth was found in a Danish grave of the later Bronze Age, wrapped around cremated bones. It was certainly made in Scotland as late as the 18th century. The Scottish poet, Thomas Campbell, wrote then of sleeping in nettle sheets in Scotland and dining off nettle tablecloths. Records show that it was still being used in the early 20th century in Tyrol.

In the middle ages it was believed that nettles marked the dwelling place of elves and were a protection against sorcery. They were also said to prevent milk from being affected by house trolls or witches.

Settlers in New England in the 17th century were surprised to find that this old friend and enemy had crossed the Atlantic with them. It was included in a list of plants that sprang up unaided.

Before World War II, vast quantities of nettles were imported to Britain from Germany. During the war there was a drive to collect as much of the home-grown nettle as possible. The dark green dye obtained from the plant was used as camouflage, and chlorophyll was extracted for use in medicines.

SPECIES

Urtica dioica
Stinging Nettle
Hardy perennial. Ht 1.5m (5ft), spread infinite on creeping root stock. The male and female flowers are on separate plants. The female flowers hang down in clusters, the male flower clusters stick out. The colour for both is a yellowish green.
The leaves are green toothed and have bristles. This is the variety that can be eaten when young.

Urtica pilulifera
Roman Nettle
Hardy perennial. Ht 1.5m (5ft), spread infinite on creeping root stock. This looks very similar to the common stinging nettle, but its sting is said to be more virulent.

Urtica urens
Small Nettle
Hardy annual. Ht and spread 30cm (12in). The male and female flowers are in the same cluster and are a greenish white in colour. The green leaves are deeply toothed and have bristles.

Urtica urentissima
Devil's Leaf
This is a native of Timor and the sting said to be so virulent that its effects can last for months and may even cause death.

CULTIVATION

Propagation
Seed
Nettles can be grown from seed sown in the spring. But I am sure any of your friends with a garden would be happy to give you a root.

Division
Divide established roots early in spring before they put on much leaf growth, and the sting is least strong.

Pests and Diseases
Rarely suffers from pests and disease, well not ones that one would wish to destroy!

Maintenance
Spring: Sow seeds, divide established plants.
Summer: Cut plants back if they are becoming invasive.
Autumn: Cut back the plants hard into the ground.
Winter: No need for protection, fully hardy.

Garden Cultivation
Stinging nettles are the scourge of the gardener and the farmer, the pest of children in summer, but are very useful in the garden, attracting butterflies and moths, and making an excellent caterpillar food. They will grow happily in any soil. It is worth having a natural corner in the garden where these and a few other wild flowers can be planted.

Harvest
Cut young leaves in early spring for use as a vegetable.

CULINARY

Nettles are an invaluable food, rich in vitamins and minerals.
  In spring the fresh leaves

Nettle soup

may be cooked and eaten like spinach, made into a delicious soup, or drunk as a tea.

Nettle Soup
Serves 4

When cooked, I am pleased to say, nettles lose their sting.

250g/½lb young nettle leaves
50g/2oz oil or butter
1 small onion, chopped
250g/½lb cooked potatoes, peeled and diced
900ml/1½ pints/3¾ cups of milk
1 teaspoon each (mix, fresh, chopped) sweet marjoram, sage, lemon thyme
1 dessertspoon fresh chopped lovage
2 tablespoons, cream and French parsley, chopped, optional

Pick only the fresh young nettle leaves, and wear gloves to remove from stalks and wash them. Heat the oil in a saucepan, add the chopped onions, slowly sweat them until clear. Then add the nettles and stew gently for about a further 10 minutes. Add the chopped potatoes, all the herbs and the milk and simmer for a further 10 minutes. Allow to cool then put all the ingredients into a liquidizer and blend. Return to a saucepan over gentle heat. Add a swirl of cream to each bowl and sprinkle some chopped French parsley over the top. Serve with French bread.

MEDICINAL

The nettle has many therapeutic applications but is principally of benefit in all kinds of internal haemorrhages, as a diuretic in jaundice and haemorrhoids, and as a laxative. It is also used in dermatological problems including eczema.
  Nettles make a valuable tonic after the long winter months when they provide one of the best sources of minerals. They are an excellent remedy for anaemia. Their vitamin C content makes sure that the iron they contain is properly absorbed.

WARNING

Do not eat old plants uncooked, they can produce kidney damage and symptoms of poisoning. The plants must be cooked thoroughly to be safe.

Handle all plants with care; they do sting.

Nettle rinse and hair conditioner

OTHER USES

Whole plants yield a greenish/yellow woollen dye.
  Nettles make a good spray against aphids, especially blackfly. Pick a bucket full of nettles, pour (soft/rain) water over them. Cover the container and allow to soak for a week. Strain the liquid, and put it into a spray. Spray on infected plants.
  Nettles have a long standing reputation for preventing hair loss and making the hair soft and shiny. They also have a reputation for eliminating dandruff.

Nettle Rinse and Conditioner
Use it as a final rinse after washing your hair or massage it into your scalp and comb through the hair every other day. Keep it in a small bottle in the refrigerator.

1 big handful size bunch of nettles
½litre/1 pint of water

Wear rubber gloves to cut the nettles. Wash thoroughly and put the bunch into an enamel saucepan with enough cold water to cover. Bring to the boil, cover and simmer for 15 minutes. Strain the liquid into a jug and allow to cool.

Valeriana officinalis

VALERIAN

Also known as All Heal, Set All, Common Valerian, Garden Heliotrope, Cut Finger, Fragrant Valerian, Cat's Valerian and St. George's Herb. From the family Valerianaceae.

Valerian is a native of Europe and West Asia and is now naturalized in North America. It is found in grasslands, ditches, damp meadows and close to streams.

The name may come from the Latin 'valere' to be healthy, an allusion to its powerful medicinal qualities. Or from an early herbalist, Valeris, who first used it medicinally.

Fresh valerian roots smell like ancient leather, but when dried they smell more like stale sweat. In spite of this, valerian is still used to add a musky tone to perfume. Cats and rats are attracted to the smell and The Pied Piper of Hamelin is said to have carried the root. A tincture of valerian was employed in the First and Second World Wars to treat shell-shock and nervous stress.

COMPANION PLANTING

If planted near other vegetables, it boosts their growth by stimulating phosphorus and earthworm activity.

OTHER USES

Infuse root and spray on the ground to attract earthworms. Add mineral-rich leaves to new compost. Use the root in rat traps.

MEDICINAL

The root is a calmative. Its sedative and anti-spasmodic effects are of benefit in the treatment of a wide range of nervous disorders and intestinal colic.

Decoct the root or, more effectively, crush 1 teaspoon (5ml) of dried root and soak in cold water for 12-24 hours. Drink as a sedative for mild insomnia, sudden emotional distress, headaches, intestinal cramps and nervous exhaustion.

SPECIES

Valeriana officinalis
Valerian
Hardy perennial. Ht 1-1.2m (3-4ft), spread 1m (3ft). Pale pink/white flowerheads in summer. Leaves deeply toothed and mid-green.

CULTIVATION

Propagation
Seed
Sow the fairly small seeds in early spring, either in seed or plug trays. Press the seeds into the soil but do not cover, as this will delay germination. When the seedlings are large enough to handle, transplant to the garden at a distance of 60cm (24in) apart.

Valerian *Valeriana officinalis*

Division
Divide the roots in spring or autumn. Replant after division in a prepared site.

Pests and Diseases
Valerian is mostly free from pests and disease.

Maintenance
Spring: Sow seed. Divide roots.
Summer: Cut back after flowering to prevent self-seeding.
Autumn: Divide establish plants if needed.
Winter: A very hardy plant, no need for protection.

Garden Cultivation
Valerian is one of the earliest flowering, tall, wetland plants. As long as its roots are kept cool. (which is why it prefers to be near water) it can be grown successfully in almost any garden soil in sun or deep shade, You can sow seeds direct in spring, leaving uncovered, but for a more guaranteed result start off in plug trays. Remember that cats love the scent when choosing the planting site

Harvest
Dig up complete root in late autumn of the second and third years. Wash and remove the pale fibrous roots, leaving the edible rhizome. To dry this rhizome, cut it into manageable slices (see drying).

WARNING

Valerian should not be taken in large doses for an extended period of time.

Centranthus ruber (Valeriana ruber)

RED VALERIAN

Also known as American Lilac, Bloody Butcher, Bouncing Bess and Bouncing Betsy. From the family Valerianaceae.

A native of central and southern Europe cultivated widely in temperate climates, this cheerful plant was a great ornament in Gerard's garden, but he described it in 1597 as 'not common in England'. However, by the early 18th century it had become well known.

SPECIES

Centranthus ruber (Valeriana ruber)
Red Valerian
Perennial. Ht 60-90cm (2-3ft), spread 45-60cm (18-24in). Showy red fragrant flowers in summer. They can also appear in all shades of white and pink. Fleshy, pale green, pointed leaves.

CULTIVATION

Propagation
Seed
Sow the small seeds in early autumn in seed or plug trays, using the bark, peat, grit mix of compost. Cover lightly with compost and leave outside over winter, covered with glass. As soon as you notice it germinating, remove the glass and place in a cold greenhouse. Prick the seedlings out when large enough to handle and pot up using the same mix of compost. Leave the pots outside for the summer, watering regularly until the autumn. No need to feed with liquid fertilizer. Plant out 60cm (2ft) apart.

Pests and Diseases
This plant does not suffer from pests or diseases.

Maintenance
Spring: Dig up self-sown seedlings and replant if you want them.
Summer: Dead head to prevent self-seeding.
Autumn: Sow seeds. Plant previous year's seedlings.
Winter: A very hardy plant.

Garden Cultivation
Red valerian has naturalized on banks, crumbly walls and rocks in coastal regions. It is very attractive to butterflies. As an ornamental, it thrives in poor, well-drained, low fertile soil, and especially on chalk or limestone. It likes a sunny position and self-seeds prolifically.

Harvest
Dig complete root up in the late autumn of the second and third years. Wash and remove the pale fibrous roots, leaving the edible rhizome. If you want to dry this rhizome, cut it into manageable slices (see drying). Pick young leaves as required.

CONTAINER GROWING

Make sure the container is large enough and use a soil-based compost. No need to feed, otherwise you will inhibit its flowers. Position the container in a sunny spot and water regularly.

CULINARY

Very young leaves are eaten in France and Italy. They are incredibly bitter.

Red Valerian
Centranthus ruber

MEDICINAL

A drug is obtained (by herbalists only) from the root, which looks like a huge radish and has a characteristic odour. It is believed to be helpful in cases of hysteria and nervous disorders because of its sedative and anti-spasmodic properties.

WARNING

Large doses or extended use may produce symptoms of poisoning. Do not take for more than a couple of days at a time.

Verbena officinalis

VERVAIN

*Also known as Holy Herb, Simpler's Joy,
Pigeon's Grass, Burvine, Wizard's Herb,
Herba Sacra, Holy Plant, European Vervain,
Enchanter's Plant and Herba the Cross.
From the family Verbenaceae.*

This herb is a native of Mediterranean regions. It has now become established elsewhere within temperate zones or, for that matter, wherever the Romans marched.

It is a herb of myth, magic and medicine. The Egyptians believed that it originated from the tears of Isis. The Greek priests wore amulets made of it, as did the Romans, who also used it to purify their altars after sacrifice. The Druids used it for purification and for making magic potions.

Superstition tells that when you pick vervain, you should bless the plant. This originates from a legend that it grew on the hill at Calgary, and was used to staunch the flow of Christ's blood at the Crucifixion.

In the Middle Ages it was an ingredient in a holy salve, a powerful protector against demons and disease: 'Vervain and Dill hinders witches from their will.'

Vervain *Verbena officinalis*

SPECIES

Verbena officinalis
Vervain
Hardy perennial. Ht 60-90cm (2-3ft), spread 30cm (12in) or more. Small pale lilac flowers in summer. Leaves green, hairy and often deeply divided into lobes with curved teeth. This plant is not to be muddled with Lemon Verbena, **Aloysia Triphylla**.

CULTIVATION

Propagation
Seed
Sow the small seeds in early spring in a prepared seed or plug tray. Cover with Perlite. No need for extra heat. When the seedlings are large enough, and after a period of hardening off, plant out in a prepared site, 30cm (12in) apart.

Division
An established plant can be divided either in the spring or autumn. It splits easily with lots of roots.

Pests and Diseases
If the soil is too rich or high in nitrates, it can be attacked by aphids.

Maintenance
Spring : Sow seeds. Divide established plants.
Summer : Cut back after flowering to stop it self-seeding everywhere.
Autumn : Split established plants.
Winter : No need for protection; fully hardy.

Garden Cultivation
Vervain can be sown direct into the garden in the spring in a well-drained soil and a sunny position. It is better to sow or plant in clumps because the flower is so small that otherwise it will not show to advantage. But beware its capacity to self-seed.

Harvest
Pick leaves as required. Cut whole plant when in bloom. Dry leaves or whole plant if required.

CONTAINER GROWING

Vervain does nothing for containers, and containers do nothing for vervain.

MEDICINAL

Vervain has been used traditionally to strengthen the nervous system, dispel depression and counter nervous exhaustion. It is also said to be effective in treating migraines and headaches of the nervous and bilious kind.

Chinese herbalists use a decoction to treat sup-pressed menstruation, and for liver problems and urinary tract infections.

CULINARY

In certain parts of France, a tea is made from the leaves. Use with caution.

WARNING

Avoid during pregnancy.

Viola tricolor

HEARTSEASE

Also known as Wild Pansy, Field Pansy, Love Lies Bleeding, Love in Idleness, Herb Trinity, Jack Behind the Garden Gate, Kiss Me Behind the Garden Gate, Kiss Me Love, Kiss Me Love at the Garden Gate, Kiss Me Quick, Monkey's Face, Three Faces Under a Hood, Two Faces in a Hood and Trinity Violet. From the family Violaceae.

CONTAINER GROWING

Heartsease look very jolly in any kind of container. Pick off the dead flowers as they appear to keep the plant flowering for longer.

Heartsease is a wild flower in Europe and North America, growing on wasteland and in fields and hedgerows.

In the Middle Ages, due to the influence of Christianity and because of its tricolour flowers – white, yellow and purple – Heartsease was called Trinitaria or Trinitatis Herba, the herb of the Blessed Trinity.

In the traditional language of flowers, the purple form meant memories, the white loving thoughts, and the yellow, souvenirs.

SPECIES

Viola arvensis
Field Pansy
Hardy perennial. Ht 5-10cm (2-4in). The flowers are predominantly white or creamy, and appear in early summer. The green leaves are oval with shallow, blunt teeth.

Viola tricolor Heartsease

Viola lutea
Mountain Pansy
Hardy perennial. Ht 8-20cm (3-8in). Single coloured flowers in summer vary from yellow to blue and violet. The leaves are green and oval near the base of the stem, narrower further up.

Viola tricolor
Heartsease
Hardy perennial, often grown as an annual. Ht 15-30cm (6-12in). Flowers from spring to autumn. Green and deeply lobed leaves.

CULTIVATION

Propagation
Seed
Sow seeds under protection in the autumn, either into prepared seed, plug trays or pots. Do not cover the seeds. No bottom heat required. Winter the seedlings in a cold frame or cold greenhouse. In the spring harden off and plant out at a distance of 15cm (6in).

Maintenance
Spring: Sow seed.
Summer: Dead head flowers to maintain flowering throughout the season.
Autumn: Sow seed for early spring flowers.
Winter: No need to protect.

Garden Cultivation
Heartsease will grow in any soil, in partial shade or sun. Sow the seeds from spring to early autumn where they are to flower. Press into the soil but do not cover.

Harvest
Pick the flowers fully open – from spring right through until late autumn. Use fresh or for drying.

The plant has the most fascinating seed capsules, each capsule splitting into 3. The best time to collect seeds is midday when the maximum number of capsules will have opened.

CULINARY

Add flowers to salads and to decorate sweet dishes.

MEDICINAL

An infusion of the flowers has long been prescribed for a broken heart. Less romantically, it is also a cure for bed-wetting.

An ointment made from it is good for eczema and acne and also for curing milk rust and cradle cap.

Herbalists use it to treat gout, rheumatoid arthritis and respiratory disorders. An infusion of heartsease leaves added to bath water has proved beneficial to suffers of rheumatic disease.

Warning: In large doses, it may cause vomiting.

OTHER USES

Cleansing the skin and shampooing thinning hair.

Viola

VIOLET

From the family Violaceae.

There are records of sweet violets growing during the first century AD in Persia, Syria and Turkey. It is a native not only of these areas but also of North Africa and Europe. Violets have been introduced elsewhere and are now cultivated in several countries for their perfume.

This charming herb has been much loved for over 2,000 years and there are many stories associated with it. In a Greek legend, Zeus fell in love with a beautiful maiden called Io. He turned her into a cow to protect her from his jealous wife Juno. The earth grew violets for Io's food, and the flower was named after her.

The violet was also the flower of Aphrodite, the goddess of love, and of her son, Priapus, the god of gardens. The ultimate mark of the reverence in which the Greeks held sweet violet is that they made it the symbol of Athens.

For centuries perfumes have been made from the flowers of sweet violet mixed with the violet scented roots of orris, and the last half of the 19th century saw intense interest in it – acres were cultivated to grow it as a market garden plant. Its main use was as a cut flower. No lady of quality would venture out without wearing a bunch of violets. It was also customary in gardens of large country houses to move the best clump of violets to a cold frame in late autumn to provide flowers for the winter.

Common Dog Violet *Viola riviniana*

SPECIES

Viola odorata
Sweet Violet
Also known as Garden Violet Hardy perennial. Ht 7cm (3in), spread 15cm (6in) or more. Sweet-smelling white or purple flowers from late winter to early spring. The leaves are heart-shaped and form a rosette at the base, from which the long-stalked flowers arise.
Viola odorata is one of the very few scented violets. It has been hybridized to produce Palma violets, with a single or double flower, in a range of rich colours. Recently there has been a revival in interest in this plant and it is being offered again by specialist nurseries.

Viola reichenbachiana
Wood Violet
Hardy perennial. Ht 2-20cm (1-8in), spread 15cm (6in) or more. Pale lilac/blue flowers in early spring. Leaves are green and heart-shaped. The difference between this plant and the common dog violet is the flowering time; there is also a slight difference in flower colour but is difficult to discern.

Viola riviniana
Common Dog Violet
Also known as Blue Mice, Hedging Violet, Horse Violet and Pig Violet. Hardy perennial. Ht 2-20cm (1-8in), spread 15cm (6in) or more. Pale blue/lilac flowers in early summer. Leaves are green and heart-shaped. This violet does not grow runners.

CULTIVATION

Propagation
Seed
The small seed should be sown in early autumn in prepared seed or plug trays. Use a soil-based compost; I have found violets prefer this. Water in and cover with a layer of compost, and finally cover with a sheet of glass or polythene. Put the trays either in a corner of the garden or in a cold frame (because the seeds germinate better if they have a period of stratification, though it will still be erratic). In the spring when the seedlings are large enough to handle, prick out into pots. If grown in cells allow a period of hardening off. Plant out as soon as temperatures have risen at a distance of 30cm (12in).

Cuttings

These can be taken from the parent plant, with a small amount of root attached, in early spring and rooted in cell trays, using the bark, peat mix of compost. Harden off and plant out into a prepared site in the garden in late spring when they are fully rooted. Water in well.

When using runners to propagate this plant, remove them in late spring and replant in a prepared site in the garden, 30cm (12in) apart. Plant them firmly in the ground, making sure that the base of the crowns are well embedded in the soil; water in well.

Runners can be grown on in pots in early autumn. Remove a well-rooted runner and plant in a pot of a suitable size. Use the bark, peat, grit mix. (See Container Growing for further information.) Over-winter in a cool greenhouse, watering from time to time to prevent red spider mite. Bring into the house in the spring to enjoy the flowers. After flowering, plant out in the garden into a prepared site.

Division

Divide well-established plants as soon as flowering is over in early summer. It is a good idea to plant 3 crowns together for a better show and as an insurance policy against damage when splitting a crown. Replant in the garden in exactly the same way as for runners.

Pests and Diseases

The major pest for container-grown violets in mild weather is red spider mite. A good way to keep this at bay is to spray the leaves with water. If it is persistent, use a liquid horti-cultural soap (again, as per manufacturer's instructions).

In propagating violets, the disease you will most probably come across is black root rot, which is caused by insufficient

drainage in the compost.

Young plants can also be affected by damping off root rot, which is caused usually by too much water and insufficient drainage.

Maintenance

Spring: Take cuttings from established plants. Remove runners, pot or replant in the garden.
Summer: Divide well-established plants, and replant.
Autumn: Sow seed. Pot up root runners for wintering under cover.
Winter: Feed the garden with well-rotted manure.

Garden Cultvation

Violets thrive best in a moderately heavy, rich soil in a semi-shaded spot. If you have a light and/or gravelly soil, it is a good idea to add some texture – a mulch of well-rotted manure – the previous autumn. In spring dig the manure in.

Plant out in the garden as soon as the frosts have finished, allowing 30cm (12in) space between plants. When they become estab-lished, they quickly create a carpet of lovely sweet-smelling flowers. There is no need to protect any of the above-mentioned violets, they are fully hardy.

Harvest

Pick the leaves in early spring for fresh use or for drying.

Gather the flowers just when they are opening, for drying or crystallizing.

Dig up the roots in autumn to dry for medicinal use.

Container Growing

Violets make good container plants. Use the bark, peat, grit mix of compost. Give them a liquid feed of fertilizer (following the manufacturer's instructions) after flowering. During the summer months, place the container in partial shade. In winter they do not like heat, and if it is too warm they will become weak and fail to flower. So, it is most important that they are in a cool place with temperatures no higher than 7°C (45°F). There must also be good air circulation, and watering should be maintained on a regular basis.

Culinary

The flowers of sweet violet are well known in crystallized form for decorating cakes, puddings, ice-cream and home-made sweets. They are also lovely in salads, and make an interesting oil – use an almond oil as base.

The flowers of common dog violet can also be added to salads and used to decorate puddings. Their flavour is very mild in comparison to sweet violet, but they are just as attractive.

Sweet Violet *Viola odorata*

Medicinal

Only sweet violet has been used medicinally. Various parts are still used, most commonly, the rootstock. It is an excellent, soothing expectorant and is used to treat a range of respiratory disorders, such as bronchitis, coughs, whooping cough and head colds. It also has a cooling nature and is used to treat hangovers.

Made into a poultice, the leaves soothe sore, cracked nipples. Also they have a reputation for treating tumours, both benign and cancerous. Strong doses of the rhizome are emetic and purgative.

The flowers have a reputation for being slightly sedative and so helpful in cases of anxiety and insomnia.

Other Uses

The flowers of sweet violets are used in potpourris, floral waters and perfumes.

TROPICAL HERBS

The following herbs grow in tropical areas of Australia, Africa, South America, the West Indies, Florida in North America, and the tropical jungles of China and India.

Outside these climates they can be grown as greenhouse plants and houseplants.

Ginger root

SPECIES

All the heights are those attained in their natural environments. In cooler conditions they will be smaller.

Elettaria cardamomum
Cardamom
Also known as Illaichi, Elaichi, Kravan, Buah pelaga and Kapulaga. From the family *Zingiberaceae*. Perennial. Ht to 3m (10ft). White flowers with a lip that is blue with white stripes and a yellow margin. The pod bearing stalks sprawl along the ground. Next to saffron, this is the world's most expensive spice. As cardamoms thrive in shady mountain forests with an average rainfall of 3.5m (12ft) and an average temperature of 23°C (73°F), they are not easy to cultivate or harvest, and this is the reason they are so expensive.

Curcuma longa
Turmeric
Also known as Haldi, Wong geung fun, Kamin and Fa Nwin. From the family *Zingiberaceae*. Perennial. Ht 1m (3ft). Flowers in bracts tipped with white, with deep yellow lip. Large tubers, which are deep yellow. Long green oblong slender leaves.

Cymbopogon citratus
Lemon Grass
Also known as Sera, Takrai and Zabalin. From the family *Gramineae*. Perennial. Tall grass with sharp-edged leaves that multiply into clumps. The whitish, slightly bulbous base is used to give a lemony flavour to curries.

Zingiber officinale *Ginger*
Also known as Adrak, Gin, Khing, Jeung, and Shoga. From the family *Zingiberaceae*. Perennial. Ht to 3m (9ft). The flowers are yellowish-green, the lip is deep purple with yellow spots and strips. It grows like a reed and has spiky green leaves and mauve and yellow flowers. The rhizomes are the part used.

Lemon grass

CULTIVATION

Propagation
Division
This is best done in spring, all the mentioned plants should be re-potted each year, the old compost shaken off the roots and the plants divided. They divide easily. Re-pot using compost made up of 2 parts peat, 1 part sterile loam, mixed with a little grit or sharp sand. A word of warning, all are damaged by remaining too long in wet soil. Watering them is an art.

Garden Cultivation
Only in tropical climates can these plants be grown outside; elsewhere, treat as container plants.

CONTAINER GROWING

When grown in containers these plants are unlikely to reach their natural heights, or flower or produce the rhizomes for culinary use. However, they are still worth growing for their attractive foliage, and Ginger and Cardamom are also aromatic.

Turmeric

The compost needed is 2 parts peat, 1 part loam, with some sharp sand or grit mixed in, and they all need atmospheric moisture. In winter, keep them on the dry side; in spring, shake out and re-pot them (see Division).

Lemon Grass is easily grown in containers. I have even found that if you buy some fresh in the supermarket and put it in a jar of water, after a week or two some will produce roots that can then be potted up.

Pests and Diseases

In their natural habitat these plants are not prone to pests or disease. Grown as container plants, they are prone to greenfly and red spider mite. Use a liquid horticultural soap spray as soon as you notice these pests, taking care to follow the manufacturer's instructions.

Harvest

Cardamom & Turmeric
It is difficult to harvest the seeds, roots or leaves from these plants unless you live in the tropics.

Ginger
To preserve fresh ginger, scrape the skin from the rhizome, divide into sections and pack into a clean dry bottle. Pour some dry sherry or wine vinegar over these to cover the ginger completely, cover tightly and store in the refrigerator.

Lemon Grass
Cut just 1 stem with a sharp knife close to the root, and use about 10-12cm (4-5 in) of the stalk from the base; discard the leaves.

CULINARY

Cardamom
The whole seed-pod is used as a spice more often than the individual seeds. There are different coloured pods: white cardamoms are merely bleached versions of the widely available green (and have less flavour), the black variety looks like a conglomeration of black beetles. These have an earthier, deeper flavour than the green. Use only the small black seeds for ground cardamom (the pods themselves are not edible), and for best flavour grind (using mortar and pestle) only as needed.

Cardamom can be acquired from Indian grocers, and is a crucial ingredient in biryanis, pilaus, dals, curries and pickles.

Ginger
The pungently flavoured rhizomes are essential to most Asian dishes; fresh ginger root only should be used, the flavour of powdered ginger is quite different. Scrape off the skin of the rhizome with a sharp knife and either chop finely or grate, depending on the recipe. The roots are used in many Eastern dishes, and the stems are crystallized for use in confectionery.

Lemon Grass
This can now be bought fresh or dried from supermarkets. If buying it in Asian shops, it is often called 'Sereh'. Fresh leaves are peeled, sliced or chopped for culinary purposes; dried they are used tied in a bunch and removed after cooking, like bay leaves. The powdered form is very strong, so use sparingly. Possible substitutes are Lemon Balm, Lemon Verbena, and the rind of a lemon.

Black cardamoms

Green cardamoms

Turmeric
Turmeric is made from the powdered rhizome, which is an orange-yellow colour and widely used as a food colouring in curries, garam masala, lentil, rice and grain dishes.

Ginger tea

MEDICINAL

Cardamom
This plant stimulates the digestion, and is used as a calmative for flatulent dyspepsia. Herbalists often combine cardamom with bitter remedies and use it to prevent the griping effects of laxatives.

Turmeric
This is used in China to treat various cramping pains.

Ginger
This is good for indigestion, flatulence, nausea and poor circulation. Chewing a piece of any ginger (crystallized stem ginger is just as good) is an effective deterrent for travel sickness. Ginger tea is good for colds and flu.

OTHER USES

Turmeric
The herb was used to dye the robes of Buddhist monks.

PROPAGATION

One of the great joys of gardening is propagating your own plants. Success is dependent on adequate preparation and the care and attention you give during the critical first few weeks. The principles remain the same, but techniques are constantly changing. There is always something new to discover.

The three main methods of propagating new plants are by Seed, Cuttings and Layering.

This chapter provides general, step-by-step instructions for each of these methods. As there are always exceptions to a rule, please refer to the propagation section under each individual herb.

SEED

Sowing Outside

Most annual herbs grow happily propagated year after year from seed sown directly into the garden. There are two herbs worth mentioning where that is not the case – sweet marjoram, because the seed is so small it is better started in a pot; and basil because, in damp northern climates like that in Britain, the young seedlings will rot off.

In an average season the seed should be sown in mid- to late spring after the soil has been prepared and warmed. Use the arrival of weed seedlings in the garden as a sign that the temperature is rising. Herbs will survive in a range of different soils. Most culinary herbs originate from the Mediterranean so their preference is for a sandy free-draining soil. If your soil is sticky clay do not give up, give the seeds a better start by adding a fine layer of horticultural sand along the drill when preparing the seed bed.

Preparation of Seed Bed

Before starting, check your soil type (see page 220-221), making sure that the soil has sufficient food to maintain a seed bed. Dig the bed over, mark out a straight line with a piece of string secured tightly over each row, draw a shallow drill, 6-13mm (¼/½in) deep, using the side of a fork or hoe, and sow the seeds thinly, 2 or 3 per 25mm (1in). Do not overcrowd the bed, otherwise the seedlings will grow leggy and weak and be prone to disease.

Protected Sowing

Starting off the seeds in a greenhouse or on a windowsill gives you more control over the warmth and moisture they need, and enables you to begin propagating earlier in the season.

Nothing is more uplifting than going into the greenhouse on a cold and gloomy late-winter morning and seeing all the seedlings emerging. It makes one enthusiastic for spring.

Preparation of Seed

Most seeds need air, light, temperature and moisture to germinate. Some have a long dormancy, and some have hard outer coats and need a little help to get going. Here are two techniques.

Scarification
If left to nature, seeds that have a hard outer coat would take a long time to germinate. To speed up the process, rub the seed between 2 sheets of fine sandpaper. This weakens the coat of the seed so that moisture essential for germination can penetrate.

Stratification (vernalization)
Some seeds need a period of cold (from 1 to 6 months) to germinate. Mix the seed with damp sand and place in a plastic bag in the refrigerator or freezer. After 4 weeks sow on the surface of the compost and cover with Perlite. My family always enjoys this time of year. They go to the freezer to get the ice cream and find herb seed instead.

Preparation of Seed Container

One of the chief causes of diseased compost is a dirty propagation container. To minimize the spread of disease, remove any 'tidemarks' of compost, soil or chemicals around the insides of the pots and seed trays. Wash and scrub them thoroughly with washing up liquid, rinse with water and give a final rinse with diluted Jeyes fluid. Leave for 24 hours before re-use. Old compost also provides ideal conditions for damping off fungi and sciarid flies. To avoid cross-infection always remove spent compost from the greenhouse or potting shed.

Compost

It is always best to use a sterile seed compost. Ordinary garden soil contains many weed seeds that could easily be confused with the germinating herb seed. The compost used for most seed sowing is 50per cent propagating bark and 50per cent peat-based seed compost and unless stated otherwise within the specific herb section, this is the mix to use. However, for herbs that

Misting Unit

prefer a freer draining compost, or for those that require stratification outside, I advise using a 25 per cent peat-based seed compost: 50 per cent propagating bark and 25 per cent horticultural grit mix. And if you are sowing seeds that have a long germination period, use a soil-based seed compost.

Sowing in Seed Trays

Preparation: fill a clean seed tray with compost up to 1cm (½in) below the rim and firm down with a flat piece of wood. Do not to press too hard as this will over-compress the compost and restrict drainage, encouraging damping off disease and attack by sciarid fly.

The gap below the rim is essential, as it prevents the surface sown seeds and compost being washed over the edge when watering, and it allows room for growth when you are growing under card or glass.

Water the prepared tray using a fine rose on the watering can. Do not over-water. The compost should be damp, not soaking. After an initial watering, water as little as possible, but never let the surface dry out. Once the seed is sown lack of moisture can prevent germination and kill the seedlings, but too much water excludes oxygen and encourages damping-off fungi and root rot. Be sure to use a fine rose on the watering can so as not to disturb the seed.

Sowing Methods

There are 3 main methods, the choice dependent on the size of the seed. They are, in order of seed size, fine to large:

1 Scatter on the surface of the compost, and cover with a fine layer of Perlite.

2 Press into the surface of the compost, either with your hand or a flat piece of wood the size of the tray,

and cover with Perlite.
3 Press down to 1 seed's depth and cover with compost.

The Cardboard Trick

When seeds are too small to handle, you can control distribution by using a thin piece of card (cereal cartons are good), cut to 10cm x 5cm (4in x 2in), and folded down the middle. Place a small amount of seed into the folded card and gently tap it over the prepared seed tray. This technique is especially useful when sowing into plug trays (see below).

Sowing in Plug (Module) Trays (Multi-cell Trays)

These plug trays are a great invention. The seed can germinate in its own space, get established into a strong seedling, and make a good root ball. When potting on, the young plant remains undisturbed and will continue growing, rather than coming to a halt because it has to regenerate roots to replace those damaged in pricking out from the seed tray. This is very good for plants like coriander, which hate being transplanted and tend to bolt if you move them. Another advantage is that as you are sowing into individual cells, the problem of overcrowding is cut to a minimum, and damping-off disease and sciarid fly are easier to control. Also, because seedlings in plugs are easier to maintain, planting out or potting on is not so critical.

Plug trays come in different sizes; for example, you can get trays with very small holes of 15mm (½in) x

15mm up to trays with holes of 36.5mm (1¼in) x 36.5mm. To enable a reasonable time lapse between germination and potting on, I recommend the larger.

When preparing these trays for seed sowing, make sure you have enough space, otherwise compost seems to land up everywhere. Prepare the compost and fill the tray right to the top, scraping off surplus compost with a piece of wood level with the top of the holes. It is better not to firm the compost down. Watering in (see above) settles the compost enough to allow space for the seed and the top dressing of Perlite. For the gardener-in-a-hurry there are available in good garden centres ready-prepared propagation trays, which are plug trays already filled with compost. All you have to do is water and add the seed.

The principles of sowing in plug trays are the same as for trays. Having sown your seed, DO label the trays clearly with the name of the plant, and also the date. The date is useful as one can check their late or speedy germination. It is also good for record keeping, if you want to sow them again next year, and helps with organizing the potting on.

Seed Germination

Seeds need warmth and moisture to germinate.

The main seed sowing times are autumn and spring. This section provides general information with the table below providing a quick look guide to germination. Any detailed advice specific to a particular herb is provided in the A-Z Herb section.

Quick Germination Guide

Hot 27-32°C (80-90°F)
Rosemary

Warm 15-21°C (60-70°F)
Most plants, including those from the Mediterranean, and Chives and Parsley.

Cool 4-10°C (40-50°F)
Lavenders. (Old lavender seed will need a period of stratification).

Stratification
Arnica (old seed), Sweet Woodruff, Yellow Iris, Poppy, Soapwort, Sweet Cicely, Hops (old seed), Sweet Violet.

Scarification
All leguminous species, i.e., broom, trefoils, clovers and vetches.

Need Light (i.e., do not cover)
Chamomile, Foxglove, Thyme, Winter Savory, Poppy and Sweet Marjoram.

In a cold greenhouse, a heated propagator may be needed in early spring for herbs that germinate at warm to hot temperatures. In the house you can use a shelf near a radiator (never on the radiator), or an airing cupboard. Darkness does not hinder the germination of most herbs (see table above for exceptions), but if you put your containers in an airing cupboard YOU MUST CHECK THEM EVERY DAY. As soon as there is any sign of life, place the trays in a warm light place, but not in direct sunlight.

Hardening Off

When large enough to handle, prick out seed tray seedlings and pot up individually. Allow them to root fully.

Test plug tray seedlings by giving one or two a gentle tug. They should come away from the cells cleanly, with the root ball. If they do not, leave for another few days.

When the seedlings are ready, harden them off gradually by leaving the young plants outside during the day. Once weaned into a natural climate, either plant them directly into a prepared site in the garden, or into a larger container for the summer.

CUTTINGS

Taking cuttings is sometimes the only way to propagate (e.g. non-flowering herbs, such as **Chamomile Treneague**, and variegated forms, such as Tri-color Sage).

It is not as difficult as some people suggest, and even now I marvel at how a mere twig can produce roots and start the whole life cycle going again.

There are 4 types of cutting used in herb growing:

1 Softwood cuttings taken in spring

2 Semi-hardwood cuttings taken in summer

3 Hardwood cuttings taken in autumn

4 Root cuttings, which can be taken in spring and autumn.

For successful softwood cuttings it is worth investing in a heated propagator, which can be placed either in a greenhouse or on a shady windowsill. For successful semi-ripe, hardwood and root cuttings, a shaded cold frame can be used.

Softwood Cuttings

Softwood cuttings are taken from the new lush green growth of most perennial herbs between spring and mid-summer, a few examples being Balm of Gilead, Bergamot, the Chamomiles, the Mints, Prostanthera, the Rosemarys, the Scented Geraniums, the Thymes, Curly Wood Sage and Wormwood. Check under the individual herb entries in the A-Z section for more specific information.

1 The best way to get a plant to produce successful rooting material is to prune it vigorously in winter (which will encourage rapid growth when the temperature rises in the spring), and to take cuttings as soon as there is sufficient growth.

2 Fill a pot, seed tray, or plug tray with cutting compost – 50 per cent bark, 50 per cent peat. It is important to use a well-draining medium rather than standard potting mixes as, without root systems, cuttings are prone to wet rot.

Firm the compost to within 2cm (¾in) of the rim and water as for sowing.

If space is limited or pots are unavailable, you can pack the base of several cuttings in damp sphagnum moss (rolled up firmly in a polythene strip and held in place by a rubber band or string) until the roots form.

3 Collect the cuttings in small batches in the morning. Choose sturdy shoots with plenty of leaves. Best results come from non-flowering shoots with the base leaves removed. Cut the shoot with a knife, not scissors. This is because scissors tend to pinch or seal the end of the cutting thus hindering rooting.

4 Place the cutting at once in the shade in a polythene bag or a bucket of water. Softwood cuttings are extremely susceptible to water loss; even a small loss will hinder root development. If the cuttings cannot be dealt with quickly, keep them in the cool (e.g. in a salad box from a refrigerator) to prevent excessive water loss.

5 To prepare the cutting material, cut the base of the stem 5mm (¼in) below a leaf joint, to leave a cutting of roughly 10cm (4in) long.

6 If the cutting material has to be under 10cm (4in), take the cutting with a heel. Remove the lower leaves and trim the tail which is left from the heel.

7 Trim the stem cleanly before a node, the point at which a leaf stalk joins the stem. Remove the leaves from the bottom third of the cutting, leaving at least 2 or 3 leaves on top. The reason for leaving leaves on cuttings is that the plant feeds through them as it sets root. Do not tear off the base leaves as this can cause disease; use a knife and gently cut them off.

8 Make a hole with a dibber in the compost and insert the cutting up to its leaves. Make sure that the leaves do not touch or go below the surface of the compost; they will rot away and may cause a fungus condition which can spread up the stem and to other cuttings. Do not overcrowd the container or include more than one species, because quite often they take different times to root. (For instance, keep box and thymes separate.)

Hormone rooting-powders that some gardeners use, contain synthetic plant hormones and fungicide and are not for the organic grower; following my detailed instructions you should find them unnecessary. However, they may help with difficult cuttings. The cutting should be dipped into the rooting-powder just before inserting into the compost.

9 Label and date the cuttings clearly, and only water the compost from above if necessary (the initial watering after preparing the container should be sufficient). Keep out of direct sunlight in hot weather. In fact, if it is very sunny, heavy shade is best for the first week.

Either place in a heated or unheated propagator, or cover the pot or container with a plastic bag supported on a thin wire hoop (to prevent the plastic touching the leaves), or with an upturned plastic bottle with the bottom cut off. If you are using a plastic bag, make sure you turn it inside out every few days to stop excess moisture from condensation dropping onto the cuttings.

10 Spray the cuttings every day with water for the first week. Do this in the morning, never at night. Do not test for rooting too early by tugging the cutting up, as you may disturb it at a crucial time. A better way to check for new roots is to look underneath the container. Average rooting time is 2-4 weeks.

The cutting medium is low in nutrients, so give a regular foliar feed when the cutting starts to root.

11 Harden off the cuttings gradually when they are rooted. Bring them out in stages to normal sunny, airy conditions.

12 Pot them on using a prepared potting compost once they are weaned. Label and water well after transplanting.

13 About 4-5 weeks after transplanting, when you can see that the plant is growing away, pinch out the top centre of the young cutting. This will encourage the plant to bush out, making it stronger as well as fuller.

14 Allow to grow on until a good-size root ball can be seen in the pot – check occasionally by gently removing the plant from the pot – then plant out.

Semi-hardwood Cuttings or Greenwood Cuttings

Usually taken from shrubby herbs such as Rosemary and Myrtle towards the end of the growing season (from mid-summer to mid-autumn). Use the same method (steps 2-8) as for softwood cuttings, with the following exceptions:

2 The compost should be freer-draining than for softwood cuttings, as semi-hardwood cuttings will be left for longer (see 10

below). Make the mix equal parts peat, grit and bark.

9 Follow step 9 for softwood cuttings, but place the pot, seed tray or plug tray in a cold greenhouse, cold frame, cool conservatory, or on a cold windowsill in a garage, not in a propagator, unless it has a misting unit.

10 Average rooting time for semi-hardwood cuttings is 4-6 weeks. Follow step 10 except for the watering schedule. Instead, if the autumn is exceptionally hot and the compost or cuttings seem to be drying out, spray once a week. Again, do this in the morning, and be careful not to over-water.

11 Begin the hardening off process in the spring after the frosts. Give a foliar feed as soon as there is sufficient new growth.

Hardwood Cuttings
Taken mid- to late autumn in exactly the same way as softwood cuttings steps 2-8, but with a freer draining compost of equal parts peat, grit and bark. Keep watering to the absolute minimum. Winter in a cold frame, greenhouse or conservatory. Average rooting time can take as long as 12 months.

Root Cuttings
This method of cutting is suitable for plants with creeping roots, such as Bergamot, Comfrey, Horseradish, Lemon Balm, Mint, Soapwort and Sweet Woodruff.

1 Dig up some healthy roots in spring or autumn.

2 Fill a pot, seed tray or plug tray with cutting compost – 50 per cent bark, 50 per cent peat, firmed to within 3cm (1in) of the rim. Water well and leave to stand while preparing your cutting material.

3 Cut 4-8cm (1.5-3in) lengths of root that carry a growing bud. It is easy to see the growing buds on the roots of mint.

This method is equally applicable for all the varieties mentioned above as suitable for root propagation, with the exception of Comfrey and Horseradish, where one simply slices the root into sections, 4-8cm (1½-3in) long, using a sharp knife to give a clean cut through the root. Do not worry, each will produce a plant!
 These cuttings lend themselves to being grown in plug trays.

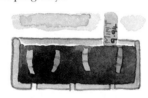

4 Make holes in the compost with a dibber. If using pots or seed trays these should be 3-6cm (1-2½in) apart. Plant the cutting vertically.

5 Cover the container with a small amount of compost, followed by a layer of Perlite level with the top of the container.

6 Label and date. This is most important because you cannot see what is in the container until the plant begins to grow and it is all too easy to forget what you have planted.

7 Average rooting time 2-3 weeks. Do not water until roots or top growth appears. Then apply liquid feed.

8 Slowly harden off the cuttings when rooted.

9 Pot on in a potting compost once they are weaned. Label and water well after transplanting. You can miss this stage out if you have grown the root cuttings in plug trays.

10 About 2-3 weeks after transplanting, when you can see that the plant is growing away, pinch out the top centre of the young cutting. This will encourage the plant to bush out, making it stronger as well as fuller.

11 Allow to grow on until a good-size root ball can be seen in the pot. Plant out in the garden when the last frosts are over.

LAYERING

If cuttings are difficult to root you can try layering, a process that encourages sections of plant to root while still attached to the parent. Bay, Rosemary, Sage are good examples of plants that suit this method.

1 Prune some low branches off the parent plant during the winter season to induce vigorous growth and cultivate the soil around the plant during winter and early spring by adding peat and grit to it.

2 Trim the leaves and side shoots of a young vigorous stem for 10-60cm (4-24in) below its growing tip.

3 Bring the stem down to ground level and mark its position on the soil. Dig a trench at that point, making one vertical side 10-15cm (4-6in) deep, and the other sloping towards the plant.

4 Roughen the stem at the point where it will touch the ground.

5 Peg it down into the trench against the straight side, then bend the stem at right angles behind the growing tip, so that it protrudes vertically. Then return the soil to the trench to bury the stem. Firm in well.

6 Water well using a watering can and keep the soil moist, especially in dry periods.

7 Sever the layering stem from its parent plant in autumn if well rooted, and 3-4 weeks later nip out the growing tip from the rooted layer to make plant bush out.

8 Check carefully that the roots have become well established before lifting the layered stem. If necessary, leave for a further year.

9 Replant either in the open ground or in a pot using the bark, grit, peat mix of compost. Label and leave to establish.

Mound Layering
A method similar to layering that not only creates new growth but also improves the appearance of old plants. This is particularly suitable for sages and thymes, which can be woody in the centre.

1 In the spring, pile soil mixed with peat and sand over the bare woody centre until only young shoots show.

2 By late summer, roots will have formed on many of these shoots. They can be taken and planted in new locations as cuttings or by root division.

3 The old plant can then be dug up and disposed of.

PLANNING YOUR HERB GARDEN

Herbs are so versatile that they should appeal to anyone, be they a cook, a lover of salads, or just wanting to enjoy the rich scents of plants and watch the butterflies collecting nectar from the flowers. And there are herbs for every space; they will grow in a window-box or in a pot on a sunny window ledge; and some can be grown indoors as houseplants as well as outside in gardens, small or large.

The best way to grow herbs is the organic way. Quite apart from the fact that if you use natural products, the soil remains clean and free from chemical pollutants, in organic herb gardens there is no chance of contaminating a plant before you eat it. Organic methods also encourage bees and other insects to the garden, which in turn helps maintain the healthy natural balance of predator and pest.

Back row, left to right: **Mint 'Eau de Cologne'**, *Mentha* x *piperita citrata*, **English Mace**, *Achillea ageratum*, **Scented Pelargonium 'Mabel Gray'**, **Orange-scented Thyme** *Thymus* x *citriodorus* 'Fragrantissimus'; front row, left to right: **Creeping Savory**, *Satureja spicigera*, **Chives**, *Allium schoenoprasum*, **Lady's Mantle 'Conjuncta'**, *Alchemilla conjuncta*, **Curry Plant Dartington**, *Helichrysum italicum* 'Dartington'.

CONDITIONS

As herbs are basically wild plants tamed to fit a garden, it makes sense to grow them in conditions comparable with their original environment. This can be a bit difficult, for they come from all over the world. As a general rule, the majority of culinary herbs come from the Mediterranean and prefer a dry sunny place. But herbs really are adaptable and they do quite well outside their native habitat, provided you are aware of what they prefer.

CHOOSING THE SITE

Before planning your site, it is worth surveying your garden in detail. Start by making a simple plan and mark on it North and South. Show the main areas of shade – a high fence, a neighbouring house and any high trees, noting whether they are deciduous or evergreen. Finally, note any variations in soil type – wet, dry, heavy etc. Soil is one of the most important factors and will determine the types of herb you can grow.

SOILS

There are basically four types of soil.

Chalk or Limestone soil

This soil tends to be light and very well drained. But its inability to hold moisture can cause problems in a hot summer. It is alkaline in character and is sometimes difficult to lower its pH level, so some plants become stunted and leaves go yellowish in colour, because the minerals, especially iron, become locked away. If you find the plants are not thriving, I recommend a raised bed where you can introduce the soil you require.

Herbs that like these conditions are the Box family, *Buxus sempervirens*; Catnip, *Nepeta cataria*; Chicory, *Cichorium intybus*; Cowslip, *Primula veris*; Hyssop, *Hyssopus officinalis*; Juniper, *Juniperus communis*; Lily of the Valley, *Convallaria majalis*; Lungwort, *Pulmonaria officinalis*; the Marjoram family, *Origanum*; the Pink family, *Dianthus*; the Rosemary family, *Rosmarinus*; and Salad Burnet, *Sanguisorba minor*.

Clay soil

This soil is made up of tiny particles that stick together when wet, making the soil heavy. When dry, they set rock hard. Because it retains water and restricts air flow around roots, it is often known as 'a cold soil'. It may have a natural reserve of plant food, but even so it is better to work compost into the first few centimetres as this will help get the plant established and improve drainage. If you continue to do this every year, it will gradually become easier to cultivate. My nursery is on heavy clay and when planting out herbs that prefer a free-draining soil, like lavenders, I add some sharp sand to the site when preparing it.

Herbs that like these conditions are the Bergamots, *Monarda*; the Comfreys, *Symphytum*; the Mints, *Mentha*; and Wormwood, *Artemisia absinthium*.

Loam soil

This soil is a mixture of clay and sand. It contains a good quantity of humus and is rich in nutrients. There are various types of loam: heavy, which contains more clay than loam and becomes wet in winter and spring; light loam, which has more sand than clay and is the very best for herbs; and medium loam, which is an equal balance of clay and sand.

Herbs that like these conditions are the Basil family, *Ocimum*; Bay, *Laurus nobilis*; Betony, *Bettonica officinalis*; Caraway, *Carum carvi*; Catmint, *Nepeta racemosa*; Chervil, *Anthriscus cerefolium*; Chives, *Allium schoenoprasum*; Coriander, *Coriandrum sativum*; Dill, *Anethum graveolens*; Lady's mantle, *Alchemilla mollis*; Lovage, *Levisticum officinale*; Parsley, *Petroselinum crispum*; Rue, *Ruta graveolens*; and the Sage family, *Salvia*.

Sandy soil

This is a very well drained soil, so much so that plant foods are quickly washed away. A plus point is that it warms up quickly in the spring. For fleshy herbs you will need to build the soil up with compost to help retain moisture and stop the leaching of nutrients. But the Mediterranean herbs will thrive on this soil.

Herbs that like sandy soils are Arnica, *Arnica montana*; Borage, *Borago officinalis*; the Chamomile family, *Chamaemelum*; Evening Primrose, *Oenothera missouriensis*; the Fennel family, *Foeniculum*; the Lavender family, *Lavandula*; the Marjoram family, *Origanum*; Tarragon, *Artemisia dracunculus*; the Thyme family, *Thymus*; and Winter Savory, *Satureja montana*.

USE

Next, decide what you want from your herb garden. Do you want a retreat away from the house? Or a herb garden where the scents drift

Preparing the site

indoors? Or do you want a culinary herb garden close at hand to the kitchen door?

STYLE

Then think about what shape or style you want the garden to take. Formal herb gardens are based on patterns and geometric shapes. Informal gardens are a free-for-all, with species and colours, all mixed together. Informal gardens may look un-planned, but the best that I know have been well planned. This is worth doing even if it is just to check the height and spread of the plant. I know only too well how misleading it can be buying plants from a garden centre – they are all neat, uniform and fairly small. After hearing me give a talk, one woman asked if she should remove the lovage she had just planted in the front of her rockery.

The plants have to be accessible, either for using fresh or to harvest, so paths are a good idea. They also introduce patterns to the design and can help to define its shape. For convenience, herbs should be no more than 75cm (30in) from a path, and ideally the beds no more than 1–1.2m (3–4 ft) wide. If

they are more than 1.2m (4ft) wide, insert stepping stones to improve access.

PREPARING THE SITE

Having chosen your sites, and having decided what you are going to do, you really have got to condition your soil.

ELIMINATE WEEDS

If you do this at the start, you will not have the hassle of trying to remove couch grass, bindweed or ground elder. (By the way, ground elder was a herb...! It was said to have been used by the Romans to feed their livestock. So the next time you are grappling with this weed, you can thank your ancestors.) Weeds do not emerge until the spring, and continue well into the season. If you wish to get rid of them successfully, it is best to cover the plot with black plastic the previous autumn. Dig a shallow trench around the area and bury the sides of the plastic in it to keep it secure. Starved of light, the weeds will eventually give up. This will take until the following spring, so if you do not like the sight of the black plastic,

position a few paving stones (taking care not to make any holes because the weeds will find them and come through), cover the plastic with bark, and place terracotta pots planted up with herbs on top of the stones.

If you do not have the patience, use a weedkiller instead. There are NO organic weedkillers but you can use Ammonium Sulphamate, which is sold as white crystals in hardware shops. Read the instructions carefully, dissolve it in water and spray the weeds. It is effective against most perennial plants, so do not get it on any you wish to keep. You will notice the difference in about 1-2 weeks but it is not safe to plant for 2-3 months. However, it is safer than modern weedkillers, both for the environment and for us, because as the plants die down the ammonium sulphamate breaks down to ammonium sulphate, which is a fertilizer used by gardeners. So, despite the fact that this is not totally organic it is beneficial in the end. But even this process does take time. There is no short cut to eradicating weeds.

CHECK THE SOIL

Find out whether your soil is acid or alkaline. Herbs generally do best in a soil between 6.5 and 7.5pH (fairly neutral). To measure the pH of your soil you will need a reliable soil-testing kit, available from any good garden centre.

Acid soil (0-6.5 pH)

The soils in this category, on a sliding scale from acidic to nearly neutral, are sphagnum moss peat, sandy soil, coarse loam soil, sedge peat and heavy clay.

Plants that will tolerate these conditions are Arnica, *Arnica montana*; Dandelion, *Taraxacum officinale*; Comfrey, *Symphytum officinale*; Foxglove, *Digitalis purpurea*; Honeysuckle, *Lonicera periclymenum*; Pennyroyal, *Mentha pulegium*; Sorrel, *Rumex rugosus*; Buckler Leaf Sorrel, *Rumex scutatus*; and Sweet Cicely, *Myrrhis odorata*.

Alkaline soil (7.7-14 pH)

The soils in this category tend to contain chalk or lime and are of a fine loam. Herbs that like these conditions are already listed under Chalk soil types.

A reading that approaches either end of the pH scale indicates that the soil will tend to lock up the nutrients necessary for good growth. If it is very acid, you will need to add lime in the late autumn to raise the pH. Fork the top 10cm (4in) of the soil and dress with lime. Clay soils need a good dressing, but be careful not to over-lime sandy soils. It should not be necessary to do this more than once every 3 years unless your soil is very acid. Never add lime at the same time as manure, garden compost or fertilizer, as a chemical reaction can occur which will ruin the effects of both. As a general rule, either add lime 1 month before, or 3 months after manuring, and 1 month after adding fertilizers. If the soil is alkaline, dress it every autumn with well-rotted manure to a depth of 5-10cm (2-4in), and dig over in the spring.

Check the ground has good drainage especially in winter and early spring.

A clay soil restricts air circulation around the roots, which not only restricts the growth but also means that the soil stays cold which will delay spring growth and germination. To help lighten the soil dig in some leafmould, or if it is a small area, some peat, prior to planting.

Check that the ground can retain some moisture during the growing season. If the soil is sandy, it may dry out in summer, so again, dig in some well-rotted manure or garden composts.

Dig the site over. If the soil is heavy the best time to dig is in early winter, so that the frosts can break up the clods of earth. If the soil is light, early spring is best, because this will allow the soil some protection during the winter against leaching of the nutrient. No matter what type of soil you have, it is beneficial to lay a good layer of well-rotted manure or garden compost over the surface in winter and dig it in the following spring. Both soil types benefit from a good digging in the spring.

LAYING PATHS

No matter whether you are planning a formal or informal herb garden, you will need paths. There are a number of choices

Grass

A grass path is quite easy to achieve and looks very attractive. Another plus point is the minimal cost. Make it at least as wide as your lawn mower, otherwise you will be cutting it on your hands and knees with shears. It is a good idea to edge the path either with wood, metal or, more attractively, with bricks, laid on their side end to end. Disadvantages to this kind of path are that it needs mowing and will not take heavy traffic.

Gravel

Gravel paths really do lend

themselves to being planted with herbs. Be sure to prepare them well otherwise a water trap will form, and the plants would be better off being aquatic.

First remove the top soil carefully. Then dig out to a depth of 30 cm (12in), putting the soil to one side. It is advisable to put a wooden edge between the soil of the garden or lawn and the new path. This will stop the soil falling into the path, and keep the edge neat. Fill the newly formed ditch with 14cm (6in) hard core. Mix the top soil with peat, bark and grit in the ratio 3:1:1:1, and put this mix on top of the hard core to a depth of 8cm (3in). Finish with 8cm (3in) gravel or pea shingle. There are many colours of gravel available, most large garden centres stock a good range, or if you have a quarry near by it is worth chatting them up. Roll the path before planting. Herbs that will grow happily in gravel are creeping or upright thymes, winter savory, and pennyroyal. The disadvantage of gravel is that you will find that weeds will recur, so be diligent.

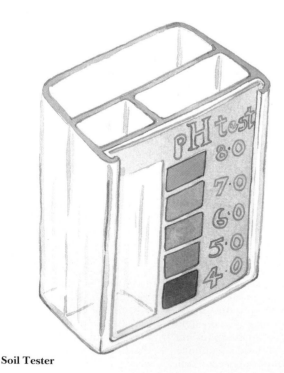

Soil Tester

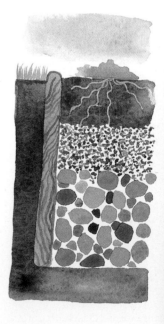

Bricks

These paths have become very fashionable. There is now a subtle range of colours available, and varied and original patterns can be made. For standard-size bricks, dig out to a depth of 10 cm (4in). As with the gravel path, include a wooden edge. Spread 5cm (2in) of sharp sand over the base; level and dampen. Lay the brick on top of the sand in the desired pattern, leaving 2-5mm (⅛-¼in) gap between the bricks. Settle them in, using a mallet or a hired plate vibrator. If you wish to plant the path with herbs, it is as well at this juncture to leave out one or two bricks, filling the gaps later with compost and planting them when the path has settled. When the whole path has been laid, spread the joints with a mix 4:1 of fine dry sand and cement, and brush it in. The mixture will gradually absorb the moisture from the atmosphere, so setting the brick.

Paving stones

These can take up a lot of space and are expensive.

Garden centres now stock a large range in various colours and shapes. Also try builders' merchants, you may get a better deal, especially if you require large quantities. Paving stones are ideal for the classic chequer-board designs and the more formal designs. If you want them to lie flush with the ground, dig out the soil to the depth of the slab plus 5cm (2in). Put 5cm (2in) of sharp sand onto the prepared area, level off and lay the slabs on top, tapping them down, and making sure they are level. If the chosen area is already level and you want the slabs to be proud, then lay them directly in position with only a small layer of sand underneath.

PLANTING THE GARDEN

The planning and hard preparation work are done, so now for the fun bit. If this is a new garden, it is worth laying the plants out on top of the prepared ground first, walking round and getting an overall view. Make any changes to the design now, rather than later. Having satisfied yourself, dig adequate holes to accommodate the plants, adding extra sharp sand or grit if necessary. Firm in, and water well. Now you can enjoy watching your garden grow.

ALTERNATIVE PLANTING

Raised beds

If your soil is difficult, or if you wish to create a feature, raised beds are a good solution. Also, plants in raised beds are easier to keep under control and will not wander so much around the rest of the garden. Finally, they are more accessible for harvesting and stand at an ideal height for those in wheelchairs.

I consider the ideal height for a raised bed to be between 30cm (12in) and 75cm (30in). If you raise it over 1m (3ft) high you will need some form of foundation for the retaining walls, to prevent them keeling over with the weight of the soil. Retaining walls can be made out of old railway sleepers (not as cheap as they used to be), logs cut in half, old bricks, or even red bricks – leave the odd one out and plant a creeping thyme in its place.

For a 30cm (1ft) raised bed, the following ratios are ideal. First put a layer of hard core (rubble) on top of the existing soil to a depth of 8cm (3in), followed by an 8cm (3in) layer of gravel, and finally 4cm (6in) of top soil mix – 1 part peat, 1 part bark, 1 part grit or sharp sand, with 3 parts top soil.

Lawns

Many herbs are excellent ground cover but, as I have already mentioned under Chamomile, beware of doing too large an area to begin with. It can be an error costly in both time and money. Small areas filled with creeping herbs give great delight to the unsuspecting visitor who when walking over the lawn, discovers a pleasant aroma exuding from their feet!

I know it is repetitious, but those of you who are gardeners will understand why I say again, 'Prepare your site well.' This is the key to many good gardens. Given a typical soil, prepare the site for the lawn by digging the area out to a depth of 30cm (12in) and prepare in exactly the same way as the raised bed: 8cm (3in) hard core, 8cm (3in) gravel, 14cm (6in) top soil mix – this time, 1 part peat, 2 parts sharp sand, 3 parts top soil. Apart from chamomile, other plants that can be used are Corsican mint, *Mentha requinni*, planted 10cm (4in) apart, or creeping thymes – see page 200-202 for varieties – and plant them 23cm (9in) apart.

HERB GARDENS

The gardens I have designed can be followed religiously, or adapted to meet your personal tastes, needs and of course space. It is with this last requirement in mind that I have specifically not put the exact size into the design and concentrated on the shape, layout and the relationship between plants. I hope these plans give you freedom of thought and some inspiration.

FIRST HERB GARDEN

When planning your first herb garden, choose plants that you will use and enjoy. I have designed this garden in exactly the same way as the one at my herb farm. Much as I would love to have a rambling herb garden, I need something practical and easy to manage, because the nursery plants need all my attention.

It is also important that the herbs are easy to get at, so that I can use it every day. By dividing the garden up into four sections and putting paving stones round the outside and through the middle, it is easy to maintain and provides good accessibility.

For this garden, I have chosen a cross-section of herbs with a bias towards culinary use, because the more you use and handle the plants, the more you will understand their habits. There is much contradictory advice on which herb to plant with which but many of these are old wives tales.

There are only a few warnings I will give: Do not plant dill and fennel together because they intermarry and become fendill, losing their unique flavours in the process. Equally, do not plant dill or coriander near wormwood as it will impair their flavour. Also, different mints near each other cross-pollinate and over the years will lose their individual identity. Finally, if you plan to collect the seed from lavenders, keep the species well apart.

Aside from that, if you like it, plant it.

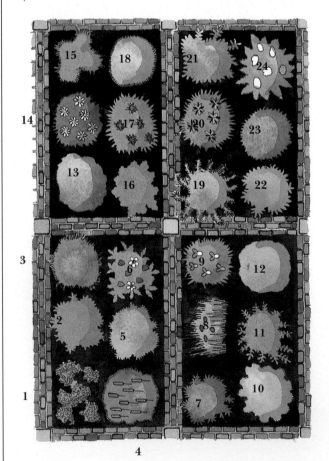

4

1 **Parsley** *Petroselinum crispum*
2 **Mint Pineapple** *Mentha suaveolens* 'Variegata'
3 **Fennel** *Foeniculum vulgare*
4 **Lavander Munstead** *Lavandula angustifolia* 'Munstead'
5 **Oregano Greek** *Origanum vulgare* ssp. hirtum
6 **Strawberry Wild** *Fragaria vesca*
7 **Sage Purple** *Salvia officinalis* Purpurascens Group
8 **Chives** *Allium schoenoprasum*
9 **Heartsease** *Viola tricolor*
10 **Marjoram Golden Curly** *Origanum vulgare* 'Aureum Crispum'
11 **Salad Burnet** *Sanguisorba minor*
12 **Thyme Lemon** *Thymus* x *citriodorus*
13 **Thyme Garden** *Thymus vulgaris*
14 **Chamomile Roman** *Chamaemelum nobile*
15 **Hyssop Rock** *Hyssopus officinalis* ssp. *aristatus*
16 **Sorrel Buckler Leaf** *Rumex scutatus*
17 **Bergamot** *Monarda didyma*
18 **Curry, Dartington** *Helichrysum italicum* 'Dartington'
19 **Rosemary** *Rosmarinus officinalis*
20 **Borage** *Borago officinalis*
21 **Lemon Balm Variegated** *Melissa officinalis* 'Aurea'
22 **Mint Apple** *Mentha suaveolens*
23 **Winter Savory** *Satureja montana*
24 **Chervil** *Anthriscus cerefolium*

HERB BATH GARDEN

This garden may seem a bit eccentric to the conventially minded but when my back is aching after working in the nursery, and I feel that unmentionable age, and totally exhausted, there is nothing nicer than lying in a herb bath and reading a good book.

The herbs I use most are thyme, to relieve an aching back, lavender, to give me energy, and eau-de-cologne to knock me out. Simply tie up a bunch of your favourite herbs with string, attach them to the hot water tap and let the water run. The scent of the plants will invade both water and room. Alternatively, put some dried herbs in a muslin bag and drop it into the bath.

Remember when planting this garden to make sure that the plants are accessible. Hops will need to climb up a fence or over a log. Again, quite apart from the fact that the herbs from this garden are for use in the bath they make a very aromatic garden in their own right. Position a seat next to the lavender and rosemary so that when you get that spare 5 minutes, you can sit in quiet repose and revel in the scent.

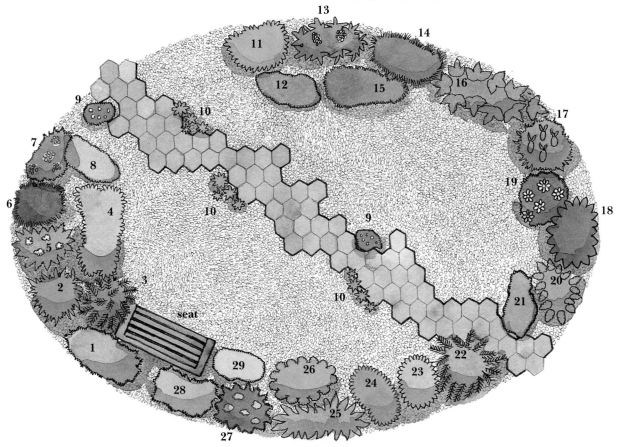

1 **Lavender Seal** *Lavandula* x *intermedia* 'Seal'
2 **Lemon Verbena** *Aloysia triphylla*
3 **Rosemary Benenden Blue** *Rosmarinus officinalis* 'Benenden Blue'
4 **Sage Gold** *Salvia officinalis* 'Icterina'
5 **Valerian** *Valeriana officinalis*
6 **Fennel Bronze** *Foeniculum vulgare* 'Purpureum'
7 **Tansy** *Tanacetum vulgare*
8 **Thyme Golden Lemon** *Thymus* x *citriodorus* 'Golden Lemon'
9 **Chamomile Double Flowered** *Chamaemelum nobile* 'Flore Pleno'
10 **Houseleek** *Sempervivum tectorum*
11 **Black Peppermint** *Mentha* x *piperita*
12 **Thyme Orange Scented** *Thymus* x *citriodorus* 'Fragrantissimus'
13 **Meadowsweet** *Filipendula ulmeria*

14 **Fennel Green** *Foeniculum vulgare*
15 **Pennyroyal Creeping** *Mentha pulegium*
16 **Hops** *Humulus lupulus*
17 **Lavender French** *Lavandula stoechas*
18 **Bay** *Laurus nobilis*
19 **Chamomile Roman** *Chamaemelum nobile*
20 **Lemon Balm** *Melissa officinalis*
21 **Thyme Porlock** *Thymus polytrichus* 'Porlock'
22 **Rosemary Prostrate** *Rosmarinus officinalis* Prostrate Group
23 **Marjoram Golden** *Origanum vulgare* 'Aureum'
24 **Mint Eau de Cologne** *Mentha* x *piperita citrata*
25 **Comfrey** *Symphytum officinale*
26 **Lady's Mantle** *Alchemilla mollis*
27 **Yarrow** *Achillea millefolium*
28 **Lavender Grappenhall** *Lavandula* x *intermedia* 'Grappenhall'
29 **Thyme Silver Posie** *Thymus vulgaris* 'Silver Posie'

AROMATHERAPY HERB GARDEN

One of the things I enjoy about growing herbs is the scent. Aroma is very evocative, and aromatherapy is growing in importance today. This garden has been designed not to create one's own oils, which is a complex process, but to have those aromas around that help our everyday lives, and to make an attractive garden, as the plants all have useful qualities apart from their aroma. The sweet marjoram, basil, thyme, fennel and rosemary are excellent culinary herbs. The chamomile and lemon balm make good herbal teas to help one relax.

I have placed paving stones in the garden to make access to the plants easier. However, when this garden becomes established, the stones will barely show.

I include a list of the herbs in this garden with the properties of the essential oil.

Herb	*Properties of the Essential Oil*
1 **Basil Sweet** *Ocimum basilicum*	Concentration
2 **Bergamot Bee Balm** *Monarda didyma*	Uplifting
3 **Chamomile Roman** *Chamaemelum nobile*	Relaxing
4 **Fennel** *Foeniculum vulgare*	Antitoxic
5 **Scented Geranium Graveolens**	
Pelargonium 'Graveolens'	Relaxing
6 **Hyssop** *Hyssopus officinalis*	Sedative
7 **Juniper** *Juniperus communis*	Stimulant
8 **Lemon Balm** *Melissa officinalis*	Anti-depressnat
9 **Lavender** *Lavandula angustifolia*	Soothing
10 **Rosemary** *Rosmarinus officinalis*	Invigorating
11 **Sweet Marjoram** *Origanum majorana*	Calming
12 **Thyme** *Thymus vulgaris*	Stimulant

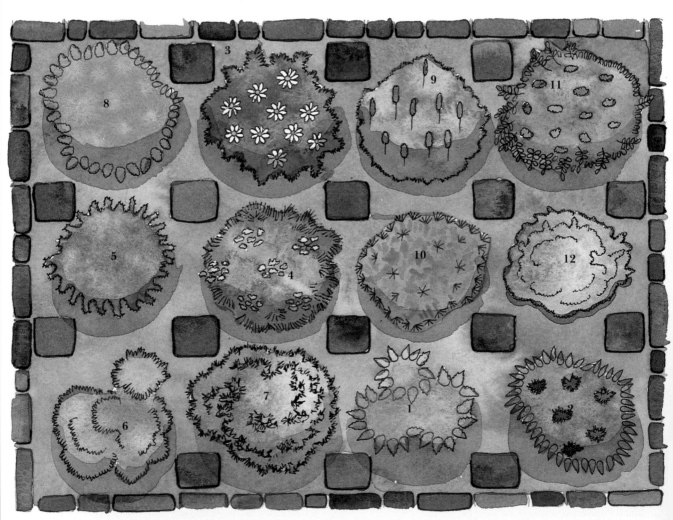

WHITE HERB GARDEN

This garden gave me great pleasure to create. For me, it is a herb garden with a different perspective.

It has a row of steps going from the road to the front door of the house. Either side of the steps is a dwarf white lavender hedge. In spring before the lavender, and just before the lily of the valley, are in flower, the sweet woodruff gives a carpet of small white flowers. This is the start of the white garden, which then flowers throughout the year through to autumn. It is a most attractive garden with a mixture of scents, foliage and flowers.

This planting combination can easily be adapted to suit a border. Even though it is not a conventional herb garden, all the herbs can be used in their traditional way. The garlic chives with baked potatoes, the horehound for coughs, the chamomile to make a soothing tea, and the lavender to make lavender bags or to use in the bath.

The great thing about a garden like this is that it requires very little work to maintain. The hedge is the only part that needs attention – trim in the spring and after flowering in order to maintain its shape.

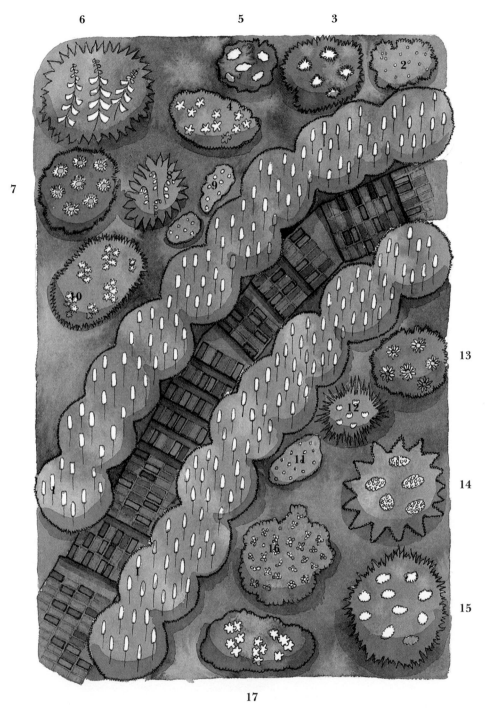

1	**Lavender White (dwarf)**	*Lavandula angustifolia* 'Nana Alba'
2	**Sweet Woodruff**	*Galium odoratum*
3	**Bergamot Snow Maiden**	*Monarda punctata* 'Schneewittchen'
4	**Jacob's Ladder (white)**	*Polemonium caeruleum* var. lacteum
5	**Yarrow**	*Achillea millefolium*
6	**Foxgloves (white)**	*Digitalis purpurea* F. *albiflora* (POISONOUS)
7	**Chamomile Roman**	*Chamaemelum nobile*
8	**Lily of the Valley**	*Convallaria majalis* (POISONOUS)
9	**Thyme White**	*Thymus serpyllum* var. *albus*
10	**Hyssop White**	*Hyssopus officinalis* F. *albus*
11	**Thyme Snowdrift**	*Thymus serpyllum* 'Snowdrift'
12	**Chives Garlic**	*Allium tuberosum*
13	**Pyrethrum**	*Tanacetum cinerariifolium*
14	**Sweet Cicely**	*Myrrhis odorata*
15	**Valerian**	*Valeriana officinalis*
16	**Horehound**	*Marrubium vulgare*
17	**Prostanthera**	*Prostanthera cuneata*

SALAD HERB GARDEN

Herbs in salads make the difference between boring and interesting; they add flavour, texture and colour (especially the flowers). There are two tall herbs in the middle, chicory and red orach (blue and red), which are planted opposite each other. Also, I have positioned the only tall plant – borage – on the outside ring, opposite the chicory so that the blue flowers

together will make a vivid splash. Again, to make access easy, there is an inner ring of stepping stones.

The herbs chosen are my choice and can easily be changed if you want to include a particular favourite. Remember to look at the heights; for instance, do not plant angelica in the outside circle because it will hide anything in the inner circle. Equally, in the inner

circle make sure you do not plant a low growing plant next to a tall spreading herb because you will never find it.

This whole design can be incorporated in a small garden or on the edge of a vegetable garden to give colour throughout the growing season. As the majority of these herbs are annuals or die back into the ground, the autumn is an

ideal time to give the garden a good feed by adding well rotted manure. This will encourage lots of leaves from the perennial herbs in the following season, and give a good kick start to the annuals when they are planted out in the following spring.

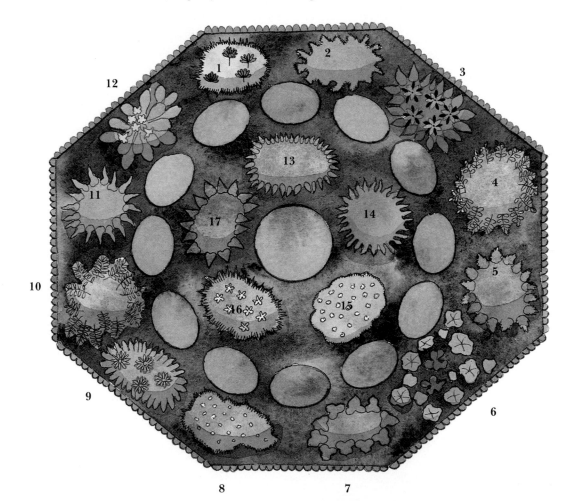

1	**Chives** *Allium schoenoprasum*	10	**Tarragon French** *Artemisia dracunculus*
2	**Caraway** *Carum carvi*	11	**Salad Rocket** *Eruca vesicaria* ssp. *sativa*
3	**Borage** *Borago officinalis*	12	**Cowslip** *Primula veris*
4	**Salad Burnet** *Sanguisorba minor*	13	**Mint Spear** *Mentha spicata*
5	**Parsley French** *Petroselinum crispum* French	14	**Chicory** *Cichorium intybus*
6	**Nasturtium** *Tropaeolum majus*	15	**Thyme Lemon** *Thymus* x *citriodorus*
7	**Sorrel, Buckler Leaf** *Rumex scutatus*	16	**Chives, Garlic** *Allium tuberosum*
8	**Hyssop** *Hyssopus officinalis*	17	**Red Orach** *Atriplex hortensis* var. *rubra*
9	**Marigold Pot** *Calendula officinalis*		

MEDICINAL HERB GARDEN

I would like this garden, not just for its medicinal use, but for the tranquillity it would bring. The choice of herbs is not only for internal use but for the whole being. I can imagine sitting on the seat watching the dragonflies playing over the pond.

Some of the herbs included are certainly not for self-administration, for instance blue flag iris, but this is a beautiful plant and would look most attractive with the meadowsweet and the valerian. Chamomile, peppermint, dill and lemon balm are easy to self-administer with care as they all make beneficial teas. One should not take large doses just because they are natural, as some are very powerful. I strongly advise anyone interested in planting this garden to get a good herbal medicine book, see a fully trained herbalist, and always consult your doctor about a particular remedy.

1	**Blue Flag Iris** *Iris versicolor*
2	**Meadowsweet** *Filipendula ulmaria*
3	**Valerian** *Valeriana officinalis*
4	**Horseradish** *Armoracia rusticana*
5	**Sage** *Salvia officinalis*
6	**Lady's Mantle** *Alchemilla mollis*
7	**Rosemary** *Rosmarinus officinalis*
8	**Dill** *Anethum graveolens*
9	**Chamomile** *Chamaemelum nobile*
10	**Horehound** *Marrubium vulgare*
11	**Comfrey** *Symphytum officinale*

12	**Feverfew** *Tanacetum parthenium*
13	**Heartsease** *Viola tricolor*
14	**Lemon Balm** *Melissa officinalis*
15	**Garlic** *Allium sativum*
16	**Black Peppermint** *Mentha* x *piperita*
17	**Fennel** *Foeniculum vulgare*
18	**Pot Marigold** *Calendula officinalis*
19	**Lavender Seal** *Lavandula* x *intermedia* 'Seal'
20	**Thyme Garden** *Thymus vulgaris*
21	**Houseleek** *Sempervivum tectorum*

COOK'S HERB GARDEN

The best site for a culinary herb bed is a sunny area accessible to the kitchen. The importance of this is never clearer than when it is raining. There is no way that you will go out and cut fresh herbs if they are a long way away and difficult to reach.

Another important factor is that the sunnier the growing position, the better the flavour of the herbs. This is because the sun brings the oils to the surface of the leaf of herbs such as sage, coriander, rosemary, basil, oregano and thyme.

The cook's herb garden could be grown in the ground or in containers. If in the ground, make sure that the site is very well drained. Position a paving stone near each herb so that it can be easily reached for cutting, weeding and feeding and also to help contain the would-be rampant ones, such as the mints.

Alternatively, the whole design could be adapted to be grown in containers. I have chosen only a few of the many varieties of culinary herb. If your favourite is missing, either add it to the design or substitute it for one of my choice.

1	**Mint Ginger** *Mentha* x *gracilis*	
2	**Chervil** *Anthriscus cerefolium*	
3	**Coriander** *Coriandrum sativum*	
4	**Parsley French** *Petroselinum crispum* French	
5	**Chives** *Allium schoenoprasum*	
6	**Rosemary Corsican** *Rosmarinus officinalis angustissimus* 'Corsican Blue'	
7	**Thyme Garden** *Thymus vulgaris*	
8	**Angelica** *Angelica archangelica*	
9	**Fennel** *Foeniculum vulgare*	
10	**Winter Savory** *Satureja montana*	
11	**Basil Greek** *Ocimum basilicum* var. *minimum* 'Greek Bush'	
12	**Sorrel Buckler Leaf** *Rumex scutatus*	

13	**Bay** *Laurus nobilis*
14	**Sweet Cicely** *Myrrhis odorata*
15	**Garlic** *Allium sativum*
16	**Oregano Greek** *Origanum vulgare* ssp. *hirtum*
17	**Tarragon French** *Artemisia dracunculus*
18	**Lovage** *Levisticum officinale*
19	**Chives, Garlic** *Allium tuberosum*
20	**Lemon Balm** *Melissa officinalis*
21	**Mint Moroccan** *Mentha spicata* 'Moroccan'
22	**Dill** *Anethum graveolens*
23	**Parsley** *Petroselinum crispum*
24	**Thyme Lemon** *Thymus* x *citriodorus*
25	**Marjoram Sweet** *Origanum majorana*

NATURAL DYE GARDEN

There has been a marked increase of interest in plants as a dye source, which is not surprising since they offer a subtle range of rich colours.

This garden includes a representative selection of those dyes that can be easily grown. It is designed with separate beds because you will need a fairly large quantity of each herb to produce the dye, and the beds make it easy to harvest the leaves, flowers and roots. You should allow sufficient space between the beds for access and maintenance.

The eight herbs I have selected give a broad range of colours. As the marigolds and the parsley are shortlived you may like to replace them with woad or even nettles. For more choice of plants, see the section on Natural Dye.

When choosing which plant goes where, the only important consideration is that the elder will grow into a fairly large tree, so plant it where it will not get in the way of the other plants or spoil the sightlines of your garden. In the present design, you will note that all with the exception of the elder die back into the ground in winter. Autumn is therefore an ideal time to give all the herbs, including the elder, a good mulch of well-rotted manure.

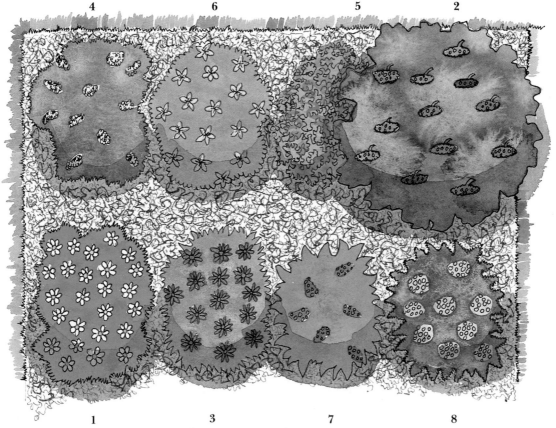

Herb		Part	Mordant	Colour
1	**Chamomile, Dyers** *Anthemis tinctoria*	Flowers	Alum	Bright yellow
		Flowers	Copper	Olive
2	**Elder** *Sambucus nigra*	Leaves	Alum	Green
		Berries	Alum	Violet/purple
3	**Marigold** *Calendula officinalis*	Petals	Alum	Pale yellow
4	**Meadowsweet** *Filipendula ulmaria*	Roots	Alum	Black
5	**Parsley** *Petroselinum crispum*	Fresh leaves	Alum	Cream
6	**St John's Wort** *Hypericum perforatum*	Flowers	Alum	Beige
7	**Sorrel** *Rumex acetosa*	Whole plant	Alum	Pale dirty yellow
8	**Tansy** *Tanacetum vulgare*	Flowers	Alum	Yellows

POTPOURRI GARDEN

Home-made potpourris are warm, not flashy in colour, and the aroma is gentle.

This garden is planted with herbs that can be dried and used in the making of potpourris. The leaves and petals should be harvested, dried and stored as per Harvesting, page 236. There is also further information under the individual species.

Position this garden in full sun to make the oils come to the surface of the leaves and get the benefit of the aroma. Also, as it has turned out to be a fairly tender garden, the soil will need a little bit of extra attention to ensure that it is very well drained. There are also some herbs that will need lifting in the autumn – lemon verbena, sage pineapple, and the scented geranium 'Attar of Roses'. Equally, if you live in a damp, cold place, the myrtle and lavender dentata will need protection. When planting, note that I have put the honeysuckle in the corner to give it a wall or fence to climb up.

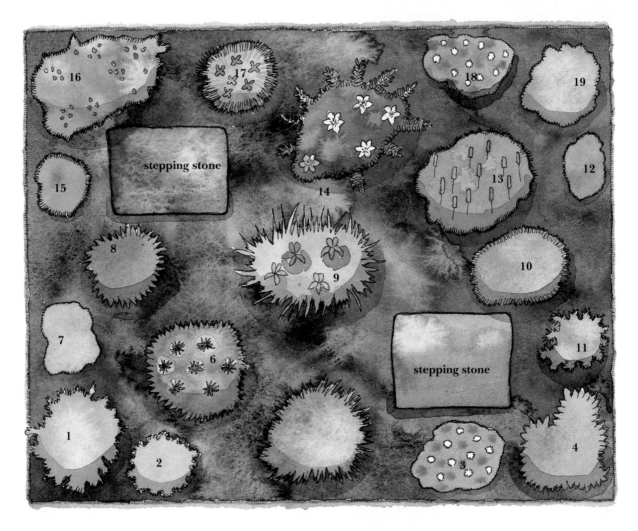

1	**Southernwood** *Artemisia abrotanum*	9	**Orris** *Iris* 'Florentina'
2	**Marjoram Golden Curly** *Origanum vulgare* 'Aureum Crispum'	10	**Alecost** *Tanacetum balsamita*
3+18	**Chamomile, double flowered** *Chamaemelum nobile* 'Flore Pleno'	11	**Scented Geranium** *Pelargonium* 'Attar of Roses'
4	**Honeysuckle** *Lonicera periclymenum*	12	**Thyme Caraway** *Thymus herba-barona*
5	**Lemon Verbana** *Aloysia triphylla*	13	**Lavender Dentata** *Lavandula dentata*
6	**Bergamot** *Monarda didyma*	14	**Myrtle** *Myrtus communis*
7	**Thyme, orange-scented** *Thymus* x *citriodorus* 'Fragrantissimus'	15	**Hyssop Rock** *Hyssopus officinalis* ssp. *aristatus*
8	**Sage, Pineapple** *Salvia elegans* 'Scarlet Pineapple'	16	**Rosemary Benenden Blue** *Rosmarinus officinalis* 'Benenden Blue'
		17	**Pinks, Doris** *Dianthus* 'Doris'
		19	**Oregano** *Origanum vulgare*

ROMAN HERB GARDEN

Over the years I have been asked by several schools to supply a list and simple plan of plants that would have been used in a Roman herb garden. This design makes use of a few of the many herbs brought to Britain by the Romans. The circular hedge is a slight cheat, as Lavender Hidcote, with its flowers a deep purple/blue, is, of course, a modern cultivar. I have chosen it because, being a small growing lavender, it is easy to maintain. To be strictly correct use *Lavendula augustifolia*, which grows much bigger. As the wormwood, elecampane, myrtle and catmint can grow to a good size, I have positioned them outside the circle to give them room to spread.

Whatever your personal preference, no good Roman would have been without his houseleek to protect him from witches, lightning and fire. Caraway was also said to give protection from witches and won its place, too, both as a fine culinary herb and as an ingredient in love potions to prevent a loved one leaving. Equally, no Roman herb garden would be complete without a bay tree, the leaves of which they used to crown their victorious soldiers. It reminded them of home and also harked back to an earlier heroic civilization – the roof of Apollo's temple at Delphi was made entirely of bay leaves. Finally, Romans would have added lavender to their baths at the end of a busy day to help them relax.

1	**Lavender Hidcote** *Lavendula augustifolia* 'Hidcote'	10	**Caraway** *Carum carvi*
2	**Wormwood** *Artemisia absinthium*	11	**Parsley** *Petroselinum crispum*
3	**Catmint** *Nepeta* x *faassenii*	12	**Rue** *Ruta graveolens*
4	**Elecampane** *Inula helenium*	13	**Pennyroyal Creeping** *Mentha pulegium*
5	**Myrtle** *Myrtus communis*	14	**Hyssop** *Hyssopus officinalis*
6	**Welsh Onion** *Allium fistulosum*	15	**Dill** *Anethum graveolens*
7	**Coriander** *Coriandrum sativum*	16	**Alecost (Costmary)** *Tanecetum balsmita*
8	**Liquorice** *Glycyrrhiza glabra*	17	**Houseleek** *Sempervivum tectorum*
9	**Savory, Winter** *Satureja montana*	18	**Bay** *Laurus nobilis*

HERBS IN CONTAINERS

In all the years I have been growing herbs I have only found a very very few that cannot be grown in containers. In the A-Z section of this book I have given details not only about each herb and what size container best suits it, but also where to place it. This section provides more general information and advice on container growing that is applicable to most herbs.

CONTAINERS

* Choose the container to suit the plant. If it is a tall plant make sure the container has a base wide enough to prevent it toppling over, even if placed outside in a high wind.

* A collection of containers is sometimes much easier to look after than a window box, and you can give each herb its own individual bit of tender loving care.

* If using unconventional containers – old watering cans, sinks, a half beer barrel – make sure they have drainage holes, and gravel or broken pots in the bottom of the container to stop the holes clogging up.

HANGING BASKETS

Herbs can suit hanging baskets, but the position is crucial. They dislike high wind and full sun all day. Also, they are mostly fast growers and if too cramped or over- or under-watered they will drop their leaves. They also benefit from being picked regularly, which is not always possible in a hanging basket.
  I can recommend the following: double flowered chamomile, creeping thymes, prostrate rosemary, catmint, creeping savory, golden marjoram, dwarf marjoram, pineapple mint, pennyroyal, and maiden pinks – to name but a few. Other candidates can be found in the A to Z section.

Preparation of Hanging Baskets
* Line the basket with sphagnum moss followed by a layer of black plastic with holes punched in it.

* Fill the basket half full with compost. Position the plants, trailers at the side, taller, more upright herbs in the middle. Do not overcrowd.

*Fill up with compost. Water in well. Let it drain before hanging.

* Check hanging position for accessibility. In the height of the season you will need to water at least night and morning. Make sure, too, that it cannot fall on anyone's head.

COMPOSTS AND ORGANIC FERTILIZER

Choosing the right compost is essential for healthy plants.

Own Mix Bark, Peat, Grit
You will have realized that I generally use the bark, peat, grit mix of compost. I have found this reliable: the open mix helps prevent over-watering; the bark retains water, which protects against under-watering and keeps the compost open to help absorb water if ever it dries out completely. It is suitable for containers and hanging baskets alike. Another plus is that you know what nutrients are in it, so will be able to feed in a balanced way.

Own Soil-based Mix
If you wish to make a soil-based compost of your own this recipe is fairly reliable.

4 parts good weed-free garden top soil
3 parts well-rotted garden compost
3 parts moist peat
1 part horticultural sharp sand

Multipurpose Potting Compost
This is usually peat based with added chemicals. Bags can be bought in numerous outlets, from garden centres to supermarkets. The bags are light and the compost is clean and easy to use. On the negative side, you will need to feed regularly as nutrients are soon depleted; also the compost is light, so watch out that large plants do not fall over. The most frequent problem is that it takes up water poorly if ever it dries out.

Fertilizer
You can buy organic fertilizer from garden centres and hardware shops. The following organic fertilizers are ideal to be added to potting or seed sowing composts when planting up.

Liquid seaweed
This contains small amounts of nitrogen, phosphorous, potassium, and it is also rich in trace elements. It not only makes a good soil feed but as the elements are easily taken in by the plant, it can also be sprayed on as a foliar feed.

Calcified Seaweed
This contains calcium, magnesium, sodium and numerous trace elements. It is ideal for adding to seed compost. Add according to the manufacturer's instructions.

Alternative Composts
Here are some alternative composts that can be used for container growing.

John Innes
This can be purchased in any garden centre or hardware store. It is soil-based and includes chemicals. On the plus side, it stays richer in nutrients longer, making feeding less critical; it holds water well and is a stable compost for a large plant. If it does dry out, it takes up water easily. The major watch point is that it is easy to over-water.
  There are usually 3 different grades of compost, though some manufacturers combine No.1 and No.2. No.1 is for growing rooted cuttings, No.2 for seedlings and No.3 for final potting. The numbers indicate the amount of nutrients. You must choose the correct one for the job. One word of warning - this is not a good compost for hanging baskets, because it is heavy when wet.

Peat-free Composts
These are becoming more readily available as we become aware of the need to conserve our diminishing peat fields. They are made of the following:

Coir

This is a by-product of coconuts. Because it is very fashionable there are quite a few product varieties on the market (at a marked-up price), some more reliable than others. I could argue that it takes a lot of natural resources to ship them from their mountain homes half way round the world, but I won't labour that.

In itself coir is worth looking at, although it does not readily decompose and water zooms through it. For this reason some manufacturers are introducing a jelly that retains water, releasing it gradually. Coir compost is light, so there may be a stability problem with tall or large plants. A final minus point – the nutrients are soon depleted so you will need to feed from the start.

Composted Bark

These composts are now becoming widely available. Although they are fine for propagating under mist, I personally do not recommend them for container growing if used straight, with no peat or soil. Watering and nutrient loss are the two major problems. Also, if the bark has not been composted for long enough, it can leach the nutrients and starve the plants. However, mixed with peat or soil, bark is a great asset.

MAINTENANCE

Spring: This is the time of year to pot on plants if necessary. A good sign of when they need this is that the roots are truly protruding from the bottom of the container. Use a pot next size up. Carefully remove the plant from its old pot. Give it a good tidy up – remove any weed, dead leaves. If it is a perennial, trim the growing tip to promote new bushy growth. Place gravel or other drainage material in the bottom of the container and keep the compost sweet by adding a tablespoon full of granulated charcoal. As soon as the plant starts producing new growth or flowers, start feeding regularly with liquid seaweed.
Summer: Keep a careful eye on the watering; make sure the pots do not dry out fully. Move some plants out of the midday sun. Dead head any flowers. Feed with liquid seaweed, on average once a week. Remove any pest-damaged leaves.
Autumn: Cut back the perennial herbs. Weed containers and at the same time remove some of the top compost and re-dress. Bring any tender plants inside before the frosts. Start reducing the watering.
Winter: Protect all container-grown plants from frosts. If possible move into a cold greenhouse or conservatory. If the weather is very severe cover the containers in a layer of sacking. Keep watering to the absolute minimum.

Back row, left to right:
Lungwort, *Pulmonaria officinalis*, **Prostanthera**, *Prostanthera rotundifolia*, **Variegated Box**, *Buxus sempervirens* 'Elegantissima', **Rosemary Benenden Blue**, *Rosmarinus officinalis* 'Benenden Blue', **Box**, *Buxus sempervirens*; front row, left to right: **Pink Prostanthera**, *Prostanthera rotundifolia rosea*, **Marjoram Golden Curly**, *Origanum vulgare* 'Aureum Crispum', **Rue Jackman's Blue**, *Ruta Graveolens* 'Jackman's Blue', **Old Warrior** *Artemisia pontica*

HARVESTING

The more you pick the healthier the plant. People are told that if their chives start to flower they will have no more fresh leaves until the following year. Rubbish! Pick some of the flowers to use in salads and, if the plant is then cut back to within 4cm (1½in) of the ground and given a good feed of liquid fertilizer, it will produce another crop of succulent leaves within a month. Keep two chive plants: one for flowering and one for harvesting.

Herbs can be harvested from very early on in their growing season. This encourages the plant to produce vigorous new growth. It allows the plant to be controlled both in shape and size. Most herbs reach their peak of flavour just before they flower. Snip off suitable stems early in the day before the sun is fully up, or even better on a cloudy day (provided it is not too humid). Cut whole stems rather than single leaves or flowers. Always use a sharp knife, sharp scissors or secateurs, and cut lengths of 5–8cm (2–3in) from the tip of the branch, this being the new soft growth. Do not cut into any of the older, woody growth. Cut from all over the plant, leaving it looking shapely. Pick herbs which are clean and free from pests and disease; they should not be discoloured or damaged in any way. If herbs are covered in garden soil, sponge them quickly and lightly with cold water, not hot as this will draw out the oils prematurely. Pat dry as quickly as possible. Keep each species separately so that they do not contaminate each other. Do not be greedy!

HARVESTING

Annual herbs
Most can be harvested at least twice during a growing season. Cut them to within 10–15cm (4–6in) of the ground, and feed with liquid fertilizer after each cutting. Do not cut the plants too low in the first harvesting as they will not be able to recover in time to give a further cutting later on. Give annuals their final cut of the season before the first frosts; they will have stopped growing some weeks before.

Perennial herbs
In the first year of planting, perennials will give one good crop; thereafter it will be possible to harvest two or three times during the growing season. Do not cut into the woody growth unless deliberately trying to prevent growth; again, cut well before frosts as cutting late in the season may weaken plants and inhibit

them from surviving the winter. There are of course exceptions; sage is still very good after frosts, and both thyme and golden marjoram (with some protection) can be picked gently even in mid-winter.

Flowers and seeds
Pick flowers for drying when they are barely opened. Seed should be collected as soon as you notice a change in colour of the seed pod; if when you tap the pod a few scatter on the ground, it is the time to gather them. Seeds ripen very fast, so watch them carefully.

Roots
These are at their peak of flavour when they have completed a growing season. Dig them through autumn as growth ceases. Lift whole roots with a garden fork, taking care not to puncture or bruise the outer skin. Wash them free of soil. Cut away any remains of top

Individual herbs laid out for drying

growth and any fibrous off-shoots. For drying cut large, thick roots in half length-ways and then into smaller pieces for ease.

DRYING

The object of drying herbs is to eliminate the water content of the plant quickly and, at the same time, to retain the essential oils. It looks pretty to have bunches of herbs hanging up in a kitchen but most of the flavour will be lost quickly. Herbs need to be dried in a warm, dark, dry and well-ventilated place. The faster they dry, the better retained are the aromatic oils. Darkness helps to prevent loss of colour and unique flavours. The area must be dry, with a good air flow, to hasten the drying process and to discourage mould.

Suitable places for drying herbs include:
* an airing cupboard

* attic space immediately under the roof (provided it does not get too hot)
* in the oven at low temperature and with the door ajar (place the herbs on a brown piece of paper with holes punched in it and check regularly that the herbs are not over-heating
* a plate-warming compartment
* a spare room with curtains shut and door open.

The temperature should be maintained at slightly below body temperature, between 21–33°C/70–90°F.

Herbs should always be dried separately from each other, especially the stronger scented ones like lovage. Spread them in a single layer on trays or slatted wooden racks covered with muslin or netting. The trays or frames should be placed in the drying areas so that they have good air circulation. Herbs need to be turned over by hand several times during the first two days.

Roots require a higher temperature – from 50–60°C/120–140°F. They are quicker and easier to dry in an oven and require regular turning until they are fragile and break easily. Specific requirements are given for each herb in the A–Z section.

Seed should be dried without any artificial heat and in an airy place. Almost-ripe seed heads can be hung in paper bags (plastic causes them to sweat) so the majority of seeds will fall into the bag as they mature. They need to be dried thoroughly before storing and the process can take up to two weeks.

TIP: An alternative method for flowers, roots or seed heads is to tie them in small bundles of 8 to 10 stems. Do not pack the stems too tightly together, as air needs to circulate through and around the bunches. Then hang them on coat-hangers in an airy, dark room until they are dry.

The length of drying time varies from herb to herb, and week to week. The determining factor is the state of the plant material. If herbs are stored before drying is complete, moisture will be reabsorbed from the atmosphere and the herb will soon deteriorate. Leaves should be both brittle and crisp. They should break easily into small pieces but should not reduce to a powder when touched. The roots should be brittle and dry right through. Any softness or sponginess means they are not sufficiently dry and, if stored that way, will rot.

A QUICK METHOD OF HERB DRYING

Microwave manufacturers have said it takes 3 to 4 minutes to dry thoroughly 10 sprigs of any herb! I have tried. It is easy to over-dry and cook the leaves to the point of complete disintegration. I have found that small-leafed herbs such as rosemary and thyme take about 1 minute, whilst the larger, moist leaves of mint dry in about 3 minutes. Add an eggcupful of water to the microwave during the process. **And be warned! Sage can ignite . . .**

STORING

Herbs lose their flavour and colour if not stored properly. Pack the leaves or roots, not too tightly, into a dark glass jar with an air-tight screw top. Label with name and date. Keep in a dark cupboard; nothing destroys the quality of the herb quicker at this stage than exposure to light.
After the initial storing, keep a check on the jars for several days. If moisture

Parsley stored in a bag for freezing, together with ice cubes for convenience

starts to form on the inside of the container, the herbs have not been dried correctly. Return them to the drying area and allow further drying time.

Most domestic herb requirements are comparatively small so there is little point in storing large amounts for a long time. The shelf life of dried herbs is only about 1 year so it is sufficient to keep enough just for the winter.

Dried herbs are usually 3 to 4 times more powerful than fresh. When a recipe calls for a tablespoon of a fresh herb and you only have dried use a teaspoonful.

TIP: If you have large dark jars, thyme and rosemary can be left on the stalk. This makes it easier to use them in casseroles and stews and to remove before serving.

FREEZING HERBS

Freezing is great for culinary herbs as colour, flavour and the nutritional value of the fresh young leaves are retained. It is becoming an increasingly popular way to preserve and store culinary herbs, being quick and easy. I believe it is far better to freeze herbs such as fennel, dill, parsley, tarragon and chives than to dry them.

Pick the herbs and, if necessary, rinse with cold water, and shake dry before freezing, being careful not to bruise the leaves. Put small amounts of herbs into labelled, plastic bags, either singly, or as a mixture for bouquet garnis. Either have a set place in the freezer for them or put the bags into a container, so that they do not get damaged with the day-to-day use of the freezer.

There is no need to thaw herbs before use; simply add them to the cooking as required. For chopped parsley, freeze the bunches whole in bags and, when you remove them from the freezer, crush the parsley in its bag with your hand. Do not be distracted in this task or you will have a herb that has thawed and is a limp piece of greenery. This technique is good for all fine-leaved herbs.

Another way to freeze herbs conveniently is to put finely-chopped leaves into an ice-cube tray and top them up with water. The average cube holds 1 tablespoon chopped herbs and 1 teaspoon water.

TIP: The flowers of borage and the leaves of the variegated mints look very attractive when frozen individually in ice-cubes for drinks or fruit salads.

HERB OILS, VINEGARS AND PRESERVES

Many herbs have antiseptic and anti-bacterial qualities, and were used in preserving long before there were cookbooks. Herbs aid digestion, stimulate appetite and enhance the flavour of food. I hope the following recipes will tempt you, because a variety of herb oils and vinegars can lead to the creation of unusual and interesting dishes. Herbs can make salad dressings, tomato-based sauces for pasta dishes, marinades for fish and meat, and can act as softening agents for vegetables, introducing a myriad of new tastes and flavours. They also make marvellous presents.

HERB OILS

These can be used in salad dressings, in marinades, sauces, stir-fry dishes and sautéing. Find some interesting bottles with good shapes.
   To start with, you need a clean glass jar, large enough to hold 500ml/¾pint/2cups with a screw top.

Basil oil

This is one of the best ways of storing and capturing the unique flavour of basil.

4 tablespoons/⅓cup basil leaves
500ml/¾pint/2cups olive or sunflower oil

Pick over the basil, remove the leaves from the stalks, and crush them in a mortar. For Greek basil, with its small leaves, simply crush in the mortar. Pound very slightly. Add a little oil and pound gently again. This bruises the leaves, so releasing their own oil into the oil. Mix the leaves with the rest of the oil and pour into a wide-necked jar and seal tightly. Place the jar on a sunny windowsill. Shake it every other day; and, after 2 weeks, strain through muslin into a decorative bottle and add a couple of fresh leaves

of the relevant basil. This helps to identify the type of basil used and also looks fresh and enticing. Label. Adapt for dill, sage, fennel (green), sweet marjoram, rosemary and garden or lemon thyme.
   Garlic makes a very good oil. Use 4 cloves of garlic, peeled and crushed, and combined with the oil.

Bouquet garni oil

I use this oil for numerous dishes.

1 tablespoon sage
1 tablespoon lemon thyme
1 tablespoon Greek oregano
1 tablespoon French parsley
1 bay leaf
500ml/¾pint/2cups olive or sunflower oil

Break all the leaves and mix them together in a mortar, pounding lightly. Add a small amount of the oil to mix well, allowing the flavours to infuse. Pour into a wide-necked jar with the remaining oil. Cover and leave on a sunny windowsill for 2–3 weeks. Either shake or stir the jar every other day. Strain through muslin into an attractive bottle. If there is room, add a fresh sprig of each herb used.

SWEET OILS

Good with fruit dishes, marinades and puddings. Use almond oil, which combines well with scented flowers such as pinks, lavender, lemon verbena, rose petals and scented geraniums. Make as for savoury oils above. Mix 4 tablespoons of torn petals or leaves with 500ml/¾pint/2cups almond oil.

SPICE OILS

Ideal for salad dressings, they can be used for sautéing and stir-frying too. The most suitable herb spices are: coriander seeds, dill seeds and fennel seeds. Combine 2 tablespoons of seeds with 500ml/¾pint/2cups olive or sunflower oil, having first pounded the seeds gently to crush them in a mortar and mixed them with a little of the oil. Add a few of the whole seeds to the oil before bottling and labelling. Treat as for savoury oils and store.

HERBAL VINEGARS

Made in much the same way as oils, they can be used in gravies and sauces, marinades and salad dressings.

10 tablespoons chopped herb, such as basil, chervil, dill, fennel, garlic, lemon balm, marjoram, mint, rosemary, savory, tarragon or thyme
500ml/¾pint/2cups white wine or cider vinegar

Pound the leaves gently in a mortar. Heat half the vinegar until warm but not boiling, and pour it over the herbs in the mortar. Pound further to release the flavours of the herb. Leave to cool. Mix this mixture with the remaining vinegar and pour into a wide-necked bottle. Seal tightly. Remember to use an acid-proof lid (lining the existing lid with greaseproof paper is a way round this). Put on a sunny windowsill and shake each day for 2 weeks. Test for flavour; if a stronger taste is required, strain the vinegar and repeat with fresh herbs. Store as is or strain through double muslin and rebottle. Add a fresh sprig of the chosen herb to the bottle for ease of identification.

To Save Time

1 bottle white wine vinegar (500ml/¾pint/2cups)
4 large sprigs herb
4 garlic cloves, peeled

Pour off a little vinegar from the bottle and push in 2 sprigs of herb and the garlic cloves. Top up with the reserved vinegar if necessary. Reseal the bottle and leave on a sunny windowsill for 2 weeks. Change the herb sprigs for fresh ones and the vinegar is now ready to use.

Seed vinegar

Make as for herb vinegar, but the amounts used are

2 tablespoons of seeds to 600ml/1pint/2½cups white wine or cider vinegar. Seeds that make well-flavoured vinegars include dill, fennel and coriander.

Floral vinegar

Made in the same way, these are used for fruit salads and cosmetic recipes. Combine elder, nasturtiums, sweet violets, pinks, lavender, primrose, rose petals, rosemary or thyme flowers in the following proportions:

10 tablespoons torn flower heads or petals
500ml/¾pint/2cups white wine vinegar

Pickled horseradish

As a child I lived in a small village in the West of England where an old man called Mr Bell sat outside his cottage crying in the early autumn. It took me a long time to understand why – he was scraping the horseradish root into a bowl to make pickle. He did this outside because the fumes given off by the horseradish were so strong they made one's eyes water.

Wash and scrape the skin off a good size horseradish root. Mince in a food processor or grate it (if you can stand it!). Pack into small jars and cover with salted vinegar made from 1 teaspoon salt to ½pint cider or white wine vinegar. Seal and leave for 4 weeks before using.

Pickled nasturtium seeds

Poor man's capers! Pick nasturtium seeds while still green. Steep in brine made from 100g/4oz salt to 1litre/1¾pints water for 24 hours. Strain the seeds and put 2 tablespoons of seeds into a small jar. Add 1 clove of peeled garlic, 1 teaspoon black peppercorns, 1 teaspoon dill seeds and 1 tablespoon English mace leaves and fill with white wine vinegar, heated to simmering point. Strain and pour over the seeds. Seal the jars with acid-proof lids and leave for about 4 weeks. After opening, store in the refrigerator, and use the contents quickly.

SAVOURY HERB JELLY

Use the following herbs: sweet marjoram, mints (all kinds), rosemary, sage, summer savory, tarragon and common thyme.
Makes 2 x 350g/12oz jars

1kg/2lb tart cooking apples or crab apples, roughly chopped, cores and all
900ml/1½pints/3¾cups water
500g/1lb/2cups sugar
2 tablespoons wine vinegar
2 tablespoons lemon juice
1 bunch herbs, approx 15g/½oz
4 tablespoons chopped herbs

Put the apples into a large pan with the bunch of herbs and cover with cold water in a preserving pan. Bring to the boil and simmer until the apples are soft, roughly 30 minutes. Pour into a jelly bag and drain overnight.

Measure the strained juice and add 500g/1lb sugar to every 600ml/1pint fluid. Stir over gentle heat until the sugar has dissolved. Bring to the boil, stirring, and boil until setting point is reached. This takes roughly 20–30 minutes. Skim the surface scum and stir in the vinegar and lemon juice and the chopped herbs. Pour into jars, seal and label before storing.

SWEET JELLIES

Follow the above recipe, omitting the vinegar and lemon juice, and instead adding 150ml/¼pint/1cup water. The following make interestingly flavoured sweet jellies: bergamot, lavender flower, lemon verbena, scented geranium, sweet violet and lemon balm.

PRESERVES

Coriander chutney

Makes 2 x 500g/1lb jars

1kg/2lb cooking apples, peeled, cored and sliced
500g/1lb onions, peeled and roughly chopped
2 cloves garlic, peeled and crushed
1 red and 1 green pepper, deseeded and sliced
900ml/1½pints/3¾cups red wine vinegar
500g/1lb soft brown sugar
½ tablespoon whole coriander seeds
6 peppercorns tied securely in a piece of muslin
6 all-spice berries
50g/2oz root ginger, peeled and sliced
2 tablespoons coriander leaves, chopped
2 tablespoons mint, chopped

Combine the apples with the onions, garlic and peppers in a large, heavy saucepan. Add the vinegar and bring to the boil, simmering for about 30 minutes until all the ingredients are soft. Add the brown sugar and the muslin bag of seeds and berries. Then add the ginger. Heat, gently stirring all the time, until the sugar has dissolved, and simmer until thick; this can take up to 60 minutes. Stir in the chopped coriander and mint and spoon into hot, sterilized jars. Seal and label when cool.

Basil oil, coriander seed vinegar and coriander oil all make delicious additions to the store cupboard

HERB DYE CHART

Herbs have been used to dye cloth since earliest records. In fact, until the 19th century and the birth of the chemical industry, all dyes were 'natural'. Then the chemical process, offering a larger range of colours and a more guaranteed result, took over. Now, once again, there is a real demand for more natural products and colours, which has resulted in a revival of interest in plants as a dye source.

The most common dyeing herbs are listed in the dye chart. You will notice that yellows, browns and greys are predominant. Plenty of plant material will be required so be careful not to over-pick in your own garden (and **please** do not pick other people's plants without permission! I plead from personal experience). To begin with, keep it simple. Pick the flowers just as they are coming out, the leaves when they are young and fresh and a good green; dig up roots in the autumn and cut them up well before use.

DYE CHART

Common Name	Botanical Name	Part Used	Mordant	Colour
Comfrey	*Symphytum officinale*	Leaves and stalks	Alum	Yellows
Chamomile, Dyer's	*Anthemis tinctoria*	Flowers	Alum	Yellows
Chamomile, Dyer's	*Anthemis tinctoria*	Flowers	Copper	Olives
Elder	*Sambucus nigra*	Leaves	Alum	Greens
Elder	*Sambucus nigra*	Berries	Alum	Violets/Purple
Golden Rod	*Solidago virgaurea*	Whole plant	Chrome	Golden Yellows
Horsetail	*Equisetum arvense*	Stems and leaves	Alum	Yellows
Juniper	*Juniperus communis*	Crushed berries	Alum	Yellows
Marigold	*Calendula officinalis*	Petals	Alum	Pale Yellow
Meadowsweet	*Filipendula ulmaria*	Roots	Alum	Black
Nettle	*Utrica dioica*	Whole plant	Copper	Greyish green
St John's Wort	*Hypericum perforatum*	Flowers	Alum	Beiges
Sorrel	*Rummex acetosa*	Whole plant	Alum	Dirty yellow
Sorrel	*Rummex acetosa*	Roots	Alum	Beige/pink
Tansy	*Tanacetum vulgare*	Flowers	Alum	Yellows
Woad	*Isatis tinctoria*	Leaves	Sodium dithionite, ammonia	Blues

FABRIC

Any natural material can be dyed; some are more tricky than others. It just takes time and practice. In the following sections I will explain the techniques connected with dying wool, the most reliable and easiest of natural materials. Silk, linen and cotton can also be dyed, but are more difficult.

PREPARATION

First time, this is a messy and fairly lengthy process, so use a utility room, or clear the decks in the kitchen and protect all areas. Best of all keep it away from the home altogether. Some of the mordants used for fixing dye are poisonous, so keep them well away from children, pets and food.

The actual dyeing process is not difficult, but you will need a few special pieces of equipment, and space.

1 large stainless steel vessel, such as a preserving can (to be used as the dye-bath)
1 stainless steel or enamel bucket and bowl
1 pair of tongs (wooden or stainless steel; to be used for lifting)

The flowrers of St John's Wort produces a beige dye

1 measuring jug
1 pair rubber gloves essential for all but Jumblies – 'Their heads are green and their hands are blue, And they went to sea in a sieve.'
Pestle and mortar
Thermometer
Water; this must be soft, either rainwater or filtered
Scales

Dyeing comprises four separate tasks –
* Preparation of material (known as scouring)
* Preparation of Mordant
* Preparation of Dye
* Dyeing Process

PREPARATION OF THE MATERIAL (SCOURING)

Prepare the wool by washing it in a hot solution of soap flakes or a proprietary scouring agent in order to remove any grease. Always handle the wool gently. Rinse it several times, squeezing (gently) between each rinse. On the final rinse add 50ml (2fl oz) of vinegar.

PREPARATION OF THE MORDANT

Mordants help 'fix' the dye to the fabric. They are available from chemists or dye suppliers. The list below includes some of the more common. Some natural dyers say that one should not use mordants, but without them the dye will run very easily.

Alum: Use 25g (1oz) to 500g (1lb) dry wool

This is the most useful of mordants, its full title being Potassium aluminium sulphate. Sometimes potassium hydrogen tartrate, cream of tartar, is added (beware! this is not the baking substance) in order to facilitate the process and brighten the colour.

Iron: Use 5g (⅛oz) to 500g (1lb) dry wool

This is ferrous sulphate. It dulls and deepens the colours. It is added in the final process after first using the mordant Alum. Remove the wool before adding the iron, then replace the wool and simmer until you get the depth of colour required.

Copper: Use 15g (½oz) to 500g (1lb) dry wool

This is copper sulphate. If you mix with 300ml (½ pint) of vinegar when preparing the mordant it will give a blue/green tint to colours. WARNING: Wear gloves; copper is poisonous.

Chrome: Use 15g (½oz) to 500g (1lb) dry wool

This is bichromate of potash and light-sensitive, so keep it in the dark. It gives the colour depth, makes the colours fast, and gives the wool a soft, silky feel. WARNING: Wear gloves; chrome is poisonous.

* Dissolve the mordant in a little hot water.
* Stir into 20 litres (4 gallons) of hot water 50°C (122°F).
* When thoroughly dissolved immerse the wet, washed wool in the mixture. Make sure it is wholly immersed.
* Slowly bring to the boil and simmer at 82-94°C (180-200°F) for an hour.
* Remove from the heat. Take the wool out of the water and rinse.

PREPARATION OF DYE

No two batches of herbal dye will be the same. There are so many variable factors – plant variety, water, mordant, immersion time.
 The amount of plant material required for dyeing is very variable. A good starting ratio is 500g (1lb) of mordanted wool in skeins to 500g (1lb) plant material.

* Chop or crush the plant material.
* Place loosely in a muslin or nylon bag and tie securely .
* Leave to soak in 20 litres (4 gallons) of soft tepid water overnight.
* Slowly bring the water and herb material to the boil.
* Reduce heat and simmer at 82-94°C (180-200°F) for as long as it takes to get the water to the desired colour. This can take from 1 to 3 hours.
* Remove the pan from the heat, remove the herb material, and allow the liquid to cool to hand temperature.

DYEING PROCESS

* Gently add the wool.
* Bring the water slowly to the boil, stirring occasionally with the wooden tongs.
* Allow to simmer for a further hour.
* Remove pan from the heat and leave the wool in the dye-bath until cold, or until the colour is right.
* Remove the wool with the tongs and rinse in tepid water until no colour runs out.
* Give a final rinse in cold water.
* Dry the skeins of wool over a rod or cord, away from direct heat. Tie a light weight to the bottom to stop the wool kinking during the drying process.

PESTS AND DISEASES

Herbs suffer from few pests and diseases, and in fact many of them can be used in the vegetable garden to protect other crops. Even so, always be on the lookout, as, in early stages of attack, they can often be dealt with by methods other than the dreaded spray gun.

GENERAL METHODS OF CONTROL

Biological Control
Many biological control methods are now available commercially. When you plant in the open, harmful pests are mostly kept under control by predators. However, in the enclosed environment of the greenhouse, the natural balance can break down. All biological control methods are relatively expensive when compared with the chemical alternatives, and nearly all are dependent on warm temperatures to work efficiently.

Organic sprays
If all else fails, there are now organic sprays for pests such as green- and whitefly, which can be purchased at any good garden centre or hardware shop. Make sure that it is an organic spray with the recognized organic symbol. We use a liquid soap called Savona, which is mixed with rainwater and sprayed on infestations of white- or greenfly. It is harmless to ladybirds, bees and other insects.

There are no organic fungicides on the market, but elder leaf is an old remedy worth trying against mildew. Spray it onto the leaves.Also, chamomile makes a good spray against the damping-off diseases in young plants.

Companion Planting
I believe that certain plants can assist other plants to thrive when planted together.

Fragrant herbs such as hyssop, thyme, marjoram, chives and parsley are beneficial in maintaining the health of a vegetable garden. There are no scientific records to back this up, but a number of gardeners have reported improvements in the general health of their vegetables when inter-planted with these herbs.

Many herbs act as an insect repellent when grown near other plants, a reason being the scent they give off. The most effective ones are *tansy, pennyroyal, nasturtiums, stinging nettle, garlic, chives, hyssop, wormwood* and *southernwood.*

Using herbs as an insecticide must be effective, because if you read this book carefully you will see that many can kill if used incorrectly. *Pyrethrum* is already used in insecticides and there are a number of others identified in the A-Z of Herbs, which can also be used in various ways. I am sure that there must be others waiting to be discovered.

Chemicals for Control of Pests and Diseases
I realize that some people need to use chemicals. However, most herbs can be grown very successfully without, and if the herbs are being used as a food crop, it is worth taking that little bit of extra care.

When choosing chemicals, choose the one appropriate to the problem. Follow the manufacturer's instructions carefully. Store the bottle after use in a secure cupboard, away from animals and children.

PESTS

There are many, many pests and I have only mentioned the few that are known to affect herbs in general.

Aphids. Greenfly, Blackfly, Black Bean Aphid
From early spring in the greenhouse, and later outside, keep a watch for greenfly. If you see a few, kill them! If there are a lot, spray them with a horticultural soap, following the manufacturer's instructions.

With blackfly, do exactly the same. Do not use a high pressure hose as you will damage the plant. If it is a pot plant, such as nasturtiums, wash them off gently under the tap; otherwise spray with a horticultural soap, as above.

Borage and runner beans thrive side by side as companion plants

Carrot Fly

The grub of this fly tunnels into the roots of plants during early summer, so herbs such as those from the Umbelliferous family, which have a long tap root, are at risk. The first sign of attack will be the yellowing or whittling of the leaves and any stunted growth. Parsley may be particularly vulnerable, and in this case the plant should be pulled up and destroyed to get rid of the pests. However, large herbs should overcome attacks, so just pick off dead leaves and boost the plant by feeding with liquid seaweed. A preventative method is to put a 75cm (30in) polythene barrier around the crop during mid-spring, or cover with agricultural fleece while the plants are young. Sowings after mid-summer should miss the first flies.

Caterpillars Cabbage White

These are attracted to herbs with large leaves, such as horse-radish, in late spring through to early autumn. Check weekly, and simply pick them off by hand and destroy. Early in the season, when the plants are small, agricultural fleece is a good barrier.

Leaf Miners

These grubs are sometimes a problem on lovage, wild celery, certain sorrels and various mints. They eat through the leaf, creating winding tunnels in the leaves like little silver tracks, which are clearly visible. Watch for the first tunnels, pick off the affected leaves and destroy them. If left, the tunnels will extend into broad dry patches, and complete leaves will wither away.

Red Spider Mite

The spider mites like hot dry conditions and can become prolific in a glasshouse. Look out for early signs of the pests such as speckling on the upper surfaces of the leaves. Look under the leaf with a magnifying glass and you will see these minute red spiders. Another tell-tale sign is the cobwebs. At first sight, either use horticultural soap in the form of a spray, or the natural predator *Phytoseiulus persimilis*, following the instructions that will come with them. Do not use both.

Scale Insects

These are often notice-able as im-mobile, waxy, brown/yellow, flat, oval lumps gathered on the backs of leaves or on the stems of bay trees. These leaves also become covered with sticky black sooty mould. Rub off the scales gently before the infestation builds up. Alternatively, use a horticultural liquid soap, following the manufacturer's instructions.

Slugs

These can only be got rid of by hand or by setting out beer traps, even better a size 10 welly boot. There is a microscopic worm that can be used as a form of biological control and infects the slugs with a bacterium that stops them feeding within a week, it actually kills them in two. This is an expensive way of getting rid of them, but worth it to protect your specimen plants.

Vine Weevil

These can be a major pest. Look out for them in the spring and early autumn. In the ground or in pots you may see horrid white grubs with orange heads. The parent is a small nocturnal beetle with a weevil's nose. The grubs eat the roots of plants, the beetles eat leaves, especially those of vines. I have tried various organic methods of irradiation, from re-potting 10,000 plants to check and get rid of the grubs, to watering with a *nematodes* (eelworms) in the autumn. This is a form of biological control the worms destroy the vine weevil grub. The temperature must be warm for them to work. The best is still a size 10 welly.

White Fly

Under protection in the glasshouse this can be a problem, less so outside. It is essential to act immed-iately, either by introducing the natural predator *Encarsia formosa*, a minute parasitic wasp that lays its eggs in the whitefly larvae, which is usually found attached to the underside of the leaves. Unfortunately, these parasites need warm temperatures to multiply so they cannot be successfully used in early spring or autumn. Alternatively, spray with a horticultural soap and repeat 7 days later.

DISEASE

Mint Rust (& other similar diseases)

Plants affected by rust should be dug up and thrown away. Alternatively, you can, in the autumn, put straw around the affected plants and set it alight. This will actually sterilize the soil and the plant. Comfrey suffers from a similar rust disease. Here the best answer is to keep the plant clipped. Cut off leaves every 4 weeks and keep well fed with manure and compost.

Powdery Mildew

This common fungal disease can occur when the conditions are hot and dry, and the plants are overcrowded. Prevent it by watering well during dry spells, following the recommended planting distances, and clearing away any fallen leaves in the autumn. Adding a mulch in the autumn or early spring also helps. If your plant does suffer, destroy all the affected leaves before spraying with elder.

YEARLY CALENDAR

This calendar assumes that the herb garden is situated in Northern Europe, the average date of the last major frost in spring being April 1st and an average date for the first frost being October 20th. Gardeners with different frost dates can adjust this calendar accordingly. But as any gardener knows, you cannot be precise. Each year is different, wetter, windier, hotter, drier, colder. So use this calendar as a general guide.

JANUARY

This is one of the quietest months. Keep an eye on the degrees of frost and protect tender herbs with an extra layer of agricultural fleece or mulch if necessary. With (one hopes) everything quiet, this is a good time to plan any additions or changes to the herb garden – like constructing new paths, steps, arches etc. It is also the time to order seeds for spring sowing.

Fresh Herbs Available
With a little bit of protection in the garden, Bay, Hyssop, Rosemary, Sage, Winter Savory, Thyme, Lemon Thyme, Chervil, Parsley.

Cultivation
Seed with Heat
Parsley.

Seed Outside in the Garden
If not sown in the autumn, sow Sweet Cicely, Sweet Woodruff, Cowslip, to enable a period of stratification.

Force in Boxes in the Greenhouse
Chives, Mint, Tarragon,

Containers
Keep watering to a minimum. Clean old pots ready for the spring 'pot up'.

Garden
Nothing to do other than keep an eye on the garden to ensure no damage is being caused by the weather.

FEBRUARY

As the days begin to lengthen, and if the weather is not too unpleasant, this is a good time to have the final tidy up before the busy season starts. If you want to get an early start in the garden and you have prepared a site the previous autumn, cover the soil now with black polythene. It will warm up the soil and force any weeds.

Fresh Herbs Available
With a little bit of protection in the garden, Bay, Hyssop, Rosemary, Sage, Winter Savory, Thyme, Lemon Thyme, Chervil, Parsley.
  Chives start to come up if they are under protection, and mint can be available if forced.

Hardy vervain needs no protection from winter frosts

Cultivation
Seed with Heat
Borage, Dill, Parsley.

Seed in Cold Greenhouse
Chervil.

Division
Herbaceous perennial herbs can be divided now, as long as they are not too frozen and are given added protection after replanting. Chives, Lemon Balm, Pot Marjoram, Mints, Oregano, Broad Leafed Sorrel, Tarragon.

Containers
As the containers have been brought in for the winter, new life may be starting. Dust off, and slowly start watering. Not too much.

Garden
Check that any dead or decaying herbaceous growth is not damaging plants. Check for wind and snow damage.

MARCH

Spring is in the air, everything is Go. Even with a cold March it is still worth getting started, even if the worst comes to the worst and the seed has to be sown again in April. Gradually uncover tender plants outside and look for hopeful signs of life. Give them a gentle tidy.

Fresh Herbs Available
Angelica, Lemon Balm, Bay, Chives, Fennel, Hyssop, Mint, Parsley, Peppermint, Pennyroyal, Rue, Sage, Savory, Sorrel, Thyme.

Cultivation
Seed with Heat
Borage, Fennel, Coriander, Sweet Marjoram, Rue and Basil – towards the end of the month.

Seed in Cold Greenhouse
Chervil, Chives, Dill, Lemon Balm, Lovage, Parsley, Sage, Summer Savory, Sorrel.

Seed Outside in the Garden
Chervil, Chives, Parsley (cover with cloches), Chamomile, Tansy, Caraway, Borage, Fennel.
  Check seeds that have been left outside from the previous autumn for the purpose of stratification. If they are starting to germinate, move them into a cold greenhouse.

Root Cuttings
Mint, Tarragon, Bergamot, Chamomile, Hyssop, Tansy, Sweet Woodruff, Sweet Cicely.

Division
Mint, Tarragon, Wormwood, Lovage, Rue, Sorrel, Lemon Balm, Salad Burnet, Camphor Plant, Thyme, Winter Savory, Marjoram, Alecost, Horehound, Pennyroyal.

Layering
This is a good time to start mound layering on old sages or thymes.

Containers
Tidy up all the pots, trim old growth to maintain shape. Start liquid feeding with seaweed. Re-pot if necessary. Pot up new plants into containers for display later in the season.

Garden
Clear up all the winter debris, fork the garden over and give a light dressing of bonemeal. If your soil is alkaline, and you gave it a good dressing of manure in the autumn, now is the time to dig it well in.

Remove black polythene, weed and place a cloche over important sowing sites a week before sowing to raise the soil temperature and keep it dry.

Towards the end of the month, if the major frosts are over, you can cut lavender back and into shape. This is certainly advisable for plants 2 years old and older. Give them a good mulch. Equally, sage bushes of 2 years and older would benefit from a trim – not hard back because sage does not recover well when cut into the old wood. Cut back elder and rosemary; neither minds a hard cutting back, in fact, quite often they benefit from it. Transplant the following if they need it: Alecost, Chives, Mint, Balm, Pot Marjoram, Sorrel, Horehound, and Rue.

APRIL

Suddenly there are not enough hours in the day. This is the main month for sowing outdoors, as soon as soil conditions permit. It is also now possible to prune back to strong new shoots the branches of any shrubs which have suffered in winter.

Fresh Herbs Available
Angelica, Balm, Bay, Borage, Caraway, Chervil, Chives, Fennel, Hyssop, Lovage, Pot Marjoram, Mints, Parsley, Pennyroyal, Peppermint, Rosemary, Sage, Winter Savory, Sorrel, Thyme, Tarragon, Lemon Thyme.

Cultivation
Seed with Heat
Basil.

Seed in Cold Greenhouse
Borage, Chervil, Coriander, Dill, Fennel, Lemon Balm, Lovage, Pot Marjoram, Sweet Marjoram, Sage, Summer Savory, Winter Savory, Sorrel, Buckler Leaf Sorrel, Horehound, Rue, Bergamot, Caraway, Garden Thyme.

Seed Outside in the Garden
Parsley, Chives, Hyssop, Caraway, Pot Marigold.

Seedlings
Prick out the previous month's sown seeds, pot on, or harden off before planting out.

Softwood Cuttings
Rue, Mint, Sage, Southernwood, Winter Savory, Thymes, Horehound, Lavender, Rosemary, Cotton Lavender, Curry.

Root Cuttings
Sweet Cicely, Fennel, Mint.

Division
Pennyroyal, Chives, Lady's Mantle, Salad Burnet, Tarragon.

Containers
You should be able to put all containers outside now; keep an eye on the watering and feeding.

Garden
This is a busy time in the garden. If all the frosts have finished the following will need cutting and pruning into shape: Bay, Winter Savory, Hyssop, Cotton Lavender, Lavenders, Rue especially variegated Rue, Southernwood and Thymes.

Comfrey 'Goldsmith' nestling in a shady corner makes an attractive border plant

MAY

Everything should be growing quickly now. The annuals will need thinning; tender and half-hardy plants should be hardened off under a cold frame or beside a warm wall. A watch must be kept for a sudden late frost; Sir Basil is especially susceptible. Move container specimens into bigger pots or top dress with new compost.

Fresh Herbs Available
Nearly all varieties.

Cultivation
Seed Outside in the Garden
Keep sowing Coriander, Dill, Chervil, Parsley, Sweet Marjoram, Basil, and any other annuals you require to maintain crop.

Seedlings
Prick out and pot on or plant out any of the previous month's seedlings.

Softwood Cuttings
Marjorams, all Mints, Oregano, Rosemarys, Winter Savory, French Tarragon, all Thymes.

Containers
These should now be looking good. Keep trimming to maintain shape; water and feed regularly.

Garden
Trim southernwood into shape.

Harvest
Cut second-year growth of angelica for candying. Cut thyme before flowering for drying.

JUNE

This is a great time in the herb garden. All planting is now completed. Plants are beginning to join up so that little further weeding will be needed. Many plants are now reaching perfection.

Fresh Herbs Available
All.

Cultivation
Seed Outside in the Garden
Basil, Borage, Chives, Coriander, Dill, Fennel, Sweet Marjoram, Summer Savory, Winter Savory, and any others you wish to replace, or keep going.

Cuttings
With all the soft new growth available this is a very busy month for cuttings. Make sure you use material from non-flowering shoots.

Softwood Cuttings
All perennial Marjorams, all Mints, all Rosemary, all Sage, Lemon Balm variegated, Tarragon (French), all Thymes.

Division Thymes.

Layering Rosemary.

Containers
Plant up annual herbs into containers to keep near the kitchen. Basil, Sweet Marjoram, etc.

Garden
If you must plant basil in the garden, now is the time. This is also a good time to nip out the growing tips of this year's young plants to encourage them to bush out.
   Trim cotton lavender hedges if flowers are not required and to maintain their shape; clip box hedges and topiary shapes as needed. A new herb garden should be weeded thoroughly to give the new plants the best chance.

Harvest
Cut second-year growth of angelica for candying. Cut sage for drying.

JULY

The season is on the wane, the early annuals and biennials are beginning to go over. It is already time to think of next year and to start collecting seeds. Take cuttings of tender shrubs as spare shoots become available.

Fresh Herbs Available
All.

Cultivation
Seed Outside in the Garden
Chervil, Angelica (if seed is set), Borage, Chervil, Coriander, Dill Lovage, Parsley.

Softwood Cuttings
Wormwood, Scented Geraniums, Lavenders, the Thymes.

Layering
Rosemary.

Containers
Keep an eye on the watering as the temperatures begin to rise.

Garden
Cut all lavenders back after flowering to maintain shape. If this is the first summer of the herb garden and the plants are not fully established it is important to make sure they do not dry out, so water regularly. Once established many are tolerant of drought.

Harvest
Drying
Lemon Balm, Horehound, Summer Savory, Hyssop, Tarragon, Thyme, Lavender.

Dyeing and Potpourris
Lavender, Rosemary.

Seed
Caraway, Angelica.

AUGUST

Traditionally a month for holidays but it is also time to harvest and preserve many herbs for winter use. Collect and dry material for potpourris, and collect seeds for sowing next year.

Fresh Herbs Available
All.

Cultivation
Seed Outside in the Garden or Greenhouse
Angelica, Coriander, Dill, Lovage, Parsley, Winter Savory.

Softwood Cuttings
Bay, Wormwood, Rosemary, the Thymes and Lavenders, Scented Geraniums, Balm of Gilead, Pineapple Sage, Myrtles.

Containers
If you are going away, make sure you ask a friend to water your containers for you.

Garden
Give box, cotton lavender, and curry, their second clipping and trim any established plants that are looking unruly. Maintain watering of the new herb garden and keep an eye on mints, parsley, and comfrey, which need water to flourish. There is no real need to feed if the ground has been well prepared, but if the plants are recovering from a pest attack they will benefit from a foliar feed of liquid seaweed.

Harvest
Drying
Thyme, Sage, Clary Sage, Marjoram, Lavender.

Freezing
The mints, Pennyroyal.

Oils
Basil.

Seed
Angelica, Anise, Caraway, Coriander, Cumin, Chervil, Dill, Fennel.

SEPTEMBER

By mid-month, basil should be taken up and leaves preserved. Line out semi-ripe cuttings of box, cotton lavenders, etc, in cold frames, under cloches or in polythene tunnels for hedge renewal in the spring.

Fresh Herbs Available
Lemon Balm, Basil, Bay, Borage, Caraway, Chervil, Chives, Clary Sage, Fennel, Hyssop, Pot Marigold, Marjoram, the Mints, Parsley, Pennyroyal, Peppermint, Rosemarys, Sages, Winter Savory, Sorrels, the Thymes

Cultivation
Seed Outside in the Garden or Greenhouse
Angelica, Chives, Coriander, Parsley, Winter Savory.

Softwood and Semi-ripe Cuttings
Rosemary, the Thymes, Tarragon, the Lavenders, Rue, the Cotton Lavenders, the Curry Plants, Box.

Division Bergamot.

Containers
Towards the end of this month take in all containers, and protect tender plants like bay trees, myrtles, and scented geraniums.

Garden
At the beginning of the month give the shrubby herbs their final clipping (bay, lavender, etc). Do not leave it too late or the frost could damage the new growth.
   Put basil into glasshouse or kitchen. Top dress bergamots if they have died back.
   If Lemon Verbena is to be kept outside make sure it is getting adequate protection.

Harvest
Drying or Freezing
Dandelion (roots), Parsley, Marigold, Clary sage, Peppermint.

Seed
Angelica, Anise, Caraway, Chervil, Fennel.

OCTOBER

The best time in all but the coldest areas to plant hardy perennial herbs.

Fresh Herbs Available
Basil, Bay, Borage, Chervil, Fennel, Hyssop, Marigold, Marjoram, Parsley, Rosemary, Sage, Winter Savory, Sorrel, the Thymes.

Cultivation
Seed with Heat
Parsley.

Seed Outside in the Garden
Catmint, Chervil, Wormwood, Chamomile, Fennel, Angelica.

Softwood and Semi-ripe Cuttings
Bay, Elder, Hyssop, Cotton Lavender, Southernwood, Lavenders, the Thymes, Curry, Box.

Root Cuttings
Tansy, Pennyroyal, the Mints, Tarragon.

Division
Alecost, the Marjorams, Chives, Lemon Balm, Lady's Mantle, Hyssop, Bergamot, Camphor Plant, Lovage, Sorrel, Sage, Oregano, Pennyroyal.

Containers
Start reducing the watering.

Garden
Clear the garden and weed it well. Cut down the old growth and collect any remaining seed heads. Cut back the mints, trim winter savory and hyssop. Give them all a leaf mould dressing. Dig up and remove the annuals, dill, coriander, borage, summer savory, sweet marjoram. and the second-year biennials, parsley, chervil, rocket etc. Protect with cloches or agricultural fleece any herbs to be used fresh through the winter, like parsley, chervil, lemon thyme, salad burnet. Dig up some French tarragon, pot up in trays for forcing and protection.

Check the pH of alkaline soil every third year. Dress with well-rotted manure to a depth of 5-10cm (2-4in) and leave the digging until the following spring. Dig over heavy soils; add manure to allow the frost to penetrate.

Back row: **Curly Wood Sage** *Teucrium scorodonia* 'Crispum'; **Lawn Chamomile** *Chamaemelum nobile* 'Treneague'; front row: **Variegated Meadowsweet** *Filipendula ulmaria* 'Variegata'; **Houseleek** *Sempervivum tectorum*; **Dwarf Marjoram** *Origanum vulgare* 'Nanum'

NOVEMBER

The Days are getting shorter and frosts are starting. The garden can be tidied up and planting of hardy herbaceous herbs can continue as long as the soil remains unfrozen and in a workable condition.

Fresh Herbs Available
Basil, Bay, Hyssop, Marjoram, Mint, Parsley, Rosemary, Rue, Sage, Thyme.

Cultivation
Seed
Sow the following so that they can get a good period of stratification: Arnica (old seed), Sweet Woodruff, Yellow Iris, Poppy, Soapwort, Sweet Cicely, Hops (old seed), Sweet Violet.

Sow in trays, cover with glass and leave outside in a cold frame or corner of the garden where they can not get damaged.

Containers
Cut back on all watering of container grown plants. Give them all a prune, so that they go into rest mode for the winter.

Garden
This is the time for the final tidy up. Cut back the remaining plants, Lemon Balm, Alecost, Horehound, and give them a dressing of leaf mould. Give the elders a prune. Dig up a clump of mint and chives, put them in pots or trays and bring them into the greenhouse for forcing for winter use.

DECEMBER

This is the start of the quiet time in the herb garden.

Fresh Herbs Available
Bay, Hyssop, Marjoram, Oregano, Mint (forced), Parsley, Chervil, Rosemary, Rue, Sage, Thyme.

Garden
Even though the garden is entering its dormancy period it does not mean you can put your feet up and watch television.

Remove all the dead growth that falls into other plants, add more protective layers if needed. Wrap the terracotta or stone ornaments in sacking if you live in extremely cold conditions. Bring bay trees in if the temperature drops too low. Keep an eye on the plants you are forcing in the greenhouse – you will need your Fresh Green Stuffing for the turkey.

REFERENCE

Encyclopedia of Herbs and Herbalism ed. Malcolm Stuart, Black Cat, 1979

Encyclopedia of Medicinal Plants Roberto Chiej, Macdonald, 1984

Evening Primrose Oil Judy Graham, Thorsons, 1984

Royal Horticultural Society *Gardeners' Encyclopedia* Oxford Press, 1951

Royal Horticultural Society *Dictionary of Gardening* Dorling Kindersley, 1989

Plant Finder, The, 1993/4 MPC

BIBLIOGRAPHY

Modern Herbal, A M. Grieve, Peregrine, 1976

Complete Book of Herbs Lesley Bremness, Dorling Kindersley, 1988

Complete Herbal Culpeper, J. Gleave & Son, 1826

Complete New Herbal, The ed. Richard Mabey, Penguin, 1988

Complete Cookery Course Delia Smith, BBC Books, 1982

English Man's Flora, The Geoffrey Grigson, Paladin, 1975

Herball John Gerard, 1636; Bracken Books, 1985

Herb Book, The John Lust, Bantam, 1974

Herb Book, The Arabella Boxer & Philippa Black, Octopus, 1980

Herb Gardening at its Best Sal Gilbertie with Larry Sheehan, Atheneum/smi, 1978

Herbs for Health and Cookery Clair Loewenfeld & Philippa Black, Pan, 1965

Herbs in the Garden Allen Paterson, Dent, 1985

Organic Gardening, Month by Month Guide to Lawrence D. Hills, Thorsons, 1983

Pelargoniums Derek Clifford, Blandford, 1958

Planning the Organic Herb Garden Sue Stickland, Thorsons, 1986

Plants from the Past David Stuart & James Sutherland, Viking, 1987

Vanishing Garden, The Christopher Brickell & Fay Sharman, John Murray, 1986

Vegetarian Cookbook, The Sarah Brown, Dorling Kindersley, 1984

Your Kitchen Garden George Seddon, Mitchell Beazley, 1975

GLOSSARY

Agricultural fleece There are many different manufactured forms of this light, woven fleece. When used to cover crops it protects them from frost, wind, hail, birds, rabbits and other pests that eat or chew the leaves. It allows a light transmission of around 85 per cent and can be permeated by rain.

Analgesic A substance which relieves pain.

Annual A plant which completes its life-cycle from germination to flowering and death in one growing season.

Antidote A substance which counteracts or neutralizes a poison.

Apothecary An old term for a person who prepared and sold drugs and administered to the sick.

Aromatherapy The use of essential oils in the treatment of medical problems and for cosmetic purposes.

Astringent A substance which contracts the tissues of the body, checking discharges of blood and mucus.

Atropine An alkaloid obtained from members of the Solanaceae family.

Biennial A plant which produces roots and leaves in the first growing season, then flowers, seeds and dies by the end of the second.

Bolting What happens when a plant produces flowers and seeds prematurely.

Bulbil A small bulb rising above the ground in the axil of a leaf or bract.

Carminative A substance which allays pain and relieves flatulence and colic.

Columnar Column-shaped.

Cultivar A cultivated or horticultural variety of a species which may have originated either in the wild or in cultivation.

Deciduous Describes a plant which loses its leaves annually at the end of the growing season.

Decoction An extract of a herb (when the material is hard and woody, i.e. root, wood, bark, nuts) obtained by boiling a set weight of plant matter in a set volume of water for a set time. An average decoction would be 25g (1oz) of herb to 600ml (1pt) water, brought to the boil and simmered for 10-15 minutes. The decoction should be strained while still hot.

Diuretic A substance that increases the frequency of urination.

Emetic A substance that induces vomiting.

Essential oil A volatile oil obtained from a plant by distillation, and having a similar aroma to the plant itself.

Genus The botanical name for a group of species with common structural characteristics.

Globose Spherical, globe-like.

Herbaceous Relating to plants which are not woody and which die down at the end of each growing season.

Herbicide A substance that kills plants.

Homeopathy A system of medicine pioneered by Samuel Hahnemann, based on the supposition that minute quantities of a given substance, such as that of a medicinal plant, will cure a condition which would be caused by administering large quantities of the same substance.

Infusion An infusion is made by pouring a given quantity of boiling water over a given weight of soft herbal material (leaves or petals) and infusing. An average infusion would be 25g (1oz) dried herb or 75g (3oz) fresh herb to 600ml (1pt) boiling water. Leave the infusion to steep covered for 10-15 minutes before straining.

Knot garden A decorative formal garden popular in the 16th century and normally consisting of very low hedges in geometric patterns.

Leaf mould Partially decomposed leaves.

Mordant A substance used in dyeing which, when applied to the fabric to be dyed, reacts chemically with the dye, fixing the colour.

Mulch A substance spread around a plant to protect it from weeds, water loss, heat or cold, and in some cases to provide nutrient material. Materials ranging from sawdust and pine needles to black plastic can be used as mulches; leaves and old straw are most commonly employed. Mulches should only be applied to moist soil.

Perennial A plant which survives for 3 or more years.

Perlite Expanded volcanic rock. It is inert, sterile and has a neutral Ph value (i.e. it is neither acidic nor alkaline).

Rhizome A swollen underground stem which stores food and from which roots and shoots are produced.

Runner A trailing shoot which roots where it touches the ground.

Salve A soothing ointment.

Saponin A substance which foams in water and has a detergent action.

Shrub A perennial plant with woody stems from or near the base.

Species A plant or plants within the same genus. These can be grown from seed and in the main run true to type.

Stamen The pollen-producing part of the plant.

Stigma The part of a pistil (the female organs of a flower) which accepts the pollen.

Tap root The main root, which grows larger than any of the secondary roots and is usually swollen with food.

Thymol A bactericide and fungicide found in several volatile oils.

Tincture A solution which has been extracted from plant material after macerating in alcohol or alcohol/water solutions.

Tisane A drink made by the addition of boiling water to fresh or dried unfermented plant material.

Topiary The art of cutting shrubs and small trees into ornamental shapes.

Umbel An inflorescence with stalked flowers arising from a single point.

Vermifuge A substance that expels or destroys worms.

Vulnerary A preparation useful in healing wounds.

BOTANICAL NAMES

The herbs in the A-Z section have been listed alphabetically by their botanical (Latin) name; also given is the family name and the other species within that genus which also have herbal properties. I know this can be very confusing, so I will explain.

Plants are usually listed in reference books under their botanical names. This is because one plant may have several common names, as you will see when reading the A-Z section. For instance Elder is also known as Dogtree, Judas Tree, Score Tree, Gods Stinking Tree, Black Elder, Blackberried, European Elder, Ellhorne. Even greater confusion can occur when a common name in different parts of the world refers to a different plant. For instance in England Meadowsweet (*Filipendula ulmaria*) is often called Queen of the Meadow, while in America, Queen of the Meadow is Gravelroot or Joe Pie Weed (*Eupatorium purpureum*).

Latin is the universal language for naming plants. The system used today is known as the 'Binomial System' and was devised by the famous 18th century Swedish botanist Carl Linnaeus (1707-78). In this system, each plant is classified by using two words in Latin form. The first word is the name of the genus (e.g. *Thymus*) and the second the specific epithet (e.g.*vulgaris*): together they provide a universally known name *(e.g. Thymus vulgaris).*

The Linnaean system of plant classification has been developed so that the entire plant kingdom is divided into a multi-branched family tree according to each plant's botanical characteristics. Plants are gathered into particular **families** according to the structure of their flowers, fruits or seeds (see table). A family may contain one **genus**, e.g. Cannacease of which Hops is a **species**, or many e.g. Compositae of which there are over 800 genera, including *Achillea, Arnica, Artemisia* to name a few, and over 13,000 species.

Plants are cultivated for the garden from the wild to improve either their leaf or their flower. This can be done either by selection from seedling or by spotting a mutation. Such plants are known as **cultivars** (a combination of 'cultivated varieties'). Propagation from these varieties is normally done by cuttings or division. Cultivars are given vernacular names, which are printed within quotes, e.g. *Thymus* 'Doone Valley', to distinguish them from wild varieties in Latin form appearing in italics i.e. *Thymus pulegioides*. Sexual crosses between species, usually of the same genus, are known as hybrids and are indicated by a multiplication sign e.g. *Thymus x citriodorus.*

For each of the herbs in the A-Z section the following information is given at the beginning of each section.
Genus or Botanical Name: Thymus
Common name: THYME
Other Names: (that the Genus is known by)
Family: Labiatae

In a following section entitled 'species' I list a selection of other species of the same genus which have similar herbal properties. In this section the following information is given as appropriate.

Botanical name: **Thymus praecox ssp. arcticus (Thymus serpyllum)**
Common name: Wild Creeping Thyme
Other names: Mother of Thyme, Creeping Thyme

Finally , a problem that seems to be getting worse. Many plants, including herbs, are undergoing reclassification and long established names are being changed. This is the result of scientific studies and research whereby it is found either that a plant has been incorrectly identified or that its classification has changed. In this book I have used the latest information available, but I am aware that within the next few years there are going to be yet more changes. Where there has been a recent change in the botanical name, this is shown in brackets.

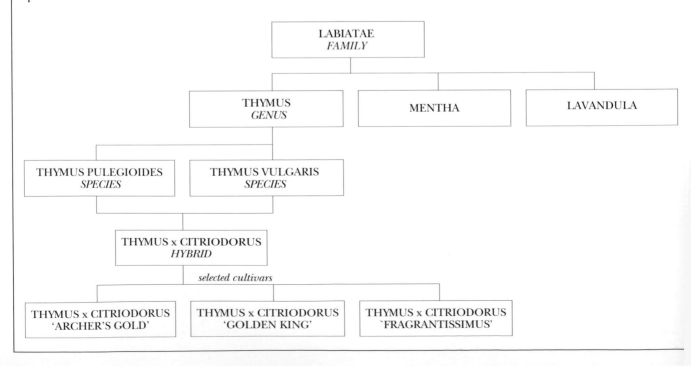

CLIMATE

Climate is a major factor in determining what plants you can grow successfully. Most perennials are hardy , but those which are Mediterranean in origin (over half of those mentioned in this book) can suffer due to their shallow roots. Plants such as Bay Tree, Rosemary and the Thymes may therefore, be affected in prolonged wet and cold winters.

On the other hand perennial herbs grown from bulbs can suffer from warm winters as the plants need to hibernate (die back) during the winter months to give the plant time to rest and regenerate.

I have indicated the hardiness of each herb in the A-Z section. The following are the minimum temperatures that the plant can withstand for short periods without serious damage.

Half-Hardy (Tender) 0°C (32°F)
Hardy -5°C (23°F) to -15°C (5°F)
Fully Hardy below -15°C (5°F)

If your climate is not suitable for a particular herb, I suggest that you grow it either in a pot or as an annual rather than struggle each winter to keep the plant alive.

The other important climatic factor that must be taken into consideration are your frost dates. These dates are important both when planting out annuals, and when harvesting both perennials and annuals. The seedlings of annual plants, if planted out too early, are most likely to be killed by a late frost and very tender plants like Basil can be killed if the night temperature falls to below 4°C (39°F).

For harvesting perennial herbs you should ensure that your last cutting is at least one month before the first winter frost, otherwise the severed stems will not have enough time to heal and the frost may damage or even kill the plant.

In my region the last frost in spring is towards the end of April and the first serious frost starts at the end of October; therefore I do not start planting out annuals until the beginning of May and complete any harvesting of perennials by mid-September to be on the safe side. As a precaution I advise that you keep a roll of agricultural fleece available. This is a marvellous material that can make all the difference between death and survival when placed over young plants if an unexpected late frost occurs at the beginning of your season.

Information from *The Complete New Herbal* , ed. Richard Mabey, is reproduced by permission of Gaia Books Ltd.

INDEX